The Stuart Century
1603 – 1714

By

S. REED BRETT M.A.

FORMERLY CHIEF HISTORY MASTER
KING EDWARD VI SCHOOL
NUNEATON

GEORGE G. HARRAP & CO. LTD
LONDON TORONTO WELLINGTON SYDNEY

First published in Great Britain 1961
by GEORGE G. HARRAP & CO. LTD
182 High Holborn, London, W.C.1

Reprinted 1964

Composed in Linotype Caledonia and printed by
William Clowes and Sons, Limited, London and Beccles
Made in Great Britain

Contents

Maps

Note

References for abbreviated titles used in footnotes throughout the book

Carlyle: *Letters and Speeches of Oliver Cromwell*
Clarendon: *History of the Great Rebellion* (ed. Macray 1888)
Gardiner: *Constitutional Documents of the Puritan Revolution*, 1625–60
H.M.C. Report: *Historical Manuscripts Commission's Reports*
Parliamentary History: ed. William Cobbett (1806–20)
Prothero: *Statutes and Constitutional Documents*, 1558–1625
Robertson: *Select Statutes, Cases, and Documents*, 1660–1832
Rushworth: *Historical Collections*, 1659–1701
Gardiner: Civil War: *History of the Great Civil War*

1*

consequence was that, instead of being on the world's fringe, she became the hub of the trade-routes which spread out between east and west, and English seamen were soon taking a full share in the new opportunities, thus adding to the nation's wealth and prestige. Indeed, as her new maritime and commercial importance received gradual recognition, England acquired a prestige out of all proportion to her geographical size. Thus the Stuarts succeeded not only to the southern half of an island-kingdom but also to a State of European importance and to the beginnings of an overseas Empire.

The relationship of the later Tudors with Continental Powers had been largely influenced by religion, and in particular by the religious movement known as the Reformation. Henry VIII's breach with the Papacy over his separation from Catherine of Aragon had opened the way, under Edward VI, for thorough-going Protestantism. This was strengthened by Mary's persecution of the Protestants: not only did she thereby intensify the convictions of the sufferers and their fellows, she also alienated the mass of moderate-minded Englishmen including not a few moderate Catholics. So Elizabeth was able to establish firmly a reformed Church comprising all but a small minority of the nation. The essence of Protestantism was —and is—the exercise of individual judgement in matters of religion; and even in the early years of Elizabeth some Protestants were beginning to criticize the Established Church to which they themselves belonged. As the reign continued, such criticism grew wider and more insistent. A considerable section desired what they regarded as its further purification of elements still savouring too strongly, as they thought, of Romanism. The advocates of purification—hence known as Puritans—remained during Elizabeth's reign and on into the early Stuarts, members of the Established Church. Not until what they regarded as the increasingly Romish tendencies of Archbishop Laud, in Charles I's reign, did the more extreme Puritans begin to form sects outside the Church.

The effects of Puritanism were not limited to religion. Men who had learned to think vigorously in religious matters would similarly think for themselves in the then very closely allied subject of politics. That the sharpest critics of Stuart Government were Puritans was not an accident.

England's acceptance of Protestantism under Elizabeth resulted also in drawing the country into European politics. On the Continent the initial sweep of the Reformation had by that time been slowed down. The Roman Church authorities, at the time that Luther published his Ninety-Five Theses in 1517, had known only one treatment for the "turbulent monk"—to suppress him as a heretic. But not a few keen Catholics recognized the existence of some of the abuses against which Luther's followers "protested." So there began a movement called the Counter Reformation which aimed at countering the Reformation by reforming the Roman Catholic Church from within, and by sharply defining the Church's doctrines. So far-reaching was this movement that there was even a succession of reforming Popes of whom one of the most notable was Sixtus V (1585–90). The whole Roman Church experienced the vigour of new life. Within the Empire the advance of Protestantism was halted: while some states within the Empire (mainly in the north) professed Protestantism, others remained staunchly Roman Catholic. Between the two there was a long-standing antagonism which in 1618 broke into open conflict, and so began the Thirty Years' War (1618–48).

Outside the Empire the leading protagonist of Roman Catholicism was Philip II of Spain; and the real reason for England's struggle with Spain during Elizabeth's reign was that England was regarded as the champion of Protestantism. The culmination of the struggle was the Spanish Armada, the defeat of which freed England for the moment from the menace of the forces of the Counter Reformation.

The foreign relations of England, thus complicated by the religious issue, proved to be a tortuous maze through which the Stuarts threaded their way only with great difficulty and never very successfully.

The economic effects of the sixteenth century upon the seventeenth may be summarized under the general term of inflation, expressing itself in a fall in the value of money and a rise in the level of prices. This condition had several contributory causes during the sixteenth century. Perhaps the beginning can be traced to Henry VIII's spending—mostly upon wars and preparations for wars—of the large treasure inherited from his father. When this was exhausted in 1526 Wolsey introduced a new coinage wherein the weight of silver coins was reduced so that the royal coffers profited by the difference in weight between the old coins and the new. Later Henry VIII carried out a series of debasements until by the end of his reign the silver content of his coinage was only a fraction of what it had been at the beginning. During Edward VI's reign the process was carried still farther. These debasements would not have been serious if coins had been regarded—as they now are—as being mere tokens of value. But then the intrinsic worth of the metal in a coin was supposed to correspond to its face-value, so that any considerable debasement undermined confidence in the currency and hampered trade both at home and abroad. Its other inevitable result was to drive up prices not only because sellers of goods demanded more cash to compensate them for the debasement but also because there was more nominal money in circulation. Though in the sixteenth century the effect that the amount of money in circulation had upon price-levels was not generally understood, that effect nevertheless inevitably operated. Further, as the century wore on, the influx of precious metals from Spanish possessions in the New World increased beyond calculation the amount of them in Europe. The consequent price-rise on the Continent had its effect also on England through her wool-trade contacts with Continental business. In 1560 Elizabeth's Minister, William Cecil, soundly reformed the coinage, but by that time the anti-inflationary effect of such a reform was being more than counter-balanced by the heavy influx of gold and silver from overseas.

The results of the price-rise were not all bad. The increase of money in circulation encouraged investment in commercial enterprises of many various kinds. Hence, for example, the considerable expansion of trade and maritime activity during the second half of the sixteenth century. Men who had goods to sell, whether landowners or merchants, received higher prices, and so in turn could take advantage of the new opportunities. The people who suffered were those who were buyers and not sellers—that is, people whose incomes were fixed, and who were workers with wages that lagged a long way behind prices.

Herein lay the root explanation of the land-enclosures which troubled all Tudor Governments from the days of Wolsey onward, and the results of which continued to affect the Stuarts also. Landowners, both large-scale and small-scale, like every one else, were affected by the general price-rise. Everything that they bought, for their households and their farming, cost more and more. They therefore were driven to farm for profit more keenly than ever before. To this end they adopted various expedients. Many owners ceased to be content to accept pre-inflation rents from tenants who were selling their produce at the newly enhanced market-prices. Demands for increased rents therefore became common. Also larger-scale farming could be more economical and could yield larger profits. This was achieved partly by small tenants or owners who added adjoining lands to their own and who put a boundary around their whole enlarged holdings which they thus 'enclosed.' More commonly a large owner determined to take advantage of the new conditions and to share in the opportunities to gain large profits by farming all his lands himself. He therefore evicted tenants whenever he could. Some such owners continued arable farming, though introducing more efficient methods than had been possible for their small-scale tenants. Others economized still further by turning their enclosed properties into pasturage so as to produce wool for which there were high demands and high prices. The result was to throw many of their labourers out of work, and to force them and their families to the precarious existence of vagrancy or worse. This evil was greatest when the landowner enclosed also common lands and woodlands along with his own properties and so prevented the villagers from grazing their own few animals as they had been accustomed to do.

It is now clear that the total areas thus enclosed were not very large, and these were limited mainly to the midlands of England. But the unsettling social effects of enclosures spread far beyond the districts immediately affected, and were among the main causes of discontent and rebellion in Tudor England.

By the end of the sixteenth century the new agricultural situation had mostly become stabilized. The results of the economic changes, however, remained, with unpredictable but decisive reactions for all the Stuart monarchs. The new methods of farming brought considerable prosperity to landowning families generally. It was from these that Members of Stuart Houses of Commons were mainly recruited, including representatives of the boroughs as well as of the counties. These were the men who opposed the Stuarts' attempts to impose taxation without Parliament's consent. If the motives of this opposition were partly selfish they were also natural, since a large proportion of the taxation was levied upon the landowning class from whom the Commons were drawn.

By contrast, among those most adversely affected by the inflation was the Crown. All the expenses of government rose during Elizabeth's long reign, especially those connected with national defences against the perpetual threat from Spain and with the costly repression of rebellions in Ireland. On the other hand, the Crown's sources of income remained relatively stable so that as the reign proceeded the Queen found greater and greater difficulty in meeting her current expenses. By various devices she managed to stave off the inevitable day of reckoning. She sold Crown lands (thereby, incidentally, forfeiting the yearly revenue from them), she sold offices and monopolies, and she pared her spending to the bone. In spite of it all, at her death she bequeathed to James I a debt of £400,000. The one real solution would have been that Parliament should realize the root cause of the Crown's difficulties and should grant a substantial increase in taxes. But Parliament had no clearer understanding of the working of economic processes than anyone else had. As the next section of this chapter will show, the Queen and Parliament were often at loggerheads over other matters, so that if the Queen had shown too great financial dependence upon Parliament she would have had to make concessions in directions where she was determined to stand firm. The legacy of debt and, more serious still, of very inadequate income, had significant adverse effects upon the Stuarts who followed. Indeed, the situation grew worse as soon as James I mounted the throne. Not only did the price-rise continue, but James had no understanding of the nature of the problem. He seems to have regarded his new kingdom, in contrast to his native one, as a limitless mine of riches which he expended without any regard to balancing his accounts. In a word, where Elizabeth had been frugal, James was extravagant. The result was to place James and, still more in due course, his son Charles, at Parliament's mercy. Financial disputes may not have been the root cause of the struggle between King and Parliament, but it is doubtful whether other causes would have brought the issues to the climax of civil war apart from the ultimate financial dependence of the King upon Parliament. This dependence was the long-term result of the general inflation of the previous century.

This has brought us to the constitutional aspect of our subject. Tudor rule had been based upon the principle that government was exercised by the King, although, at his discretion, he could summon and consult, and also dismiss, Parliament. In so doing the Tudors were but continuing practices already long established. The most common motive for summoning Parliament was the King's need of money. During the Middle Ages the King had been expected to "live of his own." A monarch was not then regarded as a sacrosanct person set apart from the rest of mankind. He was but the greatest of the barons, the "first among equals." Just as any other baron maintained his household and his armed followers out of the produce and the revenues from his own estates, so the King was expected to support his greater expenses out of his proportionately greater territories, though his personal income was supplemented by certain permanent customary dues. Only when some exceptionally heavy expense had to be met —most probably arising from a war—was the King expected to call for further, temporary, parliamentary grants. It was at such times chiefly that a parliament was summoned. Its life was usually short, for as soon as it had fulfilled its immediate purpose it was dissolved. Thus, during the forty-four and a half years of Elizabeth I's reign there were only ten Parliaments. The length of their lives varied from (nominally) eleven years, in one instance, to little more than one month in another.

But the time during which they were actually in session has been computed to average out at only three weeks for each year of her reign.

Moreover, Parliament's activities were strictly limited. Certain matters, such as foreign affairs, were outside its purview. During the intervals between Parliaments, and at all times in those matters from which Parliament's influence was excluded, government was directed by the Monarch and the Ministers whom he chose, with little more than the passive acquiescence of the nation. Nevertheless, though this practice continued throughout the Tudor period, there was a strong undercurrent which none of the Tudors could ignore, and against which their successors, the Stuarts, struggled only to find themselves at last overwhelmed. Gradually, unobtrusively, and for the most part unintentionally, throughout the sixteenth century Parliament was increasing its share in the government of the State. Henry VII, even before the sixteenth century had dawned, had owed his position as King not to hereditary right but to Parliament's recognition of him. Even Henry VIII, most autocratic of all the Tudors, carried through his religious changes, and his bewildering changes in making and unmaking legitimate heirs, by means of Parliamentary statutes.

Under the last of the Tudors difficulties with Parliament were intensified by uncertainties about the succession to the throne. Because Elizabeth was the last surviving child of Henry VIII, if she died—as, more than once during the early years of her reign, she seemed about to do—or was assassinated by a Roman Catholic agent, no one could say with certainty who the rightful successor would be. A disputed succession would invite chaos at home, embittered by religious antagonism, and the danger of attack from abroad. The nation's welfare thus made it urgent that the succession should be settled before such a need could arise.

Only one wholly satisfactory solution of the problem was possible—namely, that the Queen should marry and produce a direct heir. Hence Parliament after Parliament besought, and sometimes almost commanded, her to marry. Though Elizabeth used all her Tudor and womanly wits to evade a positive answer, her Parliaments persisted. Their spokesmen —notably Paul and Peter Wentworth and William Strickland —did not mince words in the matter. Sometimes even their own fellow-Members were aghast at their boldness; and nothing that Pym and Eliot later said to Charles I was plainer than what had already been said to Elizabeth.

Thus the Elizabethan marriage-question had its effects on the constitutional struggle between the Stuarts and their Parliamentary opponents. Elizabeth's native adroitness, and the prestige that she enjoyed because of her successful and long reign, enabled her to keep her sovereign power almost undiminished. But no matter who her successor might be, he would have a thorny political problem to handle.The political incapacity of the early Stuarts merely determined the form of, and gave bitterness to, the postponed struggle.

The factor that no one could eliminate and that bedevilled the efforts of successive Stuarts to shake themselves from Parliamentary control was their perpetual need of money, the reason for which need and its results we have examined already.

In practice the succession-problem solved itself. Well before the end of Elizabeth's reign there had ceased to be any doubt that James VI of Scotland would become King of England. James had carefully nursed his chances. For example, his acquiescence in the execution of his mother, Mary Stuart, in 1587, was largely due to his desire not to cause offence either to Elizabeth or to her Ministers who, he hoped, might some day become his Ministers. Long before Elizabeth's death her chief Minister, Sir Robert Cecil, had been secretly communicating with James as had many other English officials and nobles. That Elizabeth had no personal antipathy to James—whom she never met—was shown by the substantial annual allowance she had made, during a number of years, to enable him to suppress disorders in Scotland. She must have known that the most influential of her subjects were looking to James as the next King; and if she did not acknowledge him publicly it was at least partly because his succession was a foregone conclusion.

Chapter 2

King James I: The Ministry of Salisbury

1603–12

1. The Reign Opens

The reigns of the first two Stuart Kings, James I and Charles I, form together a single, undivided historical period. The great political and religious issues of James' reign continued into, and came to a head during, the reign of Charles. Moreover, for some time before James' death, Prince Charles and his favourite, Buckingham, had been the virtual rulers of England, so that they did little more than continue the same methods of ruling when the Prince became King. The distinguishing character of the two reigns was the resistance of the Parliaments to what they regarded as the excessive use of the royal prerogative.

The clash between King and Parliament was provoked by the Stuarts' claim to rule by Divine Right. Their insistence upon the divine origin of their authority meant that the dispute became a religious one. Not the least influential of the King's supporters were the bishops; and this intensified the support which the Puritans gave to Parliament. Further, it was Archbishop Laud who, by his Church reforms in England, and his attempted reforms in Scotland, finally precipitated hostilities. Thus, on account both of the fundamental principles involved and of the immediate cause of the dispute, the Civil War became, for most of those who engaged in it, a religious rather than a political conflict.

Nevertheless, though the dispute had religious causes, the issue itself went even deeper than that. It was concerned with nothing less than the possession of sovereignty in the State.

The Stuarts claimed that sovereignty was theirs by Divine Right. Parliament claimed that whatever prerogative the King possessed was to be exercised for the welfare of his subjects and in accordance with the nation's rights established by charters, statutes, and precedents. For itself, as the representative body of the nation, Parliament claimed an essential part in the work of government.

At the outset we need to be clear that, to whatever extent the Stuarts were giving a new emphasis to royal supremacy, Parliament's claim to a directive share in government was at least equally without precedent. Both James I and Charles I committed some unpardonably foolish blunders; yet, according to the letter of the law at least, the King was in a sounder position than Parliament. Stuart Parliaments would need such experiences as their failure to substantiate their impeachment of Strafford before this fact was brought home to the average Member and even to many of the leaders.

James I's reign is divisible into two almost equal parts—namely, 1603–14, and 1614–25. The dividing-point was the Addled Parliament of 1614, which quarrelled with the King over irregular taxation and was dissolved after sitting for only two months. During the first half of the reign James' chief Minister was Sir Robert Cecil, who had been Secretary to Elizabeth. During the second half of the reign James allowed himself and the Kingdom to be ruled by personal favourites irrespective of their capacity to govern.

When James ascended his new throne he was not without certain advantages. To the problems that Elizabeth had bequeathed to him he brought considerable experience both as a man and as a monarch. Born in 1566, he had been crowned King of Scotland in the following year after the enforced abdication of his mother, Mary, following her defeat at Carberry Hill and her imprisonment in Lochleven Castle. Intellectually, too, he had gifts above the average. As a theologian he could hold his own with learned divines; and as a political philosopher he had few equals among contemporaries—witness his *True Law of Free Monarchies* published in 1598. Further, in an age when Court morals were commonly, almost unashamedly, lax, James' personal life was apparently untouched by such evils.

Yet with all his gifts, James lacked two which made the rest ineffective—namely, strength of will to carry out the truth he saw, and ability to judge the characters of other men. Highly susceptible to flattery, he was an easy prey to anyone with a smooth tongue and persuasive manner. In consequence he was vacillating in policy and the victim of unworthy favourites. He suffered the further disadvantage of being doctrinaire in disposition: even when his judgement was sound (as often it was) he rarely understood how or to what extent to apply his theory so as to achieve his purpose. Personally, also, he had some unattractive traits. Clear talking was made difficult for him by a tongue too large for his mouth, though in spite of this defect he was incorrigibly garrulous, using the broadest of Scots speech. His gait was an awkward shamble. The sight of a naked sword sent him into a nervous shiver. This last characteristic was perhaps a reflex of his sincere devotion to peace, but it was not likely to deepen the average seventeenth-century Englishman's respect for him. James I was as sharp a contrast to the kingly—and queenly—Tudors as could well be imagined.

2. Religious Issues

The importance which religion was to have during the new reign was plainly indicated by its opening events. James was still on his way to London when a petition was presented to him supposedly representing the views of one thousand Puritan clergy and hence known as the Millenary Petition. The terms of the petition were scrupulously respectful towards the monarch and moderate in their demands for reform.[1] Its first paragraph included the following:

In the church service, that the cross in baptism . . . and confirmation, as superfluous, may be taken away. . . . The cap and surplice not urged. . . . That divers terms of priests and absolution and some other used, with the ring in marriage, and other

[1] Prothero, pp. 413–416.

such like in the book may be corrected. The longsomeness of service be abridged. Church songs and music moderated to better edification. That the Lord's day be not profaned: the rest upon the holidays not so strictly urged. That there be an uniformity of doctrine prescribed. No popish opinion to be any more taught or defended: no ministers charged to teach their people to bow at the name of Jesus. That the canonical scriptures only be read in the church.

For James the petition was in the nature of a test-question. Inoffensive though many of its terms may have been to large numbers of English people, to grant them would have seemed to show that the new King was an active sympathizer with the Puritans. This would offend a numerous and influential section of the nation, and would be a disastrous opening of the new reign. Moreover, to give a direct answer to a question, especially to a religious question, was not in James' nature. He would much prefer a long debate in which he could adjudicate and air his own theological learning. He therefore ordered a conference to consider the petition and relevant ecclesiastical matters.

The Hampton Court Conference met in January 1604. The Archbishop of Canterbury and eight bishops headed the eighteen members representing the orthodox Church party, while the Puritans were limited to four. This sufficiently indicated the line that the proceedings were likely to take. During the opening deliberations, however, James held the balance fairly even. In the end Dr Reynolds, the Puritan leader, delivered himself into his enemies' hands by referring to the "Bishop and his Presbyters." At the word Presbyter James rose in anger that was half-frightened and half-indignant. To James, a Presbyter pointed in one direction—namely, to the Presbyterian Church in Scotland where the Church was supreme and the King subordinate. During the months since his coming into England James had tasted enough of the sweets of English Episcopacy, which recognized the monarch's pre-eminence, to make him determined never to return to the humiliations of Presbyterianism. "A Scottish Presbytery," he declared, "agreeth as well with a monarchy as God and the Devil." Thereupon he rated the Puritan divine roundly and even coarsely. The climax of the King's outburst was this ominous declaration: "If this be all your party hath to say, I will make them conform themselves, or else will harry them out of the Kingdom."

James' reasons for this attitude are easy to understand. He himself summed them up in the heat of the argument: "I thus apply it. . . . No bishop, no King." But it was a short-sighted policy. At the outset of his reign he had lost a never-to-be-repeated opportunity to effect a reasonable compromise within the Church. Out of the parties which from that time grew more and more pronounced, there sprang the Civil War and much subsequent strife.

The one good result of the conference was the order for a new translation of the Bible. This arose from Dr Reynolds' plea that "there might be a new translation of the Bible because those which were allowed in the reign of Henry VIII and Edward VI were corrupt and not conformable to the truth of the original." The suggestion pleased James who, in spite of the grumble of Bancroft, Bishop of London, that "if every man's humour should be followed, there would be no end of translating," ordered the work to proceed. Fifty of the most eminent Bible-scholars of the day, divided into six groups, laboured almost continuously until 1611 to produce the Authorized Version of the Bible whose influence, in providing a matchless example of English prose and in moulding the religion of generations of English people all over the world, is beyond calculation.

In February 1604 the death of Archbishop Whitgift snapped an important link with Elizabethan England, for he had been Primate since 1583. It was an ominous sign that his successor was Bishop Bancroft, who had been the bitterest opponent of the Puritans during the Hampton Court Conference. His influence soon made itself felt. Even before his elevation he had been instrumental in drawing up the Canons of 1604, which defined Church practice and discipline afresh. The Canons enjoined that every clergyman should assent to every one of the Thirty-Nine Articles of the Church as being in agreement with the Word of God. In July a proclamation was issued that after November 30 every clergyman must either conform to the

Canons or leave his living. When December 1604 came a large body of clergy—probably three hundred, though the number is not precisely ascertainable—refused to conform, and shortly afterwards they were ejected. The ejected clergy became a body of non-conformists outside, instead of inside, the Established Church. It was the first secession, but by no means the last. The Church most certainly had the right to demand that its clergy should conform to its standards of belief and practice. But the Church was to pay a high price for its rigidity.

3. Plots

The Puritans were not the only people to suffer religious disabilities. The Roman Catholics also laboured under a sense of grievance, particularly because James continued to collect recusancy fines—that is, fines for non-attendance at English Church services. Nor were these the only reasons for general discontent. About the Court were many men disgruntled from various causes with the new regime. Sir Walter Ralegh, for example, was the centre of a group angered by the new King's policy of peace with Spain. So uncompromising was Ralegh on this subject that James' accession had been followed almost at once by Ralegh's disgrace. He was deprived of all the offices he had held at Elizabeth's Court, and henceforward was a violent opponent of James and Cecil. Lord Cobham, who shared Ralegh's political views, had also a personal grievance in that James had refused to grant him an office promised by Elizabeth. Different groups of such malcontents toyed with ideas of how to obtain redress for their wrongs. Some of these ideas were foolish and slightly criminal; others were plainly treasonable. Cobham, for example, had a scheme to remove James and his Minister, Cecil, and to enthrone Arabella Stuart. Some attempt to sort out these various schemes resulted in two being known as the Bye Plot and Main Plot; but the plotters of them overlapped so bewilderingly that neither at the time nor since has anyone been able to make clear sense of the whole business. There is a strong suspicion that Cecil purposely confused the evidence so as to rid the Court of his opponents.

Not unnaturally, when Cecil heard of the plots, Ralegh and Cobham were among the arrested persons. Cobham, on trial, attempted to shuffle out of the affair by accusing Ralegh of leading him into the plot. Ralegh was even charged with plotting with Spaniards, which is enough to show the absurdity of the proceedings. Three of them were actually executed. Cobham and Ralegh were led out to execution but were reprieved and placed in the Tower, where they remained until 1619. Ralegh spent the thirteen years of his imprisonment in writing his *History of the World*.

What had been known as the Bye Plot of June 1603 was revealed to James by Jesuits. James, as a reward for the loyalty of his informers and of the mass of his Roman Catholic subjects, promised that the recusancy fines should not in future be collected. One effect of this was that large numbers of Roman Catholics who had hitherto disguised their faith came out in their true colours. The sudden revelation of the large numbers of Catholics in England took James so much by surprise, and caused him so much apprehension, that he went from one extreme to the other. In February 1604 all priests were ordered to leave the country, and in November the collection of recusancy fines was resumed. This change of policy embittered Roman Catholics, and a small band of them formed a desperate plan to cure their ills by violence: they would overthrow the Government that was persecuting them. Out of this resolve sprang the Gunpowder Plot.

The arch-plotter was Robert Catesby, who conceived the idea of blowing up the King and his Ministers as they were assembled for the opening of Parliament, so making a clean sweep of the Protestant leaders. To take advantage of the resulting confusion, a rising of Roman Catholic gentry and their retainers was to be organized so as either to seize the Government or to obtain favourable terms for Roman Catholics. The scheme was hopelessly fantastic: the explosion-plot might or might not succeed in its immediate objective, but a rising of Catholics must inevitably be crushed, and the only effect would be heavier penalties than ever upon Catholics in general. Yet the men who planned and executed the scheme did not lack intelligence, good breeding, or experience. The depth of their folly was a measure of their desperation. Whatever our views on the justice or injustice of their cause, and however we may condemn their methods, we must admire their unquenchable bravery.

Catesby's closest associates were his cousin, Thomas Winter, and Thomas Percy, cousin of the Earl of Northumberland. Gradually certain others were brought into the plot. In May 1604 Percy hired a house next to the Parliament House, and mining operations were begun. These were carried out under the direction of Guy Fawkes, who had been brought up a Yorkshire gentleman, but who, a dozen years before the Plot, had sold his property and enlisted in the Spanish Army in Flanders. His combination of Roman Catholic zeal with expert knowledge of siege-tunnelling made him ideally suited for the work. The task of digging through a nine-foot wall was terrific, and progress was necessarily slow. Also, a long prorogation of Parliament, in July 1604, and other difficulties, caused various changes of plan.

The final plan was for Sir Everard Digby to hold a hunting-party at Dunchurch, near Rugby, on the appointed day; for Digby then to reveal to the assembled Roman Catholics the nature of the plot; and then, as soon as news of the explosion reached them from London, for them to raise a general rebellion. The day finally fixed for the opening of the new session of Parliament was November 5.

One of the men associated with Digby in organizing the rebellion was Francis Tresham. His brother-in-law was Lord Monteagle, for whose safety Tresham was deeply concerned. On the evening of October 26 Monteagle received a mysterious note urging him to find some excuse for absence from the opening of Parliament. "Think not slightly of this advertisement but retire yourself into the country, where you may expect the event in safety, for though there be no appearance of any stir, yet I say they shall receive a terrible blow this Parliament, and they shall not see who hurts them." Monteagle passed on the note to Cecil (lately created Earl of Salisbury) who thus gleaned his first information of the plot. Though the conspirators learned that Monteagle had received a letter, they gave themselves away in two respects. First, the dauntless Guy Fawkes insisted upon staying at his post hoping that he would be able to carry out the explosion before he was detected; and just before midnight of November 4 he was discovered and carried off. Second, Catesby and the other leaders decided to continue the other part of the plot. Setting out from London, they rode to Dunchurch but no one rallied to them. They became fugitives, and were rounded up at Holbeche House, in Staffordshire, where most of the ringleaders—including Catesby, Percy, and Wright—were shot dead during the attack. Fawkes, subject to long and horrible torture, gradually revealed the names of the conspirators. Those who remained alive were put on trial and executed early in 1606.

So ended what is perhaps the most famous plot in English history. It had disastrous effects on the Catholic cause. New and severe penal laws were enacted. The recusancy fines were enormously increased; recusants were forbidden to practise law or medicine and to hold any commission in the Army or Navy; and recusants could be required to take an oath that the Pope had no power to depose a king and that they would defend the king to the utmost of their ability. The last provision was an attempt to distinguish between those Catholics who were loyal to the King and the State and those who were disloyal. It was against the latter that the Penal Laws were to be enforced. This position continued until 1619 when James' anxiety for a marriage between Prince Charles and a Spanish princess necessitated some improvement in the lot of English Roman Catholics.

But the real effect of the plot was to be seen not so much in Parliamentary statutes as in the reaction of the mass of the people. A howl of execration against Roman Catholics went up on every side. The common folk did not stay to draw nice distinctions between different kinds and degrees of Catholics. In the eyes of the nation all Catholics were alike traitors. The Marian persecution had already made Roman Catholicism odious and precluded its return as the State religion. These effects were confirmed and intensified by the Gunpowder Plot.

4. First Parliament, 1604–11

The Parliament which Catesby and his fellow-conspirators had intended to blow up had first met on March 19, 1604. Already we have seen that influences had been at work during the closing years of the sixteenth century to produce a clash between Monarch and Parliament. Only Elizabeth's consummate statecraft and the nation's habitual loyalty to its great Queen had prevented the clash from coming in her lifetime. James I's accession brought this unstable equilibrium to an end. The Members of his first Parliament met under a sense of being on the verge of decisive events. The new King seemed to go out of his way to justify the sense of crisis. His insistence upon his Divine Right was a virtual challenge to his Parliaments to counter his claim by asserting their own rights and privileges.

Further, the persecution of the Puritan clergy, foreshadowed during the Hampton Court Conference, and the growing High Church influence at Court, provided Parliament with an active motive which sprang from the deepest convictions; for a large proportion of its Members were drawn from the middle classes, who were the strongest supporters of Puritanism.

The Commons' jealousy for its traditional privileges showed itself by the action it took in two cases only three days after the Parliament opened. The first was the case of Sir Thomas Shirley who, after being elected a Member, had been arrested for debt and confined to the Fleet prison. The Commons, asserting the right of its Members to freedom from arrest during Parliamentary sessions, had the Warden of the Fleet committed to the Tower and so, after a struggle, procured Shirley's return to the House.

The second case related to the election of Sir Francis Goodwin for the County of Buckingham. The Court of Chancery refused to recognize the election since Goodwin was an outlaw. A new election was ordered, and Sir John Fortescue was declared to be the new Member. The Commons, claiming to be the sole judge of its own election-returns, ordered Goodwin to take his seat. King James emphatically supported his Court of Chancery, and so Goodwin's case developed into a dispute between King and Parliament. During the proceedings James sent to the Commons a message which included the following unmistakable sentence as reported to the House by the Speaker:

> That for his part he was indifferent which of them was chosen, Sir John or Sir Francis. . . . That he had no purpose to impeach their privilege but since they derived all matters of privilege from him and by his grant, he expected they should not be turned against him.[1]

The King further desired that the Commons should hold a conference with the Judges to discuss the case. This the Commons refused to do, since to concede the principle that they were the sole judge of election-returns would enable the Crown in future to nominate Members to the House. Finally, after long disputes, James suggested a compromise:

> He granted it [the Commons] was a court of record and a judge of returns. He moved, That neither Sir John Fortescue nor Sir Francis Goodwin might have place. Sir John losing place, his Majesty did meet us half-way.[2]

This course of compromise was followed. Both King and Commons, by a wise spirit of moderation, had avoided an irremediable breach. But the substance of victory rested with the Commons: the King had granted the principle that the Commons was the sole judge of its own returns. Moreover, as though to seal its privileges, on April 13, 1604, the very day on which a new writ was issued for Buckinghamshire, the House began an inquiry into two other disputed elections—namely, for Cardigan and Shrewsbury.

A clash between King and Commons on a different issue, also in 1604, evoked from the Commons a significant statement of the principles on which it claimed that its privileges were based. The subject under discussion was wardship. Tenants-in-chief who were minors were royal wards. A ward's lands were administered by the King (who pocketed the profits from them); and if the inheritance to such an estate fell to a female

[1] Prothero, p. 326.
[2] Prothero, p. 330.

her marriage was subject to the King's arrangement (also with suitable profits). These royal rights, a relic of feudal customs, were legally incontestable. Nevertheless they had been long out of date and were a source of annoyance and abuse. For example, the rights of wardship were commonly used as rewards to courtiers and were even bought and sold. The Commons, while acknowledging the royal right to wardship, suggested that James should exchange the right for a Parliamentary grant of a sum greater than he had been receiving in wardships. James not only rejected the proposal but also rated the Commons for its temerity in making it.

The Commons abandoned the scheme but drew up an Apology setting out the nature of its privileges. This statement included the following clauses:

> With all humble and due respect to your Majesty our sovereign lord and head, . . . we most truly avouch, first, that our privileges and liberties are our right and due inheritance, no less than our very lands and goods. Secondly, that they cannot be withheld from us, denied or impaired, but with apparent wrong to the whole state of the realm. . . .
>
> In the first Parliament of the happy reign of your Majesty the privileges of our House, and therein the liberties and stability of the whole kingdom, have been more universally and dangerously impugned than ever (as we suppose) since the beginning of parliament.[1]

Though the Commons firmly professed its loyalty to James —who was referred to as "a King of such understanding and wisdom as is rare to find in any prince in the world"—the meaning of the clear enunciation of privileges was unmistakable. Further, the Apology was an uncompromising summary of the principles which were to be at stake during the following forty years and were to end in the Civil War. That the Commons could so succinctly express its views in the first parliamentary session of the first Stuart sovereign showed that already there existed an understanding of the nation's political rights and a determination to secure them. There is no evidence that the Apology was ever presented to James; hence there was no formal reply.

[1] Prothero, pp. 286–293.

The opening session of James' first Parliament ended on July 7, 1604. The interest of the second session (1605–6) centred in the Gunpowder Plot. When on November 19, 1606, James opened the third session, he referred at some length to the relations between his two Kingdoms of England and Scotland. Ever since his accession in England James had cherished the hope that the two might be fully united. As early as April 1604 he had brought the subject to Parliament's notice, and twenty-eight commissioners (fourteen from the Lords and fourteen from the Commons) had then been appointed to discuss the subject with Scottish commissioners. Their report, presented to Parliament in November 1606, included the recommendations that there should be free trade between England and Scotland, and that Scots born after James' accession (and hence called *post-nati*) should be considered as naturalized Englishmen. But Parliament rejected the proposals. The traditional antagonism between the two nations was still strong; and the English, as the richer nation, were jealous lest the Scots should gain unfairly from the union.

Actually, the status of the *post-nati* was settled in a manner beyond Parliament's control. The test case of whether Robert Colvill, or Calvin, could own land in England was brought before the English judges. Though Colvill had been born in Edinburgh, in 1605, the judges ruled that, in accordance with English Common Law, he was a natural subject of the English King. Henceforward this rule would apply to all *post-nati*.

The judges' verdict was sound in law, but the process of securing the royal will by appealing to the law-courts to override, or to evade, the will of Parliament was capable of serious abuse. The method was to be a favourite one of James and of the Stuarts generally in their disputes with Parliament. The judges' verdict in Colvill's case was not delivered until June 1608. Already two years earlier James had used a similar method to evade the Commons' control of finance.

The case in question had arisen indirectly from the dissolution of the Levant Company. This company, formed during the latter part of Elizabeth's reign, had secured for its members a monopoly of English trade with Venice and Turkey. The company had a varied and not very prosperous history, and in

2 + s.c.

1603 it surrendered its charter. As a consequence, the King would lose the annual payment of £4000 which the company had been paying to the Crown in return for its privileges. This was the more serious because James was spending considerably in excess of his income. Hence, though the Levant trade was thrown open, the King tried to compensate himself by levying a customs duty on imported currants, which were one of the most valuable elements in Levant trade.

Previous to the formation of the Levant Company, a similar duty had been levied; and for that reason the duty might be regarded as legitimate now that the company no longer existed. On the other hand, the duty was not part of the customary standing revenue of the Crown, nor was it granted by Parliament. Such a duty, imposed by the King's arbitrary power, was known as an "imposition."

One merchant, named John Bate, refused to pay the duty which the customs officers demanded on a cartload of currants. This challenge to the Crown's right to levy impositions could not be ignored, and Bate was tried before the Exchequer Court which gave judgement for the King. But the court was careful to make clear the legal reasons for its decision. It claimed that the King had the right to levy customs duties without Parliament's consent because such duties were a means of regulating foreign trade, and the direction of all foreign affairs was within the royal prerogative. Thus the verdict was far from allowing to the King indiscriminate authority to impose any kind of tax or duty irrespective of Parliament's wishes.

Nevertheless the effect of Bate's case was to open the way for further arbitrary taxation that would not always keep within the limits of the Exchequer definition. The immediate effect was the issue in 1608 of a new *Book of Rates* sanctioning further impositions which were calculated to bring in £70,000 annually.

Even this addition to the revenue was not enough to meet all the King's expenses. In 1610 Salisbury—who two years earlier had become Lord Treasurer while retaining the Secretaryship—tried to make with Parliament a settlement, called the Great Contract, which would place the King's revenue on a sound basis. His scheme was that the King should renounce the income he derived from out-of-date feudal aids, and in return should receive from Parliament a fixed annual amount, which, when added to income derived from other sources, would assure to the King £600,000 annually, which with care would suffice for all his needs. Long discussions took place about the particular dues which the King should renounce and about the exact amount which Parliament was to grant in exchange. Finally, in July, agreement was reached on all points, and the Commons drew up a statement embodying the terms.

While discussing the Great Contract, Parliament had been calling attention to many grievances in matters of religion. These included the continued silencing of the Puritan ministers who had refused to conform to the Canons of 1604, and the pluralities and non-residence commonly practised by the clergy. By this time James and the Established Church were too closely wedded to make concessions. As a result, the breach between King and Parliament widened, and the Great Contract remained unconfirmed. Such an atmosphere of mutual distrust made the continuance of parliamentary business unprofitable, and in February 1611 James dissolved the first Parliament of his reign.

With the exception of the Addled Parliament, which sat for a few weeks in 1614, there was no further Parliament until 1621. During the ten-year interval James raised money by non-parliamentary means and ruled mainly through favourites until the pressure of circumstances abroad made substantial grants once more necessary. In order to understand these circumstances we have to survey James' foreign policy during the early part of his reign.

5. Foreign Affairs, 1604–12

James I was genuinely a man of peace. Military force was repugnant to him, and was to be used only when other means had failed. Profoundly convinced of his own God-given wisdom, he believed himself capable of achieving the objects of national policy abroad by peaceful negotiations. The foreign relations of England during James' reign consisted of his sustained and obstinate efforts to this end. In carrying out this policy James had to deal with conditions which he inherited. This was particularly true in three spheres—namely, Spain, the Netherlands, and France.

Philip II of Spain had died in 1598 and had been succeeded by his son, Philip III. Though Spain was still at war with England and the Netherlands, her new King was incapable as a monarch, and was not the man to maintain an energetic war-effort. Also, a strong party among his Ministers favoured a period of peace to enable Spain to recover her economic prosperity. Such was the position at the time of James' accession.

One of James' first concerns was to negotiate with Spain for a treaty of peace. With a will to peace on both sides, no great difficulty seemed likely, especially as neither side was seeking territorial gains from the other. The chief difficulty concerned the Netherlands whom Spain had regarded as rebellious subjects but with whom England was closely allied. Negotiations finally resulted in the Treaty of London of August 1604. By its terms England was to continue to have commercial dealings with the Netherlands, and Englishmen were to be allowed still to serve in Dutch armies. James did, however, undertake to remain neutral as between the Netherlands and Spain, and to allow Englishmen also to serve in Spanish armies.

More important than the particular terms of the treaty was the fact that the long war between England and Spain was at last brought to an end.

In March 1607 hostilities came to an end between Spain and the Netherlands; and it was largely owing to Salisbury's efforts that the ensuing negotiations resulted in the Truce of Antwerp of April 1609. This truce was to last for twelve years. Its terms included a recognition of the Netherlands' independence, though this independence was not made formal or permanent until the Treaty of Westphalia, in 1648, at the close of the Thirty Years' War.

The other Power which, along with England, was interested in opposing Spain was France. Though she too was predominantly a Roman Catholic country, her position, both in religion and in politics, was different from that of Spain. In France the

Reformation had made some progress though, measured by the numbers of its adherents, French Protestantism was never strong. That is to say, French Protestants never numbered more than a small minority of the population. This minority, however, included some of the nation's most vigorous elements and also a proportion of the nobility. But, owing to the successive deaths of the royal brothers—Francis II in 1560, Charles IX in 1574, and Henry III in 1589—none of whom had a son, the French Crown fell to the House of Bourbon in the person of Henry of Navarre, who was the leader of the Protestants. Thus in 1589, the year following the defeat of the Armada, a Protestant King, Henry IV, ruled Roman Catholic France.

Henry's position was difficult in the extreme. The vast majority of his subjects would regard him as a heretic to whom allegiance was not due; and these subjects would certainly receive the support of the Catholic Philip II of Spain. This, in fact, was exactly what took place. Finally, in 1593, Henry professed allegiance to the Roman Catholic Church, and next year he entered Paris in triumph. In 1595 the Pope withdrew the excommunication previously laid upon Henry. Thus his position as King was firmly established.

The extent to which Henry IV had genuine religious convictions, whether Protestant or Roman Catholic, has always been a subject for debate. One fact is plain: after his acceptance of Roman Catholicism he did not display the bigotry which often characterizes the convert to any faith. On the contrary, in 1598 he promulgated the religious settlement commonly known as the Edict of Nantes. By its terms, Huguenots were granted the rights of freedom of conscience and private worship throughout France, and public worship was to be allowed in places where it had been conceded by a Treaty of 1577. Further, the Edict allowed the Huguenots to fortify La Rochelle and certain other towns, and the King undertook to make grants towards the cost of their garrisons. These last provisions were intended to safeguard to the Huguenots their religious rights against any possible attack from the Roman Catholic majority.

These events in France are important for our purpose because they helped to shape English relations with France during the reigns of both James I and Charles I. During the early period of James I, which is our immediate concern, the only relationship of any consequence was that England joined with the French and the Dutch in a League which Henry IV had formed for the protection of certain small Lutheran states of the Empire against the growing aggressiveness of the Roman Catholic Emperor. This League had been formed early in 1610. In May of that year, as Henry was preparing to lead his armies, he was assassinated by a priest in Paris. The League, thus left leaderless, at once dissolved.

The new French King was Henry's nine-year-old son, Louis XIII, during whose minority the regency was exercised by the Queen-Mother, Marie de Medici. The young King had been brought up a Roman Catholic, and neither he nor his Ministers had his father's tenderness for the Huguenots. Strife between Huguenots and Government was not long in breaking out. When that happened England, as the leading Protestant Power, could hardly avoid being concerned.

One other connexion which England made with the Continent during this early period of James I was also to influence profoundly her foreign relations at intervals during the following thirty years. The aim of Salisbury's foreign policy was that England should take her place as the leader of European Protestantism. One of the means to this end was the marriage of the King's daughter, Elizabeth, to a Protestant prince, and in May 1612 Salisbury was able to secure the signature of a marriage-contract between Elizabeth and Frederick V, Elector of the Rhine Palatinate. The marriage took place in February 1613.

A week after the signing of the marriage-contract Salisbury died. His death meant more than the passing of a distinguished politician: it marked the dividing-line between one historical period and another. Salisbury was the last of the Elizabethan statesmen, the last representative of a tradition which, though not free from human foibles and ambitions, did place the welfare of the State before the enrichment of individuals, however exalted. Salisbury's death was followed by a scramble for office, and for the spoils which office could supply. This scramble was encouraged by the credulity of James, who had been growing increasingly impatient of what he regarded as Salisbury's undue restraint. As a result, during the remainder of James I's reign England was virtually ruled by favourites, for the most part personally ambitious and unscrupulous. Here was a main root of the evils which ultimately were to lead to the Civil War.

Another event which made 1612 a historical dividing-line was the death of Henry, Prince of Wales, on October 6. Princes who have died young have not uncommonly been the subjects of legends and speculations about the noble rulers they would have become had they lived longer. But so universal were the good opinions held by various types of people concerning Prince Henry that there seems some justification for believing that if he, instead of his brother, Charles, had been the next King, England's political life would have been diverted into channels very different from those that it actually followed. He was passionately devoted to open-air sports, and outspoken and affable in his dealings with his fellows. In matters of religion he was a convinced Protestant, so much so that when a marriage was suggested between him and a French princess he is reputed to have declared that "two religions should not lie in his bed." The impetuousness of such a nature in a King might in due course have opened the way for troubles for the nation, but at least it would have avoided the royal subservience to unworthy favourites and uncertain dealings with Roman Catholic Powers which characterized the career of Charles I. Certainly, Prince Henry's death removed the last possible restraint upon King James' vacillating course and the last barrier to the succession of Charles.

Chapter 3

King James I: The Rule of Favourites

1612–25

1. The Addled Parliament, 1614

The first of King James' favourites after Salisbury's death was Robert Carr. Carr was a Scot who, as a page, had accompanied James to the English Court in 1603. After spending some time in France, Carr returned to England where he was soon in high favour with the King. In 1607 he was knighted. In 1611 he was raised to the peerage as Viscount Rochester, and so became the first Scot to sit in the English House of Lords. Salisbury's death in the following year left the way clear for Rochester's further rise at Court. This did not mean that he would step into all the offices that Salisbury had vacated. The Treasury was not given to any individual but was put into commission (that is, was administered by a committee); and James himself acted as Secretary of State. The result in both offices was inefficiency: at the Treasury the lack of individual responsibility caused wastefulness and debt; and James lacked the self-discipline necessary to attend both to the direction of policy and to the multifarious details of the Secretaryship. By 1614 the system broke down and new appointments were made. But during those two years Rochester was the King's assistant and confidant in matters both personal and official.

The rapid rise of a Scottish upstart gave great offence to the English nobles. One noble family, however, did not fail to ingratiate itself with the new favourite. This was the Howard family, who held numerous State offices. The Howards were a Roman Catholic family, but they had felt no compunction in accepting Protestantism so as to qualify for royal honours. But they were also in the pay of Spain and led the English Court-faction that favoured friendship with Spain.

Rochester's connexion with the Howards proved to be something more than political. He became infatuated with Frances Howard, who had been married to the Earl of Essex in 1606 when they were both little more than children. The lady on her part was nothing loth to respond to his advances. The Countess of Essex was a wild, undisciplined girl; whereas the Earl was a man of sober qualities which were to show themselves fully when, thirty years later, he became the General of the Parliamentary armies. The Countess therefore determined to secure a divorce so that she might be free to marry Rochester. Even James smiled upon the scheme. In May 1613 a commission was appointed to try the case, and in September a majority of the commissioners voted in favour of allowing the divorce. Rochester was raised to be Earl of Somerset, and on December 26 he married Lady Frances Howard.

The interval between the divorce in May and the marriage in December had been occupied by an event which was to bring down Somerset's fortunes to the ground. During his rapid rise Somerset had enjoyed the counsel of Sir Thomas Overbury, a shrewd and experienced friend. Overbury was strongly opposed to the marriage between Somerset and the divorced lady. The latter, resenting this opposition even more bitterly than Somerset did, planned to murder Overbury. Numerous poisoning attempts were made, and at last, in the middle of September, Overbury died. For two years the cause of his death remained a secret to all but the perpetrators and their accomplices.

Meanwhile James' second Parliament had met and been dissolved. In the events leading to the summoning of that Parliament Somerset had played an important part. His marriage-connexion with the Howard family resulted in his advocating their policy of friendship with Spain. In 1613 the Court of Spain sent as its Ambassador to England one of its most able representatives, Don Diego Sarmiento de Acuña, better known by the title of Count Gondomar, awarded to him four years later. From the moment of his arrival in England Gondomar began to exercise over James an influence which increased steadily as time passed. With consummate craft he played upon the various qualities, good and otherwise, of

James' nature, his personal vanity on the one hand and his genuine love of peace on the other. Suiting his moves to the occasion, Godomar used all to serve the interests of Spain and of Roman Catholicism.

His first aim was to detach James from his friendship with France. James, however, hesitated. Friendship was traditional between the French and the Scottish royal houses, and he was anxious to cement the friendship by a marriage-alliance between his son Charles and a French princess. By the end of 1613 negotiations for a marriage were far enough advanced to lay before Parliament.

A further reason for summoning a Parliament was that the royal exchequer was exhausted. Impositions and the sale of much Crown land had failed to meet the King's financial needs. Heavy borrowing had only added to his embarrassments. In February 1614, therefore, the King decided to summon a Parliament. Among those who were then elected for the first time to the House of Commons were Sir John Eliot and Sir Thomas Wentworth, two men whose careers were to be closely linked together.

On April 5 James delivered his opening speech in which he referred to the need for supplies which he hoped would be granted not because of his demands but because of the Commons' love. If James hoped thus to cajole the Commons a rude shock awaited him. The House had no intention of granting supplies until it had secured the redress of certain grievances. Accordingly, a Bill was introduced to abolish impositions, and reference was made to exclusive privileges, granted to individuals, which were virtually monopolies. As the days passed the debates became constantly fiercer in tone; and the repeated demands by Sir Ralph Winwood, the new Secretary of State, for supplies only added fuel to the fire.

The conviction that money would not be forthcoming from the Commons except on terms which the King would never accept, led the Court to look round for some other source of income. The King's project of a marriage-alliance with France was abandoned, and was replaced by a suggestion of an alliance between Prince Charles and the Spanish Infanta whose dowry, it was hoped, would be substantial enough to supply the King's needs. James consulted Gondomar about such an alliance. Though the wily Ambassador would give only a non-committal reply, James, with his usual credulity, was encouraged to feel already independent of the Commons' grants, and on June 7 he dissolved his second Parliament. It was well named the Addled Parliament for not a single Bill was placed on the Statute Book during its life-time.

The temper in which James ended this Parliament was shown when immediately afterwards he committed four Members of the Commons—including Wentworth—to the Tower for words spoken in the House, and by forbidding five others to leave London without permission. Though the prisoners were released one by one during the next few months, this infringement of the Commons' privileges would not be forgotten when another Parliament met.

Nor did dissolution of Parliament solve the King's problems. On the contrary, he was still without Parliamentary supplies, and his alternative method of trying to obtain money from Spain would deliver him into Gondomar's ever-tightening clutch. Meantime his subjects would grow increasingly estranged so that, when eventually another Parliament had to be called, he would face an opposition much more determined than the one he was now evading. Such, in brief, was the history of the seven years between the second and third Parliaments of the reign.

2. Parliamentary Interlude, 1614–21

One of the most significant events of the interval was the rise of a new royal favourite, George Villiers. Villiers was the son of a Leicestershire gentleman and was first introduced to James in August 1614 during a royal progress. Though then only twenty-two years of age, he had a singular charm of manner and the promise of graceful dignity which fuller manhood would develop. One of James' foibles was that he found a handsome man irresistible. The moment his eyes rested upon young George Villiers James' heart was conquered. And all too often his heart ruled his head. Unfortunately, he failed to recognize that the man whom the King delighted to honour as a personal friend was not necessarily the man fitted to bear high responsibilities of State. Titles, wealth, and offices were showered upon Villiers in such profusion as would have turned the head of more sober and capable men than he. Indeed, he deserves considerable credit for not allowing himself to become completely unbalanced and corrupted. Not the least important result of the King's favour was that Villiers was thereby introduced to Prince Charles. Though the Prince was slow to thaw towards him, Villiers' natural charm gradually broke through the Prince's reserve until ultimately the two youths became inseparable friends.

Villiers' rise as Court favourite was facilitated by the sudden fall of Somerset. During the latter part of 1615 the proverb that "murder will out" was literally exemplified. Information that Overbury had been poisoned was received by the Secretary of State: and finally the guilt was fixed upon the Earl and Countess of Somerset, who were arrested and sent to the Tower. They were tried and found guilty. The King remitted the death penalty against them, but they remained prisoners in the Tower until 1622. Even after their release their movements were restricted until James, shortly before his death, issued a complete pardon.

Such was the end of the first favourite after Salisbury's death. Henceforward the unhindered rise of Villiers in Court circles was assured. Honours fell upon him thick and fast. In April 1615 he had received a knighthood; in August 1616 he became Viscount Villiers; in the following January he was raised to be Earl of Buckingham; and in January 1618 he became Marquess of Buckingham. Twelve months later he was appointed to the office of Lord High Admiral. In 1623, while at Madrid with Prince Charles, he was promoted to the highest rank that a subject can hold, with the title of Duke of Buckingham.

The Earl of Somerset's fall from favour in 1616 coincided in time with the fall of another, but very different, high official —namely, Chief Justice Coke. Coke had been born in 1552, and as long ago as 1593 had been Speaker of the House of Commons. He had had a highly distinguished legal career: in 1592 he was Solicitor-General, in 1594 Attorney-General, and in 1606 was appointed Chief Justice of the Common Pleas. Coke was anything but a pleasant individual to deal with. He was rancorous and ambitious, caring for the face of no man, not even of the King. One thing alone did he respect more than his own will, and that was the Common Law of England. James doubtless anticipated that Coke's appointment as Chief Justice would ensure that his great abilities would be at the King's disposal. Even James never made a greater error of judgement. Coke's view was that his new position constituted him the champion of the law against anyone who should infringe it—including the King himself. Thus James' conviction that Divine Right placed the King above the law was squarely challenged by Coke's view that even the King was bound to act within the law.

In numerous cases in which Coke had to adjudicate, his principles were unmistakably expressed. In 1610 the Commons protested against the King's use of proclamations of which some had imposed penalties beyond what the law allowed and others had created offences unknown to the law. James therefore asked Coke's opinion about the legality of two proclamations prohibiting respectively the building of new houses in London and the manufacture of starch. Coke, after consulting with three other judges, delivered their unanimous decision that though a royal proclamation could enjoin subjects to keep an existing law it could not create any new offence, since the King's only prerogative was what the law itself allowed.

The next outstanding case which brought Coke into conflict with the King occurred in 1611 when he denied the authority of the Court of High Commission to punish by fines or imprisonment. The Council sought the opinion of all the judges on the point: though the judges' opinions varied, Coke, as usual, was adamant on the side of law.

In 1613 the Chief Justiceship of the King's Bench fell vacant, and Coke was promoted to fill it. Every one was fully aware —and no one more so than Coke himself—that the "promotion" was only the Court's move to send him to a sphere where he would have less opportunities than hitherto of maintaining the liberties of subjects against the King. But in his new office Coke was neither subdued nor muzzled. Only two years later further resistance to the King resulted in his dismissal from the Chief Justiceship.

The interval between the Addled Parliament of 1614 and the opening of James' third Parliament in 1621 saw the removal of yet another notable Elizabethan, Sir Walter Ralegh, who had been confined to the Tower since his implication—real or supposed—in the plots of 1603. The root cause of his imprisonment, as we have seen, had been his opposition to the peace with Spain advocated by James and Cecil. Gondomar's ever-growing influence over James ensured Ralegh's continued exclusion from royal favour. Ralegh tried to counter this influence by asserting that if he were allowed to lead an expedition to Guiana he would be able, from a secret goldmine, to bring back sufficient to fill the King's treasury.

As long ago as 1595 Ralegh had explored the Orinoco, and had written a book entitled *The Discoverie of Guiana* describing his search for gold and for the Inca city called Eldorado about which he had heard stories from Indians. While in the Tower, Ralegh had repeatedly besought James to allow him to lead a fresh expedition in search of the goldmine, but James as repeatedly had refused, partly because he disbelieved Ralegh's fantastic account of the gold, and also because an English expedition to South America could not fail to come into conflict with the Spaniards, and this James would in no circumstances allow. Yet by 1616 James' financial embarrassments were so serious that he was inclined to give Ralegh his chance, always provided that peace with Spain was not imperilled. Ralegh asserted that the mine was outside Spanish territory, and he undertook to avoid conflict. The fact was that he was saying anything that would make an expedition possible. In March 1616 Ralegh was released from the Tower, though he remained under surveillance, in order to prepare for the Orinoco.

The expedition was thoroughly foolish. The King tried to safeguard his policy by authorizing Ralegh to visit only those territories which did not belong to a Christian prince, and by demanding a pledge that Ralegh would not injure subjects of Spain. Further, Ralegh was warned that he would pay with his life for any breach of these stipulations. James must have known that the conditions were impossible of fulfilment.

At last, in June 1617, Ralegh, commanding fourteen vessels, set sail from Plymouth. Having arrived off the mouth of the Orinoco, he sent part of his forces up the river to attack the town of St Thomè. Fierce fighting ensued, and the rumour of approaching Spanish reinforcements compelled the English to return to Ralegh. Discontent verging upon mutiny began to spread among the crews, and no alternative remained but to sail back to England. Plymouth was reached again in May 1618.

Gondomar forthwith demanded Ralegh's execution for the breach of the peace at St Thomè. As Ralegh's death-sentence of fifteen years before had never been repealed, no further trial was necessary or even possible. On October 29, 1618, Ralegh was executed in Palace Yard. His death may fairly be regarded as the passing of the last of the Elizabethans.

After the dissolution of the Addled Parliament the King's financial needs grew increasingly serious. This was due less to insufficient revenue than to extravagance and corruption in administration. In 1617, however, a movement was set on foot to reform the royal finances so as to restore them to solvency. In this movement the chief part was played by Sir Lionel Cranfield.

Cranfield had once been a draper's apprentice in the City. Then, after marrying his master's daughter, he had set up in business on his own account. In due course some commercial transactions brought him to the notice of the Earl of Northampton who introduced him to the King. The latter, impressed by the young man's shrewd and ready speech, took him into the royal service. In 1605 he was appointed Receiver of Customs for Dorset and Somerset; and in 1613 he was promoted to be Surveyor-General of the Customs. Two years later he was knighted.

Cranfield was thus an obvious man to overhaul the royal finances. He began with the royal household. Unnecessary offices, and extravagances of all kinds, were swept away, the result being an annual saving of many thousands of pounds.

The Navy was the next important department to come under

review. In 1619 a commission of investigation was appointed, Cranfield being the chief commissioner. The inquiry revealed the Admiralty as being in a state of appalling corruption and muddle. The superior Admiralty officers were appointed because of noble rank or royal favour irrespective of whether they had any knowledge of naval affairs; and the inferior officers took advantage of their superiors' ignorance and slackness in order to plunder the department. Poor-quality stores were regularly bought at high prices; and many of the ships were rotting. The Commission recommended far-reaching reforms, including a five-year plan for building ten ships a year while reducing the Admiralty expenditure from £50,000 to £30,000 yearly. These reforms could be carried out only by new men: the Lord Admiral, Nottingham, resigned office, and Buckingham was appointed to the post. During the five-year period the plan, both of building and of economy, was faithfully carried out.

As events were to show, the financial reforms were put in hand in circumstances that would make financial efficiency even more necessary than was foreseen when the reforms were first projected. The year 1618 saw the outbreak of the war which, during the remainder of James' reign, was to put his peace-policy to the test, and finally was to drive him to abandon it.

The struggle began in Bohemia, whose people, staunchly Protestant, were suffering persecution at the hands of their King, the Habsburg Matthias, who was also Archduke of Austria and Holy Roman Emperor. Though the Bohemian Crown was elective, for several generations the Bohemians had chosen the Emperor as their King. This had been satisfactory until, as a result of the Reformation, the Bohemians became Protestants while the Emperor remained Roman Catholic. Matthias was an old man, and his death could not be long delayed. In 1617 his cousin, Ferdinand of Styria, was presented to the Bohemian Estates for election. He was accepted, but when the choice became generally known a wave of indignant apprehension swept through Bohemia, for Ferdinand was a bigoted and persecuting Catholic. In 1618, therefore, the Bohemians revolted against Matthias and elected the

Protestant Frederick V, Elector of the Rhine Palatinate, to be King. Matthias died in March 1619, and in August Ferdinand was elected Emperor. Frederick was unwise enough to accept the proffered Bohemian crown.

Misfortunes befell him in rapid succession. In November 1620, at the battle of the White Hill just outside Prague, the Protestants were routed by the Emperor's forces which then overran the whole country. Frederick took refuge with the Dutch in the Hague. Even before the battle Spanish troops from the Spanish Netherlands had invaded the Western Palatinate. In September 1621 the Emperor Ferdinand had invaded the Eastern Palatinate; and thus Frederick lost not only his new Kingdom but also his inherited homeland.

We have already seen that James' daughter, Elizabeth, had married the now exiled Frederick V, and James could not but be torn by conflicting feelings as these blows fell upon them. He was genuinely anxious to help his daughter and her husband; but the only effective method of doing so was to send large armies to Bohemia and the Palatinate. This would involve England in war with the Empire and Spain. From such a step James shrank, and wisely so; for England had no interests that could be furthered by the conflict, nor had she the prepared resources for carrying it to a successful issue. Where James was foolish was in imagining that, without the use of force on a large scale, he could achieve his purpose in any other way. He proposed, for example, a marriage between Prince Charles and the Spanish Infanta, one of the conditions of the marriage being that the Spaniards should withdraw from the Palatinate. Unfortunately for James, Gondomar had taken his measure too accurately to be influenced by any such scheme: Gondomar was convinced that, though James might threaten, he would never carry out his threats.

The mass of James' subjects did not share his illusions. Englishmen, still thinking in terms of Elizabethan antagonism to Spain and to Roman Catholicism, had no room for James' pro-Spanish policy: they were deeply suspicious of Gondomar's growing influence in the royal counsels, and they were angered by the misfortunes suffered by the English princess and her Protestant husband at the hands of Roman Catholic armies.

But the popular view showed no better understanding than the King's of the practical difficulties of the situation—of the national unpreparedness for a large-scale Continental war against united Roman Catholic forces. Indeed, on the immediate issue, the peace-loving King was wiser than his warlike subjects. Yet the nation's political intuition on the general situation was sound: if Protestantism were crushed on the Continent England might stand in greater jeopardy than even in the days of the Armada. And scarcely less dangerous was the Spanish Ambassador's insidious ascendancy over royal policy.

Even James, deeply moved by his daughter's fugitive condition after 1620, began to consider methods of raising money to meet the cost of intervening on their behalf. At the end of September 1620 a Benevolence was raised; but, though the Crown put pressure on wealthy individuals all over the country, the total contributions were less than £35,000. Such a sum was altogether inadequate for a war. A Parliament was the only alternative, and writs were issued for a new Parliament to meet in January. From James' point of view, however, a Parliament would have its drawbacks: it would grant money only on its own terms, and many issues would be raised besides that of the war.

3. Third Parliament, 1621–22

King James opened the third Parliament of his reign on January 30, 1621. Among Members then returned to the Commons for the first time were John Pym and John Hampden. Along with them sat Sir Thomas Wentworth. No less significant was the re-appearance in the Commons of Sir Edward Coke, now verging on seventy years of age. One notable member of the 1614 Parliament was absent from this of 1621— namely, Sir John Eliot.

In one respect the King had an easy task in facing the new Parliament. He had been converted to the popular policy of war in support of the Palatinate; and so great was the enthusiasm for this policy that a bold lead by the King, coupled with moderate concessions on certain grievances, would have rallied the Commons and the nation behind him, and might have given a new direction to the remainder of the reign. But bold leadership was beyond James' capacity. Now, as always, he allowed opportunity to slip through his fingers.

James' speech at the opening of the Parliament was typically ambiguous. He urged substantial grants of supply which would be required especially to reach a settlement of the Bohemian dispute, but this general statement was not accompanied by any explanation of specific measures to be taken, or by any estimate of war-expenditure. Hence Parliament, though approving the King's sentiments, felt no confidence in his carrying them into practice. The Commons therefore debated the matter during the first fortnight in February, and then voted the little more than nominal grant of two subsidies (about £160,000).

No sooner was this grant made than the Commons turned to the subject uppermost in its mind—namely, the redress of grievances, the implication evidently being that the grant of more substantial supplies would depend upon the King's response to the Commons' complaint.

The first grievance was monopolies. The granting to individuals of exclusive rights to trade or manufacture had always been a source of abuses, notably of high prices and bad quality in the monopolized goods. In 1601 the Commons had so fiercely debated such abuses that Elizabeth had placated them by this assurance: "That my grants should be grievous to my people, and oppressions privileged under patents, our kingly dignity will not suffer it." James I's reign saw a recurrence of the evil. The sale of monopolies was one of the expedients whereby the King tried to cure the emptiness of his exchequer during the years without a Parliament.

The first monopoly with which the Commons dealt was that for granting licences to inns. This was held by Sir Giles Mompesson. The Commons could bring him to book because he was a Member of the House. Evidence before the investigating committee showed his misuse of the patent—oppressive charges to would-be inn-keepers, prosecution of inn-keepers under obsolete statutes, the employment of rascally agents to spy on inns, and the like. The committee also discovered that a certain Justice named Sir Francis Michell had repeatedly extorted money from applicants for ale-house licences. The Commons removed Michell from the roll of Justices and sent him to the Tower. In so doing the House was exceeding its just powers, since the only offences for which it could impose punishments were those involving breaches of its privileges. As soon as their first anger had cooled Members realized their error, and tried to cover it by seeking a conference with the Lords. Nevertheless the Commons proceeded against Mompesson, whose iniquities were found to concern other patents beside that for inns, notably for gold and silver thread. So scared was Mompesson that he forestalled arrest by fleeing overseas. The Commons could then only vent its rage by formally expelling him from the House. The Lords then degraded Mompesson from the order of knighthood, outlawed him (all his goods being forfeited to the King), and declared that if taken he should be fined £10,000 and imprisoned for life. Four days later the King issued a proclamation revoking the patents for gold and silver thread and for inns. Early in May the Lords also sentenced Michell to a fine of £1000, to permanent exclusion from public office, and to degradation from knighthood.

Even more important than the revocation of the patents and the punishment of individual malefactors was the vindication of the Commons' powers to investigate grievances against the King's servants and, further, the fact that the King had made substantial concessions to the Commons' claims.

Meanwhile proceedings were being taken against a more exalted servant of the Crown, no less a person than Lord Chancellor Francis Bacon, Viscount St Albans. Bacon's prosecution arose from the inquiries into monopolies. Repeatedly the Commons found that its investigations could be carried only up to a certain point. The monopolists and their agents could be traced and examined; but the power behind the throne, recommending these individuals for privileges, too often baffled discovery. Since what was in question was the legality of monopolies, the ultimate responsibility was with the law-officers, and supremely with the Lord Chancellor.

But behind the immediate occasion of the attack there were

deeper reasons. Bacon had influential personal enemies. His
bitterest opponent was Coke. For many years the two men
had been rivals. In 1594 they had both hoped for the office
of Attorney-General which Coke secured. Four years later
Coke also won the second round in the contest by marrying
Lady Kathleen Hatton, for whom Bacon had been a suitor.
Then Coke's dismissal from the Chief Justiceship in 1616 was
quickly followed by Bacon's rise: in March 1617 Bacon was
made Lord Keeper, and in January 1618 Lord Chancellor.
The debates on monopolies in 1621 gave to Coke the opportunity to score against his old rival, and he made the fullest
use of it.

The most powerful of Bacon's opponents was the royal
favourite, Buckingham, who was quick to see how to divert
attention from his own dealings in monopolies by attracting
attention to Bacon. In political and constitutional principles
Coke and Buckingham were poles apart. Their momentary
union against a common enemy was enough to seal his fate.

To these influential opponents of Bacon was added yet a
third—namely, Sir Lionel Cranfield, whose dislike of the Lord
Chancellor was due to the latter's interference with the Court
of Wards of which in 1619 Cranfield had been made Master.

The upshot was that Bacon was impeached for receiving
bribes from suitors in cases brought before him for trial. So
plain was the evidence of such malpractices that Bacon
admitted to the Lords his guilt, hoping thus to ward off too
heavy a sentence. What could not be proved was that his
acceptance of bribes had influenced the judgements which he
had delivered. The King intervened to try to get the case into
his own hands, but in vain. On May 1, 1621, at the House of
Lords' request, the King deprived Bacon of his office of Lord
Chancellor. Two days later the Lords delivered sentence
against him: he was to be fined £40,000, to be imprisoned in
the Tower during the King's pleasure, and to be incapable of
holding office in the State.

The loss of office was a terrible shock to a man of Bacon's
rank and attainments. The King did his best to soften the blow
by exercising his prerogative in the matter of the other penalties. Bacon's stay in the Tower was short, and he was soon

allowed to move to the country. By the end of 1621 the King had remitted the huge fine, and early the next year Bacon was allowed to return to London.

Nevertheless other effects of Bacon's fall were highly significant. First, the case was a healthy assertion of the principle that the first duty of an administrator of English law is to keep his own hands clean, and that no man, however exalted his rank, who violated this principle, would escape due punishment. The verdict was the more striking when we remember that the acceptance of presents in connexion with services and offices was then a matter of course in every rank of life. Second, the Lord Chancellor was a royal servant. Bacon's impeachment was thus an assertion that even the King's Ministers were accountable to Parliament for their official actions. This weapon of impeachment, though not uncommon in the fourteenth and early fifteenth centuries, had fallen into disuse. Its revival in the reign of the first Stuart was a portent of the control which successive Stuart Parliaments would claim over the King's advisers and over the King himself. One of the ironies of history was that the two men against whom the process of impeachment was next set in motion were those who had been most anxious to revive it—namely, Cranfield and Buckingham.

On June 3, 1621, Parliament adjourned and did not meet again until November 20. A fortnight after the adjournment Sir Edwin Sandys was arrested and imprisoned for a speech delivered in the Commons. The purport of the speech had been that Protestantism had been defeated in Germany and that England was herself in danger. Along with Sandys went the Earl of Southampton (in whose house had been held meetings of Buckingham's enemies) and John Selden. The latter was not a Member of the Commons, and the reason for his imprisonment was obscure. Their imprisonment did not last more than a month, but this did not alter the fact that it was extremely impolitic and would produce a barrier of mistrust between King and Commons when the latter re-assembled.

The opening speech to the Houses in November was delivered by Lord Keeper Williams. He urged the postponement of all business except the voting of supplies for the Palatinate.

He was followed in a similar strain by Cranfield, who in July had been raised to the peerage as Earl of Middlesex, and subsequently had been made Treasurer.

Next day, when the Commons met, attention was called to Sandys' imprisonment, and hopes were expressed that in the coming debate on the King's message there would be no interference with Members on account of opinions voiced in the House. Though Sir George Calvert, the Secretary of State, assured the Commons that Sandys' imprisonment had not been due to words uttered in the House, Members remained sceptical, and were with difficulty persuaded to allow the subject to drop.

Even apart from any specific grievance, Parliament was at the same disadvantage as when it had first met—namely, that the King gave no indication of what his policy was for the Palatinate or of what its cost was estimated to be. During the debate on supply the mind of the House was plainly expressed by a speaker who declared that Members could not be expected to make a grant for the war until they knew who the enemy was. He further urged that an assurance should be given to them that the supply would be used to make war on Spain, and that the Prince would marry a Protestant. Many speakers supported these views.

At the close of the debate a committee was formed to draw up a petition to the King on the subject of religion. The petition, as finally agreed in December 1621, made various requests, including:

> That . . . your Majesty would resolve to pursue and more publicly avow the aiding of those of our religion in foreign parts. . . .
> That, for securing of our peace at home, your Majesty would be pleased . . . to put in execution the laws already and hereafter to be made for preventing of dangers by popish recusants and their wonted evasions.[1]

The petition's attempt to determine foreign policy, and its strong implication that the King was not carrying out existing laws against recusants, raised the King's anger to such a pitch

[1] Prothero, p. 307.

that, before officially receiving the petition, he addressed to
the Speaker of the Commons a letter which bade the Speaker
inform the House:

> . . . that none therein shall presume henceforth to meddle with
> anything concerning our government or deep matters of state,
> and namely, not to deal with our dearest son's match with the
> daughter of Spain, nor to touch the honour of that king or any
> other our friends and confederates.[1]

Then, after referring to the imprisonment of Sir Edward
Sandys, the King continued:

> You shall resolve them in our name, That we think ourselves
> very free and able to punish any man's misdemeanours in Parlia-
> ment as well during their sitting as after; which we mean not
> to spare hereafter, upon any occasion of any man's insolent
> behaviour there that shall be ministered unto us. And, if they
> have already touched any of these points which we have for-
> bidden, in any petition of theirs which is to be sent unto us, it is
> our pleasure that you shall tell them, That, except they reform
> it before it comes to our hands, we will not deign the hearing
> nor answering of it.

The astonishing terms of this letter were a denial of the
Commons' most cherished privileges. Strictly enforced, they
would have put an end to freedom of speech without which
all other privileges would be valueless. Members were deeply
moved; but the seriousness of the issue prevented them from
hasty action. For three days the Commons debated the terms
of a second petition which was intended to explain the first.
After asserting the Commons' "loyalty and dutifulness," the
petition begged that:

> . . . whereas your Majesty doth seem to abridge us of the ancient
> liberty of parliament for freedom of speech . . . a liberty which,
> we assure ourselves, so wise and so just a king will not infringe,
> the same being our ancient and undoubted right . . . without
> which we cannot freely debate nor clearly discern of things in
> question before us . . . we are therefore now again enforced, in

[1] Prothero, pp. 310–312.

all humbleness, to pray your Majesty to allow the same, and thereby to take away the doubts and scruples your Majesty's late letter to our Speaker hath wrought upon us.[1]

When the deputation of twelve Members bearing the petition reached the King at Newmarket James jestingly called out: "Bring stools for the Ambassadors!" In the letter which he sent in reply James refused to give any undertaking about his foreign policy or his son's marriage, for "these are unfit things to be handled in Parliament except your King should require it of you." As to the Commons' privileges, the King, though regarding them as "derived from the grace and permission of our ancestors and us," was yet pleased to give his royal assurance:

... that as long as you contain yourself within the limits of your duty, we will be as careful to maintain and preserve your lawful liberties and privileges, as ever any of our predecessors were, nay, as to preserve our own prerogative.

The more the Commons examined this letter, the less satisfactory they found it; and on December 18, 1621, they drew up, and entered upon their Journals, their famous Protestation:[2]

That the liberties, franchises, privileges, and jurisdictions of parliament, are the ancient and undoubted birthright and inheritance of the subjects of England; and that the arduous and urgent affairs concerning the king, state, and defence of the realm, and of the church of England, and the maintenance and making of laws, the redress of mischiefs and grievances which daily happen within this realm, are proper subjects and matter of counsel and debate in parliament: and that in the handling and proceeding of these businesses every member of the House of Parliament hath and of right ought to have freedom of speech, to propound, treat, reason and bring to conclusion of the same.

The next day Parliament was prorogued until February. During the interval James was ruminating on the situation. Then on December 30 he decided to act. He sent for the

---

[1] Prothero, pp. 311–312.
[2] Prothero, pp. 313–314.

Commons' Journals, and with his own hand tore out the page on which the Protestation had been entered.

The King could hardly meet again the Parliament whose records he had thus violated; and Parliament was accordingly dissolved.

Had all the facts been known to the Commons, Members would have been even more suspicious and angry than they had been. Throughout the proceedings James had been prompted by his evil counsellor, Gondomar, who, after the dissolution, wrote:

> It is certain that the King will never summon another Parliament as long as he lives, or at least not another composed as this one was.[1]

Such a remark reveals how little true insight Gondomar had into the character of the English people or the nature of English government. We may doubt whether James was any more perspicacious. Even before the Parliament's dissolution three Members of the Commons—Coke, Phelips, and Mallory —were arrested and sent to the Tower; and Pym was ordered to remain in his London house.

This episode of the series of petitions and letters is worth study at some length because it exemplifies what were the points of view of King and Parliament respectively during the remainder of James I's reign and throughout the reign of Charles I.

Two general aspects of the 1621–22 Parliament call for notice before we leave it. First, there can be no doubt that the Commons' claim to a voice in foreign policy, including the Prince's marriage, was unprecedented. In this respect at least James' view was historically more correct than the Commons'. Equally certain is it—as the tone of the Parliamentary debates makes clear—that the Commons did not realize how novel their claims were, nor had they any intention of infringing royal prerogative. James' error was in his misjudging the Commons' motives and the strength of Members' convictions.

Second, we must avoid reading back into this and other early Stuart Parliaments certain factors whose significance

[1] Quoted by Gardiner in *History of England*, vol. IV, p. 266.

became apparent only as the result of the experience of some twenty years later. This is true, for example, in the matter of Parliamentary leadership. We are not to imagine that Pym, Hampden, and Wentworth were at once and generally recognized as the leaders of a majority section of the Commons. Two of them were new Members, and the third had had only the three weeks' experience of the Addled Parliament seven years previously. The rarity and brevity of Parliaments hitherto had made impossible the growth of Parliamentary leadership in anything like the modern sense of the term. Such leadership could evolve only in frequent Parliaments sitting continuously for long periods. Not the least noteworthy aspect of the 1621 Parliament was that it was the first of a series of Parliaments in close succession. Between 1621 and 1629 (when another long Parliamentary break began) there were five Parliaments. In addition, therefore, to raising questions of political principle, the 1621–22 Parliament served to mark out some of the men who were to be the champions of Parliamentary government, and provided them with an apprenticeship for their task.

4. The Spanish Marriage

During the interval between the dissolution of James' third Parliament on January 6 and the meeting of his fourth on February 19, 1624, public attention was occupied largely by foreign affairs. It was these affairs which shaped Parliament's attitude to the King during the closing months of the reign.

During 1622–23 the Imperial forces drove Frederick V out of his Palatinate and gave it and his Electorship to Maximilian of Bavaria. This marked the end of the Bohemian revolution. But instead of bringing an end to the dispute, Maximilian's triumph marked only the close of the first stage in what was to become a general German, and later a European, struggle. The other German Protestants feared that their turn might come next, and there was a growing unrest and resort to arms throughout Germany, with clashes between Roman Catholic and Protestant forces.

To James I the uncertainties of the time seemed to provide

ideal opportunities for the exercise of his peculiar diplomatic genius. He was still infatuated with the notion that Catholicism in the Empire could be countered by a marriage-alliance between England and Spain. In this notion he had been encouraged by Gondomar, who had spread his influence also over Prince Charles and Buckingham. On pretence of considering details about the marriage and about negotiations concerning the Palatinate, the Spanish Court recalled Gondomar in May 1622. Before his departure he had secured a promise that Prince Charles would visit Madrid incognito, accompanied by two servants, if events in Spain made the visit advisable. The wily Ambassador's hope was that the young Prince, thus severed from English Protestantism and surrounded by the fascination of Roman Catholic ritual, would be converted to Catholicism. Clearly the English and the Spanish Courts were viewing the projected visit from diametrically opposite points of view.

Early in 1623 Buckingham and Charles urged the King to allow them at once to go to Madrid. James did his utmost to dissuade them from their intention. He was impressed by the dangers of the journey, and by his conviction that the Spaniards, as soon as the Prince was in their midst, would demand further concessions for English Catholics as the price of the marriage. Events proved the wisdom of James' judgement; but, as so often, James lacked the moral courage to carry out what he knew to be the right course. To hold out for long against the persistent requests of his favourites was impossible to the vacillating King. With much hesitation and misgiving, he at last consented to the preposterous exploit.

On February 19, 1623, Prince Charles and Buckingham, under the assumed names of John and Thomas Smith, crossed from Dover to Boulogne. Along with them went the Prince's secretary, Sir Francis Cottingham, Buckingham's Master of Horse, Sir Richard Graham, and Endymion Porter, who had lately returned from a mission to Spain where he had been sent to gauge the attitude of the Spanish Court towards the marriage-project. From Boulogne they rode across France *via* Paris and Bayonne, and so into Spain and to Madrid, which they reached on March 7. There they made themselves known to the English Ambassador, the Earl of Bristol.

In Madrid Charles and Buckingham found themselves narrowly restricted by rigid Court formalities. Not only did the Spanish social code prevent the Prince from private interviews with the Infanta, but he and his suite were hedged about at every turn by Ministers and courtiers appointed to attend them. The Spaniards deliberately prolonged the negotiations in the hope of effecting the Prince's conversion to Catholicism, and Charles seemed to encourage the idea by declaring himself willing to secure concessions for Roman Catholics in England. Finally Charles undertook that the English penal laws against them should at once be suspended, that they should be repealed by Parliament within three years, that the Infanta should enjoy her own form of worship which members of the public should be allowed to attend, and that she should have control of their children until they reached the age of twelve.

Both Charles and Buckingham must have known that there was not the remotest chance that either Parliament or the nation would allow these pledges to be fulfilled. Nor were the Spaniards deceived in the matter. They went on to demand that after the marriage had taken place the Infanta should remain in Spain for at least twelve months during which period complete toleration should be granted to English Roman Catholics and be assured by Parliament.

This stand by the Spaniards at last convinced both the Prince and his Ministers that their mission was futile, especially as, meantime, the Spaniards had refused to consider any action to help Frederick to recover the Palatinate. Buckingham flew into a violent rage of protest against the trickery of which they had been the victims, and preparations began for the return of the mission to England. Even when matters had reached this stage the Spanish Court, acting chiefly through Olivares, chief Minister of King Philip IV, continued negotiations to keep the Prince in Spain and hence to postpone as long as possible a breach with England. The Prince's anxiety to marry the Infanta blinded him to the Spaniards' duplicity, so that he went on making promises of concessions. Hence he did not leave Madrid until September 2, reaching London on October 6.

The news that the Prince had returned still a Protestant and without the Infanta evoked from the Londoners an unprecedented outburst of rejoicings—public feastings, illuminations, bonfires, and even the release of prisoners. These spontaneous demonstrations revealed how deep-seated was the nation's anxiety lest the country should be tied to Romanist Spain.

The immediate reason for the breakdown of negotiations was that both Prince Charles and Buckingham were hopelessly incompetent diplomatists. The Prince, his judgement warped by what he believed to be his passion for the Infanta, was an easy tool in the hands of the astute Spanish Ministers. Buckingham was as ill-suited an adviser to such a prince as could have been found. He lacked diplomatic experience and training. Nor did this defect find any compensation in his natural gifts. He combined the two characteristics most likely to antagonize the Spaniards—rashness and arrogance. His being raised to a Dukedom in May 1623 merely increased his imprudent arrogance towards the Spanish nobles whom it was intended to impress favourably. This effect was tersely summed up in the Spaniards' remark—as later reported by Bristol to King James—that "they would rather put the Infanta headlong into a well than into his hands."

The fundamental cause of the mission's failure, however, went deeper. It was the clash between the mutually incompatible objects of James and of the Spaniards. James' purpose was the restoration of the Palatinate to Frederick and Elizabeth. The Spaniards could not be expected to advance the interests of one whom they regarded as a Protestant rebel against the Roman Catholic Emperor. On the contrary, the Spaniards' aim was to use James' desire for the match as a means towards Charles' conversion, and hence ultimately towards England's restoration to the true Church.

Charles and Buckingham, having returned to London, became warm advocates of a new foreign policy involving a breach with Spain. Two motives prompted the change. First, both Prince and Duke were bitterly incensed by realizing at last that they had been elaborately duped by the Spaniards.

Second, the demonstrations of wild joy with which the Londoners had greeted the Prince on his return had a significance too plain to be missed even by Buckingham. James was less difficult to convert to the new policy than might have been expected. As soon as he was convinced that the Palatinate could not be freed through a Spanish marriage, he began to consider other means of achieving his aim. Buckingham was ready with a scheme to suit the situation. This was none other than a European alliance against Spain, the basis of which was to be a marriage between Charles and the French Princess, Henrietta Maria.

Such a policy would need Parliamentary sanction and support, and, as war against Spain was certain to be a popular programme, the decision was taken to summon a Parliament without delay. The order for the issue of writs was signed on December 28, 1623, and on February 19, 1624, the new Parliament was opened.

5. Fourth Parliament, 1624–25

The King's speech delivered to Parliament on February 19 must have bewildered many Members who listened to it. James, who had marked the close of the previous Parliament by imprisoning Coke, Phelips, and Mallory in the Tower, and by confining Pym to his London house, opened this Parliament by promising Members that the Duke of Buckingham would give to them an account of events in Spain and by encouraging them to express their views thereon. Said he:

> I shall entreat your good and sound advice. . . . Never king gave more trust to his subjects than to desire their advice in matters of this weight; for I assure you ye may freely advise me, seeing of my princely fidelity ye are invited thereto.[1]

Buckingham's apologia was delivered five days later. No reference was made to the many promises that the Prince had given of concessions for English Catholics or to the Prince's apparent indecision between Protestantism and Roman Catholicism as his personal faith. All the emphasis in Bucking-

[1] *Parliamentary History*, I, 1372.

ham's recital was placed upon the Spaniards' duplicity in making half-promises which events proved they had no intention of keeping. Accurately sensing the response of his audience as he drew to a close, Buckingham summarized the whole matter by demanding:

> Shall we endure further Spanish diplomacy, or, setting treaties aside, let His Majesty trust his own strength and stand upon his own feet?

The cheers with which this declamation was greeted left no doubt as to the feelings of Parliament. Buckingham had suddenly stepped into the limelight of national popularity. In that light the weakening king was to bask during the brief remainder of his reign. After long interviews between the English Court and the Spanish representatives, early in April 1624 a despatch was sent through the English Ambassador at Madrid announcing the end of negotiations.

One man stood out against the anti-Spanish flood. This was the Lord Treasurer Middlesex who had fallen foul of both the Prince and Buckingham. On the Spanish marriage Middlesex had gone so far as to express the opinion that if there were good reasons of State for friendship with Spain the Prince ought to subordinate his personal feelings and marry the Infanta. As the guardian of the royal exchequer, Middlesex inevitably opposed Buckingham's extravagance. During the Madrid expedition Middlesex had been sparing in the money sent out to meet the expenses of the insatiable Buckingham. Also, Middlesex opposed the projected Spanish war which threatened to eat up the exchequer surplus which Middlesex's economies had carefully hoarded in place of the deficiency that he had found. Moreover, Middlesex had no confidence in Buckingham's ability to conduct a war. To drain the exchequer for a victorious war might be a painful necessity. To revert to national bankruptcy through mismanagement and defeat would be a national disaster of the first magnitude.

Buckingham therefore took advantage of his own sudden popularity with Parliament to bring about Middlesex's downfall. In the middle of April the Commons, influenced by Buckingham, brought before the Lords charges of impeachment

against the Lord Treasurer. The charges concerned the appropriation to his own use of large sums out of the King's revenue.
The upshot of the proceedings was the sentence delivered on
May 13, whereby Middlesex was condemned to imprisonment
in the Tower during the King's pleasure, to the payment of a
fine of £50,000, to dismissal from all his offices, and to being
prohibited for the future from holding any office of State, and
from sitting in Parliament.

More important than these immediate results was the wider
significance of the trial itself. The impeachment of the Lord
Treasurer reinforced the implication of Bacon's trial—namely,
that the King's Ministers were accountable to Parliament for
their conduct of State business. Buckingham, in using such an
instrument to crush a personal enemy, was acting with short-
sighted imprudence. The only member of the Court to appre-
ciate this implication seems to have been the King himself,
who is reported as exclaiming angrily to Buckingham:

> "By God, Steeny, you are a fool and will shortly repent this
> folly, and will find that in this fit of popularity you are making
> a rod with which you will scourge yourself." And turning in
> some anger to the Prince, told him, that he would live to have
> his bellyful of Parliaments; and that, when he should be dead,
> he would have too much cause to remember how much he had
> contributed to the weakening of the Crown by this precedent
> he was now so fond of.[1]

A truer judgement on the proceedings would have been
difficult to frame: Buckingham was the next to be impeached.
Once again James had shown clearness of mind and feebleness
of will—the "wisest fool in Christendom."

With national attention centred on foreign affairs, legislation on domestic matters tended to be pushed into the background. Nevertheless the Commons took advantage of its
alliance with the Court favourite in order to secure certain
legislation which it had long desired. After negotiations between Commons and Court, an Act was passed making monopolies illegal. In order to secure the King's consent to the
measure the Commons agreed to exempt certain existing

---

[1] Clarendon, Book I, Section 44.

monopolies from the Bill. Also, to encourage new commercial processes, monopolies were to be allowed for a specified time (up to fourteen years) to genuine inventions.

Almost as soon as the Act was passed, on May 29, the session was closed, and Parliament was to stand prorogued until November. Two further prorogations prevented another session of Parliament during James' life-time.

The reason for the successive prorogations was that the Court was negotiating with France for the betrothal of Charles with the Princess Henrietta Maria. The French demands were similar to those of the Spaniards. Throughout the negotiations the French had the advantage over the English. Not only was French diplomacy in the capable hands of Cardinal Richelieu, but the French knew that the alliance was more necessary to the English Court than to themselves. A second rebuff abroad might well prove fatal to Buckingham's prestige at home. Moreover, the breach with Spain made an ally essential to England. France was also conveniently situated for waging war on the Palatinate which Buckingham had determined to support. Hence the French were able to drive their own bargain. The marriage treaty was signed by the Ambassadors in November and ratified by King James in December. Prince Charles secretly undertook that the Roman Catholic subjects of the Crown should have religious liberty so long as they remained loyal to the King. Within a fortnight of the ratification orders were given to the English law-courts that prosecution of recusants was to cease, and that Roman Catholics in prison for offences connected with religion were to be released.

In return for such wide concessions all that Louis XIII would grant was a vaguely termed promise to contribute towards the support of the Protestant Count Ernst Mansfeld, one of the first of the adventure-leaders of the Thirty Years' War.

In November 1624 Mansfeld had landed in England to take command of twelve thousand pressed men who were to be sent over to the Palatinate. They were a motley crowd—unwilling, untrained, ill-provided. The English exchequer contained no resources sufficient to support such a force. Large numbers of them deserted while waiting for ships to carry them across the Channel. When at last, in February 1625, the remains of the force reached Holland—Louis having raised difficulties about its going through French territory—the half-starved men became a prey to sickness and a great many perished. Only a small proportion of the twelve thousand were fit to bear arms. The expedition proved a disgraceful failure.

Meanwhile James had been negotiating for help elsewhere. In June 1624 he had sent envoys to Gustavus Adolphus of Sweden and to Christian IV of Denmark, both of whom were enthusiastic Protestants.

These negotiations did not reach a tangible stage until February and March 1625. By that time King James had little need to worry about European diplomacy. Early in March he became the victim of an acute ague. In spite of several rallies he weakened, and on March 27 breathed his last.

There is no need to moralize over the passing of the first of England's Stuart kings. Though James had lived only fifty-nine years, he already had the characteristics of old age and had lost his grip on life. Perhaps it was a merciful dispensation that removed him before the full reactions of his infirm will, both at home and abroad, could be fully evident. At home, particularly, his policy—or, more accurately, his lack of policy—had sown the wind, and the son and the favourite on whom he had doted would assuredly reap the whirlwind.

Chapter 4

King Charles I: The Rule of Buckingham

1625–29

1. Foreign Affairs, 1625–30

It was a fair prospect that spread out before the new King as he mounted the throne. Court and people were united as never during the whole twenty-one years of his father's reign. The echoes of the nation's rejoicing that had greeted his return from Spain could still be heard. His chief Minister and most intimate friend was at the moment the people's darling. In the Parliament which then stood prorogued the one-time champions of popular liberties had vied with one another in approving the desire of the Prince and his favourite for war against Spain.

Events were soon to show that this placid prospect was an illusion. The national unity was superficial only. Between the nation, as represented in Parliament, and the King there were fundamental differences. Not the least of them was that Parliament was predominantly Puritan while the King was Anglican. Even the agreement on foreign policy would raise problems. A war would involve expenditure which could be met only by parliamentary grants; and if Parliament voted supplies for war it would demand some control over the policy and conduct of the war. The result would be a new clash with the King.

The basic principle of Charles I's government was identical with that of his father. Both alike believed passionately and religiously in the Divine Right of their kingship. The one sphere of politics in which James and Charles differed fundamentally—at least during the first section of the latter's reign, 1625–29—was that of foreign affairs; and in the last resort it was the disasters of his war-policy which produced the breach finally between Charles and Parliament.

The root reason for the breach over foreign policy was that Charles' Parliaments, like their Elizabethan predecessors, still regarded Roman Catholic Spain as the supreme enemy of Protestant England, and urged naval expeditions on the lines of those led by Drake and the other Elizabethan sea-dogs. Charles, on the other hand, thought in terms of restoring his brother-in-law, Frederick, to the Palatinate, and he regarded Spain as an enemy only because Spanish troops had invaded the Palatinate. Yet Charles and Buckingham failed to use the only means of expelling them—namely, to ally effectively with Sweden or Denmark.

The first event with foreign implications in Charles' reign was his marriage with the French Princess Henrietta Maria. The ceremony took place by proxy in Paris on May 1, 1625, and six weeks later Henrietta landed at Dover where Charles met her. On June 16 the King and Queen entered London.

The King was twenty-four years of age; the Queen was fifteen. That fact was symbolical of their relationship. They were an ill-assorted pair. Charles had the seriousness that accompanies the conscious regal dignity that was one of his most marked characteristics. Henrietta had the vivacity to be expected of a French girl brought up in the Bourbon court. Charles was a sincere unwavering Protestant. Henrietta was a devout Roman Catholic. Charles, in spite of his belief in Divine Right, found himself King of a nation accustomed, during several centuries, to express its will through a Parliament which, by its control of supplies, could assert its will against the King. Henrietta had known only the autocratic government of France, and she never understood the English parliamentary system.

These contrasts caused Henrietta to be as dangerous a consort to Charles as could have been found. During the early part of the reign Charles found so little in common between himself and his youthful wife that he either ignored her or treated her with deliberate displeasure. Though Henrietta could be fretful and provoking, the chief fault for much of the discord was Charles': his unimaginative mind made him unable to realize what it meant to a young girl to be exiled from her home and country. This showed itself especially when, in

August 1626, he compelled the French members of the Queen's household, other than a few personal attendants, to return forthwith to France. In the nation at large the Queen was regarded with deep suspicion on account of her Roman Catholicism.

Later in the reign, after Buckingham's death, Charles and Henrietta became not merely reconciled but warmly attached to each other. Charles grew accustomed to seeking, and often accepting, his wife's advice about matters of State. The sequel will show that this was the period when she was most dangerous to him. Her advice—for example, that Charles should arrest the Five Members—was often based upon complete misunderstanding of English political tradition. Thus the catastrophe which finally overtook both King and nation was in no small degree due to the ill-advice of Henrietta.

At this point, however, we must be concerned primarily with the marriage as an episode in foreign politics. Henrietta was the symbol of and—so Charles and Buckingham hoped— the security for, a French alliance in the effort to recover the Palatinate for Frederick. But for that alliance Charles had been compelled to pay a high price, and would yet have to pay a still higher one.

Before Henrietta left for England Buckingham had gone to Paris in the hope of arranging a combined attack by a French army and an English fleet against the Spanish Netherlands. The bait he held out was that France should obtain the Province of Artois; and he hoped to please English opinion by persuading Louis XIII to grant concessions to the French Huguenots. In 1622 the Huguenots had lost part of the privileges which Henry IV had promised in the Edict of Nantes of 1598, though La Rochelle still remained as a city of refuge. In 1624 their prospects were worsened by the accession to power in France of Cardinal Richelieu. One of his objects, as a means to greater unity within France, was to abolish the semi-independence of the Huguenots. They therefore, appreciating their danger, decided to strike before it was too late, and a religious civil war in France was the result. Richelieu, realizing the impossibilty of capturing La Rochelle while the port was open to the sea, and having no adequate navy of his own, sought help from England. Buckingham at once promised the use of English ships, hoping thus to secure French help against Spain. But, though accepting the promise of the ships, Richelieu evaded any definite undertaking in return. Buckingham was no more successful with France than he had been two years earlier with Spain. As a diplomatist, dealing with trained, experienced statesmen, his career was an almost unrelieved failure.

Eight English vessels sailed across to Dieppe early in June under the command of Vice-Admiral Pennington. Because his orders were vague and ambiguous, and his relations with the French proved equally so, within a fortnight Pennington brought back his ships to England. Then, in mid-July, terms of peace having been made between Louis and the Huguenots, the fleet was sent back to Dieppe to be delivered to the French in the expectation that it would be used in a war that the French were believed to be about to declare against Spain. Unfortunately for Buckingham's calculations, the vessels were put to a very different use. The agreement between Louis and the Huguenots lasted only a short time. The civil war was renewed, and early in September the Huguenots were defeated in a naval action near La Rochelle. Louis' fleet on that occasion included the English vessels. As though to complete Buckingham's disillusionment, in April 1626 Spain and France made peace. Before that date his efforts abroad had suffered severe shocks elsewhere.

Buckingham had continued to press forward the preparations for the naval attack on Spain, which was the only project of foreign policy upon which he and the Commons were agreed. By the end of the summer of 1625 the fleet at Plymouth was as nearly ready as it was likely to be. Sir Edward Cecil was appointed to command it. On October 8, 1625, the fleet sailed out of Plymouth Sound for the Spanish coast. No definite objective had been decided upon beforehand. An attack was made on some Spanish ships sighted at Cadiz, but they eluded capture by taking refuge in the harbour. A direct attack on Cadiz itself was equally fruitless. Cecil therefore determined upon an alternative plan of intercepting the Plate treasure-fleet. With this intention he moved off towards Cape St

Vincent. Hardly had he sailed out when the Plate fleet, unknown to him, sailed into Cadiz harbour.

These operations revealed the weaknesses of the English fleet. Water was short; many of the provisions were bad; and the resulting sickness ended in deaths so numerous that scarcely enough men remained to work the ships. To return at the earliest possible moment was imperative, and on November 16 Cecil issued orders to this effect. The final catastrophe was a storm which scattered the fleet so that each vessel had to make its own way to port.

Though the command of the expedition had been Cecil's, the ultimate responsibility for its failure rested upon Buckingham. As Lord High Admiral since 1619, he was responsible for the deplorable condition of both the men and the stores in the fleet. Moreover, as the King's chief adviser, the foreign policy which led to the attack was his also. Buckingham had shown himself incompetent equally as a diplomatist and as an administrator. The popularity which he had enjoyed on his return from Madrid in 1623 was already evaporating. The failure at Cadiz—remembered as the scene of one of Drake's most famous exploits—damaged Buckingham's reputation still further.

One of Buckingham's most dangerous characteristics was his boundless optimism. The possibility of failure seems never to have entered into his calculations. What to a normally prudent man would have been a defeat calling for a thorough overhaul of policy and procedure, was to Buckingham only a momentary check which would not occur again. So, without grasping the significance of the Cadiz defeat, he plunged confidently into a new conflict before he had settled the existing one. This was nothing less than a war against France.

Several causes combined to bring about the breach. In November 1625 Buckingham arranged at the Hague a treaty between England, Denmark, and Holland for the prosecution of the Palatinate war. The very existence of a Protestant league was an implied threat to Roman Catholic States. Also, Richelieu's use of English ships against the Huguenots in September 1625 had both roused bitter resentment among the English people and made Buckingham realize that he had been duped.

Matters connected with Charles I's marriage were further causes of friction. On the one hand, the promise to remove English penal laws against Roman Catholics was not, and could not be, fulfilled. On the other hand, Charles was aggrieved by the interference at Court of the Queen's attendants whom, as we have seen, he finally sent back to France in August 1626.

Not least among the causes of a breach were disputes about shipping. In September and October 1625 the English seized several French ships which were believed to be carrying goods to the Spanish Netherlands. In November Charles ordered that £20,000—which he needed for subsidies to Denmark—should be raised by selling cargoes from the French ships. In December the French authorities retaliated by seizing two English ships at Rouen and by threatening to take English property in France. The climax came in November 1626 when the French took possession of the whole English wine-fleet at Bordeaux consisting of some two hundred vessels. The English reprisal was to take all possible French ships in English waters. War was thus made inevitable, and both countries hurried forward their preparations.

In England the Navy was overhauled, and efforts were made to expand it considerably. These preparations and, still more, the conduct of the war itself would cost more money than the King would know how to provide. The obvious source of supply was a parliamentary grant; but Charles knew that to summon Parliament would create more difficulties than it would solve. As later sections of this chapter will show, his second Parliament, which had lasted from February to June 1626, had been occupied almost solely by the King's demands for money and by the Commons' retaliatory impeachment of Buckingham. Charles had saved his Minister by dissolving Parliament. To summon a new Parliament would be to advertise the King's financial dependence and to invite renewed, and more embittered, attacks on Buckingham. Charles therefore tried to raise the necessary money by a Forced Loan. The Loan met with such opposition that the war-preparations were starved, and supplies of every kind were poor in quality and small in quantity. The fact was that to undertake a war against

3*

France in addition to the war against Spain, without any prospect of adequate supplies for either, was blind folly. It was a perfect example of Buckingham's light-hearted optimism.

Buckingham's new scheme was for a relieving expedition to La Rochelle, his hope being that the Huguenots of southern France would thus be encouraged to rise, and that the English ships at Bordeaux would be released. This time Buckingham, as Lord High Admiral, determined to lead the expedition himself. His force consisted of about six thousand men aboard one hundred vessels. These he led out of Stokes Bay on June 27, 1627, and on July 10 he arrived off the Isle of Rhé, two miles outside La Rochelle harbour. This was to be the English base of operations, and there, after some resistance from the French garrison, the English troops landed. Beyond that, the expedition achieved almost nothing.

The obstacle to the possession of Rhé was the island's chief town, St Martin, to which Buckingham laid siege. As the siege dragged on, his forces gradually melted away. From La Rochelle very few Huguenots came out to him, and from England he received only the slightest help of either men or supplies. The result was that the French were able to land reinforcements of men and stores in such quantities as to make Buckingham's task hopeless.

The one redeeming feature of the expedition was Buckingham's own conduct. As a commander he showed energy, not a little ability, and continual interest in his men. As an individual he repeatedly showed high courage and little care for his own safety. These qualities, if properly supported, might have brought success. Without such support Buckingham's position became desperate. A last effort on October 27 to storm St Martin was driven off, and almost at once the English forces began to re-embark. The French seized the opportunity to attack while the operation was in progress, and a great slaughter of English troops resulted. On November 11 Buckingham sailed into Plymouth bringing with him less than half the men he had taken out. For the policy which led to the disaster Buckingham alone must bear the responsibility which no amount of personal valour during the siege could diminish.

The collapse of the expedition to La Rochelle did not diminish Buckingham's determination to carry on the war for the restoration of the Palatinate, and for the relief of the Huguenots whom he had encouraged to rebel.

In the Palatinate war Charles' uncle, Christian IV of Denmark, was his chief ally. The subsidies of £30,000 a month, promised to him by Charles, ceased almost as soon as they began. The Danish campaigns had had scant success, and during Buckingham's expedition to Rhé Christian had suffered complete defeat. He was driven back to his own dominions; and of the remainder of the wretched English levies that had been sent to help him, some were shut up in Germany and others made their way out as best they could. On every side Buckingham's foreign policy had suffered disgraceful defeat.

Yet he still determined to pursue the attack against France, and preparations for another expedition to La Rochelle were put in hand. It was to be commanded by the Earl of Denbigh who was Buckingham's brother-in-law and had been one of the leaders of the Cadiz fiasco—neither of which facts was a very encouraging qualification for supreme military command!

Meanwhile Charles and Buckingham were trying various expedients to raise money, but in the end they had to recognize that only a Parliament could grant supplies sufficient for a war. Hence the third Parliament of the reign was summoned to meet on March 17, 1628.

Though the leaders of the new House of Commons decided not to revive Buckingham's impeachment, this did not imply that they were reconciled to the King's irregular methods of government. On the contrary, the Commons proceeded at once to discuss grievances, and refused to grant supplies until grievances were redressed. The climax of the disputes was the Petition of Right[1] which was first introduced in the Commons on May 8, 1628, and to which Charles gave assent on June 7.

On the very day that the petition was introduced yet another proof of the Court's incompetence was forthcoming. Denbigh had appeared with his fleet off La Rochelle on May 1. There he found himself faced by defences—men, ships, harbour-

[1] See p. 86.

moles—quite beyond the capacity of his force to overcome. On May 8 he sailed from La Rochelle and made for England. Probably the decision was a wise one, but it was not likely to raise Buckingham's prestige in the eyes of the English people. So far as Charles and Buckingham were concerned, the effect was to increase their resolution to relieve the Huguenots who were suffering terrible privations from the siege. Efforts were therefore made to raise yet another expedition, which Buckingham was to lead in person. His resolve was never to be carried into effect. In August he went down to Portsmouth to superintend the final preparations of his fleet. There on August 23, 1628, in the hall of the house which he was temporarily occupying, he was stabbed to death. The murderer was John Felton, an army lieutenant, whose motives appear to have been a mixture of personal grievance, patriotism, and religion. Felton's stroke changed the whole tenor of the reign. Here we are concerned only with its effect on foreign policy.

The immediate effect was that a new leader had to be found for the projected expedition. The Earl of Lindsey was appointed to the thankless task. He set out early in September but his force was no more adequate than Denbigh's had been. After a few fruitless attacks on the fortifications he desisted. Charles tried to negotiate with Louis XIII in the Huguenots' interests, but Louis was not likely to raise the siege when the town was on the point of collapse. On October 18 La Rochelle capitulated. The terms which Richelieu, through Louis, imposed showed a genuine desire for a peaceful settlement: though La Rochelle lost its peculiar privileges, Protestants retained the right to freedom of worship in those places where they had enjoyed it before.

The end of the dispute between the French Government and the Huguenots, and the complete defeat for the moment of the German Protestants, removed every reason for continuing the war against both France and Spain.

With France a treaty was signed at Susa in April 1629. Louis abandoned his claim for toleration to English Roman Catholics, and Charles in return abandoned similar claims for French Huguenots.

Peace with Spain was more difficult because Charles still insisted on Spanish help for the restoration of the Palatinate. Finally, on November 4, the Treaty of Madrid was signed. Its terms restored the relations between Spain and England to those which had existed before the war—that is, to those laid down in the treaty of 1604.

These two treaties together summarize the results of Charles I's foreign policy. The chief end of that policy—the restoration of the Palatinate—had been completely abandoned. All the struggles abroad of both James and Charles had gained nothing. Thereafter Charles gave up the pursuit of any foreign policy, and for the remainder of his reign he was closely occupied with problems at home. Upon these problems, as the opening paragraphs of this chapter pointed out, the failure of foreign policy had a direct bearing: the cost of the wars against Spain and France drove Charles into Parliament's hands for supplies of money; and the failure of the wars gave an added reason for Parliament's mistrust. It is to the story of the relationship between Charles and his Parliaments that we have now to turn.

2. First Parliament, June 18–August 12, 1625

The first House of Commons of Charles I included men who were to be the most famous Members not only of that Parliament but of the subsequent Parliaments of the reign—Sir Edward Coke, Sir John Eliot, John Hampden, John Pym, and Sir Thomas Wentworth. It was of ill omen for the King's fortunes that not one of these, the most capable Members of the Commons, was a supporter of the Court. To present his case to the House, the King had to rely upon such mediocrities as his Chancellor of the Exchequer, Sir Richard Weston.

In his first contact with Parliament Charles made a tactical mistake of a kind that characterized his dealing with all his Parliaments: he failed to give clear leadership. While referring vaguely to the financial support which his foreign policy would need, he neither explained his plans nor specified what sums of money any plans were estimated to cost. Parliament therefore concluded that the King had not made any plans, or else that he was deliberately hiding them. Whichever of these alternatives was the true one, it was not likely to inspire Parliament to trust the King. Here, at the outset, lies one of the clues to the misfortunes of the reign. Charles was not moved so much by calculating duplicity as by an inherent lack of imagination to sense how his actions would be interpreted by other men of varying views. The result was that his friends were embarrassed, his would-be friends bewildered, and his opponents lashed into bitter rage.

The Parliament, hoping for fuller information later, occupied its time by going into committee on questions of religion and supply. This action was typical of what happened in all the Parliaments of the reign: the Members regarded questions of religion as fundamental to, and paramount over, all other questions of State. Matters of religion were given precedence even over those of supply. After a keen debate, in which Eliot took a prominent part, the Committee drew up a petition asking the King to enforce the existing laws against Roman Catholics. This petition went up to the Lords for their support. Only then did the Committee consider the question of supply.

Nearly a fortnight had passed since Parliament had opened, and it was still awaiting guidance. Its only course seemed to be to make a small grant to meet the King's immediate needs. After further debate the Commons granted two subsidies which would suffice for only a fraction of the King's foreign commitments.

By the beginning of July the plague was spreading so dangerously in London that many Members had left the capital. The remaining Members gave their attention to another financial problem connected with tunnage and poundage, which were ancient duties on certain specified imports and exports. Traditionally these duties were granted to each King for life by the first Parliament of his reign. This custom had continued unbroken since Henry VI's reign and so had come to be regarded by successive kings as not dependent upon Parliamentary grant but as a hereditary perquisite of the Crown. James I's levy of impositions and other non-Parliamentary taxes, added to the suspicion which Charles' vagueness had already roused, led this first Parliament of the latter's reign to take an unusual course. The Commons voted tunnage and poundage to Charles for one year only. This was intended to render him more dependent than his predecessors upon Parliament. In doing so, the Commons were acting contrary to precedent, and the resentment which the action raised in the King's mind is easy to understand. The Commons, on the other hand, believed that if they had the right to make the grant they had equally the right to withhold or to limit it. Whatever view be taken of it, it was a bad start to the reign.

Even the first year's grant of tunnage and poundage was never made valid. When the Bill embodying the grant was carried to the Lords its passage was so long delayed that the session ended before all its stages were complete, so that even that grant never became law.

Because of the small numbers of the Commons remaining in London, both houses were adjourned in preparation for a reassembly at Oxford on August 1. Before the adjournment the King promised that the penal laws against Roman Catholics should be carried out.

On August 1 Charles again addressed the Houses. He reminded them afresh of Parliament's desire for war, and he appealed for substantial supplies so that the war might be successfully conducted. Once more, failing a clear explanation of policy from the King, the ensuing debate took place in an atmosphere of uncertainty and of growing animosity towards Buckingham, who was held responsible for royal policy. For the first time in Commons' debates he was named as responsible for the nation's ill-fortunes. Sir Francis Seymour, who throughout the session had been outspoken in his opposition to the Court, declared boldly: "Let us lay fault where it is. The Duke of Buckingham is trusted, and it must needs be either him or his agents"; and Sir Robert Phelips exclaimed: "It is not fit to repose the safety of the Kingdom upon those that have not parts answerable to their places."

These outbursts convinced the King that nothing was to be gained from further dealings with this Parliament, and he therefore resolved upon its dissolution. The short-sightedness of dissolution was obvious: no supplies in any way adequate to national expenditure had been granted, and a quarrel with the first Parliament might vitiate relations with all succeeding Parliaments of the reign. Though Lord Keeper Williams, and even Buckingham, urged this point of view upon the King, the latter refused to alter his decision. On August 12, Charles' first Parliament was dissolved.

If the dissolution removed an immediate embarrassment to the King at home it added considerably to his embarrassments abroad. His financial liabilities abroad, made in anticipation of parliamentary support, were heavy. But Charles decided to proceed with schemes already projected, in the hope that some of them at least would be successful enough to recover popularity for the Court and so would induce the next Parliament to grant supplies for the expenses incurred. It is not difficult to detect Buckingham's rose-coloured optimism in such a policy. Buckingham's plans went farther—namely, to make the war pay for itself by plundering Spanish ports and shipping.

The results we have already traced: Sir Edward Cecil's disastrous failure at Cadiz and the widening breach with France. Parliamentary grants were the only alternative means of meeting all the demands upon the exchequer. Writs were therefore issued for a new Parliament to meet in February 1626.

3. Second Parliament, February 6–June 15, 1626

There was no reason for thinking that the new Parliament would be any more compliant towards the King and his Minister than its predecessor had been. On the contrary, the abrupt dismissal of the former Parliament, and the recent failure of the Court's policy, would intensify the opposition in the second Parliament. One step the Court had already taken to render the opposition leaderless: in November 1625 Coke, Phelips, Seymour, and Wentworth were pricked as sheriffs and would thus be unable to leave their respective counties. This was yet another instance of the King's ineptitude. The trick embittered the Commons without achieving its purpose, for the men who were to prove the most dangerous of all the opposition leaders—Eliot and Pym—were allowed to take their seats. Moreover, neither the King nor Buckingham had yet learned that the opposition to their government was broader-based than a small faction in the House of Commons: events would show that the bulk of the Commons, and by no means a negligible part of the Lords, was solid in its mistrust of Buckingham as the King's chief Minister. One other step had been taken by the King to try to strengthen his hold over Parliament: Bishop Williams, whose opposition to Buckingham's ill-considered projects had become more and more pronounced, was replaced as Lord Keeper by Sir Thomas Coventry.

Within a few days of the opening of the Parliament the Secretary, Sir John Coke, asked for a supply. This immediately drew Eliot to his feet demanding that the accounts of the previously granted subsidies should be laid before the Commons, and that an inquiry into the reasons for past misfortunes should precede further supplies. Eliot had in mind particularly the failure at Cadiz.

As a young man Eliot had travelled on the Continent in company with young George Villiers, now become Duke of Buckingham; and the latter's appointment as Lord High Admiral in 1619 was followed in the same year by Eliot's appointment as Vice-Admiral of Devon. Thus Eliot had begun with friendship for Buckingham rather than with prejudice against him. But his position as Vice-Admiral in Devon had given him peculiar opportunities to see the condition of the ships gathered for Cadiz, and the sad plight of the men who returned: the stores were rotten; some of the sails had weathered the storm that had scattered the Armada forty years before; and not a few of the seamen that managed to return from Cadiz died in the Plymouth streets through lack of food and shelter. Eliot's patriotic fervour blazed against the man responsible for such disasters.

When, therefore, on February 10 Secretary Coke asked for a supply, Eliot declared roundly:

> Our honour is ruined, our ships are sunk, our men perished; not by the sword, not by the enemy, not by chance, but, as the strongest predictions had discerned, and made it apparent beforehand, by those we trust.

The Commons' debates of the following weeks, and the investigations of the Committee of Grievances, served to focus Members' attention more and more upon Buckingham as the root of the nation's ills. Following Sir John Coke's fresh application for supply on March 27, Eliot delivered a tremendous speech on the theme that the general unwillingness to contribute to the King's needs was due to the series of national disasters which were "fixed on the person of the Lord General, who had the whole command by sea and land." His attack became more pointed when he went on to quote Henry III's Minister, Hubert de Burgh, and Richard II's Minister, the Earl of Suffolk, both of whom had to be removed from office by the King before he was granted supplies. For both Charles and Buckingham the implication of these references was too plain to be misinterpreted; and not their least sinister feature was that both Henry III's and Richard II's resistance to the Commons' demands had provoked armed revolt.

Another significance about Eliot's argument was that he avoided blaming the King for misgovernment but fixed the blame upon the King's Minister. This continued to be the attitude of the opposition leaders throughout the reign until Charles, having lost Buckingham and having consented to the removal of Strafford, left the Commons with no alternative to holding him as solely and personally responsible for misrule. Further, Eliot was in effect asserting the principle of the responsibility of Ministers which was to develop into the Cabinet system of government, and was to become the characteristic of the British Constitution as we know it to-day.

Matters were so evidently working to a crisis that Charles decided to use his personal influence upon the Commons. Two days after Eliot's outburst the Commons were summoned to Whitehall, and there were addressed by the King in terms that included the following sharp reminder:

> Remember that Parliaments are altogether in my power for their calling, sitting, and dissolution; therefore as I find the fruits of them good or evil, they are to continue or not to be.[1]

[1] Rushworth, I, 225.

As an attempt to induce the Commons to modify its opposition, no utterance could have been less persuasive. It was typical of Charles' inability to understand a situation and to deal with men. The Commons, undeterred, steadily gathered evidence against Buckingham in preparation for a formal attack. On May 8 representatives went to the Lords to impeach him.

The eight 'managers' of the Commons' case took two days to deliver their speeches. Then the King addressed the Lords in the hope of ensuring their support. This he followed up by sending two of the managers—Digges and Eliot—to the Tower. The Commons thereupon suspended their sittings until both Members were released; and the King was forced to comply. During the weeks that followed, the dispute became more and more bitter until Charles was convinced that nothing was to be gained by further negotiations. On June 15 he dissolved his second Parliament.

The dissolution was a serious tactical error on Charles' part. Once more he was left without the customary grants of supply. If he was to continue to govern his only remaining course was to obtain income from non-Parliamentary sources. To this end he tried expedient after expedient.

Tunnage and poundage were collected as though Parliament had sanctioned them. A loan of £100,000 was to be raised from the City of London, and here the King met his first rebuff: the City refused to lend even on the security of the crown jewels, and the best that could be achieved was a personal loan of £20,000 from the aldermen. The maritime counties were ordered to raise money to provide fifty-six ships: there were precedents for this levy, and, in spite of much grumbling, the greater part of it was at last raised. Next the justices were ordered to raise from their respective counties 'free gifts' in amounts equivalent to the four subsidies which Parliament had agreed were necessary but had not granted: the responses were negligible.

Charles next tried a Forced Loan. The amount raised thereby varied according to the distance of the respective counties from London: in the home counties, where royal influence could be exerted, some contributions were raised, but in the more remote counties the yield was trifling. Even the King's judges refused to recognize the legality of the loan; and in spite of the dismissal of Sir Randal Crewe, the Chief Justice of the King's Bench, his fellow-judges maintained their obdurate attitude. In order to raise appreciable amounts numerous penalties were inflicted: gentry who refused to contribute—including Eliot, Hampden, and Wentworth—were imprisoned; poor people were sent into the Army.

Among the prisoners were five knights who sued in the Court of King's Bench for a writ of *habeas corpus* so as to compel the Crown to show legal cause for their imprisonment without trial. The five were headed by Sir Thomas Darnel: hence the term Darnel's, or the Five Knights', Case. It was heard in November 1627. The King's Bench, though not denying the fundamental claim that the reason for imprisonment must be shown, ruled that reasons of State might justify a delay in ordinary legal procedure, and that the King was the proper judge of such reasons. The Five Knights were therefore refused bail.

While these and other piecemeal expedients were failing to keep the King's coffers full, the drain on those coffers was alarmingly increased by commitments abroad, notably by the help promised by Charles to King Christian IV of Denmark, and by the expedition to the Isle of Rhé during June to November 1627. A new Parliament, as the only source of substantial revenue, became inevitable. The non-Parliamentary expedients for money-raising, and the La Rochelle failure, would make a new Parliament even more bitterly incensed against the Court, and especially against Buckingham, than its predecessor had been, but the hard fact had to be faced, and the third Parliament of the reign was summoned to meet in March 1628.

4. Third Parliament, March 17, 1628–March 10, 1629

The Parliamentary history of Charles I's reign falls into three well-defined periods: between 1625 and 1629 Charles summoned and dissolved three Parliaments; in 1640 he summoned two Parliaments, the 'Short' and the 'Long,' the latter

of which remained the legal Parliament not only until Charles'
death in 1649 but further until it consented to its own dissolution in 1660; and between 1629 and 1640 was an interval
during which Charles carried on his government without a
Parliament. The 1628–29 Parliament is thus the critical
assembly of the reign because it saw the final breach between
King and Parliament preceding the 'Eleven Years' Tyranny.'

From the beginning of proceedings in this Parliament the
opposition showed a unified leadership, though not, of course,
an organized party-leadership in the modern sense of the term.
The meeting of three Parliaments within less than three years
meant that there was much continuity of membership and that
the men who had been outstanding in the first and second of
them did not need to establish their qualities in the third.
They included Eliot, Pym, and Wentworth.

Yet now, as always, Charles was incapable of either learning
from experience or reading the evident signs of the times. In
his opening speech he informed the House that the purpose
for which they had been called was to grant supply wherewith
to meet the common danger, and that, should they fail to
grant such supply, "I must, in discharge of my conscience, use
those other means which God hath put in my hands, to save
that that the follies of particular men may otherwise hazard
to lose." As though to ensure that Members should not mis-
understand the temper that lay behind his words, Charles
added: "Take not this as a threatening (for I scorn to threaten
any but my equals) but as an admonition." If his purpose were
to create a barrier between himself and his new Parliament
he could hardly have chosen words more effectively.

Throughout almost all the debates there ran a double theme:
how to prevent non-Parliamentary taxation and arbitrary imprisonment. The Commons resolved to consider grievances
before supplies. Within a fortnight the Commons passed a
series of four resolutions of which the first condemned non-
Parliamentary taxes and the other three declared respectively
that no man could be imprisoned without a stated cause, that
every prisoner had a right of *habeas corpus*, and that if neither
of these conditions was fulfilled the prisoner was to be released.
Not until the last of these four resolutions had been passed

did the Commons begin to consider the question of supply. Though the King's needs were realized, the practical problem was how to grant taxes without making the King independent of Parliament in the future. The House finally voted the considerable sum of five subsidies (about £350,000), but it forthwith agreed to Wentworth's suggestion that the vote should not become effective until the King had assented to a measure guaranteeing the liberties of the subject. After long discussions the Commons decided to draw up a petition based upon what it regarded as an Englishman's fundamental rights. Hence took shape the famous Petition of Right which was introduced into the Commons on May 8, 1628. Lords and Commons worked closely together in preparing the measure, and in its final form the petition expressed the mind of both Houses—a most important fact.

After relating at length the King's acts contrary to Magna Carta and to certain specified medieval statutes, the Houses compressed their claims into a single paragraph:

> They do therefore humbly pray your Most Excellent Majesty that no man hereafter be compelled to make or yield any gift, loan, benevolence, tax, or such like charge, without common consent by Act of Parliament; and that none be called to make answer . . . or be confined or otherwise molested or disquieted concerning the same, or for refusal thereof; . . . and that your Majesty will be pleased to remove the said soldiers and mariners, and that your people may not be burdened in time to come, and that the foresaid commissions for proceeding by martial law, may be revoked and annulled. . . . All which they most humbly pray of your Most Excellent Majesty as their rights and liberties according to the laws and statutes of this realm.[1]

Charles tried to avoid giving a direct answer. The petition had been passed by both Houses on May 28. On June 2 the King, through the Lord Keeper, delivered his answer in the following terms:

> The King willeth that right be done according to the laws and customs of the realm; and that the statutes be put in due execution, that his subjects may have no cause to complain of

[1] Gardiner, p. 69.

any wrongs or oppression, contrary to their just rights and liberties, to the preservation whereof he holds himself as well obliged as of his prerogative.

The Commons' dissatisfaction with this vague answer was voiced chiefly by Eliot who exposed in detail the unrelieved and disgraceful failures of the Court's foreign policy. It was left to Sir Edward Coke to voice the general conviction lying behind the discontent. Speaking on June 5 he declared:

> I think the Duke of Buckingham is the cause of all our miseries, and till the King is informed thereof, we shall never go out with honour, or sit with honour here; that man is the grievance of grievances: let us set down the causes of all our disasters, and all will reflect upon him.[1]

So evident was the Commons' support for this statement that Charles did not dare either to take action against Coke or to postpone further the acceptance of the Petition of Right. On June 7 he assented to the Petition in the form of words customary to the acceptance of any Bill: *Soit droit fait comme est desiré.*

Almost at the same time there was fresh trouble on a religious issue. In June 1627 Dr Roger Manwaring preached before the King two sermons whose theme was the sin of resistance to royal authority, and Charles allowed the sermons to be licensed for printing. The 1628 Parliament took note of these proceedings and set its Committee on Religion to investigate them. The result was that on June 9 the Commons impeached Manwaring before the Lords on the charge of having violated the "fundamental law" of England. The trial ended with the sentence that Manwaring should be fined £1000, be imprisoned during the pleasure of the Lords, and be suspended from all preaching for three years, and from preaching at Court for the rest of his life. Almost at once the King pardoned him, and in 1634 raised him to be Bishop of St David's. Neither the trial nor Charles' frustration of the verdict was likely to smooth out the relations between the Houses and the King.

As soon as the Commons knew that the King had assented to the Petition of Right they passed the subsidy Bill through

[1] Rushworth, I, 607.

its stages and sent it to the Lords. But whatever hopes the King may have had that relations between him and Parliament had been eased were soon shown to be false. The Commons also pushed forward a Remonstrance stating the reasons for its opposition to Buckingham. This was finally voted on June 11. On the subject of the King's Ministers it was unmistakably explicit. After referring to the evils under which the Kingdom had suffered, the Remonstrance continued:

> The principal cause of which evils and dangers we conceive to be the excessive power of the Duke of Buckingham. . . . And our humble desire is further, that your excellent Majesty will be pleased to take into your princely consideration whether, in respect the said Duke hath so abused his power, it be safe for your Majesty and for your Kingdom, to continue him either in his great offices or in his place of nearness and counsel about your sacred person.

Thus Parliament and King reverted to the impasse, on the subject of Buckingham, which had led to the dissolution of the second Parliament. Where Buckingham was concerned Charles was adamant. Without going so far as to dissolve his third Parliament, he decided to bring its first session to a close, and fixed June 26 as the date of prorogation.

The Commons, afraid that the prorogation would be turned into dissolution, tried to prevent the King from collecting tunnage and poundage. A new Remonstrance was therefore hurried forward and was voted on June 26. It declared that:

> The receiving of tunnage and poundage and other impositions, not granted by Parliament, is a breach of the fundamental liberties of the Kingdom, and contrary to your Majesty's royal answer to our late Petition of Right.

This was a position that Charles refused to accept, and in proroguing Parliament he declared that in the Petition of Right:

> I have granted no new, but only confirmed the liberties of my subjects. . . . As for tunnage and poundage, it is a thing I cannot want, and was never intended by you to ask—never meant, I am sure by me to grant.

The interval between the first and second sessions brought notable changes in the political scene. First, several changes in the bishops enabled the King to give preferments to certain leaders of the High Church party, notably to William Laud, who was promoted from the see of St David's to London. The Church party of whom Laud was the leading light had two main characteristics. That it was the bulwark of the principle of Divine Right we have seen already: it was chiefly for this reason that the party was suspect to the majority of successive Houses of Commons. Also the High Church party adopted doctrines propounded by Arminius, a contemporary Dutch theologian whose chief tenet was Free Will in contradiction to the Calvinistic doctrine of Predestination which hitherto had been the orthodox doctrine of the English Church. Moreover, the Arminian party insisted on the belief in "One Holy Catholic Church," and it used vestments and ceremonies which reminded people of the Roman Church. Consequently the staunch Calvinism—centring largely round the doctrine of Predestination—of the Parliamentary majority made the division on both the religious issue, and also on the allied political issue, still more pronounced and bitter. Laud's work as Bishop of London, and later as Archbishop of Canterbury, will be reviewed in the next chapter.

Second, Charles received a dramatic accession of strength in the person of Sir Thomas Wentworth. His work as adviser to the King was so decisive during the closing stages of the breach between King and Parliament that at this point it is useful to understand something of the man himself. To do full justice to Wentworth is not easy. His motives and character were an enigma to his contemporaries and have remained so to every succeeding generation. The pivotal event in his career, and the chief item of the mystery surrounding him, was his acceptance of the King's favour after being the champion of Parliamentary liberties. This episode is commonly called Wentworth's 'apostasy.' Such a term begs the question of Wentworth's motives in two respects: it assumes that Wentworth changed his allegiance and that the change was of a shameful nature. A knowledge of the outstanding facts of his career is essential as a basis for right judgement.

Thomas Wentworth was the son of William Wentworth of Wentworth Woodhouse, in Yorkshire, where the family estates brought in the then very considerable sum of £6000 yearly. Thomas' education included several years spent at St John's College, Cambridge, and at the Inner Temple. In 1611 he received a knighthood, his father having been created a baronet earlier in the same year: both honours were doubtless bought at the current prices which helped to swell the royal exchequer. Then, in 1614, he was for the first time returned to Parliament as one of the Members for Yorkshire. Before that year was out his father was dead, and Thomas, though only twenty-one years of age, was left as head of the family, which included his nine brothers and sisters. In 1615 he was appointed *custos rotulorum* for the West Riding of Yorkshire, and thus was at the head of the Commission of the Peace for that area before he was twenty-three years of age.

During the interval between the 1614 and the 1621 Parliaments Wentworth spent much time at Court, where his ambitions for preferment became notorious. On two occasions at least he tried to buy a peerage. But as a courtier he was a failure: his pride of ancestry and his wealth made him contemptuous of the upstarts and of the poor at Court; and his ambitions made him an object of suspicion to those already established in the royal favour. This early eagerness for notice at Court is worth remembering in view of Wentworth's later career.

In the 1621 Parliament, when he again represented his county, Wentworth followed a middle course. While opposed alike to a warlike foreign policy and to infringements of Parliament's traditional liberties, he was anxious to avoid a breach with the King. Thus, though at one point he was in favour of making "an immediate grant, leaving to the King the choice of a fit time for declaring war," he later joined with the great majority of the Commons in opposing James' contention that the House's privileges were derived from the Crown.

During the brief 1625 Parliament Wentworth acted mainly with the popular party. One result was that he was among those nominated as sheriffs and so was prevented from Membership of the 1626 Parliament. After the dissolution of the latter Parliament Charles tried to supply his exchequer by a 'free gift.' Letters were sent to the justices to notify their respective counties and to induce moneyed individuals to contribute to the gift. Those justices that were not regarded as likely to comply were removed from office: they included Eliot, Phelips, and Wentworth.

Thus once again Wentworth was classed with the leaders of the popular party. His association with them was, however, superficial rather than real. As we have seen, he had already tried to secure Court favour. In spite of his apparent identification with the popular party, and of the rebuffs which he had received from the Court, in January 1626 he applied for the position of President of the Council of the North in succession to Lord Scrope whose retirement was strongly rumoured. Actually Scrope did not at once retire. In any case it was unlikely that Buckingham would encourage the advancement of a man of indisputably greater force of character than himself, especially of one who had shown his mistrust of Buckingham's projects.

In view of Wentworth's repeated efforts to gain the favour of King and Minister, his attitude during the first session of the 1628 Parliament was extraordinary. Into all the Commons' proceedings in vindicating the liberty of people and Parliament he threw his every talent and energy. There was scarcely a debate in which he did not take a prominent part in opposition to the Court. He repeatedly carried the Commons along with him so that he and not Eliot was the leader of the House during the first session of the Parliament. The stop came at the Petition of Right which was the outcome of Charles' refusal even to consider the Commons' grievances. The petition received the royal assent on June 7, and the first session ended on June 26. On July 22 Wentworth received a peerage as Lord Wentworth. From that time he was wholeheartedly the King's man.

Wentworth's previous relations with the Court make it impossible to resist the conclusion that he had set himself deliberately to show his powers of leadership in the Commons so as to convince the King that to continue to drive such a man into the ranks of the opposition was too dangerous. Having several times failed to win royal favour by asking for it, he adopted the opposite course of compelling the King to grant his request.

If this is the true estimate of Wentworth's conduct the question of apostasy does not arise: he did not desert the popular party because he never belonged to it. Nor is there any evidence to suggest that he tried to deceive the members of that section into thinking that he was one of them. Between him and the majority of them there was a great gulf fixed: it was the gulf of religion. While the popular party was predominantly Puritan, Wentworth hated Puritanism, and was a staunch member of that section of the Church which became increasingly attached to both the policy and person of Laud. In passing this judgement on Wentworth it is but just to remember that, having achieved his long ambition, he gave himself in selfless devotion to the public service as he understood it—that is, in the service of the King. His motto was "Thorough," and efficiency was the mark of everything he touched.

One limitation to Wentworth's contentment remained— namely, the Duke of Buckingham. The solution of this problem came earlier and more drastically than Wentworth could have imagined. On August 23 Felton's dagger removed Buckingham for ever.[1]   This did not mean that Wentworth would step into the dead man's shoes as the King's Minister. No man ever replaced Buckingham in either the counsels or the affection of the King. Charles, while still a shy youth, had given himself to Buckingham unreservedly, as such a man may give himself to one friend but can never give himself to a second. But Buckingham's removal eased Wentworth's position at Court. He had been so severe a critic of Buckingham that it is difficult to see how he could have held office under the Crown if Buckingham had remained Charles' chief adviser. This embarrassment at least disappeared with Buckingham's murder.

Events since the close of the first session of the 1628 Parliament had in general worsened rather than improved the King's

[1] See p. 76.

position. Lindsey's expedition to La Rochelle was a complete failure; and in October La Rochelle capitulated to Richelieu. Thus Charles' policy of helping the Huguenots had collapsed. At home the continued attempts to levy tunnage and pound-age and impositions provoked resistance to the customs officials. Some of the recalcitrant merchants were imprisoned; others had their goods seized. Such actions caused the second session of Parliament to open in a mood of suspicious dis-content.

The session opened on January 20, 1629. The Commons' suspicion was deepened when, two days later, their notice was called to the printed copies of the Petition of Right which contained not the customary form of the royal assent but the King's first answer which had not been regarded as satis-factory. The Houses were to some extent reassured when having been summoned to Whitehall they were informed by the King that he did not mean to claim that his royal preroga-tive entitled him to levy tunnage and poundage but that he had collected it until Parliament had formally granted it.

The hopes of appeasement proved illusory. When, shortly afterwards, religious grievances were brought to the Commons' notice, the old passions burst out again. Repeatedly the sub-ject of religion was debated in the House, and a committee was appointed to prepare resolutions on the subject for the Commons' consideration. The resolutions were before the House on February 24. In strong terms they complained of the "extraordinary growth of Popery." To counteract these ten-dencies, the resolutions put forward a series of ten remedies including that existing laws should be carried out against Papists, that orthodox doctrines and ceremonies should be maintained in the Church, and that only orthodox men should be appointed to ecclesiastical offices.

The tone of the resolutions so alarmed the King that the next day he adjourned the House for a week. When the House re-assembled on March 2 it was informed by the Speaker, Sir John Finch, that it was to be further adjourned until March 10. Finch then put the formal resolution for the adjournment, but before the vote could be taken Eliot rose to speak. Finch's statement that the King had forbidden any debate on the subject was followed by a general tumult. Finch rose to leave the Chair but was held by two Members—Denzil Holles and Valentine—and forced down while Eliot addressed the House at length. He claimed that the House had the right to adjourn itself, and he brought forward a formal protestation which he had prepared on the subject of misgovernment. Finch continued to refuse to put the vote either on the adjournment or on Eliot's resolutions; and Eliot therefore threw his resolutions into the fire.

Events were brought to a climax by the arrival of two messengers from the King: first, the sergeant who had been sent for the mace, and then, the Usher of the Black Rod. Holles repeated from memory Eliot's three resolutions which are important enough to be quoted in full:

1. Whosoever shall bring in innovation of religion, or by favour or countenance seek to extend or introduce Popery or Arminianism, or other opinions disagreeing from the true and orthodox Church, shall be reputed a capital enemy to this Kingdom and Commonwealth.

2. Whosoever shall counsel or advise the taking and levying of the subsidies of Tunnage and Poundage, not being granted by Parliament, or shall be an actor or instrument therein, shall be likewise reputed an innovator in the Government, and a capital enemy to the Kingdom and Commonwealth.

3. If any merchant or person whatsoever shall voluntarily yield, or pay the said subsidies of Tunnage and Poundage, not being granted by Parliament, he shall likewise be reputed a betrayer of the liberties of England, and an enemy to the same.[1]

Holles then himself put the resolutions to the House which voted them with acclamation. Thereupon the House voted its own adjournment. On March 10 the Parliament was dissolved.

Between the adjournment on March 2 and the dissolution a week later no less than nine Members of the Commons had been imprisoned. These included Eliot, Valentine, and Strode. The other six made voluntary submission to the King and were released. Valentine and Strode remained in prison until the elections for the next Parliament in 1640. Eliot was released only by death, after much ill-health and suffering, in 1632.

[1] Gardiner, pp. 82–83.

Eliot had shown himself a great Parliamentary orator able to sway the Commons to his will. His personal courage was unflinching. But he had few of the qualities of statesmanship; and his headlong violence of speech not only offended the King but also separated Eliot from some of the wiser members of his own section of the Commons. The most prominent member of the more moderate of the popular party was John Pym. During the previous Parliaments of the reign the two men had marched together; but this third Parliament saw a widening difference between their policies. The records of the Commons show that Pym remained aloof from Eliot's violent courses towards the end of the Parliament. For example, he took no part in the disorderly adjournment-scene. That the Court recognized the distinction between the two men is shown by the fact that Pym was not one of the nine Members imprisoned.

This Parliament had brought to a climax the question at issue between King and Parliament. Charles had summoned three successive Parliaments and all of them had debated the same fundamental questions with negative results until he seemed forced to the conclusion that the only object of Parliaments was to render the King's government impossible so as to make themselves supreme. For the future, therefore, he would rule without Parliaments; and during the following eleven years he carried out his resolve. Hence resulted the longest period without a Parliament in English history.

To assess justly the rights and wrongs of the clash between Parliament and Charles is not easy. Two facts at least stand out clearly. First, both sides were sincere but blundering: each honestly believed his own view right, and neither could understand the view of the other. Second, on strictly constitutional ground the King stood more firmly than Parliament. In trying to control the King's choice of Ministers, his conduct of foreign affairs, and even his levying of tunnage and poundage, the Commons were violating customary precedents. The Tudors would certainly never have tolerated such interference. But between the Tudors and Charles there were all-important differences: whereas they carried with them the vast majority

Chapter 5

King Charles I: Arbitrary Government

1629–40

1. Political and Judicial

The main feature of the period 1629–40 was Charles I's attempt to govern by his own will independently of Parliament. His first care was to put an end to the extraordinary expenses due to foreign wars. The peace of Susa brought peace with France in April 1629. In May Christian of Denmark made peace with the Emperor, under the terms of the Treaty of Lübeck, and so relieved Charles of an embarrassing ally. In November 1630, after long negotiations, peace was signed between England and Spain. General peace afforded some hope that Charles would be able to raise enough supplies to meet his normal expenditure.

Tunnage and poundage were collected as though Parliament had granted them. Beyond this, the first general method of raising revenue was to revive ancient statutes which had fallen into desuetude. The enforcement of such statutes was within the letter of the law and therefore could not be legally resisted.

Under a 1278 statute of Edward I every freeholder of land of £20 annual value could be compelled to become a knight or pay a fine. In the seventeenth century the value of land was much higher, and the value of money much lower, than in the thirteenth century. As a result, any enforcement of this statute would bring a correspondingly larger number of land-owners within its terms: many such were far removed from the knightly class and had no desire for what in their cases would be absurd titles. Nevertheless in January 1630 all freeholders having lands worth at least £40 annually were ordered to accept knighthood or pay the stipulated fine. Though there was at first some resistance to this distraint of knighthood, the relevant statute was so clear that no redress could be obtained in a law-court, and large sums accrued to the exchequer.

Another financial expedient of a similar type was the enlargement of the royal forests. These consisted not only of actually wooded lands but also of any area which, by medieval custom, was subject to the forest law administered by the customary forest courts. In 1634 Charles revived the Crown's claim to enormous tracts of land which were declared to be Crown property. Some of it was agricultural land, some of it formed part of nobles' estates, some of it had been built upon. The owners of such lands became liable to fines in order to retain what, in some instances, had been the property of their families for perhaps three centuries.

Such financial schemes were of far larger application than the Forced Loan or the Free Gift had been, and the widespread discontent which they fomented was poor compensation for the amount of money which they brought in. This was one of the chief reasons why, when the Civil War broke out, the Parliamentarians included not only Puritans and traders but also gentry and nobles.

Side by side with these strictly legal expedients, Charles enforced others whose legality was at best doubtful. Tunnage and poundage come under this heading. So do the fines imposed by the Star Chamber. This Court, which had served a useful purpose in Henry VII's reign in keeping the nobles in order, was used irregularly by Charles I to extort money. As its judges were high officials of the Crown, and as it did not include a jury, the King could rely upon favourable verdicts in cases that he sent to it.

Perhaps the most famous of all the sufferers from the Star Chamber under Charles I was William Prynne. He was a barrister and a Puritan bitterly opposed to the Laudian Church. Among the pamphlets which he wrote was *Histrio-mastix: A Scourge of Stage-Players*, published at the close of 1632. The contemporary stage pandered to the vulgar and immoral tastes of its audiences, and Prynne had no difficulty in lashing it furiously. In particular he fumed against the recent introduction of women on the stage in female parts.

Though the book had been licensed by Archbishop Abbot, its references to women on the stage were interpreted as veiled attacks on the Queen, who was known to take part in private theatricals. Prynne therefore, in 1634, was tried by the Star Chamber. His sentence was life-imprisonment, a fine of £5000, expulsion from the legal profession, and the removal of both ears while in the pillory. The judgement was without the slightest legal justification, for Prynne had not infringed a statute of the realm. Savage though the sentence was, it failed to break Prynne's spirit. He spent his imprisonment in writing against the bishops. As a result, in 1637 he was again before the Star Chamber. Along with him this time were two others: Henry Burton, a clergyman, for two published sermons in which he attacked the Laudian ceremonies, and John Bastwick, a physician, whose *Litany of John Bastwick* included the prayer, "From plague, pestilence, and famine, from bishops, priests, and deacons, good Lord deliver us!" All three received similar sentences: a £5000 fine, the pillory, and the loss of both ears. In Prynne's case the officials had to be content with cutting off the ear-stumps remaining after his previous punishment.

In connexion with Star Chamber trials a reference may be made at this point to John Lilburne, though his case did not involve revenue for the Crown. Lilburne, a youth of twenty years of age, was accused of having printed Puritan books in Holland. When brought before the Star Chamber in December 1637 he refused to take an oath that he would answer truly all the questions put before him. Lilburne declared that this might compel him to incriminate himself which was a practice contrary to English legal principles. He was therefore charged with contempt of court. For this he was flogged, placed in the pillory, and then thrust into the Fleet prison where he was kept without food. Only the pity of his fellow-prisoners, who shared their small crusts with him, kept him alive. Thus he remained until, along with Prynne, Bastwick, and Burton, he was released by order of the Long Parliament.

Another doubtful financial expedient was that of monopolies which had been prohibited by James I's Act of 1624. This Act, however, was so framed that it applied only to monopolies granted to individuals. Charles therefore granted them to companies. Thus in 1632 he formed a company with a monopoly for the manufacture of soap. In return the company was to pay to the royal exchequer £4 for every ton of soap sold. The results included discontent about the low quality and high prices which monopolies almost inevitably breed.

Perhaps the most notorious of all Charles' methods for raising money was Ship-money. No one could give an unqualified answer to the question of its legality. That the coast-towns were liable to provide ships for the Navy in times of national danger was beyond dispute, as was also the King's right to exercise judgement about what constituted a national danger. When, therefore, in October 1634, Ship-money writs were issued to the coastal towns, the payments were made without much resistance. In August 1635 a second writ was issued, this time not only to the coastal towns but to the whole country. The amount for which each individual was liable was to be assessed by sheriffs and justices. This extension of the Ship-money demand was without precedent; but ten of the twelve judges gave their opinion that all ought to contribute towards warding off a danger by which all were threatened. Hence, despite much discontent, most of the assessed amounts were collected within about six months. But when in October 1636 another general levy was demanded the position was changed. What had always been regarded as an exceptional tax to meet an exceptional emergency was evidently becoming a regular imposition when no such emergency existed and merely to avoid dependence upon Parliamentary grants. Though the bulk even of this third levy was finally paid, there was widespread disaffection and the collection was attended by increasing difficulties.

In 1637 three individuals determined to force a decision in the courts on the principle of the tax. They were Lord Saye, the Earl of Warwick, and John Hampden, all of whom refused to pay their Ship-money assessment. The Government avoided the challenge by the first two: proceedings on another charge were taken against Lord Saye in the Star Chamber; and the Earl of Warwick's refusal was completely ignored. Hampden's resistance alone was made the test case of the King's right to levy Ship-money. Hampden was a Buckinghamshire squire whose assessment was twenty shillings. His protest therefore was not against the amount of the tax but against the principle of it. His counsel, Oliver St John and Robert Holborne, relied chiefly upon the argument that taxation must be levied through Parliament unless the suddenness of danger made the summoning of Parliament impossible, a condition which clearly was not fulfilled when the tax was levied for three years without a Parliament's being called. Learnedly and courageously did Hampden's lawyers fight the case before the Exchequer Judges. The result was that, of the twelve judges, seven gave judgement for the Crown and five for Hampden—so giving the King the smallest majority possible, if all voted, on a body of twelve. The bulk of the nation rightly hailed the result, at the hands of judges appointed by the King, as equivalent to a victory for Hampden; but Charles, ignoring this implication, continued to levy Ship-money.

One factor in the dispute needs to be remembered—namely, that investigation shows that the money raised was honestly applied to building and equipping ships. In 1635 and 1636 considerable fleets put to sea though without any very definite purpose or result. More important was the fact that the ships built by Charles formed the nucleus of the fleet which, under the Commonwealth, upheld English naval supremacy against the Dutch. Charles' use of the Ship-money levies is a further proof of his sincerity as a ruler. Regarding himself as responsible for the welfare of the State, he thought himself justified in taking such measures as were made necessary by the Parliament's refusal to co-operate.

The various expedients enforced by the Government to supply the exchequer were together so successful that by 1638 the income met the current expenses though it did not pay off the standing debt. This result was due partly to more efficient exchequer administration and partly to a large increase in trade which produced a corresponding increase in national wealth. The continuance of peace would apparently have enabled Charles to go on indefinitely meeting his ordinary expenses out of non-Parliamentary income. Only the threat of war from Scotland in 1640 upset this financial equilibrium.

Nevertheless the Government's success was no argument for either the legal or the moral principles of its policy: the system of non-Parliamentary taxation was a threat to the liberty of the nation, and the higher the system's efficiency the more serious was its threat.

2. Wentworth: in the North and in Ireland

The efficiency necessary to the King's arbitrary rule was embodied in Wentworth. It was characteristic of Wentworth that, having received his patent as President of the North on December 15, by the 30th of that month he was at York exercising the duties of his new office.

The Council of the North had been established under Henry VIII in the year 1541, its immediate purpose being to suppress the discontent following the dissolution of the monasteries. Gradually it had extended its discretionary powers until they virtually superseded the ordinary courts of Common Law. Its authority covered the four counties of York, Northumberland, Durham, and Westmorland, as well as the Bishopric of Durham and the cities of York, Hull, and Newcastle upon Tyne. The new President was faced with no easy task. During the régime of his predecessor, the aged and feeble Lord Scrope, the administration had become lax and irregular. This was largely because the members of the northern council were local landowners against whom the lesser gentry and others could not hope to secure justice in the Court. Against such partiality Wentworth set himself with unflinching vigour. He surrounded himself with semi-regal dignity, withdrawing himself from ordinary intercourse with his fellow landowners, and reserving all intimacy for a few personal friends. This roused much antipathy locally, and made the more necessary the taking of disciplinary action against some prominent individual as an example to the rest.

The individual who brought such action upon himself was Sir David Foulis, a Scot to whom James I had granted a Yorkshire estate. Jealous of Wentworth's powers, he began to spread the story that the President was appropriating to himself the distraint-of-knighthood fines and, further, that a summons issued by the Lord President need not be obeyed unless accompanied by a legal warrant. Wentworth did not hesitate. He struck, and struck hard. Foulis was brought before the Star Chamber on a charge of libel. He was fined £500, and imprisoned in the Fleet prison, where he remained until the Long Parliament met seven years later.

The assertion of authority was not Wentworth's only concern. Laws affecting the lives of ordinary people—such as the Apprenticeship and Poor Laws—were evenly enforced. In spite of the example of Foulis, these measures provoked further opposition among the gentry. In order to deal with this opposition, Wentworth repeatedly asked that the northern council's powers should be more exactly defined and increased. At last, in March 1633, the Privy Council issued new instructions which gave to the Council of the North powers which were at least as great as those of the Star Chamber.

So far as Wentworth was concerned, the new powers were almost too late. In January 1632 he had been appointed Lord Deputy of Ireland, though he retained the Presidency of the North. He left England for his new sphere in July 1633.

The task which faced Wentworth in Ireland was one to test even his mettle. Two evils particularly afflicted the country —clan-strife and plantations. During Elizabeth's reign there had been numerous rebellions, the chief rebel during the latter part of her reign being the Earl of Tyrone, head of the O'Neill clan. It was Lord Mountjoy who at last, after a two-year struggle, defeated Tyrone and secured his submission in March 1603. Mountjoy knew that James had succeeded Elizabeth six days earlier: had Tyrone known it, he might have decided to hold out a little longer to try his fortune with the new King. In fact, he would have fared no better under James, for James' policy was to Anglicize Ireland. Under his Lord Deputy, Sir Arthur Chichester (1604–14), much was done to this end. The system of landowning by common ownership was abolished in favour of the English land-system; the English shire-system was substituted for the hereditary jurisdiction of the chiefs; and the Acts of Supremacy and Uniformity were applied. In 1607 Tyrone, accompanied by the Earl of Tyrconnel, fled from Ireland to Rome. They were at once declared to be traitors, which meant that their clan-lands became forfeit. This placed the greater part of the six counties of Ulster at the Government's disposal. The result was the 1610 plantation of Ulster. Within a few years some two thousand English and Scottish families were 'planted' in the best parts of Ulster. One of the settlements made by the City of London in the town of Derry was renamed Londonderry as was also the surrounding district. Chichester disagreed with the wholesale nature of this policy, and in 1614 he resigned his office. His departure was followed by further confiscations. Tyrone's rebellion might be held to justify the confiscation of his lands and even their plantation, but no justification could be found for the treatment thereafter meted out all over Ireland to individual landowners who had not rebelled. Title-deeds were examined, and the slightest flaw resulted in the forfeiture of the lands, which were transferred to English or Scottish settlers. The discontent engendered by this accumulation of injustice was the root cause of the rebellion of 1641.

Nor were these the only evils that Wentworth inherited in Ireland. The Army, on which in the last resort his power would depend, consisted of not more than 2500 men, ill-equipped, ill-paid, and therefore ill-disciplined. So ineffective were the country's defences that pirates infested the surrounding seas to such a degree that for six months Wentworth was prevented from crossing to take up his new duties. The Church was in a similarly parlous condition. Wentworth later described it to Laud in the following terms:

> . . . an unlearned clergy . . . the churches unbuilt; the parsonage and vicarage houses utterly ruined; the people untaught thorough the non-residency of the clergy, occasioned by the unlimited shameful numbers of spiritual promotions with cure of souls, which they hold by commendams; the rites and ceremonies of the church run over without all decency of habit, order, or gravity in the course of their service.

The Government itself was thoroughly corrupt. The Lord Deputy's Council consisted of about forty members living in various parts of Ireland, and only rarely visiting Dublin. Their chief object was to serve their own interests. Wentworth wrote of them that "they are a company of men the most intent upon their own ends that ever I met with." The higher the rank and office occupied by the English officials in Ireland, the greater the opportunities, and the more eagerly seized, for corruption. This was notably true of the Lord Treasurer, the Earl of Cork, the Chancellor, Lord Loftus, and the Vice-Treasurer, Viscount Mountnorris. Wentworth would need all his wits and all his resolution if he was to solve the problems, political and personal, which these conditions involved, and was to establish throughout Ireland a government such as that for which he had been responsible as President of the North.

From the outset Wentworth made up his mind that the only system of government that could be effective in Ireland was thoroughgoing autocracy. In order to strengthen his position, he had secured from the King a promise that no land should be granted, no office be filled in Army or Church, and no appeal made to the English Crown unless the Lord Deputy had first given his permission. That Wentworth was confident of his strength was shown by his decision, which Charles reluctantly sanctioned, to call a Parliament in 1634. He so manipulated the elections that he obtained Protestant and Roman Catholic Members in nearly equal numbers. Then he divided the Parliament's work into two sessions: the first was to be devoted to supply, and the second to consideration of grievances. From the first session he obtained the substantial grant of six subsidies, but in the second he refused to consider requests. In a letter to Laud at the close of the Parliament Wentworth could comment: "So now I can say the King is as absolute here as any prince in the world can be."

As he had begun, so he continued. Not the most powerful individual in the land was allowed to thwart the Lord Deputy's will. In December 1635 Lord Mountnorris was summoned before a court-martial (he being an officer in the Army) on account of a disparaging remark made about the Lord Deputy. Though the death-sentence pronounced upon him was not carried out, he was imprisoned and dismissed from his office. Similarly the Earl of Cork, the Lord Treasurer and most powerful man on the council, was forced to disgorge numerous

4*

parcels of church-lands which he had appropriated, and to pay enormous fines.

Alongside such efforts against the mighty went much solid work for the welfare of the mass of his subjects. At his own expense, Wentworth introduced the cultivation of flax as well as looms, and foreign workpeople for its manufacture. In part, his object was the people's prosperity, in part, the resulting increase in revenue. For this latter purpose he improved the customs system and the method of collection so that during his four years in Ireland the customs rose from £22,000 to £40,000 yearly. As a further aid to Irish trade, he set about the extirpation of piracy: the pirates' nest in the Isle of Man was destroyed, and the ringleaders led captive to England for punishment.

In 1636 Wentworth returned for a period to England where he resumed actively his duties as President of the North. One of his duties was the collection of Ship-money for that year: in Yorkshire his presence was enough to ensure the payment of the impost almost without opposition. During this period he renewed a request which he had preferred two years earlier —namely, that, in order to increase his prestige in Ireland, and to silence his enemies in England, the King would grant him an earldom. To the earlier request Charles had replied with a brief, almost curt, refusal. To this second request Charles returned a more courteous but not less definite rejection. This was a bitter dose for Wentworth. That Charles, who doled out honours easily to personal favourites, should withhold a title from his most devoted and energetic servant, was almost incomprehensible. One reason almost certainly was the Queen's dislike of him. But fundamentally, it would seem that Charles still resented having been forced to admit Wentworth to high office. For years Charles had repelled Wentworth's advances to the Court, and had accepted him at last only when circumstances left no alternative; but it was as though he never forgave Wentworth for forcing his hand. Consequently he never took him fully into his confidence. The final outcome of this relationship was seen later when Charles consented to Wentworth's execution.

Within a few months of Wentworth's return to Ireland the

dispute between King and Scots became serious. It was the Scottish war resulting from this dispute which caused Charles, in August 1639, to summon Wentworth back from Ireland. The cause of the trouble was Laud's attempt to enforce upon the Scots a Prayer Book of his own designing.

3. William Laud

William Laud was the son of a Reading clothier. He was born in 1573. From the Reading Grammar School he passed, in the year following the Armada's defeat, to St John's College, Oxford, where he became successively Scholar, Fellow, and, in 1631, President.

Whence Laud derived his characteristic ecclesiastical and political views, and what was the process of their development in his mind, are quite unknown to us. When he first gave expression to his ideas they seem to have been as definite and fully formed as in the last stage of his life. This was typical of Laud's character in general: always he was self-consistent and self-contained. All that mattered to him was the rigid maintenance of principles. The clean-cut nature of these principles was the chief source of his strength. His corresponding weakness was that this absorption in principles left him neither time nor inclination for personal friendships or for recreation of any kind. Small wonder that such a man provoked many enemies and won few friends. Though the number of his admirers was large, Wentworth seems to have been the only man who could rightly be called his friend.

The man to whom Laud owed most during the early stages of his advancement was Richard Neile, who in 1608, when Bishop of Rochester, secured for Laud a chaplaincy to the King. Neile shared Laud's ecclesiastical views, and Neile's successive promotions—to Lichfield 1610, Lincoln 1614, Durham 1617, Winchester 1628, and the Archbishopric of York 1631—indicated a corresponding growth in the influence of Arminianism in the Church. Laud in 1621 became Bishop of St David's, and by Charles I's accession in 1625 he was the predominant figure in the English Church. His early promotion was therefore to be expected. In 1626 he was made Bishop of Bath and Wells, but had not had an opportunity of visiting his diocese when in 1628 he was translated to London.

It was in London that Laud began to do his distinctive work. Throughout the diocese irregular forms of services were suppressed, uniform vestments were insisted upon, the communion-table was moved from the nave, where Elizabethan custom had placed it, to the east end of the chancel where it was railed off and became an altar, and decaying church-fabrics were restored. The most notable example of such restoration was at his Cathedral, St Paul's. For many years the Cathedral had been neglected. In 1561 lightning had destroyed the spire; and since then the piecemeal repairs had not kept pace with dilapidations. Perhaps an even worse calamity for the Cathedral than the decay of its fabric was the lack of reverence which the Londoners paid to it. The west porch—Paul's Walk—was the common meeting-place for people who wanted to discuss either business or politics; and at the west end of the Church there was a constant hubbub, even during divine service, from people walking and talking, and from children playing. The scandal of this desecration Laud determined to remove. Disorder within the Cathedral was suppressed; houses which had been built up close to its walls were demolished; and a fund was energetically raised for repairs to the fabric.

The prominence of Laud in the Church was such that he over-shadowed Archbishop Abbot. Abbot, who had been at Canterbury since 1611, was out of sympathy with both the political and the religious policy of the Court and lived almost in retirement. It was generally anticipated that Laud would step into the Primacy as soon as it was vacant; and from the time of his appointment to London Laud wielded almost an archiepiscopal influence. Hence when, in May 1633, King Charles set out to visit Scotland for his coronation there, he was accompanied by Laud.

This was not Laud's first visit to Scotland. In 1617 he had accompanied Bishop Neile who had been one of those in attendance upon King James when the latter made a progress across the Border. In more respects than one this earlier visit had afforded Laud useful experience. Early in his reign James

introduced bishops with certain supervisory powers into the
Scottish Presbyterian Church, and from time to time those
powers were increased. James' intention during the 1617 visit
was to introduce also a new form of Church-service; but so
firm was the resistance of the Scots—who claimed that such
changes could be accepted only by a General Assembly of the
Church—that James failed to achieve his purpose.

One of the purposes of Charles and Laud in going to Scotland in 1633 was to renew their efforts for ecclesiastical
changes. The tone of such changes was foreshadowed by the
ceremony of Charles' coronation as King of Scotland: the
communion-table was arranged as an altar at whose centre
was a cross to which the bishops bowed. The Scots were
therefore suspicious about any changes proposed by the King.
Hence they resolutely resisted the suggestion that the English
liturgy should be enforced in Scotland. Though in July 1633
Charles returned to England with his immediate purpose un-
accomplished, during the following year plans were made to
frame a new Prayer Book whose use was to be enforced
throughout Scotland. Thus the seeds were sown which were
to produce the crop of troubles for Charles in 1640–41.

Scarcely had Charles returned to London when Abbot's
death (on August 4, 1633) cleared the way for Laud's elevation.
Two days later Charles greeted Laud with the words: "My
Lord's Grace of Canterbury, you are very welcome."

The new Archbishop lost no time in beginning reforms
throughout his Province similar to those which he had introduced into his diocese of London. As a basis for this work he
revived the practice of a visitation. Commissioners were sent
to every part of the Canterbury Province inquiring about
every possible factor affecting the condition of the Church—
fabrics, orderliness of services, orthodoxy of the clergy. In
certain quarters, notably by Bishop Williams of Lincoln and
by the two universities, Laud met with some resistance to
what was regarded as infringement of traditional independence; but his determination wore down all resistance. Following the visitation, Laud did his utmost to insist on uniformity
in services, in the ordering of the altar, and in similar matters.
Also it was largely his influence which caused Prynne, Burton,

and Bastwick to be brought before the Star Chamber for their attacks on the bishops and the Laudian ritual.[1]

Laud's position as Archbishop brought him into even closer and more constant relationship with the Court than previously. Following the death in 1635 of Lord Treasurer Portland, the difficulty of finding a suitable successor was so great that the Treasury was administered by commissioners with Laud at their head. When the inconvenience of administering the Treasury by a Commission at last made the appointment of a new Treasurer imperative it was Laud's nominee, William Juxon, Bishop of London, who received the office. Laud was widely suspected of wishing to accumulate high offices in the hands of clerics so as to increase the Church's political influence. Though Laud was naturally zealous for the Church, such zeal was not his only motive. His letters show his disgust at the current political corruption whereby Ministers of the Crown used their offices as means of enriching themselves rather than of serving the State. Laud believed that Juxon would discharge the Lord Treasurer's duties honestly as well as ably. Juxon justified Laud's expectations by pleasing the Court, and he did it without offending the Court's opponents. The Long Parliament, when attacking the bishops, specifically named Juxon as an exception; and in spite of his evidence at Strafford's trial that he did not remember hearing Strafford propose to bring over an Irish Army, and in spite of his attendance on King Charles at the latter's execution, he was unmolested throughout the period of the Commonwealth. After Laud's death in 1645 the see of Canterbury remained vacant until the Restoration in 1660, and then Juxon, though seventy-eight years of age, was appointed to fill it, thus becoming Laud's successor.

In spite of Laud's supremacy in his own sphere, his position at Court had certain weaknesses. Perhaps the chief one was the character of Laud himself. Charles I's Court was thick with intrigues, not a few of which centred round the person of the Queen. No man could hope to hold his own there unless gifted with more than ordinary charm of manner and flexibility

[1] See p. 99.

of mind. Laud had no understanding of either of these qualities. His manner was by nature brusque and his speech acrid;
and his unbending will was unable to distinguish between the
important and the unimportant aspects of a project that he
was pursuing. Of his personal sincerity and his unflinching
devotion to his adopted principles, there can be no doubt. But
his whole career showed also that he lacked the larger qualities
of statesmanship which alone entitle a public man to be considered 'great.' In brief, Laud was not big enough to carry
out effectively all the vast and multifarious schemes that he
initiated.

His most successful period was the first three years of his
Primacy during which he was able, by royal support, to bear
down all opposition. During 1637 signs of a coming change
began to appear in the fact that Laud encountered opposition
which he was unable to break, opposition which ultimately
was to break him, and his master with him. The scene of the
trouble was Scotland.

Laud's position as Primate of England did not entitle him to
any authority over the Church in Scotland. The head of the
Scottish Church was the King, and whatever influence Laud
was able to wield therein was by virtue of being Charles'
mouthpiece.

The shaping of a new Prayer Book for Scotland began soon
after Charles' visit there in 1633. As a preparation for it, in
1636, a new Book of Canons was issued for the Scottish
Church. These enjoined that the communion-table should be
placed at the upper end of the church, that confession to a
presbyter or bishop should be encouraged, that the King
should be recognized as the head of the Church, and that the
new Prayer Book, when it should appear, should be wholly
accepted. To demand acceptance of a Prayer Book which the
Scots had not yet seen was of itself enough to rouse opposition.
But to the Scots even this could not be worse than the Canons
that they already knew: the setting up of an altar and the
practice of confession were to their minds popery, and no
one who understood the Scots would have dreamed of trying
to impose such practices upon them.

The suspicion aroused by the Canons would alone have

sufficed to ensure a hostile reception for the new Prayer Book. But this hostility was intensified by two other facts: the book was to be introduced without any consultation with any representative body of the Scottish people, and it had originated in England where the ruling influence was Laud whose Arminianism was anathema to the Presbyterian Scots.

The new Prayer Book duly appeared in Scotland in May 1637. On July 23 it was for the first time used for service in St Giles' Cathedral, Edinburgh. The result was an uproar during which a woman flung a stool at the Dean's head. The uproar grew into a riot so that the magistrates had to clear the church. From Edinburgh the opposition spread through Scotland, and in February 1638 it organized itself into the Tables, which consisted of four committees designed to represent the various sections of the nation—namely, nobles, gentry, ministers, and burgesses respectively.

During the same month the Covenant—originally formed in 1581 when Scotland was menaced by papal attack and intrigue—was renewed. Every one who signed thereby pledged himself to support and defend the Scottish Church; and throughout Scotland all classes of men rushed to sign the document. Almost the whole nation was on the verge of armed revolt.

In May 1638 the Marquis of Hamilton, cousin to the King, was sent as a special commissioner to negotiate with the Covenanters' leaders. These demanded that the new Prayer Book should be withdrawn and the Court of High Commission abolished, and that a General Assembly of the Scottish Church and a free Parliament should be summoned. Not all Hamilton's efforts could induce the Covenanters to modify these demands. Three times he made the toilsome journey between the English Court and Scotland, and finally in August 1638 Charles granted the Scots' demands.

In reality Charles was playing a game he was to play many times during his subsequent career: his aim in yielding to his opponents was to quieten them while he collected forces to defeat them. But he was dealing with men who had no intention of trifling with him or of allowing him to trifle with them. The General Assembly, which met on November 21, lost no time in getting down to what it considered the roots of Scotland's troubles. It began to debate the conduct of the Scottish bishops; and when Hamilton in just over a week dismissed the Assembly the members ignored the dissolution and continued to meet as before. Within a few weeks the Assembly abolished the Prayer Book and the episcopal system and, in place of the latter, restored Presbyterianism. Since the King was the head of the Scottish Church, the Assembly's actions were tantamount to rebellion. It was a challenge which Charles could not ignore. In the last resort his only method of asserting his authority was armed force; and during the early part of 1639 both sides were preparing for war.

In every respect the Scots had the advantage over Charles. Considerable numbers of Scots had of late returned after serving in the Thirty Years' War in Germany. Most notable among them was Alexander Leslie, who had served under the great Gustavus Adolphus. Against such experienced soldiers Charles would have no one to oppose except the militia led by the nobles, the latter being summoned as the King's feudal tenants to serve at their own charges. Moreover, whereas the Scots were almost unanimously supporters of the Covenant, both the English militia and the nobles would include many malcontents against their own Government. Laud's enforcement of High Church ritual in England had offended the large Puritan element in the Church, an element which had more in common with the Scottish Presbyterians than with the English Arminians. Also the enormous loans and fines extorted by the Star Chamber from the richer people had alienated a section whose support the King would need now more than ever before: though only two nobles—Lords Brooke and Saye—refused to take the military oath in April, many others were seriously disaffected.

The collecting of forces was not the King's only difficulty. However effective an army he might put into the field, to keep them there would depend upon his ability to pay them and supply them with munitions of war. The crux of the situation would be money. Various expedients for filling the exchequer were tried—loans from the City of London, a benevolence, the sale of offices—but all alike failed. Unless the Scots could be defeated by a rapid stroke, the King's cause was lost.

By the end of March Charles was in York. Thence he marched northward, and by the end of May he was in Berwick. Within a week the Covenanters, led by Leslie, were on the Border not more than a dozen miles from the King's camp. A clash seemed inevitable. But neither side, when faced with the issue, was anxious for war. Charles lacked both an army, with which to meet the Scots at once, and the resources for a protracted campaign. The Scots were shrewd enough to see that, if they crossed the Border, their presence on English soil might rouse the English against foreign invaders. Both sides were therefore willing to negotiate. The upshot was the Treaty of Berwick signed on June 18, 1639, which thus brought to an end the First Bishops' War without a blow being struck between the main contending armies. The terms included an undertaking by both sides that the armies should be disbanded. Also, the Covenanters were to break up the Tables and to restore royal castles already seized. In return, the King would allow the meeting of the Scots' Parliament to deal with civil matters, and of a General Assembly to deal with ecclesiastical matters.

Though at first sight the terms of the treaty seemed a fair solution of the questions at issue between Charles and his northern subjects, in reality they settled nothing. They were too vague to satisfy either side. The new Assembly and Parliament would be as opposed as their predecessors to the Laudian settlement, and no mention was made in the treaty about what powers were to be allowed to these two bodies. Possibly the Covenanters had consented to vague terms in the belief that Charles, lacking resources, would have learned his lesson, and would realize the futility of imposing an alien church on Scotland. They did not yet know that Charles was incapable of learning from experience. One of the major passions of his life was devotion to the Anglican Church, and from that devotion nothing ever induced him to swerve.

The issue was soon joined. To the General Assembly which was opened in Edinburgh on August 12 Charles had summoned the Scottish bishops, an action which the Scots interpreted as a breach of the Treaty of Berwick. The Assembly abolished episcopacy and the ritual associated with it. To this abolition Traquair, the King's commissioner, signified the royal assent. When the Parliament met in Edinburgh at the end of August Charles informed Traquair that, notwithstanding his assent to the Assembly's measures, the royal assent would never be given to the repeal of the Statutes whereby Episcopacy had been established. This statement undermined the Scots' confidence in Charles. Deadlock between the King and the Parliament was inevitable, and in the middle of November the Parliament was prorogued. Henceforward the government of Scotland was in the hands of a recently appointed Committee of eight members at the head of whom were Wentworth and Laud.

Wentworth had been in touch—mainly through Laud—with the Scottish situation from the beginning. With the policy of delay and concession he had no patience. His experience in Ireland had led him to believe that Parliaments could be brought to heel if treated with consistent firmness. His fear was that the elements of opposition to the King in England would become allied to those in Scotland. To prevent this, Wentworth's policy was that Scottish government should be exercised not by the Scots but direct from England. Events in Scotland at last convinced Charles that Wentworth was right, and Wentworth was summoned home from Ireland. He reached London on September 22, 1639. From that moment his influence, not only in Scottish affairs but in general policy, was predominant.

A renewal of war between England and Scotland was only a question of time. The business of the Committee for Scotland was therefore to find means whereby to wage it. Wentworth urged that no financial expedients short of Parliamentary supply could be adequate. His argument convinced the King, and a new English Parliament was decided upon. This was not intended as a concession to the King's opponents. On the contrary, Wentworth's advocacy of a Parliament was due to his belief that the methods that had reduced an Irish Parliament to submission would succeed equally with an English Parliament if applied with equally resolute efficiency. He proposed to return to Ireland, and there to summon a Parliament from which he would obtain supplies that would be a worthy example for the proposed English Parliament to emulate.

As a mark of royal favour, on January 12, 1640, Wentworth received the title he had long coveted: he was created Earl of Strafford, and shortly afterwards was raised from being Lord Deputy to being Lord Lieutenant of Ireland. Two months later Strafford set out for Ireland.

In the meantime one noteworthy change had taken place at Court. The Secretary, Sir John Coke, had been dismissed from office partly because of old age and partly because he was opposed to Laud's ecclesiastical system. The choice of a successor was not easy. Finally, owing largely to the Queen's influence, the choice fell upon Sir Henry Vane. The appointment was of ill omen for Strafford. The two men had lately become bitter enemies. When Wentworth had received his earldom he had taken also the subsidiary title of Baron Raby. Raby Castle, in the county of Durham, had formerly been in Wentworth's family but had been lost to them during Elizabeth's reign. Subsequently the castle had come into the possession of Vane who, aspiring to a peerage, cherished the ambition of taking Raby as his title. He therefore felt that Wentworth, in adopting this title, had forestalled him. The sequel will show that Vane stored up his resentment until Strafford's trial provided him with the opportunity of giving a damning piece of evidence against the prisoner.

4. The Short Parliament

Elections for Charles I's fourth Parliament were held during March 1640. The new House of Commons met for the first time on April 13. The attitude which it was to take up was determined by a number of factors including its own composition and the circumstances attending its calling.

The outstanding fact was that eleven years had elapsed since the dissolution of the previous Parliament. The new Parliament might therefore be expected to take what measures it could to prevent a repetition of such a period of arbitrary government. The King's need of money wherewith to equip an army against the Scots would render him more helpless against this Parliament than against any of its three predecessors. If he resisted Parliament's demands for redress of grievances Parliament would not only be able to refuse supplies but would be likely to ally with the King's enemies with whom it had more in common than with the King.

A further effect of the lapse of eleven years was that the personnel of the new House of Commons was different from that of the previous one. Of the former Commons' leaders, death had removed Sir John Eliot in 1632, Sir Edward Coke in 1634, and Sir Robert Phelips in 1636. New Members who were to win reputations for themselves included Oliver St John (Hampden's counsel in the Ship-money trial), Edward Hyde (afterwards Earl of Clarendon), and Lord Falkland. Oliver Cromwell, who had represented Huntingdon in the 1628–29 Parliament, now sat for the town of Cambridge.

The Member who by immediate and common consent was the leader of the Court's opponents was John Pym. He was now fifty-seven years of age. Few could equal his Parliamentary experience: this was the sixth consecutive Parliament of which he had been a Member. The removal of other prominent figures of the previous House left Pym without a rival as the leader of the popular section. Already we have seen that his opposition to arbitrary government, though determined and persistent, was more moderate in character than that of many others, notably of Eliot from whom Pym had dissociated himself towards the close of the previous Parliament. During the Eleven Years' Tyranny Pym had matured considerably. Not only had he grown older but he had gained valuable administrative experience as treasurer of a company for colonizing the island of Old Providence off the Mosquito Coast of Central America. Incidentally, several other members of the Providence Company were men with whom Pym was to be closely associated in the struggle against the Court during the Long Parliament. These men included Hampden and Lords Brooke and Saye. There can be no doubt that their intimacy during the colonization project helped them to work together later in the political cause which they had in common. The combination of native coolness of judgement with ripe experience made Pym the statesman not only of the Short Parliament but of the even more fateful one which was to follow.

On the day that the Parliament first met it was addressed by Lord Keeper Finch (who, when Speaker of the Commons, had been held down in the Chair in 1629). Finch asked for supplies to enable the King to defeat his enemies, and he promised that when supplies had been granted the King would be willing to consider his subjects' grievances. His references to the danger from enemies left most of the Commons unimpressed. During the ensuing debate one Member voiced the feelings of others by declaring: "I am very mistaken if there be not a case here at home of as great danger as that which is already put."

Pym expressed the mind of the majority of the Commons in a speech taking two hours to deliver. It was an orderly exposition of the principles which in his view were fundamental to popular liberties in politics, justice, and religion, and it included a recital of the grievances suffered by the previous Parliament and by the nation after that Parliament's dissolution. He declared:

> A Parliament is that to the Commonwealth, which the soul is to the body. . . . It behoves us therefore to keep the faculty of that soul from distemper.

On April 18, the day following Pym's speech, the Commons began to consider the questions of Eliot's imprisonment and of Ship-money. Three days later the King, scenting danger, summoned both Houses to Whitehall, and there the Lord Keeper informed them that the King was willing to consider Parliament's suggestion for an alternative for Ship-money.

It was at this point that Strafford returned from Ireland where his plans had met with much success. By taking skilful advantage of the division between the Roman Catholic and Protestant members of the Dublin Parliament, he had secured a unanimous vote granting four subsidies which were voted amid expressions of enthusiastic loyalty to the Lord Lieutenant and to the King. Strafford also had eight thousand foot-soldiers and one thousand horse who might be conveyed to England or

Scotland should circumstances demand it. Having thus accomplished his self-appointed task, Strafford, though racked with pain and for days able to move only when carried on a litter, returned to England, finally reaching London by painful stages on April 18. For the brief remainder of his life he was the King's staunchest counsellor and the Parliament's most dangerous foe. Nevertheless the advice that he gave to the King was not always the wisest. Two factors especially warped his judgement. First, he interpreted his experience of the Irish Parliament to mean that Parliaments in general could be brought to heel if handled with sufficient firmness: he never understood the difference between the Irish and the English Parliaments in this respect. Second, the English Parliament had changed its temper since Wentworth had ceased to be a Member of the Commons: the Eleven Years' Tyranny had stiffened Parliament's determination to resist further royal oppression, and the Commons' leadership was in the hands not of the hot-head Eliot but of the statesman Pym. The difference which these facts would make would quickly become apparent.

On Strafford's advice Charles went to the Lords to urge that supply should precede the discussion of grievances, and to ask that the Lords would not join the Commons if the latter continued to demand the reverse procedure. The Lords, with even less tact than the King, on April 24 voted that supply should precede grievances, though it was not without significance that in a House of eighty-six peers there should be a minority vote of twenty-five. This vote was a clear infringement of the Commons' control over finance, and three days later the Commons drew up a formal protest against the Lords' action, and Pym was sent to present it to the Upper House.

The Commons' unyielding attitude led Strafford to advise that the King should frankly abandon the right to levy Ship-money in return for a grant of subsidies. Accordingly on May 4 Secretary Vane informed the Commons that:

. . . upon your granting twelve subsidies to be presently [that is, immediately] passed and to be paid in three years . . . his

Majesty will not only for the present forbear the levying of any *Ship Money*, but will give way to the utter abolishing of it, by any course that yourselves shall like best.[1]

This demand for twelve subsidies proved fatal to an agreement on the subject. The Commons, lacking any means of controlling the King's use of money, feared that so great a sum would render the King independent of Parliament, and that the grant would be followed by a dissolution and by another period of arbitrary rule. Should this happen, the renunciation of Ship-money would be valueless, and the Commons, having lost both parts of the bargain, would have defeated their own ends. These fears expressed themselves in a long debate until Vane intervened to state that the King would accept nothing less than the twelve subsidies. The Commons' Committee, still hesitating to trust the King, broke off its sitting.

To the King this action appeared more sinister because he knew that the Parliament had been in communication with the Scots. The Commons had set aside May 7 on which to discuss Scottish matters; and there was reason to believe that the House would urge the King to negotiate peace with the Scots.

So critical did the King consider the situation that at 6 o'clock the next morning (May 5) the Council met to discuss the King's intention to dissolve Parliament. Though Strafford advised caution, the King persisted, and the Council finally voted for dissolution. Thereupon the King went down to the House of Lords; and the Parliament, which had opened only three weeks earlier, came to an end and was henceforward fitly known as the Short Parliament.

Charles' precipitate dissolution was something more than a mere error of judgement. It was one of the major blunders of his career, comparable to his attempt to arrest the Five Members in the Commons in January 1642. However great Charles' difficulties in dealing with the Parliament may have been, two obstinate facts remained: the Scottish Covenanting Army was still in being and would not disband until it had achieved its purposes, and only by Parliamentary grants could Charles

[1] Rushworth, III, 1154.

raise funds necessary for an army to meet the Scots. He would therefore be compelled to summon another Parliament quickly. This Parliament would know that it had the King at its mercy and would bargain with him accordingly. Had there been any doubt on this point, the failure of Charles' renewed efforts to raise money—more Ship-money, loans, and the like—would have dispelled it. Not less sinister than the failure to raise money were the signs of a rebellious temper among the masses of the people. Riots were frequent in the City.

If Charles was to re-establish his authority in Scotland the war must be waged and won quickly. Strafford, gauging the situation exactly, advised him accordingly. Secretary Vane's note of Strafford's advice was as follows:

> Go on with a vigorous war, as you first designed: loose and absolved from all rules of government, being reduced to extreme necessity, everything is to be done that power might admit, and that you are to do. . . . You have an army in Ireland that you may employ here to reduce this kingdom. Confident as anything under heaven that Scotland shall not hold out five months.[1]

The only hope of Strafford's policy being successful was that Strafford himself should carry it out. No other man of his calibre, in vision or in will, was to be found among the King's counsellors. But by this time Strafford was hopelessly broken in health: all his struggles against his infirmities only increased his sense of frustration and so made his weakness greater rather than less. Even when the royal Army moved northward, Strafford could get no farther than York.

On August 20 the Covenanting Army, led by Leslie, crossed the Tweed into England. Meeting no resistance, it marched southward, and a week later was crossing the Tyne, having overrun Northumberland and occupied Newcastle.

Meanwhile the King's opponents in London were taking advantage of the situation. Pym and St John drew up a petition for a new Parliament which should proceed against the King's counsellors and work for peace with the Scots. Twelve peers affixed their signatures to the petition. A few days later

---

[1] H.M.C. Report, III, 3.

the Scots presented a petition asking for the redress of their grievances with an English Parliament's advice.

Charles, desperately caught between two enemies, adopted the characteristic policy of compromise: instead of calling another Parliament, he decided to summon a meeting of all the peers. This would be the revival of a medieval Great Council such as had not met since Edward III's reign. What advantage the King could gain from such a meeting was difficult to see. It would carry no authority with either the English or the Scots. The King would not even enjoy the prestige of the unanimous support of the peers, for an influential section of them was opposed to him.

The proposed Great Council met at York on September 24. Charles informed it that a new Parliament was to meet on November 3, and asked for advice as to the means of dealing with the rebel Scots. The peers therefore named sixteen of their own number to act as commissioners with power to negotiate with the Scots.

The commissioners and the Scottish representatives met at Ripon. The Scots demanded £40,000 a month and their continued occupation of Northumberland until terms of peace were agreed. Presumably such terms would be negotiated with the forthcoming English Parliament. No bargaining could move the Scots from the basis of their demands though finally they reduced the monthly sum to £25,000. These terms were accepted by the English commissioners on October 21.

After that point everything awaited the meeting of Parliament on November 3.

Chapter 6

The Long Parliament

1. First Session, November 1640–September 1641

What was to be perhaps the most famous of all English Parliaments met on November 3, 1640. Though its course was interrupted during the Commonwealth by various experiments in government, this fifth Parliament of Charles I remained the only legal Parliament for twenty years—that is, until, under the terms of the Own Consent Act of 1641, it dissolved itself on March 16, 1660.

In order to ensure the defeat of Court candidates, Pym had conducted something like an election campaign over parts of the country. From the outset the Commons showed that the great majority of constituencies had fulfilled Pym's hopes. Moreover, the Parliament met in a temper embittered by the sudden dissolution of the Short Parliament and by the King's attempt to revert to arbitrary rule.

Three days after the Parliament first met Strafford set out from Yorkshire to London. Had he consulted his own wishes and judgement he would have remained in the North, for he realized something of the dangerous animosity of the Parliamentary leaders towards him. But Charles, now without anyone else on whom to lean, had bidden him come, assuring him, on a King's word, that he should not suffer "in his person, honour, or fortune." Strafford therefore obeyed the King, and reached London during the evening of November 9.

By that time debates in the Commons had shown that Members recognized Strafford as the main pillar of the King's system of government. To overthrow him therefore became the first object of their policy. No sooner had Strafford arrived at Court than, realizing the situation, he planned to strike at his enemies before they had time to strike at him. The Council, on November 10, decided to accuse the Parliamentary leaders of treasonable relations with the Scots. Though Strafford had rightly gauged his danger and how to counteract it, he seriously underestimated the determination and resource of his opponents. News of the Council's decision, like most other Court news, leaked out to the Parliamentary leaders. Pym, equally quick to sense their danger, took immediate counter-action.

That same day in the Commons Pym moved that the doors of the House be locked. This motion having been carried, Pym rose and, after referring to the danger from Strafford, called upon Sir John Clotworthy to lay certain information before the House. Clotworthy, an Irish landowner, claimed to have knowledge of Strafford's intentions to use the Irish Army against the King's enemies. To this declaration he appended a recital of Strafford's oppressions in Ireland. In the circumstances this was exactly suited to the Commons' temper. A Committee of six was appointed forthwith to frame against Strafford an accusation which should be carried to the House of Lords.

In the afternoon Pym appeared before the Lords with the impeachment-accusation, and with the request that the Earl of Strafford, as a man charged with high treason, should be imprisoned while the House of Commons prepared more exactly and fully the articles of impeachment. Tidings of what was afoot having reached Strafford, he hurried to the Lords to gain information for himself, and probably by his presence to silence his accusers. But as he entered the Lords he was met with cries of "Withdraw." Then he was recalled to hear, as he knelt, the charges against him, and to deliver up his sword to the Usher of the Black Rod into whose custody he was delivered. A crowd gathered to watch him depart, "no man capping to him, before whom that morning the greatest in England would have stood dis-covered." So dramatic a fall is hard to parallel in English history.

With Strafford thus safely in custody, the opposition leaders felt free to gather and shape information for his impeachment-charges, and also to proceed against others whom they considered dangerous. On December 18 Archbishop Laud also was impeached and placed in custody.

Orders were issued for the release of the victims of Star Chamber oppression: during November and December Prynne, Burton, and Bastwick entered London and were accorded a tremendous welcome. Other signs of increasing ferment among the people soon appeared. Thus on December 11 a petition, signed by fifteen thousand Londoners, for the abolition of Episcopacy was presented to the Commons. The association, in the people's minds, between arbitrary government and Episcopacy—the bishops being mainly Laudian—was of great significance as suggesting the course of future events.

The first definite step to secure Parliament's power and to prevent another long period without a Parliament was taken in the Triennial Bill. After declaring that the interval between two Parliaments must never exceed three years, the Bill set up machinery to summon a Parliament if this provision should be broken. On his own initiative the Lord Chancellor, or Lord Keeper, was to issue writs for an election; should he fail to do so, the peers were to attend a Parliament and the sheriffs were to issue writs for the election of Members of a House of Commons; in the last resort, if these provisions were ignored, the freeholders and burgesses were to proceed to an election. After much hesitation Charles assented to the Bill on February 15, 1641.

The complementary measure would be to prevent a repetition of the Short Parliament's experience—that is, to prevent an early dissolution. A Bill to this end took shape during the early part of May 1641 when Parliament was afraid that the King would enforce a dissolution to save Strafford. The Bill therefore provided that the existing Parliament was not to be dissolved without its own consent. Charles' hesitation to accept this measure was natural. He at last signified his assent on May 10, at the same time as he assented to Strafford's attainder.

The details of the impeachment-charges against Strafford had been presented to the Lords by Pym on January 28, 1641. The trial began on March 22 in Westminster Hall, where staging and seats were erected for the large numbers who wished to attend. The King preferred not to occupy the royal throne but to sit with the Queen where he could watch without being considered as officially present. An air of drama pervaded the proceedings.

Strafford's accusers had two fundamental difficulties to surmount. First, treason meant conspiracy against the King. In Strafford's case such a charge was manifestly absurd. His accusers tried to circumvent the problem by claiming that the conspiracy might be against the King not as an individual but as the symbol of the State. Thus interpreted, treason was conspiracy against the welfare of the State. Pym, who was the Commons' leader throughout the impeachment, summed up this interpretation in his concluding speech:

> Shall it be treason to embase the King's coin, though but a piece of twelve-pence or sixpence? And must it not needs be the effect of a greater treason, to embase the spirits of his subjects, and to set up a stamp and character of servitude upon them, whereby they shall be disabled to do anything for the service of the King and Commonwealth?

Whether as a matter of equity Pym and his followers were right or wrong in this interpretation was keenly debated at the time, and has been in dispute ever since. Even if he was right, he would have difficulty in convincing a court of law, which was what the House of Lords constituted in an impeachment-trial, for such a court was concerned only with breaches of law.

Second, Strafford's responsibility for the King's arbitrary government would be difficult to establish. He had never been on intimate terms with the Court. Charles had never taken him completely into his confidence, and the Queen (who was becoming more and more Charles' confidante) scarcely disguised her animosity. Only during the brief period following his return to England in September 1639 did Strafford really act as the King's adviser. Strafford became the focus of the popular party's spleen less because of what he had done than because he personified as no one else did the principle of arbitrary government in its most efficient form, and also because he had never been forgiven for what was commonly held to be his apostasy. But, again, neither of these considerations would secure a verdict of guilty in a law-court.

Though as a prisoner Strafford was subject to many restrictions, and though suffering constantly from increasing bodily pain and weakness, he maintained a masterly defence which not all the assaults of the prosecuting lawyers could shake. The favourable impression which his defence was making upon the peers led Pym to play a card that for some time he had been holding in reserve. During the debate on April 10, while the Commons sat with locked doors, Pym brought the younger Sir Henry Vane to explain how, during the previous autumn, he had found among his father's papers the notes of the Council-meeting when Strafford had urged that "You have an army in Ireland you may employ here to reduce this Kingdom." The elder Vane, confronted by his son's evidence and by Pym's copy of the notes, was unable to deny the accuracy of the statement. Earlier in the trial the elder Vane, under cross-examination, had admitted hearing Strafford use the words in question, but no written evidence of them had hitherto been revealed, nor had anyone else present at the Council-meeting confirmed Strafford's use of them.

Even if the newly revealed evidence of Strafford's advice to employ the Irish Army were accepted as conclusive, it still left two weaknesses in the prosecution's case. First, if Strafford had given the alleged advice, what was "this Kingdom" to which it referred? The prosecution said that the "Kingdom" was England. Strafford asserted that, even if he had used the words, they must have referred to Scotland since that was the country in rebellion. No one could prove incontrovertibly which of the two was right. Second, the law of treason required not less than two witnesses to establish a treasonable act, yet the only witness of Strafford's advice to use the Irish Army was the elder Vane. Pym's view seems to have been that Vane's notes were equivalent to a second witness. Whether a law-court would accept this view was highly doubtful.

Though Strafford's opponents were thoroughly convinced that he was a serious danger to the State, many of the more extreme among them began to fear that they had not a sufficiently clear case to secure a verdict. They therefore began to urge that a Bill of Attainder should be substituted for the impeachment-process. Such a Bill, merely asserting Strafford's guilt as a traitor, could be passed by both Houses without the need for evidence to substantiate the accusation. Though Pym and Hampden never favoured this change of policy, they were outnumbered by their own followers. On April 10, the day on which the evidence of Vane's notes was laid before the Commons, a Bill of Attainder was introduced into the House. On April 21 the Bill passed its third reading in the Commons by 204 votes to fifty-nine. The next day two thousand Londoners brought to Parliament a petition bearing twenty thousand signatures demanding Strafford's execution. On April 25 the King sent to Strafford a message assuring him that, though he could not again be employed in an office of State, "upon the word of a King, you shall not suffer in life, honour or fortune." On May 8 only forty-eight peers were present in the House of Lords when the final vote on the Attainder Bill was taken. Of these, thirty-seven voted for the Bill and eleven against.

A cruel choice was thus presented to Charles. Though he hesitated and sought for alternatives, he could find no way out. On May 10 the Attainder Bill received the royal assent. On May 12 Strafford was executed on Tower Hill in the presence of a vast concourse.

The problem of why Charles, who had refused at all cost to sacrifice Buckingham, consented to sign away the life of his staunchest Minister has never ceased to intrigue inquirers. That Charles was moved by personal cowardice is difficult to believe in view of the unflinching courage which he showed when in due course he too was brought to the block. Possibly fears for the Queen's safety, if he continued to defy the Commons and the mob, may have influenced Charles. But the working of his mind was always inscrutable, and his motives defied accurate analysis. But the fact becomes important again here that though Strafford had been taken into the King's service he had never been taken into Charles' personal affection. Probably the King's hesitation to sign away Strafford's life was due less to solicitude for Strafford than to regard for his own honour. "My lord of Strafford's condition," said Charles, while signing the Attainder Bill, "is more happy than mine." At that moment he might well reflect upon the truth of his father's warning to him at the time of the impeachment of Lord Treasurer Middlesex: "he would have too much cause to remember how much he had contributed to the weakening of the Crown by this precedent he was now so fond of."

The effect of the execution on the King's cause was decisive. No longer could Pym and his followers urge that the King's misgovernment was due to "evil counsellors." Henceforward the King had no responsible counsellor. For all future governmental policy Charles alone must bear responsibility. Thus Strafford's removal caused a hardening of the opposition against the King.

The King's helplessness in face of Parliamentary opposition encouraged his opponents to secure other legislative safeguards against a repetition of the Eleven Years' Tyranny. Thus on June 22 Charles assented to a Tunnage and Poundage Bill which, while granting those customs for a specified time, contained a provision whereby Charles renounced his claim to impose customs duties except by Parliamentary grant. On August 5 he assented to Bills abolishing the Courts of Star Chamber and High Commission. The other arbitrary courts —namely, the Council of the North and the Council of Wales, which had not been established by Act of Parliament—could not be thus disposed of; but these also ceased to function. Thus the bulwarks of arbitrary government, both political and ecclesiastical, disappeared. Two days later the proceedings against Hampden of nearly four years earlier were annulled when Charles assented to a Bill "for the declaring unlawful and void the late proceedings touching Ship-money, and for the vacating of all records and process concerning the same."

Other important business during the first session of the Long Parliament consisted of proposals which did not issue immediately in legislation. They were concerned with the Church, and their importance was not in any changes which they made but in the rift which they revealed in the opposition party. This rift became wider as time passed, and was to prove one of the determining factors in the struggle between Charles and Parliament. In February 1641 the Commons considered the London petition against Episcopacy. On the motion that the petition should be sent to a committee for report, Pym, Hampden, St John, and the younger Vane were among those who voted for the motion, while Hyde, Falkland, and Culpepper voted against it. Hitherto these seven had all voted consistently together: for example, they had all voted for Strafford's impeachment. But from this moment the two groups within the opposition became more and more distinct, and more and more widely separated. The dividing principle was that of their attitude to the Church: the Pym group, who were Puritans or closely allied to Puritans, became more extreme in their opposition to the King; the Hyde group, being staunch Anglicans who were prepared to swallow Laudianism rather than endanger the Church, in due course went over to the King's side. By the time the Civil War broke out it was the latter section which formed the backbone of the royalist party, and without whom the King would scarcely have had a party at all.

The upshot of the Commons' consideration of the London Petition was that at the end of March the House voted that bishops should be excluded from the House of Lords. The Lords, however, disagreed with this view, and on June 8 rejected the Exclusion Bill.

On May 27 a Bill to abolish Episcopacy altogether—and hence known as the Root-and-Branch Bill—had been introduced into the Commons. It owed its origin mainly to Vane the younger and to Oliver Cromwell. The vote on the second reading showed the same party-division as had the vote on the London Petition. The Bill passed its second reading by 139 to 108; but Hyde, as chairman of the Committee to which the Bill was then sent, managed to delay proceedings so long that the session ended before the Bill had completed its stages.

Thus, though the debates on Episcopacy did not produce legislation, their resulting division of the popular party was a decisive factor in the struggle which culminated in the Civil War.

While these ecclesiastical debates were taking place Parliament was being agitated on another subject—namely, the King's intention to visit Scotland. His purpose was to take advantage of a rift which had shown itself among the Covenanters also, the leaders of the two sections being Montrose

and Argyle. Moreover, the four hundred miles which separated
Edinburgh from London would almost isolate the King from
Parliament's influence. The Commons therefore repeatedly
besought the King not to make the journey; but he remained
firm, and on August 10 he left London for the North. Parliament did its best to counteract the King's tactics by appointing
six commissioners—two peers and four commoners—who also
were to visit Scotland. Their function was to watch Charles'
moves and report to the English Parliament.

On September 9 Parliament adjourned for six weeks. But
each House appointed a committee to meet during the recess,
and to keep in touch with the commissioners in Scotland.

In order to achieve his purpose in Scotland, Charles exerted
all his charm and all his adroitness. To win the goodwill of
the Scottish public he assented to every Bill which the Edinburgh Parliament presented to him, including one for the
establishment of Presbyterianism. To gain the support of
individual leaders he conferred numerous titles and favours,
including the Earldom of Leven on Alexander Leslie. Not all
these moves could deceive the Scots, who went so far as to
disband their Army so that Charles could not gain control of
it for his own purposes.

Charles then set out on his journey back to London which
he entered on November 25. By that time the second session
of the Long Parliament had been meeting for five weeks, and
the political situation in England had changed in several
significant respects.

2. Second Session, October 1641 (till January 1642)

The Long Parliament reassembled for its second session on
October 20, 1641, and immediately settled down to work. The
next day a Bill was introduced in the Commons to exclude
the bishops from the House of Lords. If this measure became
law the Court party would lose the reliable votes of the
twenty-six bishops in the Upper House. This was one reason
for the Commons' haste in passing the Exclusion Bill through
all its stages. Within two days it had passed its third reading
and was sent to the Lords. The latter, still resenting the

Commons' interference with the composition of the Upper House, and containing a larger proportion of Court supporters than did the Commons, delayed the Bill's passage as long as possible. Not until February 5, 1642—that is, later than the general events considered in this chapter—had the Bill completed all its stages in the Lords. On February 13 the Exclusion Bill received the royal assent. We have now to return to the events of the intervening weeks.

On November 1, 1641, news reached London of a rising and massacre in Ireland on an alarming scale. Strafford's absence from Ireland, and finally his execution in May 1641, had removed the brake from Irish lawlessness. His successor as Lord Lieutenant was the Earl of Leicester who, unlike Strafford, contented himself with remaining in England. Events soon showed that Strafford's work had suppressed rather than cured Irish discontent: the Roman Catholics still nursed their twin-grievances of victimization by a Protestant Government and of plantations; and the Ulster Protestants bitterly resented the introduction of the Laudian Church regime. Strafford, as we have seen, had used the divisions between Roman Catholics and Protestants to serve his own governmental ends. The withdrawal of his strong arm encouraged the malcontents to shake off English rule.

Plans for a rising had begun to take shape as early as February 1641. Not until October did events begin to move when a force actually entered Dublin preparatory to seizing the castle. News of the plan reached the Lords Justices who in the nick of time imprisoned the insurrectionary leaders and so frustrated the scheme in Dublin. Elsewhere, particularly in Ulster, the Roman Catholic Irish rose against the English and Scottish settlers, massacring many, torturing some, and turning others adrift in the open, hostile countryside without food or protection from the weather, and almost without clothes. The exact numbers of those who suffered will never be known. Five thousand is a generally accepted modern estimate of those who were killed, apart from those who died from exposure and other maltreatments. Contemporary estimates gave figures forty or fifty times as numerous as this.

These latter were the figures that filtered through to London.

The news was exactly suited to the Parliamentary leaders' purposes. Fears not unnaturally spread of similar atrocities by Roman Catholics in England, and, as the King was commonly believed to be in league with the Irish rebels, these fears strengthened the hands of the Parliamentary opposition. Also, to suppress the rebellion would involve the raising of a considerable army. Such an army in the King's hands would be a weapon with which he could destroy Parliament and all that Parliament had been contending for; yet the constitutional principle was beyond dispute that all armed forces were under the King's command.

As a way out of the dilemma Parliament voted for an army of eight thousand men and for borrowing £50,000; but coupled with this vote were Instructions to the Commons' Committee in Scotland (where Charles was still lingering). The instructions traced "the conspiracies and commotions" in Ireland to the "cunning, false, and malicious practices" of some of the King's counsellors; and they further declared that if the King continued to employ Ministers whom Parliament could not trust

> . . . we shall be forced . . . to commend these aids and contributions which this great necessity shall require, to the custody and disposing of such persons of honour and fidelity as we have cause to confide in.[1]

Whether Pym and the others realized all the implications of these instructions is impossible to say. The clause quoted was a clear enunciation of the political principle which has become one of the bases of Parliamentary government—namely, the responsibility of Ministers to Parliament and not to the King. It is noteworthy that after a fierce debate the instructions were passed in the Commons by only 151 votes to 110. These figures show not only 110 open opponents but also a large number of abstainers whose final allegiance might decide the issue as between Parliament and the King.

Evidently there was a real possibility of a swing of Members over from the popular to the royal party. Almost certainly Pym's next move was made with this fact in mind. This was to

[1] *Lords' Journals*, IV, 431, ii.

push on with a Grand Remonstrance such as had often been suggested, its purpose being to rouse the enthusiasm of the people in support of Parliament. Colour is lent to this conclusion by the further fact that the vote on the instructions was taken on November 8, and on that very day the Remonstrance was read in the Commons.

The Remonstrance is an unwieldy document of 204 clauses.[1] Internal evidence—such as repetition of subjects dealt with and variations in vocabulary—suggest that it was prepared not as a whole but by being allotted in groups of topics to separate committees of Members. The main theme of the Remonstrance was a recital of the King's illegal acts and of Parliament's proposed remedies. Its clauses group themselves, according to subject-matter, into three sections. A recital of grievances covers more than half the clauses. The next sixty clauses contain a list of the laws already passed to safeguard the people's liberty. The twenty-four concluding clauses explain Parliament's proposals in religion and politics. Among these was a renewed demand for responsibility of Ministers to Parliament.

The final debate on the Remonstrance took place in the Commons on November 22. The discussion soon revealed that both sides had mustered all their strength for what they both recognized as a decisive stage in the struggle. Beginning at noon, the debate was still in progress when darkness fell and candles had to be brought. Then it raged on again so that the final vote could not be taken until midnight. Right up to that moment the issue was in doubt, and as the votes were being counted excitement was at fever pitch. Nor was it less when the result became known: out of 307 votes cast, the Remonstrance had secured a majority of only eleven.

Even then the antagonists were not content to allow the issue to stand. A Member moved that the Remonstrance should be printed. The purpose of this motion was that copies should be distributed throughout the nation so that details of the measure might be known before it was presented to the King. Its purpose, in short, was to use the force of public opinion to

[1] Gardiner, pp. 202–232.

compel the King to sign the Remonstrance. Such a procedure was revolutionary and confirmed the belief that an appeal to the people was the original object of the Remonstrance. Finally the motion for printing was waived, but it had raised excitement to a pitch even higher than evoked by the Remonstrance itself. Swords were drawn, and the House was on the verge of a major disaster from which it was saved only by the cool courage of Hampden who persuaded the Members to disperse quietly.

According to Clarendon, as the Members were going out of the House, Oliver Cromwell "whispered in the ear of" Lord Falkland

> . . . that if the Remonstrance had been rejected he would have sold all he had the next morning, and never have seen England more; and he knew there were many other honest men of the same resolution.[1]

If Clarendon's account be accepted as fact—and there seems no reason for doubting it—it shows how sensitive Members were to the critical nature of the Remonstrance-struggle. Moreover, that struggle served to define once more the cleavage between the two sections of the former opposition party. The opponents of the Grand Remonstrance included the Hyde and Falkland section. Henceforward these latter ceased to be reckoned as among the opposition, and instead became consistent supporters of the King. The large minority in the final vote showed a considerable swing of opinion over to the royal side.

That such a swing of opinion in the King's favour was not limited to Members of Parliament but was taking place also in the nation at large was shown by the reception which had been accorded to the King when he entered London from Scotland on November 25. The Lord Mayor, the Corporation, and the City Companies turned out to give him formal welcome, while large numbers of Londoners went wild with enthusiasm. If at that point Charles had adopted a straightforward policy, nicely timed to suit passing events, he might well have won over a sufficiently large body of supporters to

[1] Book IV, Section 52.

give him a permanent majority in the nation and in Parliament. But such a policy was exactly what Charles was incapable of pursuing. Within a fortnight, by a series of foolish moves, he had thrown away every advantage already gained, and had forfeited his last chance of supremacy in the State.

Charles' first false move was taken in connexion with a protest by Archbishop Williams of York and other bishops after increasingly hostile demonstrations by the crowd as they entered the Lords' House during the closing days of December 1641. So threatening was the mob that all but two of the bishops absented themselves from the House, and Williams handed to the King a protest to the effect that all votes and resolutions taken during their enforced absence were null and void. Charles, evidently hoping to widen the rift between Lords and Commons, instructed the Lord Keeper to lay the protest before the Lords. Charles had miscalculated the direction in which the Lords would move. Instead of supporting the bishops, the Lords asked for a conference with the Commons. Pym was quick to grasp the tactical advantage thus presented to him. To concede the bishops' demand would be to bring stable government to an end: to allow an Act to be annulled for such a reason would have encouraged claims for similar annulments for all manner of reasons in the future. The King himself might claim that an Act was no longer valid since he had been compelled unwillingly to sign it. The Lords therefore agreed with the Commons in supporting Pym's motion that the twelve bishops who had signed the protest should be charged with high treason "for endeavouring to subvert the fundamental laws of the Kingdom, and the very Being of Parliament." In accordance with this motion, ten of the bishops—including Archbishop Williams—were sent to the Tower, and the other two, being of advanced age, were lodged with the Usher of the Black Rod. Thus both Archbishops were in the Tower at the same time on charges of treason.

On January 1, 1642, Charles sent for Pym to offer him the post of Chancellor of the Exchequer. Startling though such an offer appears, this was not the first occasion on which it had been made. More than once before there had been strong rumours that several of the chief Ministerial posts were to be distributed among the popular party leaders; but the idea never fructified. We may assume that the King attached to the offers certain conditions which the Parliamentary leaders refused to accept. Such a proposal had been made during Strafford's trial, Charles' intention being to award offices to Strafford's accusers on condition that Strafford's life was spared. But, as Clarendon shrewdly commented, "there were few of the persons mentioned before who thought their preferments would do them much good if the earl were suffered to live."[1] Similarly, we can only guess at the reasons for Charles' offer to Pym on January 1, 1642, and at Pym's reasons for rejecting it, but immediately following events leave little doubt what must have been in the minds of both of them. Next day Sir John Culpepper became Chancellor of the Exchequer, and Lord Falkland was appointed Secretary of State in succession to Sir Henry Vane, the elder, whom Charles had dismissed two days after his return to London from Scotland. On the day following these appointments Charles committed what may well be considered the crowning blunder of his life.

On January 3 the Attorney-General laid before the House of Lords

> Articles of high treason and misdemeanour against the Lord Kimbolton, Mr Denzil Holles, Sir Arthur Haslerig, Mr John Pym, Mr John Hampden, and Mr William Strode.

The King then impeached the Five Members of the Commons and one Member of the Lords and demanded their arrest. No matter where the Lords' sympathy might lie, their proper course in the circumstances was not easy to determine: in regular procedure the Commons, not the King, were the accusers in cases of impeachment. The Lords therefore named a Committee to examine the position. The Sergeant-at-Arms then entered the Commons' House to arrest the five accused Members. The Commons, resenting what they considered a breach of their privileges, returned answer that they would

---

[1] Book IV, Section 76.

consider the King's demand, but they also ordered the Five Members to continue to sit in their places in the House.

During the night of January 3–4 Charles was subject to his wife's persuasions. Henrietta had a strong interest in the proceedings. A belief was current that the Parliamentary leaders had intended to impeach the Queen, and that the King's real reason for arresting the Five Members had been to protect her. Never able to throw off the influence of the French absolutist regime in which she had been brought up, and never appreciating the principles of English political procedure, Henrietta repeatedly urged Charles to courses that made for his undoing. In her view, anyone withstanding the King was a traitor. So she urged Charles to assert his royal power, and, once and for all, to root out his opponents. "Go, you coward," she is reputed to have called to Charles, "and pull those rogues out by the ears, or never see my face more."

So at about 3 o'clock in the afternoon of January 4, 1642, Charles set off from Whitehall for the House of Commons. He was accompanied by his nephew, Charles Lewis (now the Elector Palatine), and some three hundred or four hundred armed men. But news of his intention sped more quickly than he did. The information was sent by Lady Carlisle who, though one of the Queen's ladies, was also warmly sympathetic towards Pym and his friends. No sooner had Henrietta excitedly confided the King's plan to Lady Carlisle than the latter found means to pass it on to the Commons. Hence, while the King was approaching the Commons the Five Members were escaping into hiding in the City.

When Charles reached the House his armed followers remained at the door while he and his nephew strode to the Speaker's chair. The Members present stood in silence while Charles vainly scanned their ranks to catch the eyes of the accused. Then, turning to Speaker Lenthall, he asked whether any of them was present. Whereupon Lenthall replied:

> May it please your Majesty, I have neither eyes to see, nor tongue to speak in this place, but as the House is pleased to direct me, whose servant I am here; and I humbly beg your Majesty's pardon that I cannot give any other answer than this to what your Majesty is pleased to demand of me.

To which Charles answered: "Well, I see the birds are flown." Then, baffled, the King turned to leave the House. As he did so the silence was for the first time broken: cries of "Privilege! Privilege!" rose from all sides. It was an ominous end to a mad adventure.

What would have happened had the Five Members remained for the King's coming can only be imagined. Terrible bloodshed could hardly have been avoided. The King might have achieved his immediate object of arresting his chief enemies, but his method of doing so must ultimately have brought disaster to his cause. To fail dramatically to achieve his object was scarcely less disastrous. He had risked everything on one bold stroke and had missed his aim.

The Commons appointed a Committee to meet at Guildhall, trusting the City's protection. On January 10 the City's trained bands were put under the command of Captain Skippon who became responsible for guarding both Houses. That same day the King and Queen moved from Whitehall to Hampton Court. Few could have guessed that Charles would never visit Whitehall again until he was brought back in preparation for his death. On January 11 the Commons returned to their own House. As they travelled by the river, with the Five Members among them, they were greeted by wildly cheering crowds on the banks and in decorated boats.

From that time onward the conviction spread among both parties that war was the only remaining solution for the nation's political differences. Accordingly, both parties began to manœuvre for opening advantages.

3. Events Leading to Civil War, January–August 1642

The first precautionary moves by both King and Parliament were for the control of strategic strongholds of which the one of most immediate importance was Hull. Hull had a double value. First, the King had sent thither the arms and ammunition that remained after the disbanding of the northern Army. Second, Hull was a convenient seaport communicating with Denmark and Holland whence the King hoped to draw armies: Christian IV of Denmark, being the brother of James I's Queen

Anne of Denmark, was Charles' uncle; and Charles' daughter, Mary, had been married, in May 1641, to Prince William of Orange. No sooner, therefore, had Charles reached Hampton Court than he appointed the Earl of Newcastle as Governor of Hull. Unfortunately for Charles, news of the plan leaked out to Parliament, which forthwith despatched orders to Sir John Hotham, M.P. for Beverley, that he should secure the town by using the Yorkshire trained bands. Parliament's messenger (Hotham's son) outstripped the King's, and so Hull passed into, and remained under, Parliament's control.

During January various communications passed between King and Parliament, but on the major issue nothing conclusive was settled. Nor did the King's attitude make any conclusion possible. He was following his usual tactics of playing for time. His immediate aim was to arrange for the Queen to leave England—so as to be out of danger, and to negotiate for foreign help—after which he would move northward to the more strongly royalist part of the country. With this in mind, Charles had stayed at Hampton Court only two days and then had moved to Windsor. On February 23 the Queen and her daughter set sail from Dover for Holland, taking with her the Crown Jewels.

From that time the King's attitude to Parliament hardened. Whereas previously he had made concessions on almost every point that Parliament had raised, now he adopted an air almost of defiance.

At about this time Hyde had a long audience with the King, and a secret arrangement was made whereby Hyde was to stay at Westminster to watch proceedings for the King. He was to keep the King regularly informed of the trend of affairs, and, whenever communications were sent from Parliament to the King, Hyde was to send detailed advice about the reply that the King should return. Hyde was a lawyer with useful Parliamentary experience. Though never showing political genius, he remained for twenty years the devoted and foremost adviser of Charles I and of his son, returning from exile with the latter in 1660, and being appointed Lord Chancellor with the title of Earl of Clarendon.

On March 3 Charles began his journey to the North, and on

March 19 entered York, which remained his headquarters until the outbreak of war five months later. London had virtually ceased to be the capital of England: and England was left without a Government. Doubtless Charles, foreseeing the situation, had reckoned that Parliament would thereby be compelled to moderate its attitude. If so, this was another of Charles' miscalculations, for the result was the reverse of what he might have expected. Pym and his followers felt themselves compelled not to capitulate but to improvise an alternative Government, and so were driven gradually to extreme courses which they had neither designed nor desired.

During March and April the pace of events quickened appreciably. On March 5—that is, almost immediately after Charles had left for the north—Parliament issued a militia ordinance nominating new Lords-Lieutenant of the counties with "power to assemble and call together all and singular His Majesty's Subjects . . . that are meet and fit for the Wars; and them to train, exercise, and put in Readiness."[1] This the King countered by a proclamation "forbidding all His Majesty's subjects . . . to rise, march, muster, or exercise . . . without consent or warrant from his Majesty." Nevertheless Parliament's preparations went on.

Parliament's next request was that the King would allow the magazine at Hull to be moved to London. When the King sent his inevitable refusal Parliament, on April 18, sent orders to Hotham for the removal of the magazine. The King decided to challenge this defiance of his command of arms. On April 23, Charles appeared before Hull demanding entrance to the town. Hotham's reply was to raise the drawbridge and shut the gates. As Charles was not yet ready to resort to war, his only course was to order his heralds to proclaim Hotham a traitor and then to retreat. For a second time the King had been compelled to retire baffled. Parliament followed up these events by sending a fresh order for the removal of the Hull magazine to the Tower. In due course the removal was carried out by ships commanded by the Earl of Warwick.

By this time few people with any knowledge of the situation

[1] *Lords' Journals*, IV, pp. 625–627.

could have seriously doubted the imminence of war. During the following weeks there was a steady flow of gentry to swell the ranks of the King's supporters at York. Among them was Edward Hyde, who now left his post at Westminster in order to attend the King in person.

On June 2, the two Houses sent to the King a document known as the Nineteen Propositions, which they begged the King to grant

> . . . as the most effective means, through God's blessing, of removing these jealousies and differences which have unhappily fallen betwixt you and your people, and procuring both your Majesty and them a constant course of honour, peace and happiness.[1]

The propositions included the demands that Ministers of State should be approved by both Houses of Parliament; that the education and marriage of the King's children should be subject to Parliament's approval; that the laws against Roman Catholics should be enforced; "that the votes of Popish lords should be taken away"; "that your Majesty will be pleased to consent to such a reformation to be made of the Church government and liturgy, as both Houses of Parliament shall advise"; and that all the Judges ". . . may hold their places *quam diu bene se gesserint* [while they behave themselves well]."

The immediate significance of the propositions was that they summarized and clarified the principles for which Parliament was contending. In a word, they were a demand for the responsibility of Ministers to Parliament. As such they were revolutionary demands for the seventeenth century, though equally Parliament might have contended that it had been compelled to make them not through revolutionary intentions or desires but through the lack of constructive co-operation by the King. Though Charles had a stronger case than Parliament if judged by constitutional tradition, we have seen that time after time his inability to understand a situation or to deal tactfully with men had led him into disastrous blunders. It is not difficult at many points in the story to see wiser courses that Charles

[1] Gardiner, pp. 249–254.

might have taken; and it was his false moves which undermined Parliament's confidence in him, and seemed to leave Parliament no practical alternative, unless it was to become a cipher, to adopting the counter-measures which step by step it took.

During June and July both King and Parliament hurriedly gathered all the resources on which they could lay their hands and placed themselves in postures of defence. On June 11 the King issued commissions of array ordering the trained bands to obey officers whom he should appoint. A week later the Earl of Newcastle seized Newcastle in the King's interest. But on July 2 the fleet rejected Charles' commander, Sir John Pennington, and accepted the Parliamentarian Earl of Warwick as its Admiral. This was a severe blow to the royalist cause. On July 4 the two Houses appointed a Committee of Safety with fifteen members—five peers and ten commoners—

> . . . to take into Consideration whatsoever may concern the Safety of the Kingdom, the Defence of the Parliament, and the Prevention of the Peace of the Kingdom, and of opposing any Force whatsoever which may be raised against them.[1]

On July 11 the two Houses issued a joint declaration recounting the King's warlike actions and declaring that:

> The War being thus by His Majesty begun, the Lords and Commons in Parliament hold themselves in Conscience to raise Forces, for the Preservation of the Peace of the Kingdom, and Protection of the Subjects in their Persons and Estates.[2]

On the following day the Houses appointed the Earl of Essex as the General of the Parliamentary forces. So matters drifted on until, on the afternoon of Monday, August 22, King Charles raised his standard at Nottingham Castle.

---

[1] *Lords' Journals*, V, p. 178.
[2] *Lords' Journals*, V, pp. 200–202.

Chapter 7

The First Civil War

1. Its Character

Before we plunge into the main story of the Civil War, this is a convenient point at which to pause to take stock of the general situation—of the composition and distribution of the contending parties, of their respective leaders, and of their resources and relative chances of success.

Of all the wars in English history this was the one that came nearest to having the evils which are inseparable from war redeemed by being fought not for selfish ends but through devotion to genuine, and even ennobling, principles. Not uncommonly, members of the same family were on opposite sides in a battle. Lifelong friends felt themselves compelled, sadly and reluctantly, to agree to go opposite ways, each respecting the views of the other. For this reason the Civil War was, on the whole, humanely conducted. As the struggle lengthened and became more and more desperate, the temperature rose, and regrettable deeds of violence were doubtless committed; but this was exceptional rather than the rule. The defeated side in a battle normally received quarter. A certain amount of plundering took place, and districts often had to support troops billeted on them. In these respects the proper test of conduct to apply is the standard current elsewhere in seventeenth-century Europe. When compared with the conduct of the contemporary Thirty Years' War which was being waged by methods of wanton barbarism, and which so devastated Germany as to leave it a desert, the English Civil War was a tournament contested by gentlemen.

Of the convictions which determined on which side individuals fought, the fundamental one was religion. The paths of those who held extreme views were plain: the out-and-out Laudian was a Royalist; the thorough-going Puritan was a

Parliamentarian. As usual in all controversies, the way of those whose views were moderate was less easy. Large numbers of people—perhaps the bulk of the nation—were devoted to the English Church as it had been under Elizabeth, but were neither Laudians nor Puritans. The course adopted by such people depended upon the particular shade of their views and upon their personal associates: Hyde and Falkland went into one camp, and Pym went into the other. The one section that was undivided on the religious question was that of the Roman Catholics: the intense hatred evinced by all types of Puritans against popery showed the Roman Catholics that their only hope of tolerable treatment lay with the King.

A factor which won to the King valuable support was that of loyal service to the Throne traditional especially in the landed families. Not a few of the gentry disliked Laudianism, and so were sympathetic to Parliament on the religious issue, yet could not bring themselves to break from the loyalty in which they and their fathers had been reared. Typical of such men was Sir Edmund Verney, who wrote to Hyde:

> I do not like the quarrel, and do heartily wish that the King would yield and consent to what they [the Parliament] desire, so that my conscience is only concerned in honour and gratitude to follow my master. I have eaten his bread and served him near thirty years, and will not do so base a thing as to forsake him; and choose rather to lose my life (which I am sure to do) to preserve and defend those things which are against my conscience to preserve and defend: for I will deal freely with you, I have no reverence for the bishops, for whom this quarrel subsists.[1]

Sir Edmund's words should be read alongside the fact that his eldest son, Sir Ralph, remained among the Puritan Parliamentarians while a younger son, Edmund, joined his father as a Royalist.

Such a family-division illustrates the fact that the dividing-line between the antagonists was primarily neither social nor geographical. A man's decision was, in the last resort, determined by his individual convictions. Further illustration of this

---

[1] See Gardiner, Civil War, I, pp. 4–6.

is to be found in the attitude of the Members of the two Houses of Parliament. Precise figures of their partisanship are not possible, partly because some Members did not show very definite adherence to one side or the other, and partly because some changed sides during the war. But we are on reasonably safe ground in reckoning that while the majority of the Lords were Royalists and the majority of the Commons were Parliamentarians, the Royalist minority in the Commons numbered as many as 175 (that is, about two-fifths of the whole), and thirty peers were more or less active Parliamentarians as against eighty Royalists and twenty neutrals. Incidentally, these figures are a warning that the term Parliamentarian must not be interpreted as referring to all Parliament-men but is only a conventional word to signify those who championed what they considered the rights and privileges of Parliament as against the King.

Although the cleavage had no hard-and-fast social basis, the broad fact remains that the aristocracy tended to favour the King while the middle classes (the trading and professional classes of the towns and the yeomen of the countryside) favoured Parliament. Even so, the main dividing motive was the religious one. Whereas the majority of the aristocracy were Anglicans, it was in the towns and among the independent-minded yeomen that Puritanism had always most of its adherents. The second was the antagonism engendered by Charles' attempts to extort money, attempts which fell most severely upon the wealthy merchants and traders. The poorer sections of the community tended to throw in their lot with the other sections to which individually they happened to be attached. Thus, while the aristocrats' gamekeepers and serving-men joined their masters in supporting the King, the traders' assistants became Parliamentarians.

In this connexion, however, we must guard against imagining that the Civil War brought the whole nation under arms. The numbers engaged even in the largest battles were small not merely by modern standards but relative to the man-power of the nation. At the Battle of Marston Moor the Parliamentarians mustered the largest force ever brought together during the whole war. Even so, including a numerous Scottish contingent, they totalled only twenty-five thousand, while the Royalists numbered about eighteen thousand. Even of those who did take part in an important battle like Marston Moor, many would return home as soon as the battle was over. Though the most prominent men in the country were active partisans on one side or the other, only a small proportion was engaged at any one time, and a much smaller fraction was under arms throughout the whole period of the war.

The vagueness of the demarcation-line between the two sides seems to apply no matter what aspect of it is considered. Geographically the same characteristic holds good. The estates of the great landowners lay mostly in the North and West; hence those areas were predominantly Royalist. Conversely, Parliament found its supporters in the South and East where most of the towns were situated and most of the industries were carried on. But even this generalization has to be modified in details. In the heart of the Parliamentary midlands was a Royalist patch including the cathedral city of Lichfield and the castles of Tamworth and Ashby de la Zouch; and in the North and West Hull, Plymouth, and Gloucester were Parliamentary strongholds.

One of the decisive factors in the war—perhaps *the* decisive factor—was that London remained staunchly Parliamentarian. For this there were two main reasons. First, since the early days of the Reformation in England, under Henry VIII and Edward VI, London had been thoroughly Protestant partly because of the influence of the numerous foreign Protestant refugees who gathered there. Second, London, more than any other part of England, had felt the effect of Charles' financial extortions. London was more than merely the largest city in the country: it was almost the only place that modern standards would consider to be a city at all—that is, it was the only place where agriculture scarcely entered at all into the lives of its inhabitants. Something like seven-eighths of all England's trade went through London, which had become one of the chief financial centres of the world. This trade went on almost uninterrupted during the war and so provided Parliament with a constant source of revenue. This was possible largely because of the almost unanimous defection of the Navy to Parliament.

Thus Parliament was able to control trade and collect customs-duties, to prevent the Royalists from obtaining the reinforce-ments they had hoped for from abroad, and also to use coastal shipping as a means of communication for their own armies. In brief, Parliament's control of the sea was a major contribution towards the final Parliamentary victory.

Nevertheless at the outset of the war the chances of victory seemed strongly on the side of the King, for the Royalist Army had distinct advantages over Parliament's. Seventeenth-century infantry consisted of pikemen and musketeers who fought in co-operation; but the infantry laboured under the disadvantage that to load and fire a musket once needed several minutes' preparation. Hence the most effective arm was the cavalry, the operation of which had recently been greatly developed, notably by Gustavus Adolphus in the Thirty Years' War, in Germany. It was in this respect that the Royalists were superior to their enemy. The gentry who joined the Royalist ranks could provide themselves and their servants with horses. Moreover, the gentry were accustomed to horsemanship, and the sort of campaigning which they were to undertake was already a second nature to them. Many of the Parliamentary townsmen, on the other hand, had no horses of their own, nor would they have been much use as horse-soldiers if mounts had been provided for them.

Another initial Royalist advantage was that the gentry possessed quantities of silver plate which was not only valuable in itself but was then the only type of easily realizable wealth. The King was therefore able to obtain arms and general supplies at a much faster rate than was Parliament. The corre-sponding disadvantage of this source of wealth was that it was strictly limited in amount and, when once used up, could never be repeated.

Parliament's resources, being derived from trade, were more slowly but continuously productive. Hence, if the King was to turn his advantages of cavalry and wealth into victory, he would need to win rapidly before his resources were exhausted and before his enemies' resources were fully developed. This was exactly what he failed to do, and this failure was one of the explanations of his final defeat.

2. Early Campaigns, 1642–44

When on August 22, 1642, the King raised his standard at Nottingham, the numbers of those who had voluntarily joined him scarcely exceeded one thousand—perhaps three hundred foot and eight hundred horse. In addition to these his only forces were the northern trained bands; but their military skill, and even their loyalty, were too uncertain for them to be of much value in warfare. The Parliamentarian Army, several times as large as the King's, lay at Northampton, and a vigorous onslaught on the Royalists might have finished the war at a stroke. But the Earl of Essex, the Parliamentary General, had not yet left London, and the opportunity was missed.

So apprehensive were the Royalists of the result of a battle that they prevailed upon Charles to open negotiations with Parliament. On August 27 the royal emissaries, Southampton and Culpepper, represented to the Lords and Commons respectively the King's desire for peace. Parliament was not likely to give much attention to the plea at a moment when the Parliamentary forces were clearly superior and before a blow had been struck. The two Houses, after conferring together, returned answer that they were unable to treat until the King had withdrawn his charges of treason against the Members of both Houses and had taken down his standard. On September 5 Charles renewed his overtures. This time his emissaries were Lord Spencer and Lord Falkland, two moderate and widely respected men. The basis of the King's offer was that both sides should withdraw their charges of treason, and that then the King would lower his standard. This offer also the Parliament rejected.

It is doubtful whether Charles expected these overtures to succeed. Writing of the first of them, Clarendon stated:

> That which prevailed with his majesty very reasonably . . . was that it was most probable . . . that, out of their contempt of the king's weakness and want of power, the Parliament would refuse to treat; which would be so unpopular a thing that, as his majesty would highly oblige his people by making the offer, so they would lose the hearts of them by rejecting it; which alone would raise an army for his majesty.[1]

[1] Book VI, Sections 10–15.

No one was in a better position at that moment than Clarendon to know what Charles' motives were. At first it looked as though his move would bring the success he hoped for. The rejection of his repeated and apparently moderate offers of peace injured Parliament's case in the eyes of many hitherto hesitant men, and there was a large influx of recruits to the royal Army which soon numbered ten thousand men. The Earl of Lindsey was appointed Commander-in-Chief of the Royalist Army, with Prince Rupert (younger son of Frederick V of the Palatinate and nephew to Charles) as General of the Horse, and Sir Jacob Astley as General of the Foot. It was typical of Charles' veneration of royal blood and of his lack of consistency that he gave to Rupert the right to take orders from the King only. The results were that Lindsey had no direct control over the most important section of his Army, and that from the outset the King's forces suffered the fatal weakness of divided command.

The Earl of Essex left London on September 9, and the next day he joined his army of some twenty thousand at Northampton. Charles, having only about half that number, planned a recruiting march towards Wales before allowing himself to face the enemy. He therefore made for Shrewsbury. The success of the march seemed assured, for the gentry of the western shires flocked to the royal standard. Indeed, its success was an embarrassment since the King's resources were unable to provide either the money or the equipment for his suddenly swollen Army.

On October 12 the King moved his Army out of Shrewsbury towards London, which he expected to be able to capture without serious difficulty. The Londoners themselves were apprehensive of a Royalist occupation, and took hasty measures of defence. During this time Essex was moving from Northampton to Worcester. Thence he marched eastward so as to intercept the King's advance towards the capital. The clash took place at Edgehill. In numbers the opposing forces were evenly matched, each having about fourteen thousand men: while the Royalist ranks had been substantially increased, the Parliamentarians had had to leave a garrison at Worcester, and

THE FIRST CIVIL WAR

the artillery under Hampden was a day's march behind the main body.

The Royalists established themselves on the crest of Edgehill. Essex, too weak to make a direct attack on this strong position, drew up his men near the foot of the hill and, thus cutting off the enemy's supplies, forced the Royalists to descend to attack him. Rupert, leading the main Royalist cavalry on the right wing, scattered the Parliamentary left, and then occupied himself with plundering the Parliamentary baggage. Essex, however, managed to control his infantry, and therewith to break the main Royalist Army. During the struggle the Earl of Lindsey was mortally wounded, and Sir Edmund Verney, the King's standard-bearer, was killed, thus suffering the fulfilment of his own prophecy [p. 145]. Only at nightfall was the battle broken off. Next day Hampden brought up the Parliamentary artillery, but Essex decided not to renew the battle. Instead he withdrew towards London. The King turned southward through Banbury to Oxford. From Oxford the Royalists moved in the direction of London, but Essex had received such large reinforcements in London that he was able at Turnham Green to draw up an Army twice the size of the King's. The King therefore had to retire to Oxford which henceforward remained his headquarters.

Perhaps the King could fairly claim to have won the action at Edgehill since his enemies had been unable to prevent his march southward. But in two respects the more far-reaching results were disastrous to his cause: he had failed to enter London, and he had failed to win the war during the first year's campaign.

For 1643 the King planned an excellent, comprehensive campaign. Still aiming to control London, he projected a threefold advance upon the capital: the Earl of Newcastle was to bring the northern Army through the eastern counties; Sir Ralph Hopton was to bring the south-western Army through Devon and Cornwall along the right bank of the Thames into Kent; and the King was to lead the main Army from Oxford to London. The scheme was based on sound strategy, but it was wrecked in practice by the unwillingness of the royal armies, being still civilians rather than soldiers, to leave their homes unprotected by moving as far away as London. Their fears for their homes were increased because Hull, in the North, and Plymouth, in the South-west, were Parliamentary strongholds.

In the North Lord Fairfax and his son, Sir Thomas, after conducting vigorous operations in Parliament's interest during the early part of the year, were besieged at Hull by Newcastle. Parliament's control of Hull had been jeopardized by overtures which, in April 1643, the Hothams, father and son, had made to the King for the betrayal of the town into Royalist hands. The plot was discovered in time, and at the end of June the Hothams were placed under arrest and sent to London where, in January 1645, both were executed. In June 1643, therefore, the citizens of Hull sent to Lord Fairfax an invitation to become their Governor, and early in July both he and his son were within the town. There, early in September, Newcastle's troops besieged them. Hull, being open to the sea which the Parliamentarians commanded, would not easily be taken by a land force alone; and on October 12 Newcastle raised the siege.

In the South-west a similar story had to be told. During May and June Hopton conducted a highly successful campaign which gave him control of Devon and Cornwall. But when in August he tried to move farther eastward the Cornishmen, fearing to leave their homes unprotected against the Parliamentary garrison that might issue from Plymouth, insisted upon returning home.

The King's part in the threefold campaign was to attack Gloucester, which was the chief Parliamentary stronghold between the West and London. Control of Gloucester might well have opened the way for Royalist control of London. On August 10 Charles summoned the Gloucester citizens to submit to his authority, and when they refused he began a regular siege. Pym and the other Parliamentary leaders were fully aware of the threat to the capital implied in the siege of Gloucester, and they made strenuous efforts to counteract it. Appeals to the Londoners to defend their City met with an enthusiastic response. The shops remained closed, the trained bands were mobilized, and recruits poured in. By the end of August Essex was able to set out westward at the head of fifteen thousand men. Charles, unable to face such an Army, on September 5, raised the siege of Gloucester.

Both armies then moved in the direction of London. When the Parliamentarians reached Newbury they found the Royalists barring their way. Essex, thus cut off from his headquarters and supply-base, was obliged to cut his way through. So the first battle of Newbury took place on September 20. Though Rupert led his cavalry into action, the nature of the country prevented his effective manœuvring. The Parliamentarians, however, pressed on steadily. Nightfall found the issue still undecided; but next morning the King withdrew to Oxford, largely because his ammunition was exhausted, and Essex was able to return to the City.

Thus the Royalists had failed to bring the second campaign also to a victorious issue. This, as we have seen, would prove fatal to their winning the war. In two other respects the 1643 operations marked an important stage in the course of the war.

First, they tested the Parliamentary military organization. During 1642 Parliament had relied upon groups of its supporters in each county to raise troops. This method had proved unsatisfactory in various ways. Some counties were so predominantly Royalist that the Parliamentary cause could do nothing. Also the troops raised on a county basis tended to think of themselves as concerned only with the defence of their respective counties which they were loth to leave. Accordingly in December 1642 Parliament had begun to form groups of neighbouring counties, and in each group to organize a military association, though in practice the only districts where the scheme could be effective were those in which adjoining counties were mainly Parliamentarian. The first was the Midland Association covering eight midland counties; the second was the Eastern Association which included Norfolk, Suffolk, Cambridgeshire, and Hertfordshire (Huntingdonshire being added in May 1643, and Lincolnshire in September 1643); and a third Association, formed a little later, was Warwickshire and Staffordshire. Though the King's 1643 campaigns were finally frustrated, they had had the effect of breaking up the Parliamentary Associations' armies other than that of the Eastern Association. The latter's strength was due largely to Oliver

Cromwell's work, to which further reference will be made later.

Second, the campaign's indecisive result caused both sides to look round for outside help. The Royalists turned to Ireland, and the Parliamentarians to Scotland.

In Ireland, during the interval since the outbreak of rebellion in October 1641, disaffection had spread from Ulster throughout Ireland. More sinister still was the fact that the Anglo-Irish Roman Catholics in the Pale had made common cause with the native Irish. In May 1642 the Roman Catholic leaders, meeting in Kilkenny, formulated an oath of association under which the Irish were to devote themselves to the re-establishment of Roman Catholicism. A Supreme Council was formed, and military leaders were appointed for the various provinces. The forces at their disposal were so numerous that they were able to hold their own against the King's armies. In October 1642 a General Assembly of Roman Catholics met at Kilkenny. While affirming both its defence of Roman Catholicism and its allegiance to the King, the Assembly ordered the restoration of Church lands to the Catholic clergy and the confiscation of lands belonging to Protestants and neutrals. In January 1643 Charles authorized the Marquis of Ormonde, his Irish representative, to open negotiations with the rebels. The negotiations were prolonged, but finally on September 15 the two parties agreed to the Cessation whereby hostilities were to cease for twelve months and the Irish were to grant £30,000 towards the royal exchequer. Charles' immediate gain was that his Army hitherto occupied in Ireland would be released for service against the English Parliamentarians. But his loss by the cessation more than counterbalanced the advantage: for his agreement with the Irish rebels fostered the idea that he was partial to Roman Catholicism, and so facilitated an agreement between Parliament and the Scots.

It was in the mutual interest of Parliament and the Scots that they should make common cause against their common opponent. But though they had a common opponent their reasons for opposing him were different: the Scots were aiming at establishing Presbyterianism; the English Puritans were nearly as averse to Presbyterianism as to Laudianism, since a growing proportion of Parliament's supporters favoured congregational independency. In short, though the Parliamentarians wanted the Scots' military alliance, they were unwilling to pay the price that the Scots would demand. Pym's clear understanding of the realities of the situation and of the need to beat the King decisively in the field caused him repeatedly to urge negotiations with the Scots. On July 19, 1643, Parliament duly appointed commissioners to go to Scotland for this purpose. Discussions, opened in Edinburgh on August 8, continued for several days. The debate centred round the terms which the Scots demanded in return for sending troops into England. Finally the two sets of commissioners found a compromise formula: the signatories pledged themselves to "a reform of religion in the Church of England, according to the Holy Word [of God] and the example of the best reformed Churches." Further, the Scots demanded £30,000 a month from the English Parliament with an advance payment of £100,000. Parliament hesitated long before accepting both the terms of the covenant and its financial corollary. Pym, however, was relentless that the price must be paid. On September 25, 1643, the Commons swore their acceptance of the Covenant at a service held at St Margaret's, Westminster. On January 19 the Earl of Leven began to lead his Army across the Tweed.

John Pym did not live to see that day. The Scottish treaty was the last contribution that he was to make to the Parliamentary cause. On December 8, 1643, the great Parliamentarian died. His passing left a gap which was never filled. Pym was more than merely a competent Member of Parliament or an effective speaker. He was the first man to realize the possibilities of government by Parliament instead of by the King with Parliament's consent. It was the realization of this governmental principle, and the adaptation of the parliamentary machine as a means of its operation, that constitute his claim to political genius. Pym's work necessarily implied a constitutional revolution, just as the work of genius implies a revolution in any sphere of life. But in Pym's case the revolution proceeded not from any preconceived idea but from circumstances in which he found himself, circumstances which had

been shaped largely by the first two Stuart Kings. Like most—
perhaps all—ardent reformers, Pym found himself driven into
courses more and more extreme; but fundamentally his aims
in both Church and State were those of a moderate and a lover
of liberty.

The nature of his loss to his party became apparent only as
time passed. Robert Baillie, who was watching events at Westminster in the interests of the Scottish leaders, wrote of the
English Parliament as he saw it eight months after Pym's
death:

> Since Pyme died, not a state head amongst them: many very
> good and able spirits, but not any of so great and comprehensive
> a braine as to manage the multitide of so weightie affaires as
> lyes on them.

The full effects of the absence of "a state head" among the
Parliamentarians after Pym's death were seen not only immediately but also in the years to come. As the Civil War proceeded, the Army became increasingly the dominant factor in
the State, and Parliament became increasingly subordinate.
This tendency, natural in any case, was encouraged by Parliament's failure to produce in succession to Pym another "so
great and comprehensive a braine as to manage the multitude
of so weightie affaires." In brief, Parliament produced no one
of the calibre to challenge Cromwell. To assert categorically
what would have happened if circumstances and people had
been different is manifestly impossible; but it is a fair guess
that, had Pym continued to live and to direct the Parliamentary war-machine, the settlement after the war would have
been made within the Parliamentary orbit, and England might
have been spared the division between Parliament and Army.
It is interesting, if not very profitable, to speculate what would
have happened if Pym and Cromwell had met later as rival
leaders. What is more likely is that if Pym's leadership had
continued Parliament would not have treated the Army as
foolishly as it did, and so a clash between them would never
have occurred.

The 1643 campaign brought the deaths of two other nota-
bilities: John Hampden succumbed to a wound received in a

skirmish at Chalgrove Field, in Oxfordshire; and Lord Falkland, divided in his loyalties, sought and found death in the first Battle of Newbury on September 20.

The Scots' appearance in England transformed the war. Henceforward the Royalists were on the defensive even in their own northern counties. By the middle of April Newcastle (now a Marquess) had led some eleven thousand troops to take refuge in York where Leven and the Fairfaxes joined forces to besiege him. Newcastle's fate, and with it the fate of the Royalist North, would be sealed unless he was speedily relieved. Rupert, who had gone to the Welsh border to recruit, turned North when he heard of Newcastle's plight. Early in June the forces of the Eastern Association, led by Manchester, their General, and Cromwell, their Lieutenant-General, arrived to reinforce York's besiegers. A month later they raised the siege to intercept Rupert as he approached. Rupert, however, avoiding an immediate encounter, slipped past the Parliamentarian armies and joined Newcastle. Then he immediately prepared to give battle to the enemy drawn up at Marston Moor, seven or eight miles west of York. There, on July 2, the two armies faced each other. Newcastle and Rupert decided that, as evening was coming on, no decisive action could take place. But as the Royalists were off their guard preparing their supper, the Parliamentarians launched the attack. Briefly expressed, the result of the battle was the rout of the Royalist forces: 3000 of them were casualties and 1500 were prisoners. Cromwell's work of disciplining the Eastern Association cavalry had vindicated itself in a big-scale battle and would be an object-lesson to the Parliamentary Army as a whole. For the King, the result of Marston Moor was that at a stroke he lost control of the loyal North. It was a stroke from which his cause never recovered.

In contrast to this success in the North, the Parliamentarians during 1644 suffered a series of reverses in the South. This was the result largely of their lack of unified command and hence of unified strategy: no sooner was Marston Moor won than the Parliamentary forces divided off into their three component parts—Leven to capture the town of Newcastle; Manchester to his command in the eastern counties; while Fairfax remained in Yorkshire to reduce some towns which were holding out for the King. Meanwhile Essex had been campaigning in the South-west. Thither a few days after Marston Moor the King set out to find him. The King's approach encouraged a fresh rising of the Cornishmen in his support. Essex thus found himself in hostile country and in danger of being hemmed in by growing Royalist forces. This threat became a reality when the latter, led by Charles, occupied high ground at Lostwithiel overlooking Fowey harbour. So desperate was the Parliamentarians' position that their cavalry, led by Sir William Balfour, was sent to cut its way through the royal lines. This it succeeded in doing, and so made towards Plymouth. But the infantry was surrounded. Essex himself took boat to Plymouth leaving his men to their fate. The King allowed them to move off on condition that they left their arms. Charles' reason for dealing thus leniently with his defeated enemy is difficult to understand. The effect was to throw away the most decisive Royalist victory of the war.

3. The Crisis of 1645

The Parliamentarians, for their part, failed to take full advantage of their undeserved escape. Their efforts were still paralysed by divided command. Essex was unswervingly loyal to the Parliamentary cause but was slow and deliberate. Manchester had little military skill, and, what was worse in a commander, had no desire to inflict decisive defeat upon the King: his object in the war was to defeat the King just enough to compel him to bargain with Parliament. Such half-hearted prosecution of a war could at best end in stalemate, and might end in a Parliamentary defeat. The most vigorous opponent of Manchester's policy was his own Lieutenant-General, Oliver Cromwell, whose plain common sense was enough to convince him that there could be no midway position between complete defeat and complete victory. More serious still as a cause of breach between them was the fact that, whereas Manchester was a Presbyterian, Cromwell was an Independent. Moreover, Cromwell, acting on his own declaration that "I desire none in my army but such as are of Independent judgement," had expelled from his command all troops who did not share both his religious and political views. By the close of 1644 these differences were coming to a head.

After the Battle of Lostwithiel Charles returned eastward to the Thames valley. By Parliament's orders Sir William Waller and the Earl of Manchester combined forces to check the King's further advance, and presently they were joined by Essex whose Army had been reorganized. Between them they commanded nineteen thousand men, while the King's forces were little more than half that number. A vigorous Parliamentary offensive would have routed the Royalists and ended the war. But the Parliamentary authorities, unable to decide which general should be given supreme command, delegated authority to a numerous commission. The inevitable result was indecisive strategy. Finally, on October 27, the Parliamentarians intercepted the King at Newbury while he was on his way to Donnington Castle. Though the Parliamentarians had many advantages, these were mostly thrown away by Manchester's dilatoriness: he refused to move against the enemy—presumably because the King was present—until the evening, by which time the Parliamentary plans had been frustrated, and there was no opportunity to gather the fruits of victory. The battle itself was indecisive, but the Royalists were able to revictual Donnington.

The ultimate results of the second Battle of Newbury were enormously greater than the immediate military result. To Cromwell and those who shared his views, it was the final straw. Convinced of the impossibility of victory while men like Manchester were in high office, Cromwell began to move for a reorganization of the Army-command.

Since the story of the second half of the Civil War, and of Commonwealth-England after it, centres round Oliver Cromwell, it is well at this point to get clear the major facts of his previous career. He was born at Huntingdon on April 25, 1599. His father was a small country-gentleman, comfortably off, yet without the rank or wealth of a noble; he served as a Justice of the Peace, and was a member of a number of commissions for draining the Fens. Oliver's mother was a woman of strong character and a staunch Puritan. There can be no doubt that it was from her that Oliver absorbed the religious convictions which were to become the basis of all his beliefs and actions.

Oliver's schooling was received at Huntingdon Grammar School, where the master, Dr Thomas Beard, also was a Puritan. In April 1616, when almost exactly seventeen years of age, Oliver entered Sidney Sussex College, Cambridge. Here the religious influence of home and school was continued, for Sidney Sussex was the centre of Cambridge Puritanism. In June of the following year his father died, and Oliver, then only eighteen years of age, returned from Cambridge to bear the double responsibility of managing the estate and of caring for his mother and sisters. The tie between mother and son was particularly intimate. The two were almost inseparable. When he became Protector he lodged his mother at Whitehall, and when at the age of ninety she died he buried her in the Abbey.

In August 1620 Oliver married Elizabeth, daughter of Sir James Bourchier, a London merchant. Five sons and four daughters were born to them, and of all these but one son grew to maturity. Robert, the eldest son, died when seventeen years old. The second son, Oliver, was a captain in the Civil War, and died of small-pox during the war. Richard, the third son, succeeded his father as Protector. Henry, the remaining son, also fought in the war, and afterwards became Lord Lieutenant of Ireland.

During the early years of his married life Oliver passed through an experience of deep religious upheaval and distress. Only very slowly and painfully did he emerge with a quiet and settled spirit. From that time he lived under the conviction of God's presence and of God's availability for all his needs. This attitude was perfectly expressed in a letter which he wrote after the Battle of Naseby:

> When I saw the enemy drawn up in gallant order towards us, and we a company of poor ignorant men, to seek how to order our battle—the General having commanded me to order all the horse—I could not, riding about my business, but smile out to God in praises, in assurance of victory, because God would, by things that are not, bring to naught things that are. Of which I had great assurance, and God did it.

He was convinced that divine guidance was unfailingly shown in all life's circumstances, and he lived under the continual urge to put into practice this guidance as he interpreted it. In brief, Cromwell was a mystic. There is no true understanding of his career that does not begin with this fact. Whatever our own individual views about the rightness or wrongness of Cromwell's religious convictions and of his political actions, we must base all our thinking about him on a recognition of his utter sincerity. From beginning to end he was acting not for personal advancement but under an impelling sense of a divine mission.

In 1628 Huntingdon sent him as one of its representatives to Parliament. So far as the Parliamentary records show, he only once intervened in debate. With the Parliament's dissolution in February 1629, Cromwell, like his fellow-Members, entered the eleven-year period of Charles I's personal rule. In 1631, having clashed with royal authority over the terms and operation of a new charter to Huntingdon, he removed to St Ives. Thence, in 1636, he moved to Ely, where he had just inherited property from his mother's brother, Sir Thomas Steward, and where he and his family remained until London called them ten years later. Soon after moving to Ely he led the cause of the small landowners and others of the Fens who claimed that the drainage of the Fens, by a company headed by the Earl of Bedford, had caused the loss of common-land rights. The result of the local protests was royal intervention in the commoners' favour. The reputation which Cromwell won throughout the Fenland as a champion of liberty was to yield its full fruit in the years to come.

In the Short Parliament of 1640, and again in the Long Parliament, Cromwell sat as one of the Members for the town of Cambridge. The twelve years that had elapsed since he had first entered Parliament had evidently seen a development of his powers and character. Though never a great Parliamentarian in the sense of being a debating orator, Cromwell several times intervened in the Long Parliament's proceedings. It was he, along with the younger Vane, who in May 1641 introduced the Bill for the abolition of Episcopacy. On November 6, 1641, he secured the passage of a motion that the Earl of Essex should command all the trained bands south of the Trent "until Parliament should take further order." During the same month he actively supported the Grand Remonstrance.

In July 1642, by which time the country was on the verge of civil war, Cromwell arranged for arms to be sent to Cambridge. In August he laid hold of the magazine at the castle there as well as of £20,000-worth of university plate that was to be sent to the King. Cromwell's leadership in the Civil War had begun.

His first military commission was as captain of the 67th troop of horse. Early in 1643 he was promoted to the rank of colonel. It was his energy mainly which was responsible for gathering and shaping the forces of the Eastern Association. The secret of his success was that from the outset he refused to enlist men haphazardly, but adopted instead a firm principle of selection. He would accept only men of decided religious persuasion and practice. He was convinced that soldiers of the type that he desired could be developed from such men. In the early weeks of the war he had expressed this view to his cousin John Hampden:

> Your troops are most of them old decayed serving-men and tapsters, and such kind of fellows, and their troops are gentlemen's sons and persons of quality.   Do you think that the spirits of such base and mean fellows will ever be able to encounter gentlemen that have honour, and courage, and resolution in them? . . . You must get men of a spirit . . . that is likely to go on as far as gentlemen will go, or else you will be beaten still.[1]

Further, in September 1643 he wrote as follows:

> If you choose godly honest men to be captains of horse, honest men will follow them; and they will be careful to mount such. . . . I had rather have a plain russet-coated captain that knows what he fights for, and loves what he knows, than that which you call 'a gentleman' and is nothing else.[2]

It was because he had men of this type that he was able to train them to perfect discipline both in general conduct and

---

[1] Gardiner, Civil War, I, pp. 40–41.   [2] Carlyle, I, p. 154.

in battle. Cromwell's were the only men on either side whom a modern army would consider regular troops.

It was at Gainsborough, in July 1643, that Cromwell's principles and methods first notably justified themselves. The town had recently been seized by Parliamentary forces, and the Royalists under Cavendish were moving to retake it. Cromwell was at Stamford. To bring his troops into action he led them by forced marches the fifty-five miles to Gainsborough. He then immediately gave battle and drove the Royalists from the field. Hardly had he done so when Newcastle appeared leading his whole Royalist Army from the North. To face this Army in open battle meant annihilation. Without hesitating, Cromwell divided his troops into two sections, allowing each alternately to retreat and then to hold the ground while its fellow retreated. By this means Cromwell's entire force—except two men!—was withdrawn in orderly fashion. It was the achievement of a tactician of the highest order. On August 9—that is, within a fortnight of Gainsborough—the Commons decided to raise the Eastern Association infantry to ten thousand men, naming the Earl of Manchester as its Major-General. Cromwell, one of the four colonels of the horse, was virtually second in command.

We have now to resume the main thread of the general Civil War narrative. We have seen that at Marston Moor, in July 1644, Cromwell's work vindicated itself in a big-scale battle but that the value of that victory was jeopardized by the subsequent separating of the Parliamentary forces into their component sections and by their generals' refusal to inflict decisive defeat upon the King. The results of these two blunders were seen respectively in Essex' defeat at Lostwithiel, in September, and in Manchester's failure to press home his opportunity at Newbury, in October. It was the latter event which brought to a head Cromwell's impatience with Manchester's dilatory and inconclusive methods.

In order to carry out his attack on his military superior, Cromwell resorted to the House of Commons. It was during this period of his career that for the first and last time Cromwell showed powers of great Parliamentary leadership, marshalling his facts, and compelling the Commons' attention by the urgency of his theme and by his personal force. On November 25, 1644, he delivered in the Commons a trenchant attack on Manchester whom he accused of being always "indisposed and backward to engagements, and the ending of the war by the sword; and for such a peace as a victory would be a disadvantage to." This charge Cromwell supported by detailed references, particularly to events between Marston Moor and the second Battle of Newbury. In order to examine the charge, the Commons appointed a committee which on December 9 duly reported its findings to the Commons.

It was Zouch Tate, the chairman of the Committee, who made a practical suggestion to solve the problem. He proposed a Self-Denying Ordinance whereby no Member of either House should be eligible for military service. Since the commanders of whom complaint was being made were Members of one House or the other, this would dispose of their services without making personal and individual mention of them. The idea was adopted, and by December 19 the ordinance had passed the Commons. But the Lords rejected it, and a second ordinance became necessary. Negotiations between Commons and Lords delayed its passage so that it was not completed until April 1645. In its final form it read:

> . . . that all and every of the members of either House of Parliament shall be . . . discharged at the end of forty days after the passing of this Ordinance, of and from every office or command military or civil, granted or conferred by both or either of the said Houses of the present Parliament.[1]

This form of the ordinance, while insisting that Members should resign their military commands, left the way open for their re-appointment should the Houses so desire.

In the meantime Parliament had passed another measure of the highest consequence in the war. On February 15, 1645, the New Model Ordinance was passed for the re-organization of the Parliamentary Army. The new Army was to consist of 14,400 foot (twelve regiments each of 1200 men), 6600 horse (eleven regiments each of 600), and 1000 dragoons, making 22,000 altogether. Of this Army Sir Thomas Fairfax was named

[1] Gardiner, p. 287.

Commander-in-Chief, with Skippon as Major-General in charge of the foot. The rank of Lieutenant-General, which would carry command of the horse, was left vacant. On April 22 Cromwell laid down his command in accordance with the Self-Denying Ordinance.

It is difficult to resist the conclusion that Parliament intended that Cromwell should continue his command. On the other hand, it must be remembered that the original ordinance would have made his reinstatement impossible. What would have been the result on the Civil War, and on the history of England, had the Lords not rejected the first ordinance, is a nice subject for speculation.

The formation of the New Model Army provided Parliament with a regular army of men no longer tied to particular localities. But this was not the only, or perhaps the most important, result. A second result was that the spirit of the Eastern Association—particularly its cavalry—permeated the whole of the new Army of which the Eastern Association had been the nucleus. In a word, the new Army was predominantly Independent in religious belief. The effect of this latter fact was to be revealed increasingly in later events. There was yet a third important result of the New Model. Since the Self-Denying Ordinance required that a Member of either House should lay down his commission, Parliament and Army tended to be sharply separated from each other. As time passed, the separation developed into mutual suspicion and then into opposition. The following chapters will show that this was largely responsible for the course of events leading to and during the Commonwealth.

During the spring of 1645 the Parliamentary armies continued to march about, chiefly in the West and the Midlands, without any central objective. But as soon as the New Model became fairly organized its commanders, having achieved some independence from Parliament's control, determined to end the war in the only way in which it could be ended—namely, by defeating the King's Army in the field.

At the end of May the Royalists had looted Leicester, carrying off as plunder every movable article of any value. Towards Leicester, therefore, Fairfax led the Parliamentary Army. He made contact with the King at Naseby, in Northamptonshire. The critical nature of the impending engagement was so apparent that Fairfax and his council petitioned Parliament for Cromwell's immediate appointment to the vacant position of Lieutenant-General. On June 10 the appointment was made. On the 13th Cromwell was hailed in the Parliamentary camp with shouts of "Ironsides is come." "Ironsides" had been Rupert's nickname for Cromwell at Marston Moor, being afterwards applied to Cromwell's troops also.

At 3 o'clock on the morning of June 14 Fairfax moved towards Naseby. His foot was drawn up in the centre: his horse, under Cromwell's command, was deployed on the wings, with Cromwell on the right and Ireton on the left. On the Royalist side, Rupert led the right, and thus he and Cromwell did not meet. The Parliamentarians, with fourteen thousand troops, outnumbered their opponents by nearly two to one.

Events in the battle were, in principle, not unlike those of Marston Moor. Rupert's charge repulsed Ireton and Rupert reached the Parliamentary baggage, but his success achieved little. In the meantime, Cromwell, having scattered the Royalist left, was attacking the left flank of the Royalist infantry-centre. Thus the King's main Army was endangered. Even so, the Parliamentarians refused to take undue risks: and when Rupert was seen returning, Fairfax and Cromwell drew up a new order of battle, including foot, horse, and guns. Against such an army Rupert would throw himself in vain. The whole remaining Royalist forces broke and scattered over the countryside. Charles took refuge in Ashby de la Zouch, nearly thirty miles away. The Parliamentarians took five thousand prisoners (including five hundred officers), the Royalists' artillery and baggage, and the King's private papers. The Royalist Army as a fighting force no longer existed.

4. The End, 1645-46

Henceforward the Royalist resistance would have to be limited to their garrisons in various scattered strong-points. The war thus entered the final stage of sieges. Two stand out as of particular importance.

The first was Bristol. Before investing the town, Fairfax summoned Rupert—who commanded the Royalist forces in the city—to surrender. Rupert was in a difficult position: he had too few men to defend the city against the Parliamentarians, yet he had no authority to yield. He tried to gain time by asking leave to communicate with the King. This request was naturally refused, and on September 10 Fairfax began to storm the place. Next day Rupert surrendered, and was allowed to leave for Oxford. When the news reached Charles he was so grievously disappointed that he dismissed Rupert from his command to which he was never restored.

The other great siege was that of Basing House, in Hampshire. It was the property of the Roman Catholic Marquess of Winchester, and was an immensely strong fortress which hitherto had defied all attempts at capture. In October 1645 Cromwell brought up heavy siege-guns against it. His offer of honourable terms of surrender having been refused, he began to pound wide breaches in the walls until, on October 14, storming-parties could be sent through them. That the defenders were Catholics added to the attackers' fury, and there was terrible slaughter. Next, the contents of the fortress were completely plundered or destroyed. Fire completed what the men had begun. In the end the whole structure was reduced to a ruin.

All over England Royalist strongholds continued to be reduced until Charles had to face the fact that further military resistance was impossible. In order to avoid the indignity of capture, he decided to give himself up, and to do so not to the Parliamentary Army but to the Scots from whom he might secure better terms. He therefore surrendered to the Scottish Army at Southwell on May 5, 1646. If he expected to be received as a kind of honourable guest he was quickly undeceived. Leven promptly marched North, and within a week was at Newcastle. On June 24 Oxford, the King's headquarters since immediately after Edgehill, surrendered to Parliament. The First Civil War was at an end.

Chapter 8

The Execution of Charles I

1646–53

1. Charles I and the Scots, June 1646–January 1647

The First Civil War was at an end. That much was certain.
But this served only to reveal the further political problem of
what settlement was to be made for the future government of
England. This problem was complicated by the fact that three
parties—Parliament, Army, and Scots—had shared in defeating the King. Each of them would expect a share in determining the resulting settlement, yet each had its own particular
views and principles. The most serious and prolonged dispute
would be between Parliament and the Army, though the clash
between them was postponed because for the moment the
centre of interest lay in the negotiations between Charles and
the Scots. Until the issue of these negotiations was known, no
constitutional scheme was worth framing. Moreover, the possibility that the Scots might agree to acknowledge the royal
authority of Charles, on terms that would be approved either
by Parliament or by the Army, tended to restrain the mutual
antipathies of the latter two bodies.

These three-cornered jealousies provided Charles with
negotiating conditions such as his soul loved. But in his negotiations, which aimed at playing off each of the three against
the others, there was one element that Charles seems never to
have understood—namely, the depth and strength of his opponents' religious convictions. On one point—his devotion to the
Established Church of England—Charles himself would never
compromise. A strange mental blindness seems to have prevented his understanding that other men's convictions, though
different from his own, might be equally strong and genuine.
It was this blindness which wrecked all his negotiations and

6*

finally led him to the block. Charles' strongest card was the apparent impossibility of any settlement apart from himself, since none but a numerically negligible body of men seriously considered either any form of government other than a monarchy or any substitute for Charles on the throne. It was on this card that Charles relied in his dealings with the Scots at Newcastle.

Charles' hope in surrendering himself had been that the Scots would use their Army to restore him to the throne. This fantastic notion ignored three all-important factors: first, that before the Scots would give any help to Charles they would demand his acceptance of the Covenant; second, that they would never lend their Army to restore Episcopacy in England; and third, that the Scottish Army would not face Cromwell and the New Model unless assured of substantial Royalist help in England, and of such help there was at the moment not the slightest prospect.

Charles did not remain long in ignorance of the Scots' intentions. Early in June he was informed that unless he fulfilled their conditions he would be handed over to the English Parliament. Charles, hoping to secure better terms by forestalling the Scots, himself sent to Parliament asking for proposals. To the task of hammering out terms for a settlement, Parliament at once gave its attention, and in the middle of May two Lords and four Commoners carried to Newcastle what came to be known as the Newcastle Propositions. The six commissioners were not empowered to bargain with Charles: they were to demand that within ten days he should accept or reject the propositions as they stood. The nineteen clauses of the proposition included the following demands:

> 2. That His Majesty . . . may be pleased to swear and sign the late Solemn League and Covenant.
> 3. That a Bill be passed for the utter abolishing and taking away of all Archbishops, Bishops . . . and all other officers, out of the Church of England and dominion of Wales, and out of the Church of Ireland.
> 5. That reformation of religion, according to the Covenant, be settled by Act of Parliament, in such manner as both Houses

have agreed, or shall agree upon, after consultation had with the Assembly of Divines.

13. That the Lords and Commons in the Parliament of England assembled shall during the space of twenty years, after the 1st of July 1646, arm, train and discipline . . . all the forces of the kingdoms of England and Ireland and the dominion of Wales.[1]

The propositions also included a long list of names or descriptions of leading Royalists who were to be exempt from Parliamentary pardon.

In spite of Parliament's demands for a categorical acceptance or rejection of the propositions, Charles managed to prolong negotiations by a series of evasive answers. In the meantime the Scots had been growing convinced that Charles would never accept the Covenant. Hence, having no other object in the struggle, they decided to 'cut their losses.' They made with the English Parliament an agreement whereby they would hand over the King on condition that Parliament in return handed over the back pay to which the Scots were entitled for the support of the Scottish Army in England. The sum agreed upon was £400,000 of which the Scots were to receive one half before leaving England and the other half later. By February 3 Parliament had paid the stipulated £200,000; whereupon the Scots transferred the King to the Parliamentary commissioners and then withdrew across the Border. The commissioners carried the King to Holmby House, in Northamptonshire.

The removal of the Scots from the arena cleared the ground for the inevitable clash between the remaining rivals for supremacy in the State—namely, Parliament and the Army. Charles' original opponent had been Parliament which, when necessity arose, had created the Army as Parliament's fighting instrument. But as the war had proceeded, the Army had become an entity with characteristics and convictions of its own which had grown increasingly different from those of Parliament. The root of these differences was religion. In order to get the nature of them clear, we must at this point interrupt the main thread of the events of 1647.

[1] Gardiner, pp. 290–306.

Earlier chapters have shown that during the years previous to the Civil War Parliament had been progressively antagonistic towards the Established Church, mainly because of the intimate association between that Church and the principle of Divine Right upon which the Stuarts' government had been based. This antagonism had expressed itself in the Root and Branch Bill for the abolition of bishops, and in the Exclusion Bill which received Charles' assent in February 1642, and which removed the bishops from the House of Lords. During the war and afterwards Parliament's antipathy to bishops expressed itself in a number of measures whose effect was virtually to abolish the Church as it had hitherto existed.

In June 1643 the Lords accepted an ordinance putting into effect a proposal mooted by the Commons as early as April 1642 for the formation of an assembly of divines to deal with ecclesiastical reforms and with matters deputed to it by Parliament. This body, known as the Westminster Assembly, numbered altogether 150 members of whom thirty were not divines but were Members of Parliament. In January 1645 Parliament resolved to establish a Presbyterian system of Church government; and by a series of ordinances the necessary reorganization was carried into effect.

The same month saw also the completion of proceedings against Archbishop Laud, who had been imprisoned since December 1640. Whether extreme proceedings would ever have been taken against him by the English Parliamentary leaders acting on their own initiative is doubtful. But Laud had enemies more bitter even than the extreme English Puritans. The Scots had never forgiven him for the part he had played in trying to enforce his Prayer Book and Episcopacy upon them: the influence which the Scots were able to exert in England after the English acceptance of the Solemn League and Covenant on September 25, 1643, gave them their chance. On October 19 the Commons resolved to proceed with Laud's impeachment. The trial did not open until March 1644 when the Archbishop was charged with trying to change the religion established by law, and to subvert the fundamental law of the kingdom. From the outset the proceedings were little better than a farce. The result was settled before the trial began.

Nevertheless the Lords, constituted as a court of law, found as much difficulty as in Strafford's case, on the available evidence, in giving the desired verdict. Consequently in November the Commons sent to the Lords an Ordinance of Attainder which the Lords finally passed on January 4, 1645. On January 10, Laud was executed.

It is impossible not to feel sorrow that the aged Archbishop, by that time powerless to harm anyone, should have been brought to so violent an end. Of his single-minded sincerity of purpose there can be no doubt. His declaration on the scaffold was a just description of his faith:

> I was born and baptized in the bosom of the Church of England, and in that profession I have ever since lived, and in that I come now to die.[1]

Nevertheless the rage of his opponents is not difficult to understand. It was his work which had intensified the religious antagonism of James' and Charles' reigns. It was the episcopal policy, personified in him, which fortified the Stuart principle of Divine Right. It was he who had persecuted the Puritans: the memory of the tortures inflicted on Lilburne, Prynne, Bastwick, Burton, and many others would not soon be dimmed. Finally, it was his interference in Scotland which had precipitated the Civil War. However warm our sympathy for Laud, we must also realize that his opponents were other than bloodthirsty bigots.

2. Parliament and the Army, January–December 1647

On the same day (January 4), as the Lords passed the ordinance of Laud's attainder, they also agreed to the final form of an ordinance whereby the Directory, prepared by the Assembly of Divines, was to be substituted for the Book of Common Prayer. This was not merely the enforcement of the very principle of religious uniformity for which Laud was being condemned; it was based on the assumption that such a uniformity of religious views existed among Puritans. Very

[1] Gardiner, Civil War, II, p. 107.

little time would be needed to show how hollow the assumption was.

The Army, on the other hand, was overwhelmingly Independent. The basis of Independency was the belief that each congregation of Christians constituted a Church with the right to order its services and corporate life in accordance with its own convictions. Such views inevitably encouraged the spread of a great variety of religious ideas and practices, and hence of a large number of sectaries all included under the general term of Independents. The Anabaptists, as their name implies, believed in re-baptism—that is, in the baptism of adults. The Antinomians ("against the law") held the view that Christians are freed from the necessity of keeping the law of God or, according to some of them, even the moral law: these ideas were the result of misinterpreting the New Testament teaching that Christians are no longer "under the Law" but live under the Grace of God, so that the more men do evil, the more opportunity God's grace has to work in forgiving them. The Seekers did not advocate any particular creed or ritual but emphasized the endless seeking after divine truth. Such were some of the chief Independent sects of which the Army was full and to which both generals and common soldiers belonged. Cromwell himself seems to have had some sympathy for the Seekers. He once wrote:

> To be a Seeker is to be of the next best sect after a Finder, and such an one shall every faithful humble Seeker be in the end.

At this point we may note also another religious sect which arose at this period, though its members were not to be found in the Army since one of their chief tenets was non-resistance. Their leader was George Fox, greatest of all the seventeenth-century Puritan leaders. He exemplified the truth that religious genius can no more be accounted for than any other variety of genius. He was born in the Leicestershire village of Fenny Drayton, his father was a weaver, and he himself was apprenticed to a shoemaker. Failing to find satisfaction in currently orthodox religious creeds and practices, for several years he strove incessantly after peace of soul. Then in 1646 (when he was about twenty-two years of age) he found rest in the essentially Protestant doctrine—which had been the basis of the teaching of Wyclif, the prototype of Protestants three centuries earlier—that every individual could have direct contact with God without the mediation of a priest or the accompaniment of formal ritual. The guidance which every Christian could thus receive was called by Fox the "inner light," a belief and practice which ever since has characterized his followers. These first called themselves Friends in the Truth and later more briefly The Friends. Their enemies, however, nicknamed them The Quakers in derision of their calling upon people to "fear and quake at the name of the Lord."

These religious variations had their political counterparts. Of Independency in general it may be said that it fostered democracy. Men accustomed to the doctrines and practices of self-government in matters of religion saw no reason why they should not exercise self-government in what they considered to be the less important matter of politics. There were, for example, the Diggers, who, believing that the common people had a right to the land of England, proceeded to plough up common land and waste land irrespective of the rights of the lords of the manor. The Fifth Monarchy men were so called because of their belief that the last of the four great Kingdoms mentioned in the Book of Daniel (interpreted to refer to the Assyrian, Persian, Macedonian, and Roman Empires) was about to pass away, and would be followed by the personal reign of Christ, whose Second Coming was regarded as imminent. For this reason they repudiated human government and looked for the Rule of the Saints.

Perhaps the most important of the political sects were the Levellers led by John Lilburne. As their name implied, the Levellers believed in the natural equality of all men notwithstanding laws and customs to the contrary, and hence they wished to dissolve Parliament, and to allow the nation to express directly its desires for government. Men holding such views would be scarcely less opposed to a Cromwellian commonwealth than to a Stuart monarchy.

If these varieties of belief offered scope for the King's scheming they would also make any permanent settlement of England difficult. The immediate problem was that of the relationship between Parliament and Army. Parliament's chance of asserting control over its servant, the Army, was greatly increased by the latter's internal religious and political rivalries. Parliament, however, was blind to the plain meaning of the situation and inept at handling it. Parliament was, in fact, bankrupt in leadership: Pym and Hampden had had no successors.

Parliament's first move, in February 1647, was to try to get rid of the Army altogether. This it proposed to do in two ways. First, it planned an army to restore order in Ireland: for this purpose, 4200 horse and dragoons, and 8400 foot were to be recruited from the New Model. Second, 6600 horse and dragoons were to be kept as a standing force in England, but the only foot-soldiers remaining were to be those necessary for garrison-work. These proposals would involve disbanding some 6000 infantry, and would break up the Army as it had previously existed. Whatever virtue the scheme may have had, it was wrecked by the fact that the Army's pay was seriously in arrears: the foot had not been paid for eighteen weeks, and the horse for forty-three. Yet all that Parliament offered on re-enlistment or on disbanding was a cash payment of six weeks' pay. Hence when, in May 1647, Parliament's proposals were communicated to Fairfax's headquarters at Saffron Walden, in Essex, the officers declared their refusal to enlist for a further period until they had received satisfaction for past services. Nor were the officers alone in their opposition to Parliament. Fearful lest the Convention of Officers would be concerned only about its own interests, the common soldiers of each troop of horse and of each company of infantry chose representatives from whom regimental representatives were in turn chosen. These men, known as Agitators—that is, agents— were thus able to voice the opinions of the rank and file of all branches of the Army. More sinister, from Parliament's point of view, was that when, on May 15, the agitators had an interview with the officers, the latter agreed with the men's complaints.

These tendencies came to a head at a great Army assembly near Newmarket on June 5, when a Solemn Engagement of the Army was drawn up. By its terms the Army declared that it would not "willingly disband or divide, or suffer itself to be disbanded or divided" until grievances were righted. Further, it demanded the formation of a "General Council of the Army" to consist of "those general officers of the army (who have concurred with the Army in the premises) with two commission officers and two soldiers to be chosen from each regiment."

Though the Army's original motive in thus organizing a representative body for itself was self-defence only, the comprehensive "General Council of the Army" would become a rival authority to Parliament. In effect, the Army would become a political body.

It was recognition of this fact which induced Cromwell to intervene in events. Hitherto he had not actively taken sides in the dispute between Parliament and Army. But when it became clear that, whether with him or without him, the Army was determined to safeguard its interests by political action, he decided to try to control what he could not prevent. It was characteristic of Cromwell that, once his mind was made up, he was not content with half-measures. Control of the King's person was the crux of the situation. Hence, on May 31 he ordered a certain Cornet Joyce to make for Holmby House with a body of horse in order to prevent Parliament from removing the King thence, as rumour said Parliament intended to do. Late on June 2 Joyce and five hundred men reached Holmby. A story that Parliament intended to rescue the King caused Joyce to ask the King to accompany him to Oxford or to some other place. Charles did not offer any serious objection to the request—doubtless scenting another opportunity to produce dissension among his enemies—but preferred Newmarket to Oxford. At his house in Newmarket, therefore, Charles arrived on June 8—that is, only three days after the promulgation of the Solemn Engagement. Thus the political centre of gravity had shifted in the Army's favour.

The Army, conscious of its power, then moved by stages towards London. By June 15 it was at St Albans. There it issued the Declaration of the Army setting forth the basis of its political policy. This asserted that the Army was not "a mere mercenary army, hired to serve any arbitrary power of a State, but called forth and conjured by the several declarations of Parliament, to the defence of our own and our people's just liberties."[1]

The Army had now virtually superseded Parliament as the ruling power in the State, and the political future of the country depended upon whether the Army could arrive at a settlement with the King. Negotiations to this end were opened, and were mainly conducted through Sir John Berkeley, a Royalist enjoying the confidence of King and Parliament alike. Berkeley's *Memoirs* contain fair statements of the moves on both sides. He records the statement of Cromwell—who took the lead as the Army's representative—that:

> . . . whatever the world might judge of them, they would be found no seekers of themselves, farther than to have to live as subjects ought to do, and to preserve their consciences; and that they thought no men could enjoy their lives and estates quietly, without the king had his rights.

Had Charles reciprocated the spirit of that statement he might have recovered his throne and reigned with dignity though not with absolute power. But Cromwell's best efforts were frustrated by Charles' evident mistrust of the officers' sincerity.

During two months negotiations between Army and King dragged on. At the end of that time they had to be recognized as abortive. The country's only hope therefore was that Army and Parliament should ignore the King and reach some mutually agreed settlement. In the middle of July Commissary-General Ireton laid before the Council of the Army a scheme for constitutional settlement. This scheme, after revision, was submitted to Charles at the end of July and was published on August 1.[2] The Council called the scheme the Heads of the Proposals, thus showing that it was intended not as a detailed constitution but as the 'headings' of the main principles of a constitution that would commend itself to the Army. It proposed that there should be biennial Parliaments, that Parliamentary seats should be redistributed on a population-basis which would also involve the disfranchisement of decayed

[1] Rushworth, VI, p. 564.   [2] Gardiner, pp. 316–326.

boroughs, that for a ten-year period Parliament should appoint Ministers of State and should control the militia, and that all Acts enjoining the use of the Prayer Book should be repealed.

The proposals obviously were a document of first-class constitutional importance. They showed an understanding of the constitutional issues at stake beyond any understanding that Parliament could show. They even foresaw accurately the lines of future constitutional developments: nearly two centuries would elapse before the "elections of burgesses for poor decayed or inconsiderable towns" were removed. Herein, indeed, lay the proposals' first weakness: though theoretically sound, they were too far in advance of contemporary ideas to be generally acceptable. Even the limited measure of religious toleration which they envisaged was several generations ahead of public opinion. Moreover, by aiming at a permanent restriction of the powers of both King and Parliament, the proposals offended both alike. Nevertheless the King's rejection of them was characteristically shortsighted. Considered as the terms offered by victors to vanquished, the proposals were moderate beyond anything that the King could have reasonably expected. Certainly they were the best terms that were ever offered to him. His rejection of them encouraged the belief that he did not intend to accept any terms at all, and therefore that he must be relying upon secret intrigue. Cromwell and the others who had tried sincerely to find a wise solution to the constitutional problem were thus driven increasingly to the view that only extreme measures—measures which excluded both King and Parliament—could save the State from chaos.

Charles was in fact relying upon a growing movement among the Presbyterians to assert themselves against the Army. The focus of this movement was Parliament, but it had two other sources of strength—namely, the City of London and Scotland. There seemed indeed some prospect of a Scottish Army to challenge the Independent Army. On July 26 a mob invaded the two Houses and compelled the Members to vote a number of resolutions including one inviting the King to return to London. When news of these events reached Fairfax at Bedford he began to move the Army towards London. Manchester and Lenthall, the Speakers of the Lords and the

Commons respectively, then withdrew from the City along with eight Independent peers and fifty-seven commoners to place themselves under the Army's protection. Thereupon the remaining Members of the two Houses and the City took measures to defend themselves against Fairfax whom they ordered to remain at least thirty miles from London. Nevertheless he pressed steadily on, and on August 6 the Army entered the City. Manchester, Lenthall, and their fellow-fugitives were restored, Fairfax was made Constable of the Tower, and the King was lodged at Hampton Court.

Even after these events the Commons, predominantly Presbyterian, showed no willingness to work with the Army to produce some form of a settled government. The long delay caused a division within the Army: the less patient section, including Cromwell, favoured purging Parliament of its refractory element; while the more peaceable section, headed by Fairfax, was willing to continue negotiations. Early in October five particularly discontented regiments elected new agitators, and these drew up a manifesto entitled The Case of the Armie Truly Stated, which was presented to Fairfax. In addition to demanding the redress of the Army's grievances, such as its arrears of pay, the document also enunciated the general principle of government that "all power is originally and essentially in the whole body of the people" whose "free choice or consent by representatives is the only originall or foundation of all just government." It even demanded certain social reforms in the interests of the poorest sections of the people. The inspiration behind The Case of the Armie evidently came from John Lilburne and the Levellers.

From the same source came, at the end of October, the Agreement of the People which was a formal statement of the Levellers' constitutional ideas. It contained only four pithily expressed articles, of which the following sentences are the essence:

I. That the people of England, being at this day very unequally distributed by Counties, Cities, and Boroughs for the election of their deputies in Parliament, ought to be more indifferently proportioned according to the number of their inhabitants. . . .

II. That . . . this present Parliament be dissolved upon the last day of September 1648.

III. That the people do, of course, choose themselves a Parliament once in two years—namely, upon the first Thursday in every 2nd March.

IV. That the power of this and all future representatives of this Nation, is inferior only to those who choose them, and doth extend . . . to whatsoever is not expressly or implicitly reserved by the represented to themselves:

Which are as followeth.

1. That matters of religion and the ways of God's worship are not at all entrusted by us to any human power.
2. That the matter of impresting and constraining any of us to serve in the wars is against our freedom.
3. That after the dissolution of this present Parliament, no person be at any time questioned for anything said or done in reference to the late public differences.
4. That in all laws made or to be made every person may be bound alike.[1]

As a constitutional document, the agreement was notable in several respects. The demand for manhood suffrage—implied in article I—and the reservation of decisions in certain matters, as being outside the purview of the representative House, were a foretaste of modern written constitutions. Moreover, no mention was made of either a monarch or a second chamber. The long debates in the Army Council, following the reception of the scheme, showed that it was in these points that opinion was most sharply divided. Cromwell, presiding over the debates, exerted a moderating influence, though even his popularity and prestige failed to produce agreement.

Meanwhile the King and his supporters had noted the growing anti-monarchical tendencies of the Army, and the growing impatience even among its more moderate elements. Moreover, the Scottish commissioners to the King were promising him that if he would satisfy them in the matter of religion they would restore him to his throne without insisting on his taking the Covenant. These two facts together indicated the desirability of Charles' freeing himself from Army surveillance in

[1] Gardiner, pp. 333–335.

order to enjoy greater independence of action. On November 11, therefore, Charles slipped away from Hampton Court and made for Titchfield, near Southampton Water, his purpose being to find shelter at Carisbrooke Castle or, if that proved inadvisable, to cross to the Continent on a vessel already ordered. Unfortunately for Charles, his friends bungled the proceedings: Colonel Hammond, Governor of Carisbrooke, was brought to the King on the assumption that he was a sympathizer, but the assumption proved illusory. Hammond carried out what he believed his plain duty and made the King a prisoner.

The only effect of the flight had been to provide a further proof of Charles' duplicity and to drive even moderate men like Cromwell in the direction of seeking a form of government that would exclude Charles altogether. While the moderates were still hesitating, their doubts were dispelled by the Second Civil War into which Charles' plottings plunged the nation towards the middle of 1648.

3. The Second Civil War, 1648

When Charles fled to Carisbrooke he left behind him at Hampton Court a letter, addressed to Parliament, promising justice to all parties in the State. Also, on November 17, the Speaker of the Lords received from the King a letter[1] offering considerable concessions, based on the terms of the Heads of the Proposals, and asking for a personal hearing in London. After scrutinizing the letter for a week the Lords formulated Four Propositions which they regarded as fundamental, the first and most important being that Parliament should control the militia for twenty years and should thereafter determine the mode of its administration.[2] These propositions were sent to the Commons who passed them as Bills to be sent to the King for his assent. Thus the Four Bills were not to be a basis of discussion between King and Parliament but would have to be accepted or rejected by the King as they stood. On December 14 the Four Bills, having passed both Houses, were sent to Carisbrooke.

---

[1] Gardiner, pp. 328–332.   [2] Gardiner, pp. 335–347.

How Charles received the Bills would depend upon his general prospects. These at the moment appeared to be fairly bright, for Charles' negotiations with the Scottish Commissioners had been going well. Among the Scots there were two rival parties: first, the clerical party led by the Marquess of Argyle; second, the nobles' party led by the Duke of Hamilton and the Earl of Lauderdale. It was the second party whose commissioners, headed by Lauderdale, were in touch with Charles. The latter, believing that he would fare better at the hands of the Scottish nobility than with either the English Parliament or the English Army, entered secretly into an agreement with the commissioners. This document was known as the Engagement.[1] It provided for the establishment of Presbyterianism in England for three years, the suppression of Independency, the disbanding of the Army, the dissolution of Parliament, and a personally negotiated treaty for Charles. In support of these terms the Scottish commissioners were willing to send an army into England. Charles signed the Engagement on December 26, 1647. Ten days later he rejected Parliament's Four Bills.

The Engagement was hidden in the gardens at Carisbrooke. But the goings and comings of the Scottish commissioners could not be hidden; and Charles' rejection of the Four Bills was enough to confirm the fears of Parliament and Army alike. Among men of all parties, outside the ranks of the Royalists, the conviction spread that the precise terms to be made with Charles mattered little, since he was unlikely to keep any terms if he thought that he could obtain better ones elsewhere. On January 3, 1648, Parliament passed the Vote of No Addresses enjoining that no further addresses should be paid to the King. An indication of Parliament's growing mistrust of the Scots was its abolition of the Committee of Both Kingdoms and its substitution of the English members only of that Committee as the body responsible for watching State business.

Any doubt remaining as to Charles' duplicity was removed when, towards the end of February, letters were intercepted from the King to the Queen showing his dealings with the

[1] Gardiner, pp. 347–353.

Scots. Further evidence came early in 1648 by outbreaks of disaffection in various parts of the Kingdom—in South Wales, in Kent, and in the North, as well as in Scotland. These almost contemporary risings suggested concerted Royalist efforts.

The first sign of open disaffection occurred in February at Pembroke Castle, whose Governor, Colonel Poyer, refused to give way to a successor appointed by Fairfax. Towards the end of March Poyer declared for the King and seized the town of Pembroke. Colonel Horton, whom Fairfax sent to deal with Poyer, found not the local mutiny which he expected but a rebellion spreading throughout Wales. At the same time Hamilton was gathering forces with which to invade England.

These risings produced one result which the King's opponents had never achieved: they caused Parliament and the Army to sink their differences, and to concert measures of defence against their common enemies. Before the Army set out to suppress the risings, a great prayer-meeting was held at its headquarters at Windsor. A member of the meeting wrote afterwards that God enabled them:

> . . . after serious seeking his face, to come to a very clear and joint resolution, on many grounds at large then debated amongst us, that it was our duty, if ever the Lord brought us back again in peace, to call Charles Stuart, that man of blood, to an account for that blood he had shed, and mischief he had done to his utmost, against the Lord's cause and people in these poor nations.

It was in the spirit of this resolve that the Army took the field in the Second Civil War—a temper in marked contrast to that of its leaders in the First War.

Early in May Fairfax sent Cromwell from London with two regiments of horse and three of foot to suppress the rising in Wales. Before he could arrive Horton had defeated Poyer at St Fagans, near Llandaff. Cromwell's task therefore was to organize the reduction of Royalist strongholds. Before the end of May Chepstow and Tenby had surrendered. Pembroke Castle, the most formidable of them all, held out until July 11. Thus Cromwell was delayed in Wales six weeks after his services had become urgently needed elsewhere.

Meanwhile revolts had occurred in Kent. More serious still,

the fleet in the Downs had declared for Charles, and had seized the castles of Deal, Walmer, and Sandown. Fairfax took vigorous action. Leading eight thousand men into Kent, he met the rebel forces at Maidstone and broke them up. Then he crossed the Thames into Essex where new disorders had broken out. Fairfax drove the insurgents into Colchester, besieged them, and prepared to starve them out. It was on August 18 that the town surrendered, and thus Fairfax was prevented from helping to crush the revolts elsewhere in England. Consequently that task devolved upon Cromwell.

The Scots, led by the Duke of Hamilton, had crossed the Border into England on July 8—that is, three days before the fall of Pembroke. Cromwell then immediately moved northward. In the belief that the Scots would move towards London by the easier road through Yorkshire—Pontefract and Scarborough being already in Royalist hands—Cromwell marched through the midlands, providing shoes for his men at Nottingham on his way, and finally, on August 12, reached Knaresborough. There he made contact with Major-General Lambert who commanded the Parliamentary armies in the north. At Knaresborough Cromwell learned that he had mistaken the Scots' plans: Hamilton, having passed through Carlisle, was following the western route through Lancashire. Hence, Cromwell had to cross the hills from Yorkshire to Lancashire in order to forestall the Scots' further advance.

Numerically the Scots were formidable: altogether Hamilton commanded twenty-one thousand men. But the quality both of the men and of their leaders seriously reduced their fighting calibre. There were in Scotland large numbers of Leven's veterans who were of the finest fighting material; but these, being staunch adherents of the Kirk, belonged to Argyle's party and therefore would not follow Hamilton. Moreover, Hamilton was a third-rate commander. At the moment when Cromwell reached Knaresborough the Scots were straggling disjointedly forward: Hamilton, with the main body of his infantry, was at Preston, his left flank being protected by some 3500 English Royalists led by Sir Marmaduke Langdale; the horse, under the Earl of Callander, was fifteen miles ahead at Wigan; while a force of several thousands was thirty miles in the rear at

Kirkby Lonsdale, in Westmorland. Such a disposition of forces invited attack; and Cromwell, though commanding only 8600 men, seized the opportunity with characteristic decisiveness.

Early on August 17, a mile or two outside Preston, Cromwell hurled himself against Langdale. The latter resisted as best he could, meanwhile sending to Hamilton urgent appeals for help but receiving nothing adequate to his needs. After four hours of stiff fighting, Langdale's division was smashed; and before nightfall Cromwell gained control of Preston. The English had thus cut off Hamilton's communications with Scotland, and had driven a wedge between his main forces south of the Ribble and his remaining forces in the North. The Scots still greatly outnumbered Cromwell's army, but Hamilton had so completely lost control of the situation that he was unlikely to re-align his scattered forces in time to deal effectively with Cromwell.

During the night Hamilton marched towards Wigan so as to join the main body of his horse. At the same time the horse were marching to join him. But, as they followed different roads, they failed to meet! During August 18, therefore, the horse had to turn southward again to catch up with Hamilton, Cromwell meanwhile worrying their rear.

Still Hamilton, fearful of facing Cromwell, was marching southward. But on the 19th Cromwell's pursuit compelled the Scots to make some sort of stand, which they did just north of Warrington. Once again Cromwell was victorious. The Scots ceased to be an army and became scattered fugitives. Hamilton gave himself up nearly a week later. This marked the end of the Second Civil War.

Even so, Cromwell did not rest but immediately after the action near Warrington he turned northward to deal with the still existing Scottish rearguard. The latter promptly retreated over the Border. Cromwell pursued them and entered Edinburgh early in October, having negotiated the surrender of Berwick and Carlisle (which Hamilton's army had seized) on the way.

The obvious policy for Cromwell was to foster the rivalry between the two Scottish parties. Fortunately for him, during September a revolution against Hamilton broke out among the

West-country Presbyterians who—for some reason never satisfactorily explained—were known as Whiggamores. Hamilton was blamed both for fomenting the war and for conducting it incompetently; and he was distrusted by the Presbyterians because his purpose had been the restoration of the Episcopalian Charles I, whose support of Archbishop Laud had been the occasion of the First Civil War. Cromwell therefore negotiated with Hamilton's rival, Argyle, whose party in the Scottish Parliament ensured the acceptance of Cromwell's terms. These were that no one who had supported the Engagement or had taken an active part in the invasion of England should be admitted to a place of public trust in Scotland. The Scots accepted these conditions on October 6, and next day Cromwell set out for England leaving Lambert and two regiments of horse to support Argyle should the need arise.

Though the immediate purpose of Cromwell and Argyle was served by their alliance, the two men's convictions were widely separated: Cromwell had no enthusiasm for the Covenant, whose enforcement was the central object of Argyle's party; and, while the Scottish Presbyterians would have countenanced no form of religion other than their own, Cromwell was an advocate of genuine and wise religious toleration—a fact which his later career would abundantly prove. How long such an alliance would stand the strain of practical politics remained to be seen.

Cromwell's immediate problem lay in the effects which the Second Civil War had had upon the political situation in England. It was that problem which was uppermost in his mind when he crossed the Border and marched towards London.

4. The Army Victorious

The outstanding result of the Second Civil War was that the Army returned with its heart hardened against the King, and with the fixed determination to bring him to judgement. In part, this determination was due to the conviction that Charles alone was responsible for the suffering which the renewed war had entailed. Charles' duplicity, leading to the Scots' invasion, was conclusive proof that further negotiations with him were

futile. But more important still was the Army's conviction that
its victory in the Second Civil War had been a sign of God's
approval so clear that to ignore it was wilful disobedience
against the light. Cromwell summed up this view with characteristic terseness:

> That fault that appeared in this summer's business is certainly
> double to theirs who were in the first, because it is the repetition
> of the same offence against all the witnesses that God had borne.

Hence, the Army went back to the resolution formed during
its Windsor prayer-meeting:

> . . . that it was our duty, if ever the Lord brought us back again
> in peace, to call Charles Stuart to an account for that blood
> he hath shed.

Yet, settled though the Army might be in its own mind as
to its responsibility to bring Charles to account, the proper
means to this end was less easily determined. Unless the Army
could carry with it the approval of the bulk of the nation, its
course would be beset with entanglements. Of such approval
there was but little likelihood. Action that seemed to threaten
the King's person would arouse intense differences of opinion.
The Army's course during the second war had been smoothed
by the support received from Parliament. But now that the
immediate purpose of the Army-Parliament alliance had been
achieved, would not the alliance dissolve into its former rival
elements?

The fact was that the alliance began to break even before
this purpose had been achieved. As early as August 1, 1648,
the two Houses of Parliament had agreed that negotiations
with the King should be reopened; and on the 24th both
Houses repealed the Vote of No Addresses. On September 18
—that is, two days before Cromwell crossed the Border into
Scotland—fifteen Parliamentary commissioners met Charles at
Newport, in the Isle of Wight. The resulting negotiations were
known as the Treaty of Newport.

The terms which the commissioners first offered to Charles
were so extreme as to be impossible for him to accept. The
King's alternatives were that he would allow Presbyterianism
to be established for three years with toleration for non-

Presbyterians, and would grant the control of the militia to Parliament for ten years. Negotiations were continued for some time, even after October 27, when Parliament rejected Charles' proposed Church settlement. Either Charles was an exceptionally good actor or the commissioners were exceptionally blind, for Charles had no other purpose than to occupy as much time as possible in the hope that some circumstances would arise to deliver him from his enemies. On October 7 he had written to a friend:

> To deal freely with you, the great concession I made this day —the Church, militia, and Ireland—was made merely in order to escape. . . . My only hope is that now they believe I dare deny them nothing, and so will be less careful of their guards.[1]

This letter justified fully the Army's convictions about the futility of negotiations with the King.

No sooner was the Second Civil War at an end than Ireton began to shape certain demands which, as finally adopted by the Council of the Army, became known as the Remonstrance of the Army. Though a lengthy document, its essential demands were that negotiations with the King should be broken off and, "that the capital and grand author of our troubles, the person of the King . . . may be speedily brought to justice for the treason, blood, and mischief he is . . . guilty of." The Remonstrance was presented to Parliament on November 20. Parliament's reply was to postpone consideration of it and to continue negotiating with the King. The Army therefore decided to take action on its own account. On December 1 the King was removed from Newport to Hurst Castle, in Hampshire; and the following day Fairfax led his troops into London. Even this did not overawe Parliament which, four days later, resolved that the King's answers were a basis for reaching a settlement of the Kingdom.

This was more than the Army could endure. It decided to deal drastically with the Commons. To cause the dissolution of the House and the election of a new one would result in a Parliament much more favourable to the King, and much more antagonistic to the Army, than the existing one. The alternative

[1] Gardiner, Civil War, IV, pp. 220–221.

was a purge of the existing Members. On December 6 a body of soldiers, under Colonel Pride's command, was posted at the approach to the Commons, and members of the Presbyterian majority in the House were prevented from entering. Just over 140 were thus excluded, and of these forty-five, who offered resistance, were placed under arrest.

Pride's Purge of the Commons brought the active life of the Long Parliament to an end. The remnant afterwards became known derisively, but appropriately, as the Rump.

The ending of Parliament's authority compelled the Army to face the problem of how to dispose of the King. Discussion revealed two main sections. Both alike favoured bringing him to trial. But whereas one section urged his execution, the other —including Cromwell—regarded his deposition only as a sufficient and wise course. For three weeks discussions on the subject went on among the Army officers. In the end, the more moderate minority was thwarted by the King's refusal to consider any terms or conditions whatever. The Army Council was therefore driven reluctantly but unanimously to extreme measures. On December 28, an ordinance was read before the Commons to set up a special tribunal to try the King. This ordinance passed the Commons on January 1, 1649; but next day the Lords rejected it unanimously.

This raised the issue of where lay the seat of final authority as between Lords and Commons. To settle the issue, the Commons, on January 4, passed three resolutions:

> That the people are, under God, the original of all just power; that the Commons of England, in Parliament assembled, being chosen by and representing the people, have the supreme power in this nation; that whatsoever is enacted, or declared for law by the Commons in Parliament assembled, hath the force of law, and all the people of this nation are concluded thereby, although the consent and concurrence of King or House of Peers be not had thereunto.

Whatever the justice or otherwise of thus excluding the king and the peers from this process of law-making, it was highly incongruous that such resolutions should proceed from so notoriously an unrepresentative an assembly as the Rump.

Nevertheless by virtue of the resolutions, ordinances of the Commons were thenceforward called Acts.

Hence, an ordinance, passed by the Commons only (on January 6), was known as the Act Erecting a High Court of Justice for the King's Trial.[1] This Act named 135 individuals who were to constitute such a court.

On January 20, 1649, the trial opened in Westminster Hall. Of the 135 judges appointed, only sixty-eight that morning answered their names. Perhaps the most notable absentee was General Fairfax. Also there had been great difficulty in finding a lawyer of high repute to preside over so irregular a court. Finally the office of President fell upon Sergeant Bradshaw.

Never throughout his whole career did Charles I show to so great advantage as during his trial and execution. In spite of the strain which the proceedings must have imposed upon him —a strain enormously increased by his loneliness—Charles maintained a regal dignity and an imperturbable courage to the end. Consistently claiming that the court had no authority to try him, for three days—January 20, 22, and 23—he refused to plead to the charges brought against him, and three times the baffled judges had to withdraw him. On the second of the days he thus summed up his case:

> It is not my case alone; it is the freedom and liberty of the people of England; and do you pretend what you will, I stand more for their liberties; for, if power without law may make laws, may alter the fundamental laws of the Kingdom, I do not know what subject he is in England that can be sure of his life, or anything that he called his own.[2]

It was a plea which conveniently forgot many of Charles' own infringements of the people's liberty, but it was well calculated to win sympathy, and to foment division among his opponents. For two more days the court sat privately and heard evidence from witnesses who had seen the King in arms against Parliament. These days were used also by the more determined members of the court in bringing pressure to bear upon their more wavering fellows. Not the least prominent in these proceedings was Cromwell who, though one of the

[1] Gardiner, pp. 357–358.   [2] Gardiner, Civil War, IV, p. 301.

moderates before the trial was opened, was now foremost in
ensuring a decisive issue.

On Saturday, January 27, Charles was brought before the
court to hear his sentence pronounced. Now he repeatedly
sought opportunity to address the court as having something
to say "most material for the welfare of the kingdom and the
liberty of the subject." Bradshaw ruled that his opportunity
for so doing had passed, and called upon the clerk to read the
sentence. This summarized the reasons for bringing the King
to justice.

> For all which treasons and crimes this Court doth adjudge
> that he, the said Charles Stuart, as a tyrant, traitor, murderer,
> and public enemy to the good people of this nation, shall be put
> to death by the severing of his head from his body.[1]

As soon as sentence had been pronounced, Charles was taken
from the court to Whitehall, where he spent that night and
the Sunday and Monday following. During those three days
he was constantly attended by Bishop Juxon, and during the
Monday he took final leave of his two youngest children,
Elizabeth—then thirteen years of age—and the Duke of
Gloucester—three years younger.

The King spent his last night at St James's Palace. About
10 o'clock on the morning of January 30 he walked briskly
across the park to Whitehall, from the Banqueting Hall of
which, about 2 o'clock, he stepped out to the scaffold. An
immense throng of people had gathered, and Charles found
that his voice was incapable of reaching the crowd. He therefore addressed his last words to Juxon and the few others on
the scaffold:

> For my people, I desire their liberty and freedom as much as
> anybody whatsoever; but I must tell you that their liberty and
> freedom consists in having good government, in those laws by
> which their life and goods may be most their own. It is not their
> having a share in government; that is nothing pertaining to
> them. A subject and a sovereign are clean different things. . . . If
> I would have given way to have all changed according to the
> power of the sword, I needed not to have come here; and there-

[1] Gardiner, pp. 377–380.

fore I tell you (and I pray God it may not be laid to your charge)
that I am the martyr of the people.

Charles then laid his head upon the block and gave the
agreed sign to the executioner who, with one blow of the axe,
severed the head from the body. As the executioner lifted up
the head and uttered the usual phrase, "Behold the head of a
traitor," a groan of grief and horror rose from the onlookers.
So marked was the crowd's hostility that soldiers were employed to clear the ground. At a stroke, the Army leaders and
the Rump had transformed a tyrant into a martyr.

Yet before we condemn the King's executioners, on the score
either of theoretical justice or of practical shortsightedness,
we do well to ask what alternative course of policy lay open
to them. From the first day of his reign to the last, all public
relationships with Charles were vitiated by his conviction that,
as King by Divine Right, there was no need for him to keep
faith with his subjects. To Charles, breaches of his pledged
word for reasons of State seemed to be not merely his privilege
but even part of his royal duty as God's vice-gerent; to his
subjects, on the contrary, such breaches seemed incorrigible
double-dealing:

> It was the deep distrust which Charles had inspired that led
> to this drastic mode of setting him aside from the exercise of
> that authority which he had so constantly abused. It was his
> avoidance of open and honourable speech which brought Charles
> to the block.[1]

The future well-being of England, and of more than England, would depend upon whether Charles' executioners had
the wisdom, and could command enough prestige, to evolve a
system of government that would disprove Charles' words on
the scaffold; a system, that is, which would give 'good government' without tyranny.

5. The Republic Challenged, 1649–53

The practical problem calling for immediate solution was
what should be the form of the country's new constitution.

[1] Gardiner, *Oliver Cromwell*, p. 150.

From time immemorial, monarchy had been the only type of government that England had known. Now the King was executed, and so thoroughly was the kingship discredited with the men in power that they were unlikely to replace one king by another. This attitude was made clear by the Acts passed immediately after Charles' execution. Within a week the Commons had passed resolutions against the continued existence of both the House of Lords and the monarchy. On March 17 the Rump passed an Act formally abolishing the monarchy. Two days later the House of Lords was similarly abolished. On May 19 yet a further Act declared:

> . . . that the people of England, and of all the dominions and territories thereunto belonging . . . are hereby constituted . . . a Commonwealth and Free State, and shall henceforth be governed as a Commonwealth and Free State by the supreme authority of this nation, the representatives of the people in Parliament.[1]

To exercise the executive functions formerly vested in the King, the Rump had passed (on February 13) an Act appointing a Council of State of fifty-one members to "direct all the militias and forces both by sea and land," and to promote trade, and to control foreign policy. The new Great Seal bore the superscription: "In the first year of freedom by God's blessing restored, 1648."

It is one of history's ironies that, however sincere were the motives of England's new Government, it was in essence not a democracy but a religio-military oligarchy. For the moment the Royalist Anglicans and the Roman Catholics were powerless, but other discontented sections did not hesitate to make themselves heard. Among these were the Levellers who regarded the Commonwealth as embodying the reverse of the principles for which they had fought. Discontent with the new constitution spread among the rank and file of the Army. In speech and writing the officers, particularly Cromwell, were bitterly attacked. In March 1649 Lilburne and others were brought before the Council of State, and were committed to the Tower. Lilburne was irrepressible. Notwithstanding repeated imprisonments, he continued to defy the Government

[1] Gardiner, p. 388.

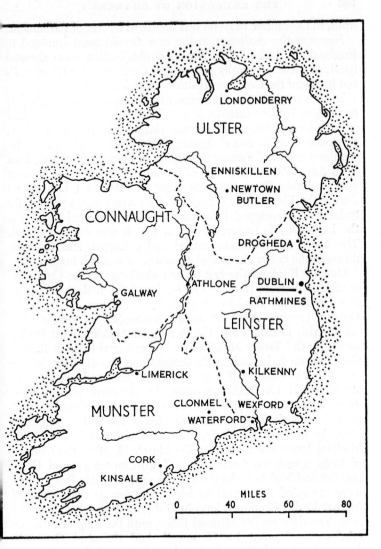

THE REPUBLIC CHALLENGED : IRELAND

until, in December 1651, he was banished by Act of Parliament.

Nor was the challenge to the new Government confined to England. In Ireland and Scotland disaffection soon showed itself; and the sympathy felt on the Continent for Charles I's son involved the Commonwealth in trouble at sea.

In two respects the Government's hands were strengthened to deal with these threats: it was financially sound and it had a magnificent Army. Its income during the first year of its existence was, in round figures, £2,000,000, made up of the regular sources of income (including customs and excise), fines from Royalists, and the sale of confiscated lands. This amount was probably three times as large as Charles I had raised during the Eleven Years' Tyranny. The Army was a splendidly trained and equipped force of forty-four thousand men. Not the least notable feature of it was that it was regularly paid. The Navy also was reorganized and enlarged, and the condition of the crews in pay and otherwise was much improved.

Outside England the first serious challenge to the Commonwealth came from Ireland. The leader of the Irish malcontents was Charles I's Lord-Lieutenant, the Marquess of Ormonde. During January 1649 Ormonde succeeded in uniting the Anglo-Irish Royalists and the Roman Catholics against Parliament: by the Treaty of Kilkenny he promised to Irish Roman Catholics an independent Parliament and the abolition of the penal laws. Charles I's execution at the end of January strengthened Ormonde's position by dividing his enemies: many Protestant English and Scots in Ireland refused to support a regicide Parliament, and almost the only stronghold securely in Parliament's hands was Dublin, where Colonel Michael Jones was Governor. On March 15, 1649, the Council of State appointed Cromwell as Lord-Lieutenant and Commander-in-Chief in Ireland for three years. Nearly five months were occupied in organizing his expedition so that not until August 15 did Cromwell land in Dublin with twelve thousand men. Ten days earlier Michael Jones, with the help of advance reinforcements sent by Cromwell, had defeated Ormonde decisively at Rathmines, and so had destroyed the only army that the malcontents could put into the field. The remainder of the war was therefore almost exclusively one of sieges.

The first siege was that of Drogheda. At the moment of Cromwell's landing, Owen Roe O'Neill, leader of the Ulster Irish, was threatening to advance southward. It was to check such a move that Cromwell advanced against Drogheda and summoned the town to surrender. Refusal of the summons was met by an order to storm. Though the garrison defended itself gallantly and warded off two assaults, it was beaten in the third. Under Cromwell's orders, the whole garrison of 2800 was butchered. According to the accepted rules of warfare, Cromwell was correct in thus putting to the sword a garrison that had refused to surrender. The humanity or otherwise of his action must be judged according to other standards.

The next siege was of Wexford which also Cromwell stormed. Here again the garrison, numbering 1500, was slaughtered. In November Waterford was attacked; but the combination of hard weather and illness among the besiegers compelled Cromwell to raise the siege.

Early in 1650 Kilkenny and Clonmel and several smaller places capitulated. By that time England was being seriously threatened from Scotland. In January Parliament had ordered the recall of Cromwell, but he did not leave Ireland until May. Ireton remained as Commander-in-Chief. In August Ireton took Waterford; and in October 1651, after a terrible five-month siege, Limerick capitulated. Next month Ireton died of fever. Ludlow and Fleetwood succeeded him as commanders. In May 1652 the surrender of Galway marked the completion of Ireland's subjugation.

The settlement of Ireland consisted of a vast scheme of plantation. The estates of outstanding rebel leaders were confiscated, and the less prominent among the disaffected lost a proportion of their lands. Even the proportion of land allowed to the disaffected was to be held in Connaught whither the unfortunate people were transported. It has been computed that something like two-thirds of Irish land changed hands. The confiscated lands were granted to English soldiers who thus were rewarded for their services and were expected to become a bulwark against Roman Catholicism in Ireland. In other respects Cromwell's settlement in Ireland was lenient and even enlightened. Ireland was allotted thirty Members in the united Parliament at Westminster; and free trade was allowed between England and Ireland. Roman Catholic services were suppressed, and Roman Catholic priests were exiled; but Catholics were not forced to attend Protestant services. Perhaps the greatest benefit conferred upon Ireland was the system of English justice and good order.

The danger from Scotland which brought Cromwell back from Ireland in May 1650 was the result of long negotiations between Prince Charles and the Scots. Within a week of Charles I's execution, and only the day after the news of it had reached Edinburgh, the Prince of Wales was proclaimed there as King of Great Britain and Ireland. Had the Scots proclaimed him as King of Scotland only, they would have been acting within their rights; but by proclaiming him as King of England and Ireland also, they put themselves in the wrong. The English Parliament and Army were able to claim that England's war against Scotland aimed not to impose a form of government on Scotland but to prevent Scotland from imposing a government on England.

An open clash between Parliament and the Scots was postponed for more than a year because Charles hesitated to bind himself to uphold the Covenant and to impose Presbyterianism on England and Ireland as well as on Scotland. He placed his hopes upon the Earl of Montrose, who had been Charles I's champion against the Covenanters. Early in 1650 from Jersey, and later from the Netherlands, Charles II communicated with Montrose, commissioning him to raise the Scottish Royalists. Though Montrose struggled valiantly to win support, he failed. On April 27 his small force was rounded up by the Covenanters; and on May 21 he was executed at Edinburgh. On June 2 Charles embarked for Scotland, and, realizing the hopelessness of struggling against the Covenanters, signed the Covenant during the voyage.

War between England and Scotland was the inevitable result of the Covenanters' implied challenge to the sovereignty of the English Parliament. The latter voted Fairfax and Cromwell to their former positions as General and Lieutenant-General respectively of the English armies. When Fairfax knew that the Government's intention was not to await a Scottish

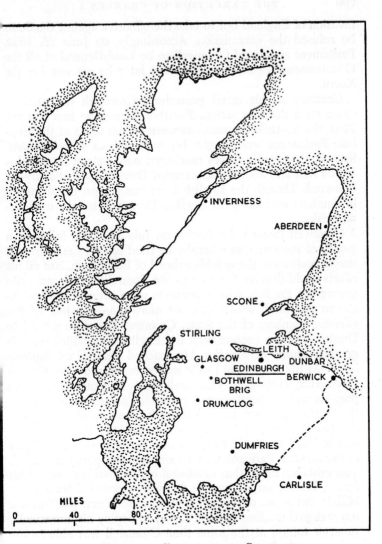

THE REPUBLIC CHALLENGED : SCOTLAND

invasion of England but to take the offensive against the Scots he refused the commission. Accordingly, on June 26, 1650, Parliament appointed Cromwell to be Lord-General of all the Commonwealth's forces. Two days later he set out for the North.

Contrary to his usual procedure, Cromwell hesitated to bring on a decisive action. For this there were two reasons. First, the Scottish Covenanters were former allies of the English Parliament and might be regarded as co-religionists. Second, Cromwell's forces numbered only sixteen thousand— 10,500 foot and 5500 horse—against David Leslie's twenty-six thousand. Though the English were fine troops, the disparity in numbers was too great to allow Cromwell to take unnecessary risks.

Cromwell crossed the Border on July 22. Then followed a month of manœuvring whereby he tried to lure Leslie from a strong position in the neighbourhood of Edinburgh. Not all his efforts could deceive the wily Leslie. Soon disease became rife among the English, whose numbers were thereby reduced to eleven thousand, which was not more than one half of the effective numbers of the Scots. Cromwell therefore moved to Dunbar to make contact with the English fleet which was his greatest source of supplies. He reached Dunbar on September 1. At the same time Leslie moved rapidly to a position on Doon Hill, cutting off Cromwell from England. Cromwell's position was desperate: apart from his immediate danger was the further fact that his failure in Scotland would encourage the Royalists to rise in England. Fortunately for him, Leslie was induced to move. This was due partly to over-confidence in the Scottish Parliamentary Committee and partly to Leslie's own mistaken belief that Cromwell was embarking some of his forces. Hence, on September 2 Leslie descended from Doon Hill. It was an act of military suicide. Leslie's new position was too cramped to allow him effectively to deploy his numerically superior forces; at the same time Cromwell was able to use his own unrivalled skill as a tactician.

Cromwell decided to forestall Leslie's offensive. Before dawn on September 3, the English moved to the attack. For some time the issue hung in doubt. But at the critical juncture Cromwell, with unerring judgement, led his reserves into action shouting: "Let God arise, let His enemies be scattered." By 6 o'clock that morning the Scots were routed. The battle added yet another to the list of Scottish routs and slaughters by English armies: three thousand Scots were killed and ten thousand were prisoners.

Leslie's movement down from Doon Hill, which alone had made Cromwell's victory possible, naturally lowered the prestige of those who had urged the movement—namely, the Presbyterian ministers. More than this, the general Scottish policy which had culminated in Dunbar had been directed by the Kirk. The disastrous defeat thoroughly discredited the Kirk party headed by Argyle. This did not mean that Scotland was ready for peace with England. On the contrary, on January 1, 1651, Charles, following traditional Scottish practice, was crowned at Scone, and so became more than ever the centre of Scottish nationalism. Partly as the result of the widespread reaction after Dunbar, and partly owing to Charles' intrigues, the leadership of the national movement passed to the Scottish nobles.

After Dunbar Leslie gathered the remnants of his forces at Stirling, while Cromwell made Edinburgh and Leith his headquarters. During the early part of 1651 there was a lull in operations owing to Cromwell's long and serious illness. Not until June was he sufficiently recovered to resume the offensive. On August 2 he took Perth, thus cutting Leslie's communications with his sources of supply in the north and east. But Cromwell's position north of Stirling left the way open for the Scots to slip into England. Cromwell must have foreseen this possibility. If the Scots should move southward Cromwell would be able to bring on a decisive engagement before the winter set in. Whatever the military possibilities of the situation, Charles was unable to resist the invitingly open door into England. On July 31 the Scottish Army at Stirling broke up and, twenty thousand strong, moved southward.

Charles followed the route through Carlisle into Lancashire and along the Welsh border so as to tap those districts which

7*

experience had shown to be most strongly Royalist, and whence he might attract bodies of recruits to his standard. Cromwell, unperturbed by the new development, left General Monk as Commander-in-Chief in Scotland with six thousand men, sent Harrison and Lambert with the horse to keep on the Scots' flank and rear respectively, while he himself followed with the foot through Yorkshire.

Charles' hope that the English Royalists would flock to his standard proved illusory. Scarcely a single recruit joined after he crossed into England. The result was that when, on August 22, Charles entered Worcester, Cromwell could command more than thirty thousand men against Charles' sixteen thousand. Battle was joined on September 3, exactly a year after Dunbar. The Scots put up a valiant fight, but the odds against them were too great to allow any but one end to the encounter. The Scots' infantry mostly surrendered; the cavalry tried to cut its way through the Cromwellians and make northward. Few of them reached their homes safely.

Charles was among the small number of Scottish nobles who managed to elude pursuit. Not all Parliament's efforts—neither the threat of the penalties of treason to anyone who helped him, nor the promise of £1000 to anyone who was the means of his capture—succeeded in discovering him. Many men and women must have penetrated the King's disguises in the course of his wanderings, but none betrayed him. At last he found a vessel, and, sailing from Brighton, he landed in France on October 22.

The breaking and scattering of the Scottish Army left Scotland at Cromwell's mercy. Monk proceeded to a systematic subjugation of the country. The principle of Cromwell's settlement of Scotland was similar to that of his settlement of Ireland —namely, that the country lost its political independence and sent representatives to the British Parliament at Westminster. But the details of his dealings with the two countries differed; for, whereas the bulk of the Irish population was Roman Catholic, Cromwell could not forget that the Scots were Presbyterians who hated Romanists and Episcopalians as much as he did. Hence, though the General Assembly of the Scottish

Church was dissolved in 1653, the synods and presbyteries were allowed to meet, the reason being that the General Assembly was more influential than the Scottish Parliament as the leader of the nation. Though the English Parliament declared the confiscation of the estates of those Scots who had invaded England, Cromwell carried out the confiscation penalty only on a small group of the leaders so that the rank and file of the Scottish people were not directly affected. Yet, however much the blow might be softened, nothing could alter the fact that Scotland, like Ireland, had at last lost her independence, and that Cromwell had succeeded where kings had failed to effect a united State of England, Wales, Ireland, and Scotland.

The end of the war against Ireland and Scotland gave to both Parliament and Army some leisure to deal with the problem of English government, a problem that had been shelved since the King's execution. The root of the problem was that, whereas the State was controlled by a republican Army, the majority of the nation was still at heart monarchical. Some means had therefore to be devised to reconcile the nation to the republic. To this end Cromwell favoured measures to conciliate the mass of moderate Royalists and to popularize the republic with the nation as a whole. This plan was supported by the Army but was thwarted continually by the Rump. The latter, in spite of Pride's Purge, was predominantly Presbyterian (and hence opposed to religious and political toleration) and was afraid of any scheme that would undermine its own powers or terminate its existence. Hence there was a division which grew increasingly acute between Army and Parliament until an open breach was inevitable.

For some causes of discontent in the nation at large, the Parliament could hardly be held responsible. Perhaps the most important was high taxation. The maintenance of the Army and Navy absorbed nearly £2,500,000 yearly, and the total national expenditure in Worcester-year was three times as large as in any year of Charles I. None the less, in most respects Parliament acted with an obstinacy that was blind to the needs of the day. For example, in 1652 it enacted that estates—numbering more than six hundred—forfeited for treason should be sold. The result was that large numbers of individuals

—some of them by this time reconciled to the Government —were turned adrift. Similarly, though demands for the reform of the law and of legal procedure, which was obscure, dilatory, and costly, were both widespread and insistent, no decisive action was taken.

The result of the Rump's procrastination was a growing demand for the dissolution of Parliament. By the Act of May 1641, it could not be dissolved except by its own consent. Repeatedly conferences of officers discussed the subject. Cromwell had been consistently on the side of toleration and reform, and in the matter of the dissolution he was fully in sympathy with the Army, yet not even his influence could induce the Rump to yield to popular clamour. On the contrary, early in 1653 it proceeded with a Bill for the new Representative. This Bill, which had been drawn up by Vane, provided that when an election took place all the existing Members should retain their seats and, further, should have the right to judge the suitability of the new Members chosen by the constituencies.

This Bill finally convinced Cromwell that the Rump's chief concern was not the nation's welfare but was to perpetuate its own existence. On April 20, therefore, when the third reading was to be taken, he occupied his usual place in the House and listened to the debate. When the Speaker was about to put the motion to the vote, Cromwell suddenly rose and began to address the House. With growing passion, he declaimed at length against the Parliament's corruption and injustice. Then he bade Harrison to call in soldiers, who had been posted at the doors, and to clear the House. The Members were quick to take the hint. Speaker Lenthall refused to move except by force; but a firm touch from Harrison caused him to change his mind: having descended from the Chair, he left the House followed by the other Members. In the midst of the scene Cromwell noticed the mace. "What shall we do with this bauble?" he exclaimed. Then, in answer to his own question, he commanded: "Here, take it away!" Thereupon, ordering the doors to be locked, he strode out of the House. Thus the Rump which had come into existence with the sword, perished by the sword.

The expulsion of the Rump provoked yet a further sharp division in the nation. Henceforward not only were Royalists divided from Republicans but the Republicans were themselves divided into those who supported the Army and those who wished for a civil regime. While this division lasted, there could be small chance of establishing a republican constitution of any kind.

Chapter 9

The Rule of Cromwell

1653–60

1. The Protectorate Established, 1653–55

Cromwell's dismissal of the Rump brought an end to the last remaining element of legally constituted authority in the State. Parliament had followed the monarchy to the grave. Once again a new form of government had to be found. Many various sections of the nation had their own solutions. The Fifth Monarchists, headed by Harrison, saw in the situation the heaven-sent opportunity for the beginning of the Rule of the Saints. At the other extreme, men of logical minds believed that the only means to restore permanent order was to set up a Government similar in form to the traditional monarchy but depending upon a written constitution which would state beyond dispute the relationship between the respective elements in the political system and between the Government and the governed. Between these two extremes there were many varieties of political theory. There was no means of discerning infallibly which was the one theory ideally suited to the England of 1653. The only possible method of discovering it was that of "trial and error": the system with the least objection to it, according to the judgement of the men then in power, would have to be tried and later be modified in the light of experience.

Herein lies the significance of the period 1653–60: it saw a series of unique political experiments. Perhaps it is well to begin study of the period by having the series clearly in mind. It may be set out as follows:

> The Little (Barebone's) Parliament, July–December 1653.
> Instrument of Government (Protectorate), December 1653.
> Major-Generals, March 1655–January 1657.
> Humble Petition and Advice, February 1657.

The last of these constitutions swung England back to a monarchy in all but name, and to a two-chamber Parliament.

After the Rump's dissolution Cromwell was the only individual with enough prestige to carry any new constitution into effect. His popularity had been recently enhanced by the ejection of the Rump. The truth of his declaration that when its members went out "there was not so much as the barking of a dog" is amply borne out by contemporary pamphlets and ballads. But Cromwell had no ready-made scheme for replacing the Rump. For himself, he believed in the "rule of the godly." As a result, the Independent congregations of each county were instructed to nominate representatives from whom the Council of Officers chose a smaller number. Thus there came into existence an Assembly of 140 members: 129 for England, six for Ireland, and five for Scotland. It became known as the Little Parliament and as Barebone's Parliament, the latter name being derived from one of its members, a London merchant, named Praise-God Barebone.

Cromwell had done his best to make the Parliament representative of those sections that had opposed Charles; but some, like Fairfax and Vane, had refused to join it. Consequently all the members were Independents who were opposed to Romanists, Episcopalians, and Presbyterians alike. The mass of English Puritans regarded the new Parliament as the beginning of a new political era. This was a view which Cromwell shared. But how long a body so narrowly constituted would be able to govern the nation effectively only experience could show.

The Parliament certainly took its office seriously. Reforms of the most far-reaching kind were tackled almost lightheartedly. The Court of Chancery—whose delays and costliness had become a by-word—was to be abolished. Civil marriages were to be allowed. Records of births, marriages, and deaths were to be kept in parochial registers. A Committee was appointed to codify the law, a hope being expressed that: "the great volumes of law would come to be reduced into the bigness of a pocket-book." Such a hope suggests zeal without knowledge. Further proposals were before the House for church-reform, including the abolition of tithes. The inevitable result was bitter sectarian controversy. Perhaps the greatest practical difficulty facing the Little Parliament was the perennial one of finance. The Dutch war, which had broken out in May 1652, was proving costly.

Very soon the belief began to spread that social order and personal freedom could be secured only by restoring the traditional form of English government—that is, by restoring the monarchy. The period of the Little Parliament was therefore one of growing royalism. Since Ireton's death at Limerick, in 1651, Lambert had come to be regarded as the leader of what might be called the 'constitutional party'; and this now resolved to end so dangerous an Assembly. On Monday, December 12, the Speaker, Francis Rous (Provost of Eton and step-brother of John Pym), and the moderate section of Parliament repaired early in the morning to Whitehall and there resigned its powers to the Lord General. Cromwell had not been a party to this move. To the next Parliament he declared: "I can say it in the presence of divers persons here who know whether I lie, that I did not know one tittle of that resignation, till they all came and brought, and delivered it into my hands." That declaration was never challenged. None the less the end of the Parliament certainly accorded with Cromwell's wishes, and he accepted the proffered resignation.

Previous to these last events, Lambert and his followers had been working on a new constitution which they now presented to Cromwell, and which came to be known as the Instrument of Government. By its terms the titular head of the State was to be the Lord Protector, to which office Oliver Cromwell was nominated. In administrative matters, both domestic and foreign, he could act only with the consent of the Council. The latter was to consist of fifteen men named in the Instrument, together with six others whom the fifteen could appoint with the Protector's consent; and, subject to good behaviour, the Councillors were to retain office for life.

The Instrument's most striking clauses were those relating to the composition and election of Parliament. It omitted the smallest boroughs which hitherto had had separate representation; and, by allotting various numbers to various counties— for example, Devon was to have eleven, and Rutlandshire two

—an attempt was made at approximately equal constituencies. To England were assigned four hundred Members, to Scotland thirty, and to Ireland thirty. These were to be elected by owners of property worth at least £200, except that no Roman Catholic was to have a vote. Otherwise there was to be liberty of conscience.

Such was the Instrument presented to Cromwell who, having signified his acceptance of its terms, was duly installed as Protector in Westminster Hall on December 16, and thence was conducted to Whitehall, his official residence.

Both in its general conception and in most of its clauses, the Instrument showed statesmanship of a high order. In its reform of the franchise and of the distribution of Parliamentary seats, as well as in the granting of a measure of religious toleration, it was several generations ahead of its time. This, however, would not necessarily ensure for it success in its own day. To be too far ahead of its time might have the reverse effect. Moreover, the new constitution had two features especially which would certainly provoke opposition and controversy. The first was the basic fact, however disguised, that it had been imposed by the Army. Second, the franchise was far from democratic: the only sections possessing political power were the well-to-do middle class and upward.

In one other respect the Instrument was notable—namely, that, being a written constitution, it necessarily defined, and therefore limited, the Protector's powers. Cromwell's ready acceptance of it was typical of his attitude. He had no ambition for dictatorial powers. On the contrary, the invariable tendency of his career was away from autocracy and towards a constitutional government which approximated increasingly to that of traditional English monarchy. That more than once he broke into the working of a constitution which he had already accepted was due to his belief that the constitution had ceased to function as it was intended to do. His interventions were not due to a hankering for autocracy for himself.

The Instrument of Government had expressly entrusted government to the Protector and his Council until the next Parliament should meet. During the intervening period—that is, from December 1653 till September 1654—Cromwell used this delegated authority in order to issue eighty-two ordinances, thereby carrying out certain reforms in which he was particularly interested. Among these were matters concerned with religion. By an ordinance of March 20, 1654, thirty-eight commissioners, some of them laymen and some clerics, were appointed to inquire into the qualifications of all applicants for church livings. The commissioners' inquiries were to be directed not into doctrinal matters—provided that the candidate was an Independent, a Presbyterian, or a Baptist—but into his manner of life and whether "the grace of God" was evident in him. In August 1654 a further ordinance appointed commissioners for each county with power to eject ministers who were immoral in life, inefficient in their administrations, Popish in their teachings, or disloyal to the Government. Such were the two sets of commissioners known as Triers and Ejectors. Their inquisitions were, of course, capable of misuse; but the available evidence seems to support the view that:

> Both bodies of commissioners did the work they were charged to do with fidelity. Some good men were expelled merely for royalism or for using the liturgy, but the bulk of those who lost their livings deserved their fate, and those admitted were generally fit for their office.[1]

Outside the State-recognized churches dissenters were allowed to gather into congregations, and, notwithstanding laws to the contrary, even Episcopalian and Roman Catholic services were allowed to continue provided that they were unobtrusive and did not raise suspicion of active disloyalty to the Government. Even the Jews were allowed to return to England, though this step was due as much to the commercial benefits likely to accrue from their presence—since they controlled trade with Spain and Portugal and with the Levant—as to the Protector's disposition to toleration.

In no part of his work did Cromwell show higher nobility of purpose or sounder political wisdom than in this of religious toleration. In a century when religious toleration was unthought of, except with abhorrence, Cromwell's career justified his declaration that: "I had rather that Mahometism was per-

---

[1] C. H. Firth, *Oliver Cromwell*, p. 360.

mitted among us than that one of God's children should be persecuted."

The first Protectorate Parliament met, as provided in the Instrument of Government, on September 3, 1654. The elections had returned a majority of Presbyterians, the result probably of the £200 property-qualification, since the Presbyterians were drawn mostly from the well-to-do sections of the nation. This boded ill for the Government: the Presbyterians were still at enmity with the Independents of the Army and therefore with the Protector.

On the second day of the session Cromwell addressed the House, appealing to the Members to pursue a policy of "healing and settling." In so doing, he castigated the Levellers as would-be disturbers of the class-divisions which were the social foundations of the State. This was a line of argument likely to appeal to his hearers. But if he expected thereby to soothe them into a compliant acceptance of his rule he was to be disappointed.

The first subject to which the Members directed their attention was the Instrument of Government, which they criticized both in principle and in detail. Objections were raised particularly to the powers which the Protector was allowed to wield independently of Parliament and against its measure of religious toleration. Cromwell realized that if the debates were not checked the constitution would be undermined. He therefore summoned the Members to his presence, reminded them that their Membership in accordance with the terms of the Instrument implied their acceptance of it and that the judges had taken out commissions and thus had tacitly acknowledged the Instrument's legal validity. Cromwell therefore insisted that the Members should not be allowed to re-enter their House until they took a pledge "to be true and faithful to the Lord Protector and the Commonwealth of England, and not to propose or give consent to alter the government as it was settled in a single person and a parliament." Nearly one hundred Members who refused to give this pledge were excluded from the House.

Even this did not mean that henceforward all would go smoothly between Parliament and Protector. No Parliament would ever be reconciled to a Protector who ruled by virtue of his command of the Army; and however the position might be disguised, the truth was that England was under military rule. Members therefore debated a proposal that the joint control of Parliament and Protector over the Army should be limited to the life-time of the present Protector. After his death the Army was to be controlled by Parliament alone. Then Parliament set to work to try to reduce the high cost of the Army by reducing its numbers from the fifty-seven thousand then in arms to the thirty thousand provided for in the Instrument. To this end it proposed to grant money sufficient for the reduced numbers. Cromwell was convinced that thirty thousand men were not enough to ensure the peace of the British Isles, in every part of which there was serious unrest: Ireland was known to be discontented; in December a plot was discovered among the Army in Scotland to depose Monk and march into England against the Government; and the Levellers were known to be joining with the Royalists against the Protector. Seriously to weaken the armed forces at such a time was, in Cromwell's view, to invite the renewal of strife, with what results to the State none could predict. Accordingly the Protector determined to end the Parliament on the earliest possible date allowed by the Instrument. Hence, on January 22 —five lunar months after the House had first met—he summoned the Members again to his presence, reproached them for the unrest that they had encouraged, and declared the Parliament dissolved.

2. Foreign Policy, 1652-58

Cromwell's foreign policy had three objectives: to support Protestantism and to strike at Roman Catholicism; to promote English trade; and to prevent foreign Powers from helping to restore the Stuarts. This threefold policy proved to have two fundamental weaknesses.

First, in two respects it was based upon ideas which had been valid a generation earlier but which by the middle of the seventeenth century had ceased to be so. To begin with, diplomacy was no longer determined by religious doctrine.

The last religious war in Europe was the Thirty Years' War of 1618-48. Even that war had lost its distinctively religious character after the death of Gustavus Adolphus at Lützen, in 1632, after which Cardinal Richelieu led Roman Catholic France to intervene on the side of the Protestants, in 1635. Thenceforward national ambitions in the realms of politics and trade had superseded religion as the chief factor in diplomacy. Cromwell was blind to this fact. The other aspect of his outmoded policy was that he still thought of Spain as being the one enemy that England had to fear. Cromwell had been born into a staunchly Protestant family in Elizabethan England, the Armada being still fresh in men's minds. He had lived through James I's reign when, owing to the abandonment of Elizabeth's policy, national prestige abroad had disgracefully declined. One of Cromwell's motives was, in essence, to re-establish England's prestige by reverting to Elizabethan policy. In so doing, he ignored not only changed conditions abroad but also a change in the views of an important section of Englishmen. Under Elizabeth there had been two chief motives for attacking Spain: the first was religion; the second was the desire to tap the sources of Spain's mineral wealth in the New World. The first of these we have seen to be an anachronism by 1650. The second was scarcely less so. Spain's goldmines and silver-mines had not saved her from poverty and weakness, and Englishmen were beginning to realize that the true source of England's wealth was trade. The real threat to English trade came not from Roman Catholic Spain but from Protestant Holland. At the moment the merchant class alone was awakening to this aspect of affairs, and that class was only a small minority of the nation and was unrepresented in the Government.

The second fundamental weakness of Cromwell's foreign policy was that its three objectives were mutually inconsistent. Since the threat to English trade came from Holland, this implied rivalry, not alliance, between the two Protestant States of England and Holland. Protestant Holland was also a staunch supporter of the Stuarts. Moreover, Spain and France, the most powerful States on the Continent, were both Roman Catholic, so that to oppose Spain would almost certainly involve an alliance with Roman Catholic France. In brief, the pursuit of Cromwell's three aims at one and the same time was impossible. The attempt to pursue them led inevitably to vacillation in his foreign policy.

In extenuation of these misjudgements, it must be remembered that Cromwell was too close to relevant events to be able to assess them justly. He could not know that there would never be another religious war in Europe. Nor could he realize the full import of Spain's decline or of Holland's rise. Cromwell was no more blind to the changed conditions abroad and at home than were the vast majority of his contemporaries. But, in so far as a statesman's business is to see farther ahead than his contemporaries, to meet the rising tide and not to follow its ebbing predecessor, Cromwell's foreign policy must stand condemned.

War between England and the Dutch broke out in 1652. There were two main reasons for it. The first was dynastic. In May 1641 Charles I's elder daughter, Mary, had married William, son of Frederick Henry of Orange, Stadtholder of the United Provinces. In March 1647 William succeeded his father as William II. It was natural that William II should espouse the cause of his royal father-in-law, Charles I. So strong was the resentment felt in Holland against the treatment received by Charles that the English Parliament's emissaries, sent to William soon after his accession, were refused an audience. In November 1650 William died. His son, the future William III, was not born until a few days later. For the time the office of Stadtholder remained in abeyance, and a republic was established under John de Witt's leadership. The opportunity seemed ripe for more friendly relations between the two republican and Protestant Governments of England and Holland. Oliver St John, now Chief Justice, and Walter Strickland, were therefore sent in March 1651 as special Ambassadors to The Hague. Yet so great were the hostility and suspicion that greeted them that after three months the negotiations broke down.

This rebuff moved the English Government to some form of retaliation—namely, an attack on Dutch trade. The Dutch were the maritime carriers of Europe. Much of their carrying trade was between England and her colonies in Newfoundland, in some of the West Indian islands, and on the eastern shore of North America, as well as to trading stations in India. So the English expressed their anger against the Dutch by trying to strike at this trade. In October 1651 Parliament passed the Navigation Act.[1] This enacted that any produce of Asia, Africa, or America imported into the British Isles must be brought in British ships or in ships belonging to British plantations, and that the majority of the crew on a ship so employed must also be British. Further, all imported products of Europe must be brought either in British ships or in the ships of the country producing the goods. The preamble to the Act stated that it was intended:

> For the increase of the shipping and the encouragement of the navigation of this nation, which under the good providence and protection of God is so great a means of the welfare and safety of this Commonwealth.

If the Act succeeded in this purpose it could do so only at the expense of the Dutch.

The Dutch, on their side, had long-standing grievances arising from maritime rivalry with the English. The latter, claiming sovereignty of the Narrow Seas, demanded that Dutch ships should lower their flag to English ships. Also, English merchant-ships not uncommonly rigged themselves out as armed privateers, the inevitable result being clashes at sea.

To what extent the Navigation Act directly crippled Dutch trade is difficult to estimate with any exactness. Its clauses cannot have been at once fully enforced because English merchant-vessels did not exist in numbers sufficient to replace all the Dutch vessels hitherto engaged in the English trade. Nevertheless the Dutch Government, anticipating that the Act would restrict their trade, in December sent envoys to ask for its repeal. Cromwell, realizing that war between the two countries would ruin his hopes of a general Protestant alliance, did what he could to bring about an understanding; but his efforts were in vain. The continued English claim to sovereignty

[1] Gardiner, pp. 468-471.

of the seas caused a breach in negotiations, and there was a drift into war.

In May 1652 the Dutch admiral, Tromp, put to sea with orders to protect Dutch shipping. Fortunately for England, the Government had done much during the previous two or three years to make up leeway in its naval resources. Immediately after Charles I's execution, the Parliament, as though realizing that this violent act might provoke a challenge from abroad, decided to add thirty ships to its fleet. The Earl of Warwick ceased to be Lord High Admiral, and a Navy Committee was appointed to administer naval affairs. Its leading member was Sir Henry Vane, the younger, who had been Treasurer of the Navy since 1642. In 1649 Colonel Blake was appointed Admiral and General-at-Sea. Blake turned out to be the man of the moment, the genius whom England then most needed. His subsequent career entitles him to rank along with Drake and Nelson, with the added distinction that he had not had the advantage of a maritime training from his youth up, for he was fifty years of age when he first put to sea in his new sphere of command. Both he and his fleet got their first experience of naval warfare in operations against Rupert off the coasts of Ireland and of Portugal. The Portuguese Government had allowed Rupert to shelter and refit in Lisbon harbour. In September 1650 Blake retorted by seizing a Portuguese treasure-fleet on its way from Brazil, capturing eleven valuable prizes which he sent to England. Hence, by the time that war broke out between England and Holland in the middle of 1652, Blake had shown himself an admiral fit for the occasion.

Soon after Tromp put to sea in May 1652 he fell in with Blake in the Downs and, refusing to strike the flag as Blake demanded, was attacked. Tromp had to retire with some loss, and open war between the two republics became inevitable. Tromp was provided with a fleet of eighty-five sail which was twice the number that Blake could command. On November 30 Blake and Tromp met off Dungeness. Tromp's numerical advantage was so enormous that his victory was almost inevitable, and during the following three months he ruled the Channel. Then in February 1653 an English fleet of seventy ships, led by Blake and Monk (who also had been transferred

from the Army to the Navy), put to sea. Off Portland they fell
in with Tromp, who was conveying a fleet of merchantmen
towards Holland. The presence of the merchantmen seriously
hampered Tromp, and, though he maintained a running fight
for three days, he suffered a severe defeat. Thenceforward the
English retained their control of the sea. They even kept up
a blockade of the Dutch coast. On July 31 Tromp, in an attempt
to break this blockade, was defeated and killed by the English
under Monk's leadership in a battle off the Texel.

This was the last battle of the war. As soon as Cromwell
became Protector in December 1653 he began to move for
peace. Long negotiations followed, and a treaty was not concluded until April 5, 1654. Its chief provisions were that there
should be a defensive alliance between the two countries, that
each should expel the enemies of the other (which meant that
Holland would not harbour the Stuarts), that the Dutch should
compensate the English for losses sustained in the East Indies
(including the massacre at Amboyna of 1623[1]), and that the
Dutch should salute the English flag but that they were not to
pay rent for fishing-rights in the North Sea. It should be noted
that the Dutch abandoned their demand for the repeal of the
Navigation Act. From the States of the Province of Holland—
by far the most wealthy and influential of the Seven United
Provinces—Cromwell further demanded an Act of Exclusion
which would for ever prevent a member of the House of
Orange from being chosen as Stadtholder or as Captain-
General. Only when the Act had been passed would Cromwell
ratify the Peace Treaty. The ratification was proclaimed on
April 26. It was an astute move designed to paralyse the Seven
Provinces by perpetuating internal political discords.

This conclusion of the Dutch war realized two of Cromwell's
aims: it brought an alliance with a Protestant State, and it
would promote English trade. A further result was that England acquired a new prestige in Europe. The basis of that
prestige was sea-power.

The return of peace left Cromwell free to pursue his project
of a general Protestant alliance. For this purpose he opened

[1] See pp. 407–408.

negotiations with Sweden and Denmark. Apart from their Protestantism, these Baltic countries were England's source of naval supplies of timber, tar, and hemp. Free access through the Sound into the Baltic was thus a necessity for the Navy.

It was to Sweden that Cromwell turned first. In April 1654, only a few days after the conclusion of peace with Holland, Cromwell secured a treaty which settled relations between England and Sweden, and provided that Sweden would not help the cause of Charles II.

Dealings with Denmark were more difficult because of the family relationships between the royal houses of the two countries. These difficulties, however, were overcome, and in September 1654 a treaty with Denmark granted to English ships the right to pass through the Sound on the same terms—that is, paying the same dues—as the Dutch.

Portugal was the next country to be brought within Cromwell's scheme of alliances. In 1640 Portugal had revolted against Spain and recovered its independence which it had lost sixty years before. Two years later the ancient alliance between England and Portugal was renewed, and English merchants were thereby granted valuable privileges in Portugal. These events made the Portuguese sympathetic towards the Stuarts. Hence the friendly reception accorded to Prince Rupert's fleet in 1650. But Cromwell's decisive defeat of the Royalists at Worcester in 1651 made Portugal, whose independence was still precarious, anxious to conciliate the Commonwealth Government. In 1652, therefore, King John of Portugal sent an Ambassador to England. The outcome was a commercial treaty whereby Portugal undertook to pay £50,000 as compensation for injuries done to English merchants while Lisbon was Rupert's base. In 1654 a further treaty granted to English merchants the right to trade with Portugal and Portuguese possessions, and guaranteed that such merchants might exercise the Protestant religion in their houses and ships.

Thus by 1654 Cromwell was at peace with the Protestant States of Holland, Sweden, and Denmark, and he had hampered Spain by advantageous treaties with Portugal.

The biggest problem of Cromwell's foreign policy still remained to be solved—namely, his relations with France and with Spain. In this matter the chief difficulty was that both countries were Roman Catholic. When religious principle failed as a guide, expediency must be the only motive.

No sooner was the Anglo-Dutch war at an end than both France and Spain began to bid for English friendship. France offered to help England to gain Dunkirk from Spain and to renounce the cause of Charles II. Spain offered to help England in the recovery of Calais from France and to subsidize English troops; but when Cromwell demanded that English merchants should be free to trade with Spanish America and to exercise the Protestant religion in Spanish ports the Spanish Ambassador replied that such demands were like asking for his master's two eyes. This was probably the decisive factor against a Spanish alliance. Other factors were that England had traditionally regarded Spain as her enemy; that Spain was more uncompromisingly Roman Catholic than France; and that, whereas Spain had no Protestant subjects, France had the Huguenots whose interests Cromwell might protect if he allied with France but not if he fought her. Hence everything tended towards an alliance with France.

This, however, did not lead to an immediate or open breach with Spain. Indeed, Cromwell still lived so much in the Elizabethan tradition that he seems to have seen no reason why clashes at sea and raids against Spanish colonies in America should involve the two Governments in a formal war in Europe. Towards the end of 1654 preparations were made for an expedition to the West Indies, and at the end of December the expedition set sail from Portsmouth. Admiral Penn was in command of the fleet of thirty-eight vessels, and General Venables of the force of 2500 soldiers. On January 29, 1655, the fleet reached Barbados. There, and from other islands, Venables recruited enough men to raise his army to seven thousand. Formidable though these numbers appeared, they were in reality deceptive: the men were ill-assorted, ill-disciplined, ill-armed, and ill-led. Even Penn and Venables were mutually jealous. In April a landing was made on the large Spanish island of Hispaniola and an attack directed against its capital, San Domingo. Three successive advances failed, and soon the lack of water and other supplies caused illness and a large number of deaths. The men were therefore embarked without having threatened San Domingo.

Penn and Venables then decided to retrieve their reputation by attacking the neighbouring island of Jamaica, and there they landed in May. The island was occupied without serious difficulty, and the Spaniards were driven out. But sickness again gripped the Army, and hundreds died. By June Penn and Venables sailed for England. Their news of failure at Hispaniola caused Cromwell much vexation. The two commanders were called before the Council and committed to the Tower. Though shortly released, they were never again given commands.

This breach with Spain naturally encouraged closer relations between England and France. A contemporary event in Europe also contributed to Anglo-French friendship. This was the massacre of large numbers of Vaudois, or Waldenses, who were Protestants in Savoy. Their name was derived from that of Peter Waldez, their twelfth-century founder. In 1581 the Duke of Savoy had granted them toleration within a specified geographical boundary. By the middle of the seventeenth century they had spread outside this boundary, and in January 1655 troops were used to drive them back into it. The result was a widespread massacre in which French troops joined. When, in May, news of these events reached Cromwell, he acted at once to protect the Waldenses. The ruling house of Savoy was related to the French Bourbons. Cromwell therefore urged Louis XIV to intervene to stop the massacre, and he refused to sign any treaty with France while the oppression continued. To his fellow-Protestant rulers he addressed letters on behalf of the Waldenses. In England he opened a subscription-list on their behalf and contributed heavily himself. French pressure induced the Savoy authorities to desist, and throughout Europe Cromwell was hailed as the great champion of Protestantism.

On October 24, 1655, the day on which the Spanish Ambassador left England, England and France signed a formal alliance. Ostensibly the treaty was a commercial one, but a secret clause provided for the exclusion of Charles Stuart and of certain other leading Royalists from France, and for the exclusion of the Prince of Condé's supporters from England.

The opening stage of war against Spain took place at sea. English fleets continued to sail around the Spanish coast with the double object of intercepting treasure from Spanish America and reinforcements from Spain to the West Indies. Not until early September 1656 was this constant watch rewarded when an English squadron under Captain Stayner fell in with eight Spanish galleons off Cadiz. Several of the galleons were destroyed, and treasure valued at several hundreds of thousands of pounds was captured.

Even then Blake remained unsatisfied and carried out the unprecedented feat of keeping at sea throughout the winter. In April 1657 news reached him of a Spanish treasure-fleet in the Canaries. Thither he sailed, and found his quarry in the harbour of Santa Cruz, at Teneriffe. The Spaniards had removed the treasure well inland. Nevertheless Blake destroyed the galleons and so prevented the transfer of the treasure to Spain. This was both the most notable and the last of Blake's exploits at sea. The ceaseless blockade had worn him out. On August 7 he died as his vessel was entering Plymouth Sound. The effects of his deeds outlived him: the Spaniards, cheated of their treasure, were unable to maintain their armies at strength, and defeats on land were the result.

In March 1657 England and France made an offensive alliance for a joint attack on Gravelines, Mardyke, and Dunkirk, the last two towns being assigned to England if the campaign was successful. England was to provide a fleet, and also six thousand soldiers whom France was to pay. During 1657 the campaign was not strikingly successful, though Mardyke was finally taken and put into English hands in October.

In 1658 the great French soldier, Turenne, laid siege to Dunkirk, and when the Spaniards sent an army fourteen thousand strong for its relief, a battle took place among the surrounding sandhills. The Battle of the Dunes (June 14, 1658) was decisive: the Spaniards were routed and suffered five thousand casualties. The Ironsides played a distinguished part in the battle; and when ten days later Dunkirk surrendered it was handed over to the English.

The following years were to show that Dunkirk's value to England was illusory. Cromwell regarded the town as a gateway into the Continent, the base whence he could operate against Spain in support of his Protestant allies. But, as we have seen, this conception of policy was an anachronism. Spain had ceased to be a source of danger to England and to Protestantism.

Three months later Cromwell died. Perhaps his death saved him from disasters abroad. Had he used Dunkirk as a base of offensive operations into central Europe the only result would have been the impoverishment of the English people for no fruitful purpose. Both before and after Cromwell's day land campaigns by an English army abroad were successful only when subsidiary to naval campaigns. That condition could not have been fulfilled if Cromwell's plans had been put into operation.

Early in 1659 France and Spain signed a truce, and the Treaty of the Pyrenees was concluded between them in November of that year. The treaty made no mention of England's possession of Dunkirk, and France specifically undertook not to help England against Spain. Such was the difference made by the death of Cromwell. The war against Spain ended without England's gaining anything substantial from it.

While these events had been taking place abroad, changes of great consequence were taking place in the Protectorate Government at home. To these we must now turn.

3. The End of the Protectorate, 1656–58

The proceedings of the first Protectorate Parliament had shown that a Parliament and rule by the Army were irreconcilable. Stability would be restored in the State only if one or other of these antagonistic elements was either removed or made strictly subordinate to the other. The first move after the first Parliament's dissolution was in the direction of the Army's supremacy and took the form of the Major-Generals.

The deficit in the exchequer, and the increasing discontent due to heavy taxation, led to a suggestion that the Army should be reduced in numbers and should be supplemented by a militia. Cromwell adopted the suggestion but decided that the militia, though consisting of local forces, should be controlled by the central Government. In the autumn of 1655 England and Wales were divided into eleven districts in each of which an officer with the rank of Major-General was appointed to organize and command the militia-levies.

This original function of the Major-Generals was soon swamped by a host of other duties assigned to them. These included the maintenance of public order and the administration of laws regulating morals and amusements. Under their supervision, drunkenness was suppressed (partly by punishing offenders and partly by abolishing many ale-houses); and bear-baiting, cock-fighting, and horse-racing were forbidden, the excuse being that the attendant gatherings were used by Royalists for plotting against the Government.

Nothing that Cromwell could have done could more effectively have turned the mass of the nation against his rule. The restrictions enforced by the Major-Generals were naturally contrasted in men's minds with the freedom of Charles I's days and with the yet greater freedom which would doubtless come with a restoration of Charles II. Many even of the Puritans regarded the restrictions as being excessive. The Royalists were hardest hit of all, for a 10 per cent. tax was levied upon their rentals in order to find money for the Major-Generals' salaries. Thus almost every class in the community was alienated by the new system of military police.

Tangible proof of the system's unpopularity was soon forthcoming. By the terms of the Instrument of Government a new Parliament need not be called until 1657. But the war with Spain had broken out in October 1655. Fresh taxes would soon be necessary, and the Instrument provided for the summoning of a Parliament as soon as possible after the outbreak of war. Hence writs for a new Parliament were issued. The Major-Generals assured Cromwell that they could manage the elections so as to ensure the return of suitable members. The results were a shock to them and to Cromwell: among those returned were a hundred republicans who were avowed opponents of the Government. The latter had a short and simple way of dealing with such malcontents: the list of Members was carefully examined, certificates were issued to the 'safe' men, and no man without the necessary document was allowed to enter the Commons' House. Those who remained were a colourless company of reliable Presbyterians and Independents. The Instrument had enjoined that the Council "shall peruse the said returns, and examine whether the persons so elected and returned be such as is agreeable to the qualifications"—that is, "persons of known integrity, fearing God, and of good conversation." Hence, the Council, in excluding the hundred members, was acting according to the letter of the constitution; but equally certainly it was offending its spirit. And if Cromwell had gained a tractable Parliament he had still further alienated the mass of moderate men and made the return of some sort of monarchy more sure than ever.

On September 17, 1656, when the second Protectorate Parliament met, Cromwell addressed the Members for three hours. His speech was intended to justify the Government's recent acts—the Spanish war, the Major-Generals, the restrictive legislation, the taxes on Royalists. But he was preaching to the converted.

Even so, as time passed this complaisant remainder of the Commons began to stiffen its attitudes. This was illustrated when, in January 1657, during a debate on the method of maintaining the new militia, the question of the 10 per cent. tax on Royalists came up for discussion. Cromwell's son-in-law, John Claypole, led the opposition to the tax, and he found such a following that the House decided against the tax by a majority of thirty-six. Cromwell had to bow to Parliament's will thus expressed. Deprived of the means of paying his Major-Generals, he had to allow the system to fall into desuetude.

Outside Parliament signs of threats to the State's stability were becoming increasingly pronounced. Several plots against the Protector's life were discovered. Some of these were hatched by religious fanatics who regarded Cromwell as an apostate. Others were the result of Charles II's offer, made in 1654, of a knighthood and £500 a year to anyone who slew Cromwell. If one of the plots should succeed no one could predict with any certainty what might result from the ensuing chaos: the Army might be able to fasten its hold on the governmental machine, or the Stuarts might be restored. None of Cromwell's subordinates enjoyed a prestige so outstanding as to win general recognition as his successor. The Republic's safety was bound up with the personal safety of the Protector. Even apart from the threat of violence, in the course of nature Cromwell's death could not be long delayed. He was fifty-eight years of age; for many years he had had a wearing life, and his physical powers were known to be declining. To avoid the uncertainties which his death, whether natural or violent, must entail, there was only one course: a form of government must be instituted whereby the succession to the headship of the State would follow a fixed order. Such a form, whatever its name, would differ little from a monarchy. It was to this solution that Englishmen were turning in increasing numbers.

The first move in Parliament to this end was made on February 23, 1657, when Sir Christopher Pack introduced an "address and remonstrance" urging changes in the constitution including one that Cromwell should take the title of king. Throughout March the Commons debated the clauses of the remonstrance which received support from moderate men of various political views. Extremists like the Fifth Monarchy Men fought against it desperately. But the weightiest opposition came from the Army, particularly from the highest ranks of officers who did their utmost, during long conferences, to dissuade Cromwell from taking the kingship. Cromwell refused to bind himself to reject a proposed constitution which had not yet been cast into final shape or been submitted to his consideration.

The final draft of what was called the Humble Petition and Advice was presented to the Protector on March 31, 1657. For several weeks he continued to debate its provisions with a Committee of the Commons, with his officers, and with himself. At last, on May 8, he announced his decision not to accept the title of king. The petition therefore was amended in this respect, and in some others, and was accepted by Cromwell in its final form on May 25. It petitioned Cromwell to designate his successor as Protector, to call future Parliaments of two

Houses, and to nominate members of the "other House" in number not more than seventy and not less than forty. It further declared Parliament's intention to settle a yearly revenue of £1,300,000 of which £1,000,000 was to be for the support of the Navy and the Army and £300,000 for the support of the Government.

On June 26 Cromwell was a second time installed as Protector in Westminster Hall. The ceremony was carried through with great pomp and pageantry. Indeed, the only outward difference between the installation and a royal coronation was the absence of a crown and an anointing. The monarchy had returned in all but name.

Immediately after the Protector's second inauguration Parliament was adjourned until January 20, 1658, when it met for its second session. One of the Government's chief items of business during the interval was the nomination of Members of the "other House." Sixty-three persons were nominated but only two-thirds of this number ever took their seats. Of the absent one-third, a few were doubtless prevented from attending by genuine reasons of duty, but the majority of them merely refused to be associated with the new order. Seven of the nominees were members of the Cromwell family, and seventeen were senior officers of the Army. It was upon these two groups that Cromwell would mostly rely, and these twenty-four would form a majority of the forty-two sitting Members.

In several respects the Government would be weaker under the new constitution than under the previous one. First, the composition of the second House conveyed the impression that, though there appeared to be something like a limited monarchy, in reality the nation was still at the mercy of the Army. Second, some thirty of the Members of the second House had previously been supporters of the Government in the Commons: in itself this transfer was natural, but the result seriously weakened the Government in the Commons. Third, the republican Members of the Commons, whom the Council had been able to exclude under the terms of the Instrument, now returned to their places: the Humble Petition did not empower anyone in the State to impose tests on elected Members of the Commons. Fourth, in neither House could the Government enlist the presence of members of the older nobility: hence, one of the State's traditional bulwarks had no place in the new regime. These conditions constituted for the new Protectorate a state of unstable equilibrium. It was only a question of circumstances and time as to just how and when another revolution would begin.

The ineffectiveness of both Houses was soon shown by their quarrels. The Commons in particular spent valuable time in debating whether the second House should be called the "other House" (which would imply the limitation of its powers specifically to those defined in the Humble Petition), or the "House of Lords" (which might lead to its assumption of the powers of the former House of that name). Even Cromwell's appeal for progress with State business—in particular for voting the pay of the Army—was of no avail. News reached Cromwell that on February 4, certain elements of the Commons were to present a petition for the restoration of the Long Parliament. That very morning, therefore, he went down to Parliament and, without any warning, dissolved both Houses. "And," said he, "let God be judge between you and me."

Cromwell was to find, as his two Stuart predecessors had found, that to dismiss a refractory Parliament was to intensify rather than to solve political problems, in particular the problem of money. The total revenue of £1,300,000 was little more than the Government's current expenses. Even the additional £600,000 which the Parliament had reluctantly granted left an annual deficit of about £500,000. This, added to the accumulated debt of £1,000,000, might well produce, in the course of a year or two, a serious situation. For the Commonwealth's advisers showed no genius in handling national finance. The only solutions that they saw were either to reduce expenditure or to secure an increase in Parliament's grants. As the Navy and Army absorbed £2,000,000, while the civil Government cost only £300,000, the only way to make a substantial saving was to reduce drastically the armed forces. Yet the combination of continued disaffection at home and of dangers abroad would make this a risky proceeding. Nevertheless so widespread was the fear of financial collapse that the Council was beginning to favour the calling of another Parliament to deal with the situation.

A new Parliament, freely elected, would almost certainly raise a further problem: it would represent the increasing demand for a full monarchy. Cromwell would therefore have to make up his mind afresh what answer he would give to a petition that he would assume the title of king.

Meanwhile he was having to face his own personal problems and losses. On August 6 his favourite daughter, Elizabeth, wife of John Claypole, died. Her last illness was distressingly painful, and, even to the neglect of State business, Cromwell spent much time at her bedside. Her death was a blow from which he never recovered. Already fast ageing, almost immediately after her funeral he began to break up completely. On August 20 he fell ill of an ague or fever. Now and again he rallied, but from the first there was little hope of a recovery. On September 3 the great Protector died. It was the anniversary of Dunbar and Worcester, and the day which for several years he had kept as a day of thanksgiving. Doubtless, had he been in a condition to consider it, he would have greeted his final release as the truly "crowning mercy" of his life, and as coming with peculiar appropriateness on his thanksgiving day.

No individual in English history has been the subject of more violently various opinions, both of his own and succeeding generations, than has Oliver Cromwell. This very diversity of view should be proof enough of his greatness. Men do not continue to debate the merits and demerits of a nonentity three centuries after his death. Cromwell may be esteemed either as pernicious or as beneficent, but he cannot be ignored. Perhaps the reason for the diversity of views about him is that he was an ordinary man, though cast in a large mould, called to deal with an extraordinary situation. His human frailties, like the wart upon his face, were plain for every one to see; and he himself, natural and unartificial, was the last man to try to hide them.

That Cromwell was no plaster saint but a full-blooded man meant that he was not faultless. But his faults were not vicious or positive: they were the reverse side of his characteristic virtues. His impatience with Parliaments, for example, was due to the clearness with which he saw to the heart of the nation's problems. Such intuitively clear-sighted men do not commonly suffer fools gladly. Similarly his severity in Ireland, though cruel and deplorable in itself, was a measure of his conviction of the peril in which England and Protestantism stood. It was precisely because he was a real and fully human person, not a flat lifeless figure, that he gives a different impression according to the angle from which he is viewed. The judgements that we pass upon him—as upon Shakespeare or Beethoven or any of the immortals—are in large measure a reflection of the quality of mind that we bring to bear upon him.

The charge most commonly brought against Cromwell has been that of personal ambition. Any man who, in any sphere of life, lifts himself above what might be considered his normal level, is likely to be regarded as ambitious. But in Cromwell the charge will not hold. Ambition implies a set purpose of self-advancement and, when the summit has been reached, a determination to stay there no matter what the cost to others. Neither of these implications held good of Cromwell. There is no evidence that he set out to achieve a high place for himself. Rather he went forward one step at a time, doing the thing that next needed to be done, and in the process his own character and abilities were so developed that the day came when he had to shoulder the highest responsibility of all. He himself once expressed the position perfectly: "No one," said he, "goes so far as he that knows not whither he is going." Moreover, no sooner was absolute political power, based upon military supremacy, within his grasp, than he set about hedging that power with limitations, and curbing the Army on which his authority rested. This was the real explanation of the successive Parliaments of various types during his period of rule. Notwithstanding his lack of Parliamentary gifts and his impatience with Parliamentary methods, he never denied the principle that Parliament alone is the source of law, especially in matters of finance. In the end, all his experiments with other types of parliaments having failed, he accepted a dual-chamber Parliament almost identical in powers with the Long Parliament which he had helped to overthrow. This was not the work of an ambitious ruler.

The first essential to a just judgement of Cromwell, both personal and political, is to see him against the background of his own age. For example, his constantly repeated asseverations of God's favour and guidance strike harshly upon a modern ear; but they were contemporary Puritanism's normal, sincere forms of expression, and not normally signs of hypocrisy, conscious or unconscious.

Perhaps the proper test to apply is not what we think of Cromwell at a distance of three centuries but what the men and women of his own generation thought of him. By this test he must be recognized one of the greatest—perhaps *the* greatest—of Englishmen of all time. He had his critics then as now, and his active supporters were a minority of the nation, but no party ever challenged his supremacy. He was forty-three years of age when he first went into battle, yet he rose to supreme command by sheer force of character combined with some native ability; and when Charles I's rule ended, Cromwell stepped into the position of chief magistrate because, by those same qualities, he stood beyond challenge above his fellows. Abroad he made a similar impression. The greatest princes of the day acknowledged the government of the regicide and sought his alliance. In that sense his enemy, Clarendon, was right: "His greatness at home was but a shadow of his glory abroad."

It is true that the Commonwealth Government in effect disappeared with Oliver, that the Stuarts against whom he had fought were restored, and that the ordinances and Acts of his Parliaments were abolished. In this sense his work was a failure. But this is only a superficial sense. Cromwell would have been among the last to claim that the Protectorate was an ideal form of government or that it ought to be permanent. He was called to it after the nation had been torn by a decade of civil strife, and his first duty was to restore order and security, not to establish an ideal or permanent form of government. Judged by that standard, his rule was outstandingly successful. Though the Protectorate bears the marks of political strain and instability, the ordinary citizen enjoyed a quiet prosperity greater than ordinary citizens had known at least since the supposedly halcyon days of Queen Elizabeth. And though Oliver's death was followed before long by the restoration of the Stuarts, Charles II and James II did not come back to the monarchy of their father, Charles I. Monarchy reappeared, but it was not the former monarchy in which the King ruled with Parliament as a more or less consenting party. It was a new monarchy in which the King could rule only through Parliament. The proof of the change in regime was that when James II tried to rule by the methods of Charles I he lost his throne. The political triumph of Oliver is to be seen in the fact that James II was succeeded by William III whose powers were defined by Acts of Parliament—the Bill of Rights and, later, the Act of Settlement—and who therefore could not, even if he would, claim to rule by Divine Right. Oliver's true successor was William III for, as the first constitutional King in English history, he was the embodiment of Cromwell's ideal of government.

Even more notable than Cromwell's contribution to future political development was his contribution to religious development. In an intolerant age Cromwell displayed an unprecedented spirit of toleration. Though there were strict limits to the scope of his toleration—it did not reach to Papists or Prelatists—what was chiefly remarkable was that he displayed it at all. But for the opposition of his Parliaments, his toleration would have been wider and more thorough-going. Even his exception of Roman Catholics and Anglicans from toleration was probably due to political considerations at least as much as to religious prejudice: the interests of both were closely bound up with the Stuart cause. One effect of Cromwell's rule was that various dissenting sects had time to establish themselves before Anglicanism was restored under the later Stuarts. Thus the principle of toleration outside the State Church was gradually maintained. These sects, also, were the forerunners of the later Nonconformists from whom have sprung many of the reforming pioneers—political and social as well as religious—of later centuries.

To the men of his own generation, Cromwell may have seemed a failure. Succeeding generations should realize that in politics and in religion alike he had built more truly than even he himself knew.

The supreme proof of Cromwell's greatness is that, almost alone among the dictators of history, he did not suffer deterioration in personal character through his possession of power. No sooner did circumstances put power into his hands than he did his best progressively to divest himself of it, and the power that remained to him he used not to satisfy selfish ambition but as a responsibility entrusted to him in the service of his subjects.

4. Richard Cromwell and the End of the Protectorate

Events following Oliver's death revealed both the strength and the weakness of his government. That his elder son, Richard, succeeded without opposition to the Protectorate for no other reason than that Oliver had named him as his heir, and in spite of having few personal qualifications for the position, was proof of the enormous personal prestige that Oliver exercised in the nation. But the serious divisions in the State, soon after Richard's accession, showed that even Oliver's government had not been exempt from the weakness in all systems of personal government—namely, that when one man is the pivot of a system his removal necessarily involves the system's collapse. Had Oliver been succeeded by a son of a different calibre from Richard's—possibly by the younger surviving son, Henry, the Lord Deputy of Ireland—events might have taken a different turn. Richard had no influence with either of the sections from whom his father had derived his most active support—namely, the Army and the 'Saints.'

Richard had been barely sixteen years of age when the Civil War broke out in 1642, and he took no active part in it. His preference was for a quiet, country life; and after his marriage in May 1649 he settled down as a country gentleman at Hursley, Hampshire, in the home of his father-in-law, Richard Major. Though the death of his brother Oliver, in 1644, left Richard as his father's heir, Richard continued to live in much the same manner as before. His father's accession to the Protectorship brought Richard into greater prominence, and he was one of the Protector's family to be nominated to the "other House" set up in 1658. None the less, it was clear to all that such publicity was due to his being the Protector's son, and not to his desires or qualifications. In particular, his lack of soldierly enthusiasm, and the fact that he had not shared the hardships and perils of the Civil War, prevented him from inheriting his father's influence over the Army.

Scarcely less of a handicap was his lack of religious enthusiasm. Though various Puritan elements and sects from time to time had quarrelled with Oliver, and a few had regarded him as apostate, they had always recognized that at least his roots and theirs were in common soil. Richard had little or nothing in common with them. He was a plain, straightforward man who showed little evidence of personal religious convictions. In the course of conversation he once turned to Colonel Ingoldsby, who was one of the group around him, and declared: "Go thy way, Dick Ingoldsby, thou canst neither preach nor pray, but I will believe thee before I will believe twenty of them." This may have been an accurate reflection of Richard's experience, but it was hardly likely to commend him to the Puritans.

Richard's first difficulties were with the Army. The officers held weekly meetings at Fleetwood's residence, Wallingford House, and there they shaped a set of demands the granting of which was to be the condition on which the Army would support the new Protector: the Protector was to cease to command the Army; Fleetwood was to be Commander-in-Chief; and no officer was to be cashiered except by court-martial. In effect, the Army would become a self-governing body, and its commander would be at least as powerful as the Protector.

To counteract the Army, Richard summoned a Parliament which met on January 27, 1659. He had not miscalculated: the majority of the Commons' Members were moderate-minded Presbyterians who had little love for the Independent Army. Unfortunately for Richard, his Parliament repeated the mistakes of most of its Commonwealth predecessors. No attempt was made to raise the money necessary to discharge the considerable arrears of pay due to the Army, and the Parliament adopted a fractious tone which embittered relations which already were strained.

Early in April a large number of officers met at Wallingford

8*

House and drew up another petition. This included the demands that the Army's arrears should be paid and that freedom of worship should be re-assured. When Richard received this petition he sent it to the Speaker. The Commons replied by voting that there should be no meetings of officers in the future except by permission of the Protector and of both Houses of Parliament. Then, on April 19, Richard went to Wallingford House and dissolved the officers' meeting. Thus the crisis of the struggle of Army versus Parliament was reached. Had Richard arrested the Army chiefs he might even yet have established himself, but this he shrank from doing. Fleetwood, when summoned to Whitehall on April 21, refused to obey. Instead, he ordered the Army in London to assemble at St James'. The Army's obedience to this summons showed that the Protector was powerless. The officers then demanded the dissolution of Parliament. Until late at night Richard resisted their demand, well knowing that to accede to it would be the end of the Protectorate. But at last he could hold out no longer; and on April 22 Parliament was declared dissolved. From that date Richard ceased to have even the semblance of power though he remained the nominal head of the State for another fortnight.

The Army had now to decide what form of government it would support. Its intention had been that Richard should remain Protector, but its republican allies would not countenance any form of Protectorate. In its place they demanded the restoration of the Commonwealth without any titular head. In order to satisfy this demand, the Army agreed to the return of the Rump Parliament. On May 7 Speaker Lenthall, now an old man, presided over forty-two members. Shortly afterwards Richard left Whitehall and retired to Hursley. Twelve months later, fearing for his personal safety, he left England and did not return for twenty years. After his return he continued to live quietly in the country until his death, in 1712.

Richard's fall was followed by a marked increase in Royalist activity. Charles and a few personal followers gathered secretly at Calais ready to cross the Channel when circumstances should be favourable. Gradually plans took shape for Royalist risings in England. August 1, 1659, was the day fixed, but the actual outbreaks proved to be few and scattered. The most serious, led by Sir George Booth in Cheshire, was routed by Lambert, and the others then died out.

The Army now felt safe in pressing its claims against Parliament. Bitter squabbles between Parliament and the Army came to a climax on October 13 when Lambert surrounded the Commons' House with soldiers and prevented Members from entering. Thus for a second time the Rump was expelled.

Once again the political pendulum began to swing: no sooner had the Army unseated its rival than a reaction set in against the Army. This reaction among most classes of the nation was strengthened by the support of certain sections even of the Army, in particular of Monk and his army in Scotland.

The geographical separation of Monk's troops from the rest of the Army had led them to feel that they were too often neglected, especially in the matter of promotion. Hence they were more prone to discontent than were their fellows. Monk had carefully preserved the soldier's correct attitude of obedience to recognized authority, and he had served in succession King, Long Parliament, two Protectors, and restored Parliament. Now, for the first time, he took an independent line. To the Speaker he sent an assurance of loyalty to Parliament; and to his Commander-in-Chief he sent a protest against the officers' usurpation of power. From among his own troops he systematically purged all disaffected elements, both officers and men, and thus welded together an army upon which he could thoroughly rely. What were Monk's intentions for the future no one knew, nor has anyone since discovered. Whether he was impelled by ambition or by genuine patriotism, or by a mixture of both, remains an inscrutable mystery. Possibly Monk himself had no very clear idea of a consistent course or even of a goal. Whatever his motives or his plans, he left no doubt as to his immediate attitude: when the Wallingford House party sent a representative to make contact with him Monk had the officer confined to prison.

This attitude encouraged widespread opposition to the Army's rule among the civil population. Even Fleetwood and the others could not be blind to the instability of their position;

and on December 26 they once more restored the Rump Parliament.

When news of this restoration reached Monk he judged that the moment had arrived for a definite move in support of Parliament. On January 2, 1660, he crossed the Tweed into England. The Army under Lambert, who had been sent to the north to negotiate with, and check, Monk, had no enthusiasm for their task and melted away. Monk had prepared for his advance by planning a rising of the northern gentry, headed by Fairfax, in the Parliament's interest. Fairfax had seized York, and Monk advanced thence unopposed towards London. Throughout the march he received petitions that the full Long Parliament might be restored and that a new Parliament might be freely elected. Still Monk preserved complete silence about his own intentions. Almost certainly he was waiting on events to show which policy to adopt. On February 3 he entered London.

Once there, he soon formed the opinion that the Rump was as selfish and as autocratic as the Army. He therefore adopted a new and definite policy. He addressed to the Rump a letter demanding that writs be forthwith issued to fill up vacancies in the House and that Parliament should be shortly dissolved. News of this move caused an immediate outburst of public rejoicing in the City—illuminations, bonfires, and, not the least significant of all, the roasting of rumps of beef. At one stride Monk and his soldiers had become the heroes of the nation.

Finally Monk summoned the excluded Members to meet him and obtained their written promise that, if restored, they would satisfy the Army's arrears of pay, issue writs for a new Parliament, and dissolve themselves at an early date. On February 21 these Members were allowed to resume their seats, and thus the full Long Parliament was in session once more for the first time since Pride's Purge of December 1648. The Parliament honoured its promises. It named Monk Commander-in-Chief, fixed April 25 as the date for the meeting of a new Parliament, and dissolved itself on March 16.

By this time events had convinced Monk that the restoration of the Stuarts was the only solution of the nation's problems. He therefore sent to Charles to urge that the King should promise a general oblivion of all offences, confirm land-sales effected during the Civil War, undertake that the Army's arrears should be paid, and grant liberty of conscience. These recommendations reveal an astute political sense, for they were likely to satisfy those sections of the community most likely to have doubts how they would be affected by the Stuarts' return —namely, the prominent Parliamentarians (both civil and military), the purchasers of Royalists' lands, the Army, and the Puritans.

Charles was wise enough to accept Monk's suggestions which were included in the declaration which Charles issued on April 4 from Breda where he was waiting ready to take the next step that events might indicate. There was, however, one important difference between Monk's suggestions and the declaration—namely, that to the terms as expressed by Monk Charles had added a proviso in each clause that he would be guided by the will of Parliament. This addition was due to the advice of Hyde, who, having shared Charles' exile, was acting now as his Lord Chancellor. Hyde was convinced that a freely elected Parliament would be strongly Royalist and therefore almost certainly would make exceptions in the King's favour to at least some of the terms of the declaration. Thus, while the references to Parliament's will were likely to make a favourable impression upon the English people, in practice they were calculated to provide the King with the means to avoid keeping the spirit of his promises while observing their letter. It was an accurate foretaste of the reign that was about to open.

The new Parliament assembled on April 25. Technically it was not a Parliament since it had not been summoned by a King, and it accordingly was known as the Convention. Under the terms governing its election, Royalists had been allowed to vote, and the Convention was strongly Royalist in tone. Monk sent copies of the declaration to both Houses. The Lords promptly voted that "according to the ancient and fundamental laws of this Kingdom, the government is and ought to be, by King, Lords, and Commons." The Commons at once concurred in this declaration. On May 8 Charles was publicly proclaimed

King, and commissioners were sent to inform him of the proclamation, and to invite him to return to England.

On May 25 Charles landed at Dover where Monk awaited him. Thence he advanced by stages to London which he entered on his birthday, May 29, the day which was to become known as Royal Oak Day, in commemoration of his famous 'hide' in the Boscobel Oak during his wanderings after the Battle of Worcester. London received the King rapturously. The houses were festooned with garlands and tapestries. Every window and balcony along the route was thronged with spectators. The fountains spouted wine. The crowds went mad with excitement. In the midst of it all Charles is reported to have remarked characteristically that he did not know why he had not returned before. At Whitehall the Lords and Commons assembled to meet him in the great room from which his father had stepped to his execution.

by his duplicity and his vacillation. In Charles II duplicity and vacillation showed themselves in no less a degree: that they did not bring him also to ruin was due to his nimbler wits and his refusal to be tied by principles, whether political or otherwise. Least of all would he allow himself to be tied to the English Church. Perhaps it was in this respect that his mother's influence showed itself. Whether or not Charles II had any sincere religious convictions has never been proved, and perhaps is incapable of proof; nor is it possible to be certain about the sincerity of his death-bed profession of Roman Catholicism. But throughout his reign he appears to have been a genuine supporter of toleration and to have tried to modify the harshness of the laws against Nonconformists, including those against Roman Catholics.

Second only to the King as a factor in the restored Stuart regime was Edward Hyde. His earlier career we have already followed, including the transference of his support from the opposition to the King after the Grand Remonstrance of 1641. In 1646 he went into exile with the then Prince of Wales whose chief adviser he became and whose sufferings and wanderings he shared. In 1658 Charles appointed him Lord Chancellor, an appointment which became effective on the Restoration. In November 1660 he was created Lord Hyde, and in the next year was raised to be Earl of Clarendon. For the sake of convenience we shall refer to him henceforward by this latter title.

In most respects Clarendon's character was in sharp contrast to the King's. He was twenty-one years older than Charles, and therefore was more firmly established in his views, and less amenable to new influences. But such firmness was due to more than age: unlike the King, Clarendon was strongly attached to certain principles, the same as those he had advocated in the Long Parliament. Politically he stood not for an absolute monarchy but for the working together of the various elements in the government—notably of King and Parliament —in accordance with historical precedent, for the nation's welfare. The extravagant claims to absolutism, whether by Monarch or Parliament, he regarded as equally a departure from the true and normal line of English government. The guiding principle of his ministry thus was, in both Church and

State, to restore what he regarded as the traditional English government based upon the rule of law to which all alike—monarch and peasant—were subject.

The two Secretaries of State at the beginning of the reign were Sir Edward Nicholas and Sir William Morice. Monk was raised to the peerage as Duke of Albemarle. Another man who was to become a prominent—perhaps the most prominent—politician of Charles II's reign was Sir Anthony Ashley Cooper. Created Lord Ashley in 1661, he was Chancellor of the Exchequer during the period 1661–72, and in the latter year was promoted to be Earl of Shaftesbury. Edward Montagu, the admiral who had led the Navy in allegiance to Charles, was rewarded with the title of Earl of Sandwich. The Earl of Southampton, one of the staunchest of the Stuarts' supporters, was given the Lord Treasurership. These men together (except Sandwich) formed the Committee of Foreign Affairs, a sort of inner ring of royal counsellors to whom some historians look as the nucleus from which the Cabinet in due course developed.

As soon as the new Government could get down to work, it found four main problems awaiting settlement—namely, those relating to the regicides, land, finance, and religion.

The term 'regicides' was properly applied to those who had composed the court that tried Charles I. Soon after Charles II returned to England he issued a proclamation calling upon Charles I's judges to give themselves up within fourteen days. Nineteen obeyed the summons. During the following weeks there were long debates in the Convention on the interpretation of the amnesty promised in the Declaration of Breda. Charles, backed by Clarendon, exercised his influence on the side of moderation. On July 27 Charles reminded the Lords of his promises made at Breda "which," said he, "if I had not made, I am persuaded, neither I nor you had been here." The upshot of the debates was the Act of Indemnity and Oblivion of August 29. By its terms, the nineteen regicides who had surrendered were exempted from the indemnity but they were not to be executed unless a special Act was passed to that effect. Four non-regicides, including Lambert and Vane, were also exempted from the indemnity, but both Houses petitioned that their lives should be spared. Nineteen other regicides who had fled abroad were attainted. Following this Act, ten persons were immediately executed; three more were seized at Delft two years later, at which time Vane also was tried and executed in spite of the King's acceptance of the Act of Indemnity which asked for Vane's exemption. On January 30, 1661—the anniversary of Charles I's execution—the bodies of Cromwell, Ireton, and Bradshaw were hanged at Tyburn and there buried.

Even more knotty than the problem of the regicides was that of the Royalists' lands. Early in the Civil War some Royalists had sold parts or the whole of their estates in order to put the proceeds into the King's coffers. Others, as the Civil War had proceeded, had been compelled to sell—and therefore had realized only low prices—either under pressure from the Parliamentarians or so as to raise money to pay taxes extorted from them. The Royalists in general not unnaturally expected that the restoration of the King would bring the restoration also of their lands. But the problem was not so simple as that. Land that had changed hands by ordinary legal process belonged, in the eyes of the law, to the person indicated on the deeds, irrespective of the price paid for it. If these deeds were to become invalid the security of all legal deeds would be jeopardized. Moreover, in some instances, estates bought from Royalists had been broken up; in others, the land had changed hands, perhaps several times. To evict all the new owners, who had paid for their land in good faith, would be to turn them into enemies of the new Government. Whatever the solution adopted of so complex a problem, injustice to certain groups would be unavoidable. The Convention—not a few of whose Members possessed property in dispute—finally settled that Crown lands, and lands confiscated from private owners, should be restored; but that all property-sales in due legal form should hold good. It is impossible to see what other course could have been adopted unless the Government had granted monetary compensation to injured Royalists. Apart from the practical difficulties of administering such compensation, the Government had no means of raising the vast amount necessary to finance it. Nevertheless the Royalists were bitterly disappointed, and this was one source of the growing discontent which showed itself as the reign proceeded.

One of the subjects of perennial dispute between Charles I and his Parliaments had been finance. This was at least partly due to the inadequacy of, and lack of system in, the King's income. Unless the royal exchequer was put upon a sound basis, a recurrence of disputes was inevitable. Charles II's finances were embarrassed at the outset by debts remaining from his father, and by the debts which he himself had contracted during his exile (amounting to £3,000,000), as well as by the need to raise money to pay off the standing Army.

Charles I's annual income from all sources was calculated to have been £900,000. This sum had never been enough to meet his expenses, and Charles II's expenses were likely to be greater rather than less. The Convention therefore agreed upon £1,200,000 as a reasonable income, and it granted to the King for life certain stipulated sources of income which, together with revenue from Crown lands, were expected to yield this total. The opportunity was taken to remove one financial anomaly—namely, the King's right to profit from wardships and certain other customary dues which were survivals from feudalism.

Though the Convention acted in all good faith in thus settling the King's income, a short time was to be enough to show that it had by no means solved all his financial problems. Three matters it had been unable to deal with. First, there was the lack of understanding of financial principles even by exchequer officials; they were incapable of estimating accurately how much money a particular operation would require, or even how much a particular tax would yield (for example, whereas the customs were expected to yield £400,000 annually, their average for the first seven years of Charles II's reign was only £285,000). Second, Charles II was incorrigibly extravagant, spending lavishly on mistresses and favourites almost without regard for the national balance-sheet. Third, corruption was rampant and was taken for granted in every office in the State: while this condition remained, financial health was impossible.

The one measure of economy undertaken was the disbanding of the Army. Enough money was raised to pay off the regiments one by one, and very shortly England would have been without an army but for an outbreak of disorder in London early in 1661. The Government, thus provided with a practical demonstration of the danger of being left without armed forces to meet an emergency, retained Monk's regiment of foot (the Coldstream Guards) and one troop of horse. This was the nucleus around which the British Army of later years was to grow.

The Convention was dissolved on December 29, 1660. New elections were held during April of the following year, and the first Parliament of the reign met on May 8, 1661. In one significant respect its composition differed from that of the Convention: the previous large Presbyterian element had been greatly reduced and had been replaced by a body of ardent Cavaliers. It was this Parliament—fitly known as the Cavalier Parliament—which made the ecclesiastical and constitutional settlement of the restored Stuarts.

As a result of the Commonwealth, at least two thousand benefices were occupied by Presbyterians and some four hundred by Independents. These together included more than one-quarter of the benefices of the Church. The first proposed settlement of this situation was a scheme of comprehension whereby Presbyterians should accept some form of Episcopacy and that bishops should accept the assistance of presbyters. A Conference met at the lodgings of Sheldon, Bishop of London, in the Savoy, to settle the details of this scheme. But the Savoy Conference achieved nothing, partly because the Presbyterian leaders showed singular tactlessness in negotiations, and partly because it soon became clear that no scheme of comprehension had any chance of being accepted by the Cavalier Parliament or by the majority of the nation.

The religious settlement which Parliament finally accepted acquired the name of Clarendon Code because it consisted of a series of four Acts passed during Clarendon's Chancellorship. In one respect at least the name is misleading: the four Acts were not planned as a whole but were introduced successively —the first in 1661 and the last in 1665—as circumstances suggested; and hence they were not properly a 'code.'

To what extent Clarendon was personally responsible for them will become more apparent as the story of them is followed.

The first item of the so-called code was the Corporation Act,[1] passed in December 1661. Its most important clause stipulated that every member of a municipal corporation should receive the sacrament according to Church of England rites. This provision would affect the composition not only of the corporations but also of the House of Commons since in many boroughs the members of the corporation alone had Parliamentary votes.

Because the Savoy Conference had broken up without reaching agreement on a form of belief or of church-practice, the revision of the Prayer Book was left to Convocation. Effect was given to the resulting liturgy by the Act of Uniformity[2] of May 1662 enacting that the Prayer Book must be used in every place of worship, that all incumbents of livings must be ordained by a bishop, and that all incumbents, as well as all university teachers and all schoolmasters, must declare their acceptance of the Prayer Book. This Act came into force on St Bartholomew's Day (August 24) 1662. When that day arrived some 1200 clergy left their livings and their homes rather than submit to a regime contrary to their conscience. Whether their views were right or wrong is a matter for individual judgement. What is beyond dispute is that men of their quality of character could ill be spared by any church. However great the temporary gain in authority, the loss in independence of thought and in moral calibre would be permanent. Henceforward the line between Anglicans and Nonconformists was clearer than ever before.

The immediately pressing problem for the 1200 seceders was how to earn livelihoods to support themselves and their families. The method most natural to them, that of teaching, was closed by the Act of Uniformity. In some instances many parishioners left the Church and formed a separate congregation supporting its former clergyman as its minister. Such a proceeding undermined the influence of the new clergyman in

---

[1] Robertson, pp. 34–37.   [2] Robertson, pp. 37–53.

the parish and went far to defeat the objects of the Uniformity Act. Consequently in May 1664 a new measure, the Conventicle Act,[1] was passed forbidding attendance at conventicles. For the purposes of the Act, a conventicle was defined as a meeting for worship, not in accordance with the Church of England ritual, at which five or more persons were present in addition to the members of one family.

In the next year London was visited by the Great Plague. During its ravages many Nonconformist ministers continued to shepherd their former flocks, and, in some instances, to hold services in their former churches from which the new incumbent had fled. The widespread respect evoked by such self-sacrificing devotion was regarded by the Cavalier Parliament as so dangerous that in October 1665 the Five Mile Act[2] was passed. It forbade nonconforming ministers to approach within five miles of any corporate town or of any place in which they had formerly ministered.

These Acts were flagrant breaches of the spirit, if not of the letter, of the liberty to tender consciences promised by the Declaration of Breda. They were base rewards of the Presbyterians without whose co-operation the Restoration would have been impossible. Whatever justification the Church may have had for insisting upon at least a minimum of uniformity in belief and practice among its clergy, it had none for persecuting those of its clergy who, unable conscientiously to accept those standards, left the ranks of the Church. The persecution was an ill omen for independence of thought in England, and for religious and mental health within the Church itself.

One further fact connected with the Code needs special emphasis—namely, that the responsibility for it rested primarily not with Charles or with Clarendon but with the Cavalier Parliament. Both King and Minister used every effort to restrain the Parliament from extreme, persecuting measures. A revealing example of Charles' policy was afforded by his action after the passing of the Act of Uniformity. On December 26, 1662—that is, during a Parliamentary recess—Charles

---

[1] Robertson, pp. 67–70.   [2] Robertson, pp. 70–74.

issued a proclamation stating that in spite of the Act he intended to honour his Breda promise to give toleration to tender consciences and that a Bill to that effect would be laid before Parliament. But when the Commons met again in February 1663 they presented to the King a demand that the Act of Uniformity should be rigidly enforced; and as Charles was dependent upon Parliament for supplies of money, he had no option but to comply. The Commons rightly judged that one of Charles' motives for toleration was his partiality for Roman Catholics, if not for Roman Catholicism. It was much to Charles' credit that he never forgot the self-sacrificing services rendered to him after the Battle of Worcester by Roman Catholics in various parts of England, and that he did his best to bring to them some amends. Clarendon's attitude was less tolerant than Charles': it can perhaps be described as midway between the Parliament's persecution and the King's indulgence. As a staunch adherent of the English Church, he refused to support the King's moves towards toleration for Roman Catholics; but he wished to include some modifying clauses in the Act of Uniformity.

Charles' partiality for Roman Catholics showed itself in his foreign not less than in his domestic policy. That is to say, he leant towards France rather than towards Holland. By this time French power was overshadowing all western Europe. By the Treaty of Westphalia (1648) at the close of the Thirty Years' War, France had acquired Alsace and the Bishoprics of Verdun, Metz, and Toul, thus having footholds on the rivers Rhine, Meuse, and Moselle. The Treaty of the Pyrenees (1659), which closed the Franco-Spanish War, gave to France the Province of Artois and a number of frontier towns in the Spanish Netherlands as well as the Province of Roussillon which commanded the road from France into Spain to the east of the Pyrenees. These acquisitions would be stepping-off places towards yet greater conquests. Louis XIV's aim was for what France called her "natural frontiers," which she interpreted as being the Rhine, the Alps, the Pyrenees, and the sea. The pursuit of these objects would involve France in clashes with the Empire, Spain, and the United Provinces. The United

Provinces were especially alarmed at the implied threat to their independence.

England's policy might well prove to be the decisive factor in the issue of these conflicting European politics. But at the opening of Charles II's reign that policy was far from certain. On the one hand, religious convictions made the majority of English people sympathetic towards the Dutch. On the other hand, English and Dutch were trade rivals, and Charles was personally attached to France, under his cousin Louis XIV, more than to the United Provinces which had excluded his brother-in-law, William of Orange, from the Stadtholderate. This sympathy of Charles II towards France was reinforced by Clarendon who, true to Elizabethan tradition, regarded an alliance with France against Spain as the pivot of English foreign policy.

The first evidence of this policy was the marriage of Charles II's youngest and favourite sister, Henrietta, to the Duke of Orleans, brother to Louis XIV, in 1661. Between that event and her death, in 1670, Henrietta played a decisive part in bringing her native and her adopted countries into a close alliance.

Two events of 1662 marked a further stage in Anglo-French collaboration. In May Charles married Catherine of Braganza, sister of King Alfonso VI of Portugal. Catherine's dowry consisted of Bombay and Tangier, and of more than £800,000 in cash. These items had attractive advantages: Bombay would please the merchant class; Tangier would be a valuable base in the Mediterranean; the money would relieve the King's financial embarrassments; and the marriage itself would please Louis XIV, whose policy included the strengthening of Portugal against Spain.

The occupation of Tangier indirectly effected a further change in English possessions. Valuable though Tangier was as a naval base, the annual cost of maintaining its garrison and fortifications would be substantial. Charles realized that to maintain both Tangier and Dunkirk would be financially impossible. Of the two he valued Tangier much the more highly, and rightly so. Cromwell's motive in acquiring Dunkirk had been to use it as a base of military operations in Europe. Even in Cromwell's time such a policy was unwise; for Charles II, who had almost no army, it would be impossible. Hence the £100,000, which Dunkirk cost the exchequer annually, was a waste. Moreover, now that Charles II had entered the orbit of Louis XIV's diplomacy, and Spain was no longer a first-rate Power, there was no need to keep an outpost against France. When Louis offered £200,000 for the cession of the place Charles wisely accepted (October 1662). By so doing he rid himself of a useless expense, gained a useful capital sum, and strengthened his friendship with Louis. The English people took a different view: they classed the sale of Dunkirk with the loss of Calais. Clarendon was popularly believed to have been heavily bribed by Louis XIV—though there is no evidence to support the charge—and the populace named the new residence that Clarendon was building for himself in London as "Dunkirk House."

The growing Anglo-French friendship could have only one result—namely, war against the Dutch. But, even apart from France, English and Dutch had plenty of quarrels of their own. Trade-rivalry was still the chief source of ill-feeling. The Navigation Act of 1651, along with other Commonwealth ordinances and Acts, became void at the Restoration, but the trading interests demanded that another Act should incorporate its provisions. Hence, in 1660 a new Navigation Act[1] included the terms of the 1651 Act and added the further restrictions that imports and exports of English colonies were to be carried only in English ships, and that sugar and tobacco and certain other commodities should be exported only to England and to other English colonies. Also, English and Dutch colonists clashed in various parts of the world—in North America between the Virginian English and the New Amsterdam Dutch, in the East Indies, and in Africa.

During 1664 there were various skirmishes between English and Dutch forces. Though the two countries were at peace, ships of the Royal Navy were sent to seize Dutch settlements on the Guinea Coast (which soon afterwards were recaptured by the Dutch admiral, de Ruyter) and New Amsterdam in

[1] Robertson, pp. 3–13.

North America, the latter town being renamed New York in honour of the Lord High Admiral, the Duke of York. Such events were obviously the prelude to war which England formally declared on March 4, 1665.

The opening battle took place in June off Lowestoft where the Duke of York defeated a Dutch fleet which he could have annihilated had he followed up his victory.

The next year was less fortunate for the English. The Duke of York had left the fleet, and the Earl of Sandwich succeeded to the command. News was received of a great Dutch treasure-fleet from the east, which, making homeward by the north of Scotland, had taken shelter in the neutral Norwegian port of Bergen. Norway was then part of the Kingdom of Denmark, and the English offered to the Danish King half the spoil gained from the Dutch ships if he would allow an attack upon them. The offer was accepted, but Sandwich was too impatient to wait until the Danish authorities in Bergen had received official instructions. When, therefore, the English attacked the Dutch on August 3, 1665, they were driven off with much loss by the land-batteries. Sandwich was relieved of his command. The Danes saved themselves from Dutch retaliation by a Dutch alliance, and so England had to face an additional enemy.

In 1666 Prince Rupert and the Duke of Albemarle led the English fleet. They might have won a decisive action had not Rupert been detached with twenty ships to ward off a French squadron (Louis XIV, for reasons of his own politics, having temporarily thrown in his lot with the Dutch). As a result, Albemarle could not withstand a vast Dutch fleet which he met on June 1. Rupert arrived after Sandwich's defeat, but even their combined fleets were unequal to de Ruyter's. In July the hostile fleets met off the North Foreland where the English won a resounding victory which gave them command of the seas.

By this time the English were feeling the severe strain not only of the war at sea but also of conditions at home. During 1665 London suffered the worst visitation of the plague since the Black Death of 1348. Plague-deaths numbered nearly seventy thousand. The uncertainty of existence, and the helplessness of the victims owing to lack of medical knowledge and treatment, induced a state of panic. People who could do so left London. Those who remained lived in constant fear. London was not the only plague-stricken town; but its dense population, its impure water-supply, and its lack of even rudimentary sanitation, all combined to encourage the plague's virulence. Not until the winter did the plague moderate, and it did not die out until well into 1666.

This latter year saw yet another catastrophe fall upon the City. On Sunday, September 2, a fire broke out in a baker's shop. An easterly wind drove the flames from house to house until it was beyond all control. The City authorities proved utterly incapable of coping with it. The King alone showed either the ability or the energy to grapple with the spreading disaster. His orders were to pull down houses so as to make gaps too wide for the flames to leap. The fire then had to burn itself out within the ring thus formed, and it took five days to do so. But for this action, it is difficult to see what could have stayed the fire before it reached the natural spaces of the countryside. As it was, some thirteen thousand houses and ninety churches (including St Paul's Cathedral) were destroyed. Two-thirds of the City had ceased to exist. The problem of rebuilding was unprecedented. Only Sir Christopher Wren's genius was equal to the situation. He prepared a comprehensive scheme for the whole devastated area in which all the main roads should converge upon a new St Paul's. This magnificent plan would have involved the abandonment of previous property-boundaries and the compensation of dispossessed owners. It was this problem of property-interests which frustrated the fulfilment of Wren's vision. Instead, he had to be content with building a new St Paul's and numerous City churches.

Just as the Plague affected the nation's nerves, so the Fire affected its financial stability. Probably half the nation's wealth centred in the City. The interference with trade and revenue added to the Government's existing financial embarrassments and made the Government anxious to bring the Dutch war to an end. In 1667, so as to save expense, the English fleet was laid up at Chatham, and a boom for its protection was flung across the Medway. In June a Dutch fleet entered the Thames estuary, broke the boom, sailed into Chatham harbour, burnt four ships, and towed away the *Royal Charles* which was the largest vessel in the English fleet. The sound of the guns, heard in London, produced panic, and had the effect that the Dutch desired—namely, of hastening the peace-negotiations already begun.

A peace-treaty was signed at Breda on July 21, 1667. Its most important terms were that England gained New Amsterdam and agreed to demand the salute of the flag in an area much more restricted than formerly. The gain of New Amsterdam—that is, New York—was important because it linked English colonies in the New England states with Virginia, and because it commanded the line of the Hudson River to the St Lawrence.

The Medway raid brought an end to more than the Dutch war: it ended also the political career of Clarendon. Clarendon's influence had been declining for a long time. The root reason was his incompatibility with the tone and trend of Restoration England. He had nothing in common with any important section of the nation. The Nonconformists, both Protestant and Roman Catholic, held him responsible for the code under which they suffered. The Cavalier Royalists blamed him for the Act of Indemnity and Oblivion. The Court was incensed by his marked disapproval of the prevailing looseness of morals; and one of his most formidable enemies was the King's mistress, Lady Castlemaine. The Commons distrusted him because of his opposition to the principle of appropriation of supplies and the audit of accounts. The King resented his refusal to promote the scheme for toleration to Roman Catholics: and he resented not less Clarendon's habit of delivering homilies on royal immorality and extravagance. And the bulk of the nation was angry at the sale of Dunkirk whose proceeds, it was convinced, were going into Clarendon's pocket.

Politically, the undermining of Clarendon's position had begun soon after the Restoration. In October 1662 the King's friend, Sir Henry Bennet, had been appointed to succeed Sir Edward Nicholas as Secretary of State; and in the next year Bennet was created Lord Arlington. Of him, Clarendon was

intensely jealous. The two men were opposites. Clarendon
was a staunch upholder of the English Church and of a rigid
code of morality (both private and public), while Arlington
was strongly suspected of dealings with Rome, and he used
the royal mistresses to ingratiate himself with Charles. Arlington was the leader of a faction which set itself to overthrow
Clarendon, and associated with him were the Roman Catholic
Earl of Bristol, Lord Ashley, and the Duke of Buckingham,
who was the son of Charles I's favourite, whose wealth and
charm he inherited. Clarendon's position was further weakened
when the Treasurer, Lord Southampton, died in May 1667.
Instead of appointing another Treasurer, the King placed the
office in commission: the most influential commissioners were
Clarendon's enemies, notably Lord Ashley and Sir Thomas
Clifford.

The climax followed the appearance of the Dutch fleet in
the Medway in June. When Parliament next met, on July 25,
the clamour against the unpopular Chancellor, who was held
to be responsible for the Dutch war and its disasters (but not,
apparently, for its successes), was irresistible. Though the King
prorogued Parliament again on July 29, he dismissed Clarendon on August 30. Clarendon's enemies, however, feared his
powers of revenge. His daughter, Anne, had in 1661 married
the Duke of York, who was heir to the throne. A slight change
of circumstances might thus bring Clarendon back into favour.
To forestall this, the Commons impeached him. The charges
were insubstantial, and it is doubtful whether the Lords would
have found him guilty. To bring the crisis to an end, Charles
induced the fallen Minister to leave the country. This, very
reluctantly, he did in November 1667. For the next seven
years he lived in France, using his time to write his *History
of the Great Rebellion*, and there in December 1674 he died.

The real reason for Clarendon's fall was his failure to realize
the changes that English politics had undergone during the
previous half-century. In 1640 his views on Parliament's
powers might have been termed 'advanced'; by 1665 the same
views were 'reactionary.' Though the return of the Stuarts, and
of the two Houses of Parliament in accordance with ancient
usage, appeared to be a reversion to Elizabethan government,

the appearance was deceptive. The Civil War, the execution of Charles I, the Commonwealth (which demonstrated that England could survive without a king), the return of Charles II on agreed terms—all these had necessarily made a difference in the relationship between King and Parliament. In spite of appearances, the inward reality of politics had changed, but Clarendon remained the same. He might put back the hands of the clock, but he could not alter either its works or the time. His failure to keep pace with the march of events, and even to realize that the march was part of a natural process, made his fall inevitable.

2. The Cabal, 1667–73

Though Clarendon's fall freed Charles from a long-standing embarrassment, to find a suitable successor would not be easy. Indeed, it proved to be impossible, not so much because of the dearth of capable men as because Charles could not safely entrust anyone to carry out his policy. Charles, whatever his motives, still clung to his idea of toleration, yet the opening years of the reign had shown that the country was not ready to adopt such a policy, especially as there was a strong suspicion that Charles' real motive was to favour Roman Catholics. The opening years had shown also that Charles could not expect adequate supplies of money from Parliament except on condition of subservience to Parliament's wishes. An alternative scheme therefore gradually took shape in Charles' mind. This was to enter into a close alliance with Louis XIV from whom he would derive supplies of money. One of Louis' stipulations would certainly be that Charles should declare himself a Roman Catholic. Such a declaration would not only satisfy Louis' religious scruples: it would ensure a breach between England and Louis' Protestant enemies, the Dutch. The independence from Parliament, which a French pension would secure, would have the added advantage to Charles of giving to him the chance to carry out his policy of toleration.

The possibility of finding one chief Minister who would identify himself with Charles' views in these matters, and to whom all the delicate complexities of resulting policy could be entrusted, was extremely remote. The King's most influential Minister was Arlington, his chief business being foreign affairs. With him were Clifford, Buckingham, Ashley, and the Scottish Secretary, Lauderdale. They were a strangely assorted quintet. Clifford and Arlington were Roman Catholics (or, what amounted to the same thing so far as practical politics were concerned, acted in intimate conjunction with Roman Catholics); Buckingham, though a man of dissolute habits, affected to be the champion of Protestant Nonconformists and had married the daughter of Fairfax; Ashley was a genuine supporter of freedom and toleration; and Lauderdale had been a prominent Scottish Presbyterian until he had adhered to Episcopacy for political reasons. For Charles' purposes, these differences had advantages and might well facilitate the tortuous policy which he was about to initiate. It was of the highest importance that not one of the five Ministers was a genuine Anglican. Whether or not that fact had governed Charles in the choice of them can only be guessed. It augured ill for the smooth running of the State that Ministers with these views should have to reckon with a House of Commons the great majority of whose Members were Cavalier Anglicans. Contemporaries were quick to note the accident that the initial letters of the Ministers' names formed the word Cabal. Hitherto the word had meant only a committee. The reputation which this particular committee eventually won for itself can be gauged from the meaning which has ever afterwards attached to the word Cabal—namely, a group of secret plotters.

Since Charles' hopes pivoted upon Louis XIV, the latter's foreign policy would necessarily help to shape events in England. Three months before Clarendon's fall Louis had taken a step which was to set the course of the remaining half-century of his reign and was to concern England scarcely less intimately than it did France. When Louis' father-in-law, King Philip IV of Spain, died in 1665, and was succeeded by Philip's son, Charles II, Louis put forward a trumped-up claim to the Spanish Netherlands on behalf of his wife, Maria Theresa, who was the daughter of Philip IV and his first wife, while Charles II of Spain was the son of Philip and a second wife. That the claim to the Netherlands was worthless mattered little to Louis, and in May 1667 his troops moved across the frontier. In normal times such a step would have provoked the opposition of both Dutch and English: the former had no wish for a strong enemy on their borders; the latter, under Elizabeth I, had feared the possession of the Netherlands by Spain in the zenith of her power, and would equally mistrust their possession by the France of Louis XIV. But in 1667 England and the United Provinces were at war, and hence were unable to hinder the advance of Louis' troops.

It was the French menace which made the Dutch anxious to hasten the end of hostilities against England—hence the Dutch exploit in the Medway, in June 1667. Their success was proved the next month by the signing of the Treaty of Breda. This Treaty changed Louis' prospects. They were further clouded when in January 1668 Sir William Temple, the foremost English diplomatist of the day, was sent to The Hague. Before the month was out he had negotiated the Triple Alliance of England, the United Provinces, and Sweden, whereby the French were to be compelled to end their war against Spain, and the French frontier was to be adjusted to a line already agreed to between the Dutch and the French.

The upshot of the Alliance's pressure upon Louis was the Treaty of Aix-la-Chapelle, signed on May 2, 1668, whereby France retained eleven towns which she had seized in the Netherlands—the most important being Charleroi, Lille, and Tournai—but returned the Province of Franche-Comté which a French army had recently overrun. These fortresses were notable gains in themselves. More important still was their value as bases for further advance as soon as opportunity should serve. Even this was not the limit of Louis' gains at Aix. Doubtless the Triple Alliance felt some satisfaction at having compelled the King of France to yield to its demands. What the Alliance did not know was that in January 1668— that is, before signing the treaty—Louis had secured from the Emperor Leopold I a secret agreement whereby Leopold undertook to allow Louis to seize Franche-Comté and the Spanish Netherlands whenever the childless Spanish King, Charles II, should die. Thus Louis had made peace for the present on terms giving him fortresses whose possession would ensure the much greater gains promised for the future.

Louis' next move was to break the Triple Alliance by detaching England from it. To this end he opened negotiations with Charles II. As we have seen, an alliance with Louis was exactly suited to Charles' plans; yet each of the wily monarchs was suspicious of the other, and during 1668–70 negotiations proceeded slowly. The fact was that in certain respects Louis and Charles were at cross-purposes. Louis had reached the view that the only way to remove the danger of the United Provinces was to defeat them in war, and it was primarily for this purpose that he wished for Charles' alliance. Charles' chief interest in a French alliance was in the money that it would yield so as to make him independent of Parliament. Even when the terms of the treaty were agreed upon, the further question had to be settled of whether Charles' public conversion to Roman Catholicism should precede or follow a declaration of war against the Dutch. The chief agent in the negotiations was Charles' sister, Henrietta, Duchess of Orleans. On May 15, 1670, Henrietta landed at Dover, and on the 22nd of that month the Treaty of Dover was signed.

The most important terms of the treaty were that Charles should announce his conversion to Rome as soon as he judged it safe to do so; if this announcement provoked disorder in England Louis was to provide Charles with six thousand soldiers and two million *livres* (rather more than £150,000); and after Charles had professed conversion France and England were to make joint war against the Dutch, at the end of which England was to receive the Zeeland Islands.

Though Louis had ensured that Charles' conversion should precede the Dutch war, Charles thereby would control the date when the war should begin. In the actual event, Charles never did make public confession, and Louis had to start his war without it. At the moment of signature neither side realized how nearly the treaty failed to be signed at all: within three weeks of its signature its negotiator, Henrietta, suddenly died.

The negotiations had been carried out in the utmost secrecy. Even the existence of the treaty was only guessed. Its provisions, by their very nature, could be revealed to very few even of the English Ministers. The only members of the Cabal who signed it were Clifford and Arlington; and to their signatures was added that of a leading Roman Catholic nobleman, Lord Arundell of Wardour. But, no matter how complete the secrecy surrounding the treaty, nothing could blind Ministers' eyes to the facts of a war against Holland and of supplies of money from Louis. Therefore, in order to allay suspicion and to involve Protestant members of the Cabal in Charles' scheme, a sham treaty was drawn up. Its terms were identical with those of the real treaty except that no mention was made of the King's conversion to Roman Catholicism; and the subsidy that Charles was to receive after profession of his faith was written down as a contribution to the war. This sham treaty was signed by all five members of the Cabal.

Charles' policy was in the highest degree astute, but to a scarcely less degree was it dangerous. Louis henceforward held him in his power. At any time that suited French policy, Louis could publish the terms of the treaty, and Charles would at once be overwhelmed by the execration of his Parliament and his people. The ensuing strife would not merely pull down Charles but would reduce England to a cipher at least long enough to enable Louis to ignore her while he achieved his objectives. Even apart from revelation by Louis, the terms might leak out. Ashley, for example, would not be an easy man to deceive for long; and if his hatred of Rome caused him to leave the Court, or if he was driven out because his knowledge was dangerous, he would be a formidable opponent, especially if the other Protestant Ministers supported him.

One certain effect of the treaty would be that England would be involved in war against the United Provinces. For this purpose, the Government's most urgent need was for money which neither Parliamentary grants nor Louis' subsidies nor both together had produced in sufficient amounts. Consequently, on January 2, 1672, the King issued a proclamation suspending for one year the payment of interest on his debt to the London bankers. The amount of this interest (nearly £1,500,000) was to be formed into a new debt to bear interest at 6 per cent. In one sense Charles is hardly to be blamed for this "Stop of the Exchequer": even the strongly Royalist Cavalier Parliament kept him ridiculously short of money. But whatever the theoretical excuse for the Stop, its practical un-wisdom was beyond question. The bankers were seriously embarrassed. From them the financial disorder spread to those who had trusted them with money, and hence bankruptcies were numerous. This in turn disorganized the country's trade and so reduced its taxable wealth. Thus the King had started a financial boomerang which would return to strike at his own head. Most serious result of all was the blow which the Stop of the Exchequer gave to the financiers' confidence in the Government. It was also in effect an overriding of Parliament's power of the purse, and even the Cavalier Parliament was not likely to submit without protest to this interference with its control over finance. The public outcry was directed mostly against Ashley as Chancellor of the Exchequer, though in fact he had opposed the policy of the Stop.

In order to show to Louis XIV some evidence of an intention to carry out the terms of the Treaty of Dover, on March 15 Charles issued a Declaration of Indulgence whereby he sus-pended "all and all manner of penal laws in ecclesiastic matters against whatever sort of nonconformists or recusants"; Protes-tant dissenters were to be allowed to obtain licences for places of worship, and Roman Catholics were to be allowed their own form of worship in private houses. This exercise of the suspend-ing power was no less a challenge to Parliamentary rights than was the Stop of the Exchequer. Whenever Parliament met again after prorogation the challenge would certainly be taken up. Charles' only hope of averting it was by carrying through with success the general policy of which the Indulgence was only a part. That is to say, Charles must either achieve so notable a victory against the Dutch that he became popular enough to warrant Parliament's reassembly, or he must obtain such subsidies from Louis as would make Parliament unneces-sary. One immediate advantage the indulgence had achieved: it had cemented the loyalty of all the Cabal to the King, though the reasons for their respective loyalties varied. The effect was seen in the shower of new dignities which fell upon Ministers. Arlington became an earl. Clifford became a baron and Lord Treasurer (in place of the previous commission). Lauderdale became a Scottish duke. Ashley was raised to be Earl of Shaftesbury and Lord Chancellor. In thus elevating Ashley, the King was doubtless laughing in his sleeve, for Ashley could have little imagined that the indulgence, which was thoroughly in keeping with his own ideas of toleration, was intended as a first step towards the return of Roman Catholicism which he hated.

Two days after the issue of the Declaration of Indulgence— that is, on March 17—following clashes at sea, war was declared against the United Provinces. The events leading to the Continental outbreak lie outside English history. In any case, Louis' steps towards war were so obviously pretexts that they do not merit detailed description here. For our purpose all that matters is that in May 1672 French armies under Turenne and Condé advanced on to the Rhine which they followed downward towards the United Provinces.

England's part in what is commonly known as the Third Dutch War was exclusively naval. On May 28 the combined English and French fleets, commanded by the Duke of York, were surprised by de Ruyter in Southwold Bay, and suffered a serious check. The Earl of Sandwich was killed in the battle.

On land the French forces carried all before them. Of the seven Provinces, only Holland and Zeeland remained outside French occupation, and even they were kept free only by cutting the dykes. These disasters completely discredited the party of the de Witts who had deliberately neglected the Provinces' armed forces so as to keep the Orange family out of power. But the crisis roused the fury of the Dutch people: William III was made Stadtholder, and the two de Witt brothers, John and Cornelius, were murdered by an angry mob on August 4, 1672. This was the turning-point of the war. The whole people rallied to its new leader. In October William was further strengthened by the alliance with him of the Emperor Leopold I, and of the Great Elector, Frederick William of Brandenburg.

During 1673 the French had some success on land, but on August 11, as French and English ships under Prince Rupert's

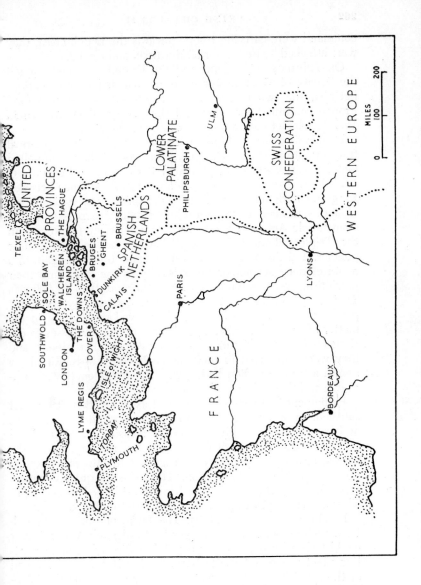

command were carrying troops towards the Dutch coast, they were attacked by de Ruyter off the Texel and routed.

On February 9 England and the United Provinces signed the Treaty of Westminster on terms which left the relations between the two countries much as they had been before. France continued the war until the Treaty of Nymwegen in 1678, to which treaty reference will be made later.

England's change of policy abroad was due to a political transformation at home. Need for money had compelled Charles to reassemble the Cavalier Parliament on February 6, 1673. During the long prorogation the former alliance between King and Parliament had been undermined. The basis of that alliance had been a common religious policy (expressed in the Conventicle Act) and a common foreign policy (expressed in the Triple Alliance). The King had abandoned both these policies, and the Members therefore came together again in a mood of deep suspicion. Their loyalty to the King, and their patriotism, were shown by their vote of more than £1,200,000. Their suspicion of the Government was shown by their suspending the grant until they had received satisfaction in the matter of the Indulgence. The Commons sent addresses to the King on the illegality of suspending Acts of Parliament, and they were supported in their action by the Lords. Finally, a month after the session had begun, the Indulgence was withdrawn and the seal upon it broken.

Parliament had won a notable victory. Even then it was not satisfied. In order to remove all Roman Catholics from office, and from influence with the King, a measure was introduced whereby every holder of office, civil and military, under the Crown must make a declaration against the Roman Catholic doctrine of Transubstantiation. The measure quickly passed through all its stages, and the King was obliged to accept it. Thus the Test Act was placed upon the Statute Book.

Its effects were momentous. The Duke of York, a staunch Roman Catholic, could no longer be Lord High Admiral. Nor could Clifford remain Treasurer. A less direct but more startling effect concerned Shaftesbury. During 1672 he had learned of the provisions of the Treaty of Dover concerning the introduction of Roman Catholicism into England. The information is supposed to have been revealed to him by Arlington who was moved by jealousy because Clifford had been given the Treasurership over Arlington's head. Partly through convinced opposition to Catholicism, and partly through anger at discovering that he had been fooled, Shaftesbury began to oppose the King's interests in Parliament. He supported the Test Act, and he opposed the Duke of York's marriage to the Roman Catholic Mary of Modena (the Duke's first wife, Anne Hyde, having died two years earlier). Such open opposition to Court policy by a Minister of the Crown was intolerable. On November 9, 1673, Shaftesbury was dismissed from office.

The immediate results of Shaftesbury's dismissal were the break-up of the Cabal and the end of the Cabal's policy of religious toleration. As an alternative, the King had to revert to something like Clarendon's policy of reliance on the Anglican Church and of (at least nominal) separation from France. The new policy met with severe opposition from a section of Parliament. The leader of the opposition to it was Shaftesbury. Hence the indirect effect of his dismissal was the beginning of a coherent party in opposition to the Court, an opposition that was inspired not merely by personal motives but by a belief in religious toleration and in resistance to arbitrary government. In a word, the indirect effect of Shaftesbury's dismissal was the gradual formation of what came to be known as the Whig Party, and hence of the party-system of government and its corollary the Cabinet. All this was to be a matter of slow growth, and only as we now look back over the intervening centuries can the full significance of the events of 1673 be understood. But it is well to have this significance in mind as we trace the story of the remainder of the period covered by this volume.

3. The Ministry of Danby, 1673–79

As Lord Treasurer in succession to Clifford, the King appointed Sir Thomas Osborne, who entered office in June 1673. In 1674 Osborne became Earl of Danby, by which name he is usually known though in 1689 he became Marquess of Carmarthen, and in 1694 Duke of Leeds. Danby was a staunch

Anglican and wished for no dealings with Roman Catholicism, whether in the form of toleration in England or of alliance with France. This policy was so exactly suited to the mood of the majority in Parliament that Danby seemed the ideal Minister to carry out the King's policy of placating all sections of its Members. Danby turned out to be a man of shrewd common sense, considerable administrative ability (particularly in matters of finance, which was his primary concern), and perfect understanding of the art of managing the House of Commons ('management' consisting largely of suiting various kinds and degrees of bribery to various Members).

Danby was fortunate that, following a period of trade depression, he took office at the beginning of economic revival. During 1674 and '75 the widespread improvement in trade brought enormously increased yields from both customs and excise. These windfalls, added to such economies as paying off troops and ships and reducing the interest on Government loans from 10 per cent. to 8 per cent., enabled Danby to restore the exchequer to solvency. Even the cost of the Dutch war was paid off. This was the only occasion in the twenty-five years of Charles II's reign when the accounts showed a genuine balance on the right side. Danby took advantage of this affluence in order, in 1675, to resume the interest-payments which had been suspended by the Stop of the Exchequer of January 1672. This resumption did more than anything else could have done to impress the City favourably, and to restore the Government's credit with the nation.

In 1677 Danby was able to negotiate a royal marriage-alliance with the Dutch. On November 4 the Duke of York's elder daughter, Mary, was married to William III of Orange. The ultimate results of this marriage were incalculably vast: it was to make possible the Protestant Revolution of 1688-89, with all that that revolution was to imply at home and abroad. These results were hidden from Danby and his contemporaries, but no one could fail to understand that the marriage implied a close alliance with Protestant Holland and a clean break from dependence upon Roman Catholic France.

This, however, did not mean that everything would be smooth running for Danby's policy. On the contrary, there was one stumbling-block which no amount of adroitness could remove—namely, the will of the King. Charles had no intention of abandoning his policy of peace coupled with a French alliance. He was shrewd enough to use even the William-Mary marriage to suit his purpose: the marriage had the double effect of satisfying Danby and the Commons that the Roman Catholic connexion had been broken, and of showing Louis that Charles could take an independent line with Parliament's support unless Louis made Charles' friendship worth while.

Relations between Charles and Louis during the Danby period (and after) were devious and complicated. We can here follow only their main stages. As soon as news of the Anglo-Dutch marriage became known in November 1677, Louis stopped the payments which he had been making to Charles; and when in March 1678 Charles approached Louis, the latter still refused to resume their previous relationship. Louis' refusal had two explanations. First, he was bringing his war against the Dutch to an end, the Treaty of Nymwegen being finally concluded in August 1678. Thus England's friendship, or neutrality, was no longer necessary. Second, Louis had found a more effective means of controlling English policy—namely, that of maintaining, by means of bribery, a compact group in the English Parliament. This group would vote in whatever way best suited French interests, usually in such a way as to embarrass Charles. Presently Louis resumed his pension-payments to Charles, and was thus able to play off Charles and the Parliamentary opposition against each other. Among Louis' pensioners were the Duke of Buckingham and Algernon Sidney. Shaftesbury and Lord William Russell (son of the Duke of Bedford) were also confederate with Louis though there seems no evidence that they accepted bribes.

While matters were thus unstable there burst upon the scene one of those unpredictable phenomena which upset conditions hitherto regarded as part of the permanent order of social life. Yet, as with most crises, its suddenness was more apparent than real. For several years the nation had been living in a state of increasing uncertainty and suspicion: the influence of Roman Catholic Ministers at Court, the Declaration of Indulgence, the mysterious power which France seemed

to exert over English policy, all these touched English suscep-
tibilities at their most sensitive point—a fear of Roman
Catholicism. Events showed that this process had produced a
condition of high nervous strain.

At this stage there appeared a rogue with all the qualifications for exploiting the national tension to his advantage. Titus
Oates had had a varied and dishonourable career. Though the
son of one of Cromwell's Baptist chaplains, he had been
expelled from a public school, and he had suffered imprisonment for perjury. In 1675 he professed conversion to Roman
Catholicism, and had entered certain Jesuit colleges, chiefly
at St Omer. Thence also he was expelled. In 1677 Oates came
to England (claiming to be a Doctor of Divinity of Salamanca
University) and began to spread rumours of a Popish Plot. His
fellow-schemer was Israel Tonge who had at least an Oxford
D.D. to his credit. To what extent Tonge was a deliberate liar
like Oates or had been duped by Oates is difficult to say.
Possibly the truth is that, having an obsession against Roman
Catholics, he lapped up Oates' stories without being too particular either to find evidence in their support or to discrimi-
nate nicely in the methods for anti-Jesuit propaganda.

Oates declared that while with the Jesuits he had learned
of a plot to kill King Charles II so as to ensure the immediate
succession of James, Duke of York. Not content with giving
details of the alleged plot, Oates was ready with a list of the
chief plotters. So persistent were his allegations that he was
brought before the King and the Privy Council. The King's
shrewd questioning easily detected the weak spots in the story.
Under cross-examination Oates was shown never to have met
certain individuals from whom he had already purported to
have learned his facts. But, quite unabashed, he adhered to his
story, and even improved on it by adding details almost from
day to day.

In normal times Oates would have imposed upon no one;
but circumstances at that particular juncture combined to
favour his scheme. First, there was the abnormal nervous condition which prevailed in England, a condition provoked by
fear of exactly the sort of scheme that Oates was alleging.
Second, men who were, or had been, about the Court—like

Shaftesbury—had evidence enough of goings and comings between England and Roman Catholic France to make the existence of a popish plot easily believable. Third, Oates had some amazing strokes of luck which seemed to corroborate his yarns. Two instances will suffice as illustrations. One of those named by Oates as a conspirator was Father Coleman, secretary to the Duke of York. Coleman was arrested and his room searched. Letters were found from Roman Catholics abroad containing references to schemes for restoring Roman Catholicism to England. But no papers were found bearing dates later than 1676. The inference drawn from this fact was that later letters had been destroyed and that these would have contained references, even more damning than those in the letters that had been found, of a conspiracy. The truth almost certainly was that Coleman's correspondence was innocent: naturally he was interested in the restoration of Catholicism, and naturally he corresponded with his friends on the subject; but not a shred of evidence was ever produced to show that he favoured treasonable methods of achieving his hopes. The other instance of Oates' good luck concerned Sir Edmund Berry Godfrey who was a well-known, staunch Protestant Justice of the Peace in Westminster. With him Oates had placed a sworn deposition of the alleged facts of the plot. Then, on Saturday, October 12, Godfrey suddenly disappeared. On the following Thursday his body was found face downward in a ditch on Primrose Hill with a sword driven right through him. From that day to this the manner of Godfrey's death has remained a complete mystery. Much ingenuity has been expended on the problem, but not one of the suggested solutions—suicide (and if so, why?) or murder (and if so, by whom?)—can be substantiated by anything approaching conclusive evidence. Whatever the truth, the general public jumped unanimously to the one obvious solution that the Jesuits had murdered Godfrey in order to repress facts that Oates had confided to him. The coroner's jury returned a verdict of "wilful murder."

The result was as though the whole nation had suddenly gone mad. Panic spread in all directions. Oates improved the shining hour by elaborating the original story and by naming more accomplices of the alleged Jesuit plotters. Most of the populace went about its work during the day, and retired to bed at night, in constant apprehension of a new and immensely grander Gunpowder Plot. Good Protestants carried with them substantial weapons, called Protestant Flails, with which to defend themselves when the terror should break upon them. Oates became a popular hero, saviour of Protestantism and of the State. He was housed luxuriously and kept at the public expense. This encouraged many imitators: a crop of informers arose to relate stories of plots, some corroborating Oates, and some on private lines of their own. On the bare word of Oates and his accomplices, thirty-five persons were convicted by law-courts of treason and executed, among them Father Coleman and Archbishop Plunket of Armagh, Primate of Ireland. How far political leaders, as distinct from the mass of the people, believed Oates is difficult to determine. Almost the only man who confidently disbelieved him was the King, though he dared not take action against the informers: to do so, in the prevailing temper of public opinion, would have invited suspicion of being a Papist, illogical as the charge would have been in view of the aims of the alleged plot.

The only party to gain advantage from the panic was that of Shaftesbury. Nothing could have suited his faction more perfectly than panic due to fear of Roman Catholicism. Shaftesbury was president of an organization calling itself the Green Ribbon Club whose members, for various reasons, were opponents of the Court. The Club, founded in 1675, was the first political party-organization in English history. Its agents were sent all over the country to mobilize support in elections; petitions and demonstrations were organized; the mobs of the London outskirts obeyed its summons. The organization became more complete as time passed, but already by 1678–79 it was sufficiently in being to exploit to its advantage the effects of the Popish Plot.

One item of the Club's propaganda concerned the succession to the throne. It was thus opening up what was to be the most important issue of the following decade. Its object was to secure a Protestant successor to Charles. On November 2, 1678, Shaftesbury moved in the Lords that Charles should be asked to remove the Duke of York from his counsels. Two days later a similar resolution was moved in the Commons. The King's reply was that he was willing to take measures for the security of Protestantism so long as such measures did not interfere with the normal order of the succession. Nevertheless Charles asked his brother not to attend meetings of the Privy Council.

This was followed by a Bill to exclude Roman Catholics from both Houses of Parliament by adding to the ordinary oaths taken by Members a declaration against Transubstantiation. The Bill passed both Houses (though the Lords insisted on an amendment to exempt the Duke of York from its provisions) and received the King's assent. Roman Catholics remained excluded from Parliament until this Act was repealed, and Roman Catholic Emancipation was granted, in 1829.

The next turn in events concerned Danby. Danby had few friends. The Green Ribbon Club hated him because he had been plainly sceptical about the Popish Plot. Even the King disliked the rigidity of his Minister's Protestantism. One of Danby's most dangerous enemies was Louis XIV, who had never forgiven him for his part in the marriage-alliance between England and Holland and who knew that he was opposed to an alliance with France. In order to remove Danby from power, Louis used Ralph Montagu, a former English Ambassador to Paris and a bitter personal enemy to Danby. On December 19, 1678, Montagu, heavily bribed by Louis, brought before the Commons a letter written by Danby to Louis in March 1678 asking for 6,000,000 *livres* for three years. The Commons' anger blazed against Danby who thus appeared to have advocated one policy in public and to have pursued the opposite one in secret. Rejecting the defence, clearly borne out by the terms of the tell-tale letter itself, that the Minister was carrying out the express orders of the King, the Commons impeached Danby. Though for some reasons Charles would not have regretted the loss of his Minister, to deliver him to his enemies (as his father had delivered Strafford) might be but the first of a series of enforced conciliations. To save Danby from Parliament's attack only one way was open—to dissolve Parliament. Accordingly the Cavalier Parliament was dissolved on January 24, 1679. During its eighteen years of existence the personnel of this Long Parliament of Charles II had undergone much change, so that only about one-half of the Commons' Members in 1679 had been Members in 1661. Nevertheless its dissolution marked the end of the third stage of Charles II's reign.

4. Three Parliaments, 1679–81

The fourth period of the reign lasted only a little more than two years but it included three parliaments, all of which were characterized by a struggle between the King and Whig majorities in the Commons.

The general election provided the electors with the first opportunity in eighteen years to express their views. The result showed a decided swing in public opinion. In the 1661 House of Commons the King had had a safe majority; in the 1679 House he had only a precarious one. Almost as soon as the Parliament met, on March 6, it returned to the attack on the King's government, concentrating particularly on opposition to Danby, and on a demand for the exclusion of the Roman Catholic Duke of York from the succession to the throne.

A general pardon which Charles had given to Danby was brushed aside as an encroachment on the Commons' customary right to impeach a Minister. As a last resort to save Danby, the King dismissed him from the Treasurership. But the Commons were not to be baulked of their prey: an Attainder Bill was introduced, and Danby gave himself up. He was sent to the Tower where he remained until February 1684. The process of the attainder was never completed because the Lords managed to drag out the proceedings. But Danby's fall was a notable step in establishing the constitutional principle of the responsibility of Ministers for all acts of State: he had been overthrown for an action carried out at the King's express command and in spite of the King's pardon.

In order to avoid a repetition of such a proceeding, Charles adopted a plan, which seems to have originated with Sir William Temple, for the reconstitution of the Privy Council. The existing Privy Council had grown too large to be efficient as the King's private council. Temple's scheme was for a new Privy Council of about thirty members. Both Court and Opposition parties were represented on the new Council, and Shaftesbury was appointed as its President. Temple hoped that such a body, intermediary between King and Parliament, and having the confidence of both, would prevent the repetition of the friction which had become chronic between them. But, however desirable such a change may have been, of far greater importance than the theory of the scheme were the practical facts that the members of the new Council still ranged themselves on party-lines, and that the King still confided in a small group of his supporters rather than on the full Council. For this Charles was hardly to be blamed: the Council was still too large, and its membership too various, for efficiency either in speedy decisions or in secret discussion.

A Bill to exclude the Duke of York from the throne was first introduced into the Commons on May 15, 1679. Perhaps the only matter on which Charles II never compromised or wavered was his insistence on the legitimate succession; and so substantial was the support which the Exclusion Bill received from the Commons that, rather than yield, on May 27 he prorogued Parliament.

In one other matter the opposition had been more successful. Since the thirteenth century a man imprisoned without trial had been able to obtain (or his friends could obtain on his behalf) from the Court of King's Bench a writ of habeas corpus whereby the gaoler was ordered to "have his body" in court for trial. This right at common law had never been secured by Act of Parliament, and by various legal devices the issue of the writ could be evaded. Shaftesbury and his friends regarded the establishment of the right as essential in a continued struggle against the King. In 1679 they therefore introduced a Bill to make enforceable at law the issue of a habeas corpus writ in favour of any person imprisoned on a charge of crime except of treason or felony. Owing largely to Shaftesbury's efforts, the measure passed the Lords as well as the Commons, and it received the royal assent on the day that Parliament was prorogued.

On July 12, while Parliament was still prorogued, a proclamation was issued dissolving it. Charles took this decision against the strong advice of his Council. A new Parliament was to meet on October 7; but on that day the new Parliament was prorogued until the following January. On October 15 Shaftesbury was dismissed from the Council; and before the Parliament met, several Council-members had resigned in protest against the King's ignoring the Council's advice about the dissolution. Thus there was an influential opposition awaiting the opportunity which the new Parliament would provide. In January there was a further prorogation, and not until October 21, 1680, did the third Parliament of the reign meet.

It was on the subject of Exclusion that the battle was to be joined. So formidable was the opposition-group, centring in the Green Ribbon Club, and so strong were its feelings, that wise leadership would have made it irresistible. A second revolution and Charles' dethronement would have been probable results. This catastrophe was averted by the folly of Shaftesbury and his fellows.

If James was to be excluded an alternative successor had to be chosen. There were two possible persons, either of whom might have secured popular respect. The first was James' elder daughter, Mary. Her succession would have maintained the normal line by merely omitting James from it. Also, as James' only children were daughters—the Princesses Mary and Anne who in 1680 were eighteen and fifteen years of age respectively —and were the children of his first wife, Anne Hyde, and as none of the children of James and Mary of Modena had survived infancy, there seemed little likelihood that there would ever be a son to upset Mary's succession to the throne. A second possible successor was William III of Orange. He was the son of Charles I's daughter, Mary, and of William II of Orange, and hence he would be next in succession to the English throne after Mary and Anne. Also, because three years previously he had married the Princess Mary, his connexion with the English throne was particularly close. Moreover, he was a staunch Protestant, the champion of Continental Protestantism against Louis XIV, and therefore his foreign policy would fit exactly the views of the Green Ribbon opposition.

By a strange aberration of judgement the Green Ribbon

faction rejected both of these possible choices and supported instead the weakest and most foolish of all possible alternatives to James—namely, Charles II's illegitimate son, the Duke of Monmouth. The only explanation of this policy seems to be that many of Shaftesbury's followers were in Louis XIV's pay and so, whatever their convictions, could not support Louis' arch-enemy, William, or William's wife, Mary.

Monmouth was the natural son of Lucy Walters and (presumably) of Charles II. In 1680 he was thirty years of age. He had seen war-service against the Dutch in 1672–73 and against the French in 1678. He had considerable personal charm but was unstable in character, extremely ambitious, and feather-brained. Perhaps he was to be pitied rather than blamed: he had lacked the discipline of firm, continuous home-training, and was thoroughly spoiled by Charles, who could deny him no indulgence. There was one thing only that Charles would never grant to his son: he would never acknowledge his succession to the throne in preference to the legal claimant, the Duke of York. In this at least Charles showed himself a wiser man and a truer patriot than the Shaftesbury faction. In 1679 Charles deprived Monmouth of his commission as a general and banished him from England. When, before 1679 was out, Monmouth returned, he was stripped of other offices that he held but was allowed to remain in the country. He spent his time in journeys, chiefly in the West, posing as the champion of Protestantism.

This was the position when Parliament finally assembled on October 21, 1680. A new Exclusion Bill was introduced and passed the Commons, but it was forthwith rejected by the Lords. So impossible was the situation, if England was to be governed at all, that Charles re-opened negotiations with Louis of France and, having the prospect of a substantial French pension, on January 10 he prorogued his third Parliament and a few days later dissolved it.

The period of this Parliament had seen the opposition-faction become more sharply defined and better organized than formerly. It was then that the terms which, for at least a century-and-a-half, were to be generally applied to the two political parties became current. The terms Whig and Tory were originally nicknames. The first sharp definition of the parties resulted from the prorogation of the third Parliament in January 1681. Following that prorogation, the Exclusion Bill's supporters continued for months to petition the King to summon Parliament, and hence they became known as Petitioners. Their opponents countered these petitions by addresses expressing their abhorrence of such infringement of royal prerogative: these opponents thus became known as Abhorrers. As party-feeling rose, the King's supporters began to call the Petitioners "Whigs," a label derived from the word Whiggamores, which was the name of some extreme Scottish Presbyterians then in revolt against the King. The Petitioners retorted by dubbing their opponents "Tories," which was the name of certain Irish Roman Catholic outlaws.

One politician calls for mention at this point as refusing to be bound by either faction. He was Sir George Savile, Marquess of Halifax, whose range of intellect and wise judgement place him among the greatest of all English statesmen. Sir Walter Raleigh, the editor of Halifax's writings, called him "the practical genius of the English Revolution, and the acutest genius among English politicians."[1] Though prominent in politics from the time that he sat in the Convention Parliament of 1660 till his death in 1695, and though co-operating now with one party and now with another, Halifax would not attach himself permanently with either. His political principle was clear to his own mind: whereas the principle of Whigs and Tories was to gain party-advantage, his was that of compromise in the interest of the State. He believed that any policy, however good in itself, if carried to extremes became a danger to national stability. His enemies scoffed at him as a Trimmer. This name he adopted, but gave it an interpretation of his own:

> This innocent word *Trimmer* signifieth no more than this,
> That if men are together in a Boat, and one part of the Company
> would weigh it down on one side, another would make it lean

[1] *The Complete Works of George Savile, First Marquess of Halifax,* ed. by Sir Walter Raleigh (Intro. p. vii), from which the other quotations are taken.

as much to the contrary; it happeneth there is a third Opinion of those, who conceive it would do as well, if the Boat went even, without endangering the passengers.

Moreover, he claimed that this motive of compromise was traceable through all English history and in all phases of English life:

> Our climate is a *Trimmer*, between that part of the World where men are Roasted, and the other where they are Frozen; That our Church is a *Trimmer* between the Phrenzy of Platonic Visions, and the Lethargick Ignorance of Popish Dreams; that our Laws are *Trimmers* between the Excess of unbounded Power, and the Extravagance of Liberty not enough restrained; That true Virtue hath even been thought a *Trimmer*, and to have its dwelling in the middle between the two Extremes; That even God Almighty himself is divided between his two great Attributes, his Mercy and his Justice.

Perhaps Halifax is best described as a political realist who would not allow his tactical freedom to be hampered by doctrine.

Halifax first became prominent as a supporter of the policy of the 1669 Triple Alliance against France. In 1673 he supported the Test Act, thereby losing the Duke of York's favour; and during the following years he was an opponent of Danby. In 1679, after Danby's fall, he was made a member of the new Privy Council of thirty. In practice the men on whose advice Charles chiefly relied were the Triumvirate of Halifax, Sunderland, and Essex. True to his principle of opposition to sudden change, Halifax opposed the Exclusion Bill, and, in its stead, advocated a plan to recognize the Duke of York as King in succession to Charles while William of Orange and his wife the Princess Mary should be regents and should exercise the government. On the day after Shaftesbury was dismissed from the Council in October 1679, Halifax was raised from Viscount to Earl. For the remainder of Charles II's reign Halifax remained generally high in favour, and in August 1682 he was created Marquess.

The opportunity for the next clash between the parties came in the 1681 Parliament. The elections had returned to the

Commons a large majority of Exclusionists, and the King's defeat seemed certain. But Charles moved with consummate skill. First, he summoned the Parliament to meet not at Westminster but at Oxford. This would put the Whigs at a serious disadvantage: it would rob them of one of their most valuable means of influencing votes in the House—the London mobs. Oxford was still a strongly Royalist university and city.

As planned, proceedings opened on March 21. Once again the central theme was Exclusion. The Council produced Halifax's scheme for the Duke of York to succeed to the title without effective power. But the Commons rejected it. It was a not unnatural decision: even if the Council's offer was genuinely intended, the plan was not likely to work, for the Duke of York, when he became King, could not be expected to tamely submit to the rôle set for him.

But if the Whigs imagined that they had thereby cornered Charles they had miscalculated their man. Charles had laid his plans, though of their nature, or even that they existed, he betrayed no trace. On the contrary, he acted so as to convey the impression that he was powerless while the Whigs were planning another Exclusion Bill. Then on March 28, without any warning, Charles struck. In ordinary clothes he went down to the Parliament's place of meeting, there changed into his State robes, ordered the Commons to the bar of the Lords, and forthwith dissolved the Parliament.

He thus demonstrated the wisdom of choosing Oxford for the Parliament. Had Parliament been suddenly dissolved in Westminster, the Whigs, relying on the mob and on the influence of the City merchants, would have challenged the King. But at Oxford, taken off their guard and lacking local support, the Whigs first hesitated and then hurried back to London. When brought face to face with the possibility of revolution the Whigs' nerve had given way. Their acquiescence in the King's manœuvre was fatal to their cause. The crisis of the dissolution thus safely passed, Charles was confident that the situation was in his hands, for he intended never to call another Parliament while Louis XIV continued to pay him his agreed pension. Its first instalment arrived on the day following the Parliament's dissolution.

5. Rule without Parliament, 1681–85

Both parties had gone to Oxford with their respective retainers in anticipation of a clash of arms; yet both sides, when faced with the issue, had shrunk from war. Charles' policy of standing aside and allowing the anti-papist storm to exhaust itself now met its reward. The country was swept by a wave of Toryism at least as pronounced as the previous wave of Whiggism. The King was deluged by a flood of loyalist addresses expressing grateful approval of his having saved the nation from the anarchic effects of selfish faction.

As week followed week the loyalist tide rose. When the tide seemed at its height Charles moved. On July 2, 1681, Shaftesbury was committed to the Tower. Not until November 24 was he brought to trial. He then appeared before the Grand Jury of Middlesex impanelled by the City of London sheriffs who were still Whigs. As a result the jury returned a no true Bill, and Shaftesbury was released.

Though the Whig leader thus enjoyed another political triumph, he was at the end of his physical resources. His strenuous life and his imprisonment had undermined his health, and he decided that, if he was not to leave his party defeated, he must hurry forward his campaign. He therefore advocated plans of violence verging on rebellion. It was a part of these plans that, during the autumn of 1682, Monmouth went on a semi-royal tour through Cheshire. The only effect was that he was arrested. The Government's next step would be to arrest Shaftesbury. To avoid ending his days in prison, if not on the block, in November Shaftesbury fled to Holland where he died in January 1683.

Thus Charles' most formidable opponent died a broken man, leaving a wrecked party. Shaftesbury had miscalculated the calibre of the King with whom he had to deal. But fundamentally his judgement was sound. Within six years of his own death the Whigs were triumphant again; the Duke of York, whom Shaftesbury had aimed to exclude from the throne, was an exile; and the Protestant Succession was assured.

Though Shaftesbury's flight had robbed the Whigs of their

founder and head, Whiggism was by no means dead. During 1683 there came to a head a scheme which had been in course of formation earlier. A number of Green Ribbon men—among them the Earl of Essex, Lord William Russell, and Algernon Sidney—had with Shaftesbury planned an insurrection to force the King to summon a Parliament. Of that scheme, Monmouth's progress through Cheshire had been the first evidence. In spite of temporary checks, the general scheme continued.

Alongside it went another scheme, a plot to assault, and possibly assassinate, Charles and James. This was at bottom a republican plot, the chief plotters being two Cromwellian officers, Rumbold and Rumsey. Their final plan was to seize Charles and James as they passed Rumbold's house, the Rye House in Herts., on their way from Newmarket in April 1683. The plot was frustrated by the accident that a large fire in Newmarket caused Charles to leave earlier than intended.

In June one of the Rye House plotters gave information to the Government. Other plotters (including Rumsey) then tried to save themselves by betraying what they knew. Arising from the orgy of confessions, knowledge emerged of the other plot by the Green Ribbon leaders. To what extent, if any, the latter had been aware of the Rye House conspiracy has never been clearly established; but the existence of two contemporary plots gave to the Government an opportunity it could not be expected to resist. All alike were treated as equally guilty. Rumbold for the moment escaped arrest by fleeing abroad. Monmouth lay in hiding. Sidney, Russell, and Essex were sent to the Tower. Essex committed suicide. Russell was executed in July 1683 and Algernon Sidney in December. Monmouth gave himself up on condition of receiving a royal pardon.

Nothing could have served the Government's purpose better than the discovery of these conspiracies. Not only were the Green Ribbon leaders eliminated or scattered so that the Club was deserted, but the Tory reaction in the country was stimulated. Taking advantage of this movement, Charles struck at one of the chief sources of Whig political influence—namely, the borough corporations. The powers of the corporations were derived from royal charters. These, having been granted at different times and in different circumstances, were not uniform in their terms, but mostly they allowed to the corporations the right to elect Members of Parliament. Moreover, as most corporations were not themselves popularly elected but were perpetuated by co-option, borough government had fallen under the control of family cliques which were beyond the influence of the townsmen on the one hand and of the King on the other. Moreover, as the towns had been the strongholds of Puritanism and Parliamentarianism, most of the corporations were Whig. While this condition remained the Court would remain powerless to influence a large proportion of Parliamentary seats.

The only means of altering the situation was to remodel the borough charters. To call in all the charters at once by royal proclamation would have provoked a resistance too wide to be safe. Charles therefore attacked them gradually and by legal process. Irregularities of various kinds, often of a trivial nature, in the exercise of the corporations' powers, under the terms of their charters, were used as excuses for the forfeiture of the charters. After a few small boroughs had been thus attacked, in 1683 a writ of *quo warranto* was issued against the City of London. Instances were collected of the City's exceeding its powers, and in June 1683 its charter was declared forfeit. The King's success in attacking London meant that no other borough in the Kingdom would dare to oppose him. Thus a wholesale attack was made on the remaining borough charters. The terms of the new charters were such as to ensure Tory corporations, which in turn would assure Tory sheriffs, Tory juries, and Tory Members of Parliament.

Thus by the middle of 1683 limitations to the King's absolute power had been removed: his income from Louis XIV was enough to allow him to dispense with Parliaments; but whenever a Parliament should become necessary his control over the borough electorates would ensure a Tory House of Commons. The King did not need to levy arbitrary taxes, or to imprison men without trial, or to institute a formal censorship of the Press, for he had less provocative and more effective means of achieving his objects. For that very reason, his subtle despotism was more dangerous to liberty than Charles I's had been. In defiance of the Test Act the Duke of York returned to Court and to the Admiralty. Danby was released from imprisonment on bail; and Titus Oates was first expelled from Court and then, in 1684, was imprisoned for failing to pay an impossibly large fine. Notwithstanding the terms of the Triennial Act, whereby a new Parliament should have been called not later than 1684, Charles continued to rule without Parliament.

One serious feature of Charles' absolutism was its effect on England's standing abroad. The continuance of the absolutism hinged upon Charles' pension from Louis XIV, and that pension would be forthcoming only so long as Charles remained passive while Louis pursued his own schemes of conquest. In 1683 French armies had entered the Spanish Netherlands; in 1684 they overran Luxemburg which was compelled to surrender. Both Spain and the United Provinces looked in vain to England for help; and Spain was compelled to make a twenty-year truce with Louis during which period certain towns were left in his hands. The practical effect would be to enable Louis to move forward thence whenever it suited his purpose to do so.

Another effect abroad of Charles' absolutism at home was the English withdrawal from Tangier, which had been part of the dowry that Charles' Queen, Catherine of Braganza, had brought to England. On the defences of the town and the improvement of the harbour Charles had expended large sums. Strategically, Tangier was in a commanding position on the Mediterranean, but Charles could not afford the cost of maintaining it if he was to govern without a Parliament. In 1683, therefore, the English withdrew from Tangier.

How long Charles would have been able to continue his absolute government is difficult to estimate. Much would have depended upon political conditions on the Continent. Even among his supporters at home there were differences of opinion on policy. Halifax was opposed to subservience to France and, believing that the royal control of boroughs would ensure the return of Tory Members, he strongly urged that a new Parliament should be summoned in accordance with the terms of the Triennial Act. The opposite policy was supported by the Earl of Rochester (formerly Laurence Hyde, son of the first Earl of Clarendon, and therefore brother-in-law to the Duke of York). Around these two rivals—Halifax and Rochester—opposing Court factions centred. During 1684 the balance between them was fairly even. The issue of their rivalry was determined in an unexpected fashion. On February 2, 1685, Charles suffered a sudden seizure, and on February 6 he died. Perhaps the only significant fact connected with Charles' death was that he accepted the last rites from a Roman Catholic priest, Father Huddlestone, whom the Duke of York had smuggled into the royal bedchamber; but what was the exact significance that Charles himself attached to this act, no one will ever know.

To die thus in his bed after a reign of twenty-five years, following the upheaval of the Civil War, was no mean personal achievement. But it had been accomplished by allowing things to take their course, and by intervening only when necessary to divert them into some desired direction. It had been a policy of putting off the evil day. For this very reason Charles left to his successor an unenviable legacy.

Chapter 11

King James II

1685–88

1. James' Tyranny

The completeness of Charles II's victory over the Whigs was shown by the peaceful succession of James whose exclusion had been the chief item of the Whigs' programme. James had not even suffered the alternative restrictions favoured by Halifax. The party-disputes about his succession would inevitably complicate the situation which he would have to face at least during the early months of his reign. But James was not an inexperienced youth. He was fifty-two years of age, and during the twenty-five years of his brother's reign he had been intimately associated with public affairs, and as Lord High Admiral had competently discharged the duties of one of the most responsible offices of State. Perhaps the best assurance that he would proceed with caution in the matter of religion was his craving for royal power. Within a quarter of an hour of Charles' death, James addressed the Privy Council, as he handed back the seals of offices to their previous holders, in the following terms:

> I shall make it my endeavour to preserve this government, both in Church and State, as it is now by law established. I know the principles of the Church of England are for monarchy, and the members of it have shown themselves good and loyal subjects; therefore I shall always take good care to defend and support it. I know, too, that the laws of England are sufficient to make the king as great a monarch as I can wish; and as I can never depart from the just rights and prerogatives of the crown, so I shall never invade any man's property. . . . I have often heretofore ventured my life in defence of this nation; and I shall go as far as any man in preserving it in all its just rights and liberties.

That these words were uttered informally, and with every mark of being extemporary, seemed to make them the more trustworthy as an expression of the new King's unaffected con-victions. Moreover, in contrast to his late brother, James had never been known as a dissembler.

Protestants who thus reflected on James' accession were doubtless brought to a pause by the news that, on the second Sunday of his reign, James had the doors of the Queen's Chapel at St James's flung open so that all might watch and, if they wished, share in the celebration of mass. Even this action might be held to accord with James' reputation for straightforwardness.

Evidence of the swing in public feeling during the previous few years was afforded by the treatment meted out to Titus Oates. Convicted of perjury on two counts, Oates was sen-tenced to unfrocking, an exorbitant fine, brutal flogging, and a spell in the pillory once a year. If Oates was to endure retri-bution for all the injustices he had brought upon others, no punishment could be too harsh. On the other hand, the cruelty of the sentence was a sinister reflection of the temper of the age and an ill omen of the treatment that opponents of the Court's religion were likely to receive.

Whatever views James' subjects might hold individually about these opening religious events in the reign, all alike approved his action in issuing writs for a Parliament which met first on May 19. This was the first occasion on which the effects of remodelling the borough-corporations had a chance to show themselves. The new House of Commons contained an almost solid phalanx of Tories. It was the most 'loyalist' House since the Civil War and probably during the whole Stuart period. Even James is stated to have confessed that there were not more than forty Members whom he could wish to change. From his point of view, the one danger-spot was the Tories' devotion to the Established Church. If James ever acted so as to threaten the Church's security he might find even a Tory Parliament unyielding.

The chief Ministers were Rochester (formerly Laurence Hyde) as Lord Treasurer, Godolphin as Lord Chamberlain to the Queen, and Sunderland as Secretary of State. With them was associated Rochester's brother, Clarendon. The two brothers were worth their places in office if only to suggest that no violence would be done to the Established Church which they consistently supported as their father had done before them. The most competent of the Ministers was Godolphin, an administrative genius who later, as Marlborough's collaborator under Queen Anne, was to exercise enormous influence in the State. But it was Sunderland who had the King's closest confidence: his great object was to oust Halifax and Rochester, and to this end he threw himself unreservedly into supporting the King and the Roman Catholic party.

In spite of the loyalty with which James was greeted, there were seriously discontented elements both in Scotland and in England. It was in Scotland that the discontent first openly burst out.

Unrest there had been smouldering ever since Charles II's accession. The Restoration settlement of the Church in Scotland had followed much the same lines as that in England, including the ejection of something like one-third of the clergy and an Act that was even more stringent than the English Five Mile Act. The result was a succession of violent outbreaks, some big some small, throughout Charles' reign—the Pentland Rising of 1666, the murder of Archbishop Sharp in 1679, followed by encounters at Drumclog and Bothwell Brig in the same year. In 1679 also the Duke of York, who had taken up his residence in Edinburgh, was made High Commissioner for Scotland. He secured the passage by the 1681 Scottish Parliament of a Test Act requiring that all office-holders in Church and State (including Members of Parliament) should take an oath both to support the Protestant religion and also to repudiate the Covenants and to recognize the principle of non-resistance to the Crown. The two parts of the oath were mutually contradictory, so that only men of undecided convictions could subscribe to it. A number of clergy relinquished their livings rather than take the oath, and when it was submitted to the Earl of Argyle he would accept it only with the reservation: "As far as it is consistent with itself and with the Protestant Religion." Argyle was the son of the great Marquess, the Covenanters' leader, who had been seized by Charles II's orders and executed in 1661. The Earl's virtual rejection of the oath was a precedent which might encourage imitators. He was therefore charged with treason and condemned to death. Having managed to escape from Edinburgh Castle, he fled to Holland. There he met other discontented exiles, including the Duke of Monmouth; and there, after James' accession, plans were hatched for joint rebellions which were to be raised by Argyle in Scotland and by Monmouth in England.

Argyle set out from Holland early in May 1685 taking with him some three hundred men who he hoped would be the nucleus of a great rising of Covenanters. His hopes were an illusion. Argyle was not fitted to be the leader of such an enterprise. Also, though there was widespread antagonism in Scotland towards James, the discontented elements were so divergent in their views that there was small chance of their making common cause together. The Government took prompt action, and by quartering troops in the district most likely to be sympathetic towards a rising, prevented any great influx of recruits. By the middle of June Argyle fell into Government hands and, without further trial, was executed under the sentence of 1681.

While Argyle's meagre forces were being dealt with in Scotland, Monmouth, having collected what arms he could in Holland, crossed over to England. On June 11, 1685, he landed with 150 followers at Lyme Regis. In the declaration which he at once issued he claimed that he was Charles II's legitimate son, and that the succession to the throne should be determined by the vote of a free Parliament. He charged James II with responsibility for the Great Fire, for the murder of Godfrey, and for poisoning Charles II. Claiming to be Protestantism's champion, he called upon Englishmen to rally to his support. In considerable numbers recruits answered his call, chiefly West-country labourers. At its best, though only for a short time, the rebel army numbered perhaps seven thousand men. Had they been well-equipped and led they might have proved formidable, but they were neither: a large proportion carried only farm-implements—scythes, forks, and the like—and so few of the gentry joined that scarcely any officers were available. The King had troops and arms in plenty. Regular soldiers, including the garrison from Tangier, were sent from London; and three regiments of Scots, serving the United Provinces, were sent over by William of Orange. Supreme command was given to the Earl of Feversham, a naturalized Englishman of French birth and in high favour at the English Court but not otherwise distinguished. His second-in-command was John, Lord Churchill.

Monmouth moved through Axminster and Taunton, where he was enthusiastically welcomed, to Bridgwater. His original plan had been to advance to Bristol; but the farther he marched thither the more hopeless his prospects appeared, so he returned through Frome to Bridgwater. At Sedgemoor, east of the town, the royal forces gathered and barred any further move. So superior were the royal troops that the rebels' only chance of success lay in a surprise attack. This was Monmouth's decision on the night of July 5. Such an enterprise, hazardous in any circumstances, needed rigid discipline and skilful leadership. Monmouth's irregulars betrayed their presence before they could deliver their attack. Though the rebels fought with the utmost bravery, selling their lives dearly against tremendous odds, their defeat was inevitable. As soon as this became plain, Monmouth fled from the battlefield to be found three days later hiding in a ditch in the New Forest. He was taken to London where he obtained an interview with the King before whom he grovelled with craven pleadings for his life. On July 15 he was executed, and in justice it should be recorded that he met his death with great courage.

The immediate effects of Monmouth's rebellion were that Colonel Kirke and his regiment lately returned from Tangier hanged the disbanded rebels wherever found, and that Chief Justice Lord Jeffreys went on the western circuit and doled out terrible punishments not only to the rebels but to all who had harboured or encouraged them. Among the latter class was Alice Lisle, who had sheltered two fugitives without at first realizing who they were. When the truth dawned on her she informed the authorities but meanwhile the men escaped. She was nevertheless put on trial. Twice the jury found her not guilty, but Jeffreys raged until he secured a verdict of guilty. He then sentenced the prisoner to be burned alive, a sentence which the King commuted to beheading. Exact records of the total number of Jeffreys' victims are not available; but probably some one hundred suffered death, and four times that number were sold into slavery in the West Indies. Jeffreys' progress was fitly known as the Bloody Assizes. Responsibility for the brutality cannot rest on Jeffreys alone. Ultimately it must rest upon the King, who not only did not check Jeffreys but on the latter's return to London raised him to be Lord Chancellor. The episode casts a sinister light on James' character, and indicates the lengths to which he would have gone in order to establish Roman Catholicism in England. A more far-reaching effect of the rebellion was that its defeat, and the consequent powerlessness of the Protestant forces, encouraged James to press on with his schemes of Romanizing all departments of State, including the Army. In this process he was further encouraged by the temporary popularity which the rebellion evoked for him in Parliament.

James' religious policy, like that of his brother before him, would of necessity be closely related to his foreign policy and to events on the Continent. Charles' independence of Parliament had been made possible by his pension from Louis XIV; and Louis' friendship had depended upon Charles' lenience towards Roman Catholics. With James these same factors obtained but to an even more marked degree. As James' Catholicism was much more pronounced and open than Charles' had been, his collaboration with Louis might be expected to be closer. In practice, however, things did not work as simply as this, for James' strong Catholicism would alienate Parliament and so would render him more dependent upon Louis than Charles had been. Immediately on James' accession, Louis transmitted, through his Ambassador, Barillon, a substantial present to James, and thus held out a bait for future subservience; but thereafter, notwithstanding James' repeated inquiries, Louis awaited the turn of events and refused further payments.

A more prudent king than James would have realized that the quickest, as well as the surest, method of achieving his object would be to proceed slowly. The proper strategy was to test the nation's feeling by first securing a general toleration and then, if this proved safe, by measures more specifically favouring Roman Catholics. But James was not prudent, and he lacked the ability to interpret the nation's attitude on the whole subject of religion. Though he began with moves for the repeal of the Test Act, he seemed blind to the meaning of the reaction which these moves provoked. When the question of repealing the Test Act and the Habeas Corpus Act was brought before the Council Halifax led the opposition, and in October 1685 Halifax was dismissed from the Council. In the same month Louis XIV revoked Henry IV's Edict of Nantes of 1598, which had granted certain rights of worship and civil liberty to the Huguenots. That the two events, in England and France respectively, almost coincided in time, was mere chance. But this did not alter the fact that evidently the French and the English Governments were moving in the same direction. In view of the relations that had existed between the two Governments during Charles II's reign, the suspicion and even alarm which spread in England was natural.

The nation's attitude was accurately reflected when Parliament met for the second session. The King's Speech on November 9 announced that, in view of the inadequacy of the militia to deal with such rebellions as that recently experienced, the regular Army had been increased, and that some of the new officers did not comply with legal requirements—that is, with the Test Act—but upon their fidelity he could rely. Long debates ensued, and Parliament showed its determination to insist upon observance of the Test Act before granting the King money. To entrust James in peace-time with an army officered by men of his own choice would be to place in his hands the supreme instrument of arbitrary government. In order to give pause to the strong anti-governmental feeling expressed in an address to the King against appointing Roman Catholic officers, the debate was adjourned on November 19 for four days. Even James could see that this would make no difference to the passing of the address, so, rather than sustain an adverse vote, on November 20 he prorogued the House until February. In actual fact, the Parliament never met again, though it was not dissolved until July 1687.

By proroguing Parliament James forfeited the £700,000

which it had proposed to grant him. But his freedom from
Parliamentary interference encouraged him to proceed with
his schemes to exalt Roman Catholicism in all departments of
national life irrespective of statutes or private rights to the
contrary.

James' first care was to organize an army on which he could
rely to carry through his Romanizing policy. Many of the new
recruits, and a large proportion of the officers, were Roman
Catholics. The Army in Ireland became predominantly Catholic, and drafts from it were sent over to England. During each
of the three summers of 1685, '86, and '87 a training-camp was
pitched on Hounslow Heath. The presence of some sixteen
thousand troops so near to London was interpreted as an
attempt to awe the City into compliance with the King's will.

In order to give some appearance of legality to these proceedings, James had a test-case (known as *Godden v. Hales*)[1]
brought before the courts. Sir Edward Hales, a convert to
Roman Catholicism, was appointed to be Governor of Dover.
In 1686 he was sued in the name of his coachman, Godden, for
having broken the Test Act by holding office under the Crown
without taking the required oath and sacrament. Tried at
Rochester Assizes, Hales was found guilty. Then, pleading a
royal dispensation, he lodged an appeal to the King's Bench.
There eleven of the twelve judges found that the Crown had
the right to use the dispensing power. In the next year Hales
was appointed Lieutenant of the Tower of London and Master
of the Ordnance. Much more important than its effect on Hales
himself was the bearing of the case upon James' designs for
arbitrary government in general. The judges' finding removed
any legal bar to his ignoring Acts of Parliament, and assured
him that he could rely on his judges if any of his subjects
should resist. Thus strengthened, he could proceed with his
methods of arbitrary government and his schemes to spread
Roman Catholicism.

The Minister that chiefly supported James in his religious
innovations was the Earl of Sunderland, who in December
1685 became Lord President of the Council (an office which

[1] Robertson, pp. 384–388.

10 + s.c.

Halifax's dismissal had left vacant), though retaining the chief Secretaryship of State. In order to make his ascendancy secure, Sunderland now needed to remove his one remaining rival, Rochester. After Parliament's prorogation James no longer needed to placate the Anglican party with which Rochester was identified—that is, the King no longer needed Rochester as a figurehead. Though for the moment Rochester retained his Treasurership, he ceased to have any active influence in the counsels of the King. Sunderland saw that his interests would be doubly served by urging James to extreme measures: he would win James' favour, and would further undermine Rochester's influence.

In July the King set up a commission for ecclesiastical affairs with powers similar to those of the Court of High Commission which had been abolished in 1641 and whose abolition had been confirmed in 1661.[1] The Archbishop of Canterbury was appointed President of the Court. Its remaining members were two other bishops, Rochester, Sunderland, Chief Justice Herbert, and Lord Chancellor Jeffreys. Without the Lord Chancellor's attendance there could be no quorum. Archbishop Sancroft, being opposed to James' religious policy, excused himself from membership on account of ill-health: a fresh lay-member was therefore appointed. The Court's first action was to suspend Compton, Bishop of London, who had displeased the King by opposing the repeal of the Test Act.

Among the chief targets for James' attack during the following months were the universities of Oxford and Cambridge. These were strongholds of Anglicanism, and their influence in training the future leaders of the nation made their conversion to Roman Catholicism essential to James' schemes. The Vice-Chancellor of Cambridge, for having refused to obey a royal order to admit a Benedictine monk to a degree, was haled before the ecclesiastical commission and deprived of his office. At Oxford, in April 1687, the Fellows of Magdalen College were ordered to elect the King's nominee to the vacant Presidency of their college. They refused—partly on account of the nominee's ineligibility under the college statutes and partly

[1] Robertson, pp. 24–25, 32–34.

because of his personal unfitness—and made their own election. The King declared the election void, and ordered the election of Samuel Parker, Bishop of Oxford. Once again the Fellows refused. Even when James went in person they remained unmoved. Finally, under a special royally appointed commission, force was used to instal Parker, and the obdurate Fellows were removed. Parker died in 1688; and then James appointed a Papal emissary, Bonaventura Giffard. No matter how successful James' browbeating methods might seem to be in the universities, it was dearly bought. The universities, especially Oxford, had consistently championed the Stuart cause; and for the King thus to intimidate them was to turn his best friends into bitter enemies.

While James was pursuing the direct methods of browbeating the Established Church into submission and of capturing key-positions in it for his Roman Catholic nominees, he was also trying the indirect method of circumscribing the Church's influence by winning to himself the alliance of the Protestant Dissenters. These latter, including the Presbyterians, were numerous and, in the aggregate, they controlled considerable resources of wealth. Though they and their beliefs were abhorrent to James, their support, added to that of the Roman Catholics, might enable him to defy the Anglicans. In one respect the interests of Protestant and of Roman Catholic Dissenters were identical—namely, that the Test Act and the penal laws should be repealed. If James could secure the support of both groups of Dissenters towards that end he would then be able to flood the State Departments, civil and military, with Roman Catholics and thereafter to ignore the Protestant Dissenters. Some of the latter were willing to give James their support for the repeal, not the least among them being William Penn, the Quaker son of the Cromwellian Admiral who seized Jamaica. William Penn was personally familiar with Court circles, and his attitude encouraged James to believe that the Protestant Dissenters could be won over.

One other step was necessary in preparation for an open declaration of religious freedom. The chief representatives of Anglicanism in Court circles were the King's brothers-in-law, Clarendon and Rochester. Hence, in order to undermine rigid

Anglicanism still further and at the same time to convince the Dissenters that the King's wish for toleration was genuine, in January 1687 Clarendon and Rochester were dismissed from their offices as Lord-Lieutenant of Ireland and Lord Treasurer respectively. Thereafter James felt that he could rely on the Dissenters and on his Court in carrying out his policy.

Accordingly, on April 4, 1687, the King issued his first Declaration of Indulgence[1] which granted full liberty of public worship both to Protestant Dissenters and to Roman Catholics, and abolished religious tests for office under the Crown, but also renewed the King's promise to maintain the established Anglican Church. Further, the Declaration affirmed that Parliament would approve the toleration.

In spite of this affirmation, James knew that the existing Parliament, notwithstanding its original loyalty, would never countenance his Romanizing intentions. Hence on July 2, 1687, the prorogation became a dissolution; and during the autumn every possible effort was made to prepare the constituencies for new elections. Whig Dissenters replaced Tory Anglicans on the borough corporations, and in the counties new Justices were appointed. In spite of these precautions the country's hostility to the Court's policy remained dangerously clear. Even the Dissenters, whose support was essential, remained suspicious of, and in many instances actively opposed to, James' plans which were regarded as thinly veiled popery. The proposed elections had therefore to be indefinitly postponed. Yet, in face of the plain implications of the situation, James pressed forward.

On April 27, 1688, he published his second Declaration of Indulgence which in the main was a repetition of the first declaration, but with the additional promise that a new Parliament should meet not later than November of that year. A further difference was that an Order in Council, drawn up on May 4 and issued three days later, enjoined that "the bishops cause the said declaration to be sent and distributed throughout their several dioceses" where, on two successive Sundays,

[1] Robertson, pp. 388–391.

it was to "be read at the usual time of divine service . . . in all churches and chapels."

The second declaration roused public opposition to fever-heat. To abrogate the Test Act by the use of the royal prerogative was evil enough. To compel the clergy to promulgate such a declaration, and the laity to listen to it, contrary to their consciences, was an insult not to be endured. On May 12 some of the London clergy consulted together at Lambeth Palace; and on May 18 a meeting of bishops at Lambeth resulted in a moderately worded protest signed by Archbishop Sancroft and six other bishops.

> The Declaration, being founded on such a dispensing power, as may at pleasure sett aside all law, ecclesiastical or civill, appears to us illegall, and did soe to the parl'mt of 72, and it is a point of soe great consequence, that we cannot soe farre make o'selves p'ties to it, as the reading of it in the Churches at ye time of divine service will amount to.[1]

By thus protesting against the declaration not on religious grounds but on the ground of its use of the dispensing power, the bishops had raised a constitutional issue of first-class importance which the King could not ignore. Moreover, the temper of the people so expressed itself as to leave no doubt that the Seven Bishops were but the nation's mouthpiece.

The petition was presented to the King on the evening of the day on which it was drawn up, Friday, May 18—that is, two days before the first Sunday on which it was to be read in the London Churches. Clearly he had to make a choice between two extreme alternatives: either he must suppress the bishops or he must abandon the Indulgence. He decided on the former course. On June 8 the Seven Bishops were summoned before the Council and sent thence to the Tower. Their trial took place on June 29. At the end of the proceedings the judges were divided on the directions to be given to the jury, and the jury itself was divided. Only after the jurymen had been shut up all night were they prepared to give a unanimous verdict, which on the 30th they did. It was a verdict of

[1] Robertson, p. 392.

Not Guilty. The whole nation seemed to go wild for joy. Not the least significant fact of the demonstrations was that they were shared by the Dissenters and by the King's Army on Hounslow Heath.

The intensity of the rejoicings at the bishops' release was heightened by an event which had brought the nation to a sense of crisis. On June 10 (two days after the Bishops had been sent to the Tower) the Queen gave birth to a son. For fifteen years the King and the Queen had been married. They had had several children but none had survived infancy, and six years had elapsed since the previous child had been born. The common belief had been that James would never have an heir by Mary of Modena, so that the heir presumptive was Mary, the elder of his daughters by his former wife, who was also the wife of William III of Orange. It was this fact which made a large proportion of the nation unwilling to offer immediate or violent opposition to James' innovations: a few years at most would bring James' death and the succession of a staunchly Protestant monarch. This prospect of a natural solution of the nation's difficulties seemed to make armed resistance not worth while. The birth of a Prince transformed this situation. The general reaction to it was first stupefaction and then incredulity. The rumour spread that the child was not the Queen's but had been smuggled into the palace in a warming-pan so as to frustrate the Protestant Succession. Support was given to this view by the fact that, owing to the Queen's unexpected and quick labour, the usual formalities of witnessing the birth were omitted. Even members of the royal family, including the Princess Anne, were frankly sceptical about the legitimacy of the so-called Prince. The Prince was, in short, held to be a pretender.

Though time and more sober counsels have discredited the general scepticism about the child's origin, that scepticism was largely responsible for a twist then imparted to the nation's constitutional development. Leading men of all views and parties realized that the appearance of a pretender made prompt action imperative. The child would be brought up a Roman Catholic and, if he were accepted as the legitimate heir to James, Roman Catholicism, instead of being only a passing phase of the declining years of the reigning king, would be fastened upon the nation for ever. Only one method of avoiding what was commonly regarded as this catastrophe presented itself: the Princess Mary and her husband, William, must be installed on the English throne. Hence, on June 30 (the very day of the bishops' acquittal), seven representative men (Bishop Compton; Lords Devonshire, Shrewsbury, Danby, and Lumley; Edward Russell, and Henry Sidney) signed a document inviting William's intervention. The letter was carried to Holland by Arthur Herbert, formerly an English admiral but dismissed for his refusal to support the repeal of the Test Act and now disguised as a common seaman.

James II's imprisonment of the Seven Bishops was the crowning blunder of his reign, comparable to his father's blunder in trying to arrest the Five Members. It had set in train a process which was to change the constitutional face of Britain and, indirectly, of the World.

2. The Coming of William and Mary

The invitation which Herbert carried to William was the end, not the beginning, of long negotiations between William and certain leading Englishmen. Since James' accession William had made himself familiar with the turns of English politics. For this interest he had two main reasons. First, the political and military situation on the Continent was so finely balanced that the attitude of England might be the decisive adjusting factor; and in that adjustment the very existence of the United Provinces might be determined. Second, the personal relationship of William and of his wife to England made English affairs a matter of natural concern to William, especially as the absence of male heirs to James made Mary heir presumptive to the English throne.

During the opening months of James' reign William's attitude was friendly. This was shown by the readiness with which William sent over the Scottish regiments from the United Provinces to help James against Monmouth. But that was during the time when James was moving slowly and without showing his hand. In such circumstances it behoved

William to move with equal caution. As James' religious policy became increasingly pronounced, William's attitude became correspondingly rigid. If James managed to re-establish Roman Catholicism, England would be drawn into the orbit of France, the mortal enemy of the United Provinces. To keep close contact with the English parties opposed to Rome therefore became an essential factor in maintaining the United Provinces' independence.

In England, similarly, James' opponents realized that the interests of their cause could best be served by collaboration with William. Not only was the Protestantism of William and Mary unimpeachable, but if the feared French support of Roman Catholicism in England ever materialized, William's military co-operation against France would be invaluable. During the early part of 1687 William kept his special Ambassador, Dykveld, in England with the object of discovering everything possible about Anglo-French relations. Dykveld used the opportunity to open up personal dealings with most of the opposition-leaders; and when he returned home he was able to place in William's hands written assurances of support, including those of Lord Churchill and the Earl of Rochester. Henceforward it was understood that William would be accepted as the leader of any open opposition to James. The point at which such opposition should declare itself, and the procedure to be adopted, would be less easy to determine. On one stipulation William insisted: he would cross to England only if he received a written invitation signed by a number of responsible leaders. The latters' signatures on a document, which William could produce at his pleasure, would compel the signatories' adherence to his cause and would encourage others to follow. Such was the document carried by Herbert when he left England for The Hague on June 30, 1688.

The receipt of the invitation raised another, and not the least, of William's difficulties: how was he to persuade the Dutch States-General to allow him to lead armed forces out of the United Provinces which thus would be left defenceless against French attack? The destiny of both England and the United Provinces might thus hang on the moves of the French King. Louis' foreign relationships at that moment were being determined by the outcome of two events of 1686. The first was the anti-French alliance between Frederick William, the Great Elector of Brandenburg, and the Emperor Leopold I. Thus Louis' threat to the German States had achieved the impossible: the leading Protestant and the leading Roman Catholic States had taken common action. This was a fact that would have caused a less egoistical person than Louis to pause. The second event of 1686 was the formation of another alliance, the League of Augsburg. Its original members were the Emperor, Spain, the United Provinces, Sweden, and Saxony; and in 1687 to these were joined Bavaria and Savoy; while Pope Innocent XI secretly encouraged them on account of the long-standing quarrel between himself and Louis, notwithstanding the latter's Catholicism. Once again we have to note a combined Roman Catholic and Protestant league against Louis. A war between Louis and a number of other European States seemed inevitable. England's fate and that of the United Provinces would depend upon the exact time at which the war broke out and the exact direction it took.

Louis' information about European politics was much fuller and more exact than was James'. While James was raising enemies against himself in England, and while William was hiring soldiers wherever possible in northern Europe, Louis was continually warning James of the danger in which he stood. James merely resented Louis' interference and informed Louis that French patronage would compromise him still further in the eyes of his English subjects. So far as the Dutch were concerned, Louis was less dangerous than he appeared to be. If he opened hostilities against the United Provinces his ships would be swept from the sea by the superior Dutch fleet. Moreover, Louis' immediate concern was with his German enemies, and he had no desire to bring about combined action between them and the Dutch. His problem therefore was how to strike against the German States in such a way as not to involve the Dutch. His solution was to direct his main armies against the fortress of Philippsburg in the Palatinate, on the Upper Rhine. This he did towards the end of September 1688 and so removed from the Dutch all fear of an immediate French invasion, thus providing conditions favourable to

10*

William's leading not only a fleet but also troops to England. Possibly Louis was not unwilling to teach James how much he depended upon French support. If so, Louis miscalculated the situation at least as seriously as James did. Louis could have had no conception of how complete William's victory in England would prove or he would never have moved his troops so as to make it safe for William to leave Holland. It was the crisis of William's foreign policy; for William's success in England, and the consequent indissoluble Anglo-Dutch alliance, frustrated all Louis' objectives, ultimate as well as immediate.

By the time that Louis took his fateful step away from Holland, even James could no longer remain blind to the evident signs of disaffection in England and of danger from overseas. During September and early October he made concessions with gathering momentum. Bishop Compton's suspension was removed. The ecclesiastical commission court was abolished. The appropriated charters of London and other towns were restored, and all town-charters granted since 1679 were cancelled. The recently removed Justices were reinstated. The Magdalen Fellows were allowed to return to their college. These and other similar hasty concessions deceived no one: they were too obviously inspired by fear; and if for any reason the fear of William's invasion should be removed, they would be cancelled with equal haste. Moreover, none of the concessions touched the root causes of the nation's grievances: they did not mention the use of the King's dispensing power or the introduction of Roman Catholicism.

Meanwhile William's preparations for an expedition to England went steadily on, and by the end of September he was only awaiting a favourable wind. Altogether he had two hundred transport vessels, with about fifty men-o'-war and many lighter craft to escort them. The English fleet was drawn up off the Sussex coast. Until October 19 a "Papist wind" kept the Dutch in port, but on that day a "Protestant wind" blew, and they were able to set sail. A sudden storm caused damage enough to compel a return to port. It was on Thursday, November 1, that William set sail a second time. He sailed past the English fleet along the south coast of England. The proceeding was extremely risky, for the unbeaten English fleet was thus in a position to cut the Dutch communications. But the risk of losing communication with Holland was almost negligible compared with the greater risk of the invasion as a whole. On the other hand, a clash with the English fleet was very undesirable. Eventually the English fleet set off in pursuit of William; but the wind veered to the south-west and compelled the English to enter Portsmouth. The same wind took William into Torbay where his mixed force of fifteen thousand troops landed without hindrance on November 5.

Perhaps the most remarkable feature of the crisis was that nowhere in the country was there a party of men prepared to strike a blow in James' support. Even those who, by virtue of office or family-relationship, had been closely identified with him, forsook him. The result was that there were no serious clashes of arms or bloodshed, and William's advance towards London resembled an orderly progress rather than the march of a conqueror.

William's chief need was that prominent men should declare in his favour and so should encourage the mass of the nation to join him. At first, as was not unnatural, such men hesitated. The Bloody Assizes were still fresh in mind, especially in the West. But after a few days a trickle of adherents began to flow into William's quarters. One of the first was Lord Cornbury, heir to Clarendon. The Earl of Devonshire was the most important recruit in the midlands. Lord Delamere raised forces for William in Cheshire; and Danby, having seized York, similarly raised William's standard in Yorkshire.

The first stage of William's journey from his landing-place at Brixham was Exeter, where he remained a fortnight. James in due course set out from London towards Salisbury whence he could bar William's advance. Having reached Salisbury on November 19, James held a council of his officers. The obvious plan was to attack the invader before he gained more recruits. But the unreliable morale of the royal troops rendered the wisdom of this plan doubtful. The loyalty of many even of the officers had been shaken by James' rejection of a petition, drawn up by the bishops, for a new Parliament. How unstable the mass of the Army was had been shown by the enthusiasm

with which it had greeted the Seven Bishops' acquittal. On
November 24 James and his council decided to leave Salisbury
and fall back to London. It was a fatal move. The retreat
encouraged the belief that James knew that he was beaten.
Even more fatal to his cause was the defection to William
during that same night of James' nephew, the Duke of Grafton, and of his ablest general, Lord Churchill. Churchill's
defection spread dismay in the royal Army. James' retreat
rapidly became a rout. When he reached London on November 26 worse news awaited him. His daughter, Anne, had
been left with her friend, Lady Churchill, with whom Lord
Churchill had concerted plans before leaving for the West.
In accordance with those plans, on the 25th the Princess Anne
and Lady Churchill left Whitehall. The facts, as afterwards
known, were that they were conducted by Bishop Compton
to the Earl of Devonshire at Nottingham. Nothing could have
demonstrated more completely the hopelessness of James'
position. Well might he cry: "God help me! My own children
have forsaken me."

On November 27 James met a hastily convened gathering
of about fifty peers. They minced no words. Even the leading
Tories like Clarendon, and others who were less definitely
attached to the party like Halifax, told James plainly that if
he was to keep his throne he must call a Parliament, dismiss
Roman Catholic officers, sever himself from France, and
negotiate with William. William's staunchest followers could
scarcely have demanded harsher terms than these, and James'
view was that a throne on such conditions was not worth
keeping. In order to give himself time for action, he agreed to
the issue of writs for an election, and promised meanwhile to
consider the peers' other demands. Next day James promised
a free pardon to all in arms against him, and sent commissioners to treat with William, the three appointed being Halifax, Nottingham, and Godolphin. On December 1 Clarendon
himself left London to join William. Very soon James would
have no party left.

James' real intention was to flee the country. The three
commissioners met William on December 8. On the 9th the
Queen and the infant Prince set sail from Gravesend for

France. James then destroyed the writs for the forthcoming
Parliamentary election and ordered the disbanding of the
Army. Having thus done everything possible to hamper his
successor, early on December 11 he set out secretly from
Whitehall, carrying with him the great seal which he threw
into the Thames as he fled across the river. At Sheerness he
boarded a customs vessel.

The King's flight left the country without any supreme
executive authority. Yet somehow the country's government
must be carried on, and the peers wisely took the first steps
towards finding a successor to James. Meeting at Guildhall,
they drew up and sent to William a declaration offering to
co-operate with him for the nation's freedom. The need for
such a step was shown during the night following James'
flight when the London mob sacked the houses of the representatives of foreign Roman Catholic Courts. This disorder
revealed also the most serious weakness of such government
as still remained—namely, the lack of sufficient armed forces
to maintain order. Whatever secret intentions William may
have cherished when he embarked for England, he now found
himself without any alternative to taking over the responsibility for the country's government.

Hardly had this position become clear when another com-
plication arose. Some fishermen discovered James on board
the vessel at Sheerness and, in an excess of zeal, brought him
ashore. On December 15 he was brought back to London. This
was the last thing that William or many of his supporters
desired. Having so nearly gained control of English politics,
thus attaining his life's ambition of checking Louis XIV, William was in no mood to relinquish his hold. Yet to get rid of
James by violence, whether by execution or by expulsion,
would alienate a large section of the nation whose support
was most important to William. William therefore decided
upon a middle course. He ordered that James should be taken
back to Rochester. There the prisoner was kept under such
slack guard that he had no difficulty in escaping. On December 22 he once more, and for the last time, embarked from
English soil.

One of William's first acts after receiving the good news of

James' flight was to order the French Ambassador, Barillon, to leave England within two days. Few episodes in his career can have afforded William such keen satisfaction.

In one respect William's government was now faced with the same constitutional dilemma as Charles II's had had to resolve: only Parliamentary recognition could make a king's accession valid, but no legal Parliament could be summoned except by a king, and the break in the succession had left the country without both king and Parliament. The solution adopted in 1688 followed the precedent of 1660. Elections were held, but the resulting assembly called itself not a Parliament but a Convention, its primary function being to recognize the new occupant of the throne. The procedure involved a legal fiction, but it did the least possible violence to constitutional custom.

The Convention met on January 22, 1689. For the first time in many years the elections had been truly free, for William had wisely made no attempt to influence the representation. Differences of views in the Convention soon showed themselves as between exclusionists and those who would have preserved the theory of Divine Right by recognizing James as King but with a regency exercising his executive powers. After long debates, two resolutions were passed by both Houses:

> That King James the Second, having endeavoured to subvert the constitution of the kingdom by breaking the original contract between king and people, and by the advice of Jesuits and other wicked persons having violated the fundamental laws, and having withdrawn himself out of the kingdom, has abdicated the government, and the throne is thereby become vacant.
>
> That it hath been found by experience to be inconsistent with the safety and welfare of this protestant kingdom to be governed by a popish prince.

This declaration that the throne was vacant left the way clear for filling it. Here another problem arose: William was only third in the order of succession, the rightful heir being his wife, Mary, and after her, her sister Anne. Various solutions were suggested, including one that Mary should be Queen with William as Prince Consort. William, however, made clear that he would never be the subject of his own wife, and that the least that he would accept would be the crown for life; otherwise he would return to Holland. This was the principle formally incorporated in the Declaration of Rights (February 1689) which, having listed James' illegal acts, stated that William and Mary should be jointly King and Queen (though William alone was to exercise administration), that the survivor should rule for life, and that the order of succession after William and Mary was to be, first, Mary's descendants, second, Anne and her descendants, and third, William's descendants. Further, the declaration defined as illegal "the pretended Power of Suspending of Laws," "the pretended Power of dispensing with Law . . . as it hath been assumed and exercised of late," and the keeping of an army in time of peace; and it asserted that the subject had the right to petition the King, that election of Members to Parliament should be free, that there should be freedom of speech in Parliament, and that excessive bail or fines or cruel punishments should not be imposed.

In these terms was summarized the settlement of the matters that had been in dispute between King and Parliament since the accession of the first Stuart King of England, in 1603.

Chapter 12

King William III, 1689–1702,
and Queen Mary II, 1689–94

1. Revolution Settlement

The unanimity with which the nation allowed James to leave England, and William to enter it, was illusory. Events would soon show that the religious and political differences which had rent the nation during two generations were not dead but only dormant. New circumstances would awaken the old issues in a new, but a no less intense, form: and William would be handicapped by peculiar difficulties in dealing with the resulting problems. Not the least of his handicaps would be himself. William had been trained in a school of bitter experience. After being excluded by the jealousy of the de Witts from what he regarded as his rightful place as Stadtholder during his youth, he had been called to lead his country in the crisis of 1672 when he was still only twenty-one years of age. The bitterness produced by these early experiences developed in him a secretiveness that hardened rather than softened as the years passed. This effect was further intensified by the ill-health which persisted from his youth up. The condition of his lungs was such that he could hardly draw breath without pain. This alone was enough to make him irascible. Moreover, his ill-health had serious political consequences. Even in the seventeenth century the atmosphere of London was so smoky that to stay in it would have been death to William. The nearest to the capital that he could live was Kensington; and whenever possible he lived still farther out at Hampton Court. There were times when to return to his native air in Holland seemed imperative. For periods William was thus removed from the hub of national life and from the personal interplay which makes up much of the fabric of political affairs.

William's need to visit Holland gave colour also to the idea that England held only a subsidiary place in his interest. It was generally recognized that his real purpose in coming to England had been the desire to assure an unbroken alliance between the United Provinces and England: while he ruled there could be no dalliance between England and France, and English forces could be used to smash French domination in Europe. Though William conscientiously discharged his duties as King of England, his English subjects knew that his heart was elsewhere; and they believed increasingly, as the reign proceeded, that English interests were subordinated to those of his native country. William's health, causing him to withdraw on occasions to Holland, fostered this idea.

From the worst consequences of his unpopularity William was saved by his Queen. Mary was thoroughly English in origin and upbringing. This, added to her personal charm, went far to counteract the effects of William's foreign attachments and his austerity. The thorough-going Tories would never be reconciled to the Revolution settlement which marked the overthrow of their political principles, and of their political supremacy; but, because Mary was the hereditary successor of James II, she retained for the Crown the loyalty of the moderate section of the Tories, and would thus preserve a balance, in Parliament and in the nation, in support of the new regime.

The first Act (February 22, 1689) of the new reign transformed the Convention into a Parliament, thus avoiding the disturbance of another election. Its business was to pass legislation which would place the new regime on a sound foundation, and would prevent a renewal of former abuses of royal power. The vexed and crucial question of the King's revenue was, for the first time, given a comprehensive answer. The King's individual expenses were separated from his governmental expenses: £700,000, the amount derived from hereditary revenues and the excise, was granted to William for life to meet his ordinary Civil List charges—that is, to pay Ministers and officials, and to meet his personal expenses; about £600,000, derived from customs, was granted for four years to maintain the armed forces; and all extraordinary expenses were to be met by specific Parliamentary grants.

Commissioners were appointed to audit public accounts and to watch appropriation of supplies. This procedure ensured to Parliament the control over the royal income, and hence over royal expenditure; and this in turn would give to Parliament a large measure of control over royal policy.

The question of the control of the Army was settled in an unexpected fashion. A Scottish regiment, raised by James II, mutinied against William and began to march towards Scotland, a move which was frustrated by Dutch cavalry led by Ginkel. This episode illustrated two dangers: first, that of leaving the country without an armed force sufficient to keep order; and, second, that of having no legal means of maintaining discipline over such forces as were in existence. The upshot was a Mutiny Act of March 1689 authorizing the continuance of the Army for six months, during which period desertion was to be punishable under martial law. Thenceforward the Mutiny Act was renewed every twelve months. The Act had two effects that could be only imperfectly anticipated by its framers: first, the Army thereby became dependent upon Parliament's authority; second, since the Mutiny Act legalized courts martial for only a year at a time, a Parliament would have to sit every year to renew the Act so as to prevent the soldiers from becoming civilians. Though subsequently there were certain years when the Army continued in existence in spite of the failure to summon a Parliament, the principle was clear, and was an important factor in developing the continuous authority of Parliament.

This is a convenient point at which to consider another proposal to strengthen Parliamentary government. To ensure that in future there should be no long interval between the dissolution of one Parliament and the meeting of another— like, for example, the interval of 1629–40 between the third and the fourth Parliaments of Charles I—was a necessary condition of such government. But scarcely less necessary was the complementary condition that no one Parliament should continue to sit for so long that it ceased to be representative of public opinion—as the Cavalier Parliament of Charles II had done from 1661–79. In 1689 a proposal was put forward to limit the life of any Parliament to three years, but it came to nothing. In 1693 a Bill for this purpose passed first the Lords and then the Commons but was vetoed by William. Later in 1693 a similar Bill was rejected even by the Commons. But in 1694 a third Bill was introduced and, having passed both Houses, received the royal assent. This Act continued in operation until 1716 when, in order to avoid a general election while the country was still in a ferment after the Jacobite Rebellion of the previous year, Parliament voted that its duration and the duration of all future Parliaments should be permitted for seven instead of three years.

In the Church, no less than in the State, the Revolution settlement was likely to evoke sharp differences of view and divided loyalties. On the whole there was no intentional persecution of religious minorities. Roman Catholics were penalized to the extent of being forbidden to carry firearms or to own a horse worth more than £5, and they were excluded by statute from London and Westminster. Even these regulations were mildly administered, and Roman Catholics were not seriously victimized.

Officials of the Established Church, like other State officials, were compelled by a further Act of March 1689 to take the oaths of Supremacy and Allegiance to William and Mary. The clergy were thereby faced with the choice between losing their livings or renouncing the oaths of allegiance already taken to James II. How keenly the clergy felt on the issue was shown by the fact that, even of the Seven Bishops who had refused to read James II's Declaration of Indulgence, five (including Archbishop Sancroft) refused to take the oath to William and Mary. Their example was followed by some four hundred other clergy, all of whom were consequently ejected. Thus began the party known as the Non-Jurors.

One reason why James' policy of indulgence had failed had been the Protestant Dissenters' refusal to be bribed by the prospect of toleration. The Dissenters were also among William III's staunchest supporters. It was fitting that they should be rewarded by some improvement in their conditions. The first proposal was that the bounds of the Established Church should be so widened as to include Protestant Dissenters within it. The plan was wrecked when Convocation refused to recognize necessary alterations in the Prayer Book, and when a Comprehension Bill failed to pass through Parliament. The alternative adopted was the Toleration Act of May 1689. By its provisions, Protestant Dissenters were allowed their own places of worship if they took the oaths of Supremacy and Allegiance, and Dissenting ministers and teachers were allowed to follow their callings if they subscribed to all but certain stipulated clauses of the Thirty-nine Articles. These benefits were specifically denied to Roman Catholics and to those who rejected the doctrine of the Trinity. The net effect of the Toleration Act was to annul the Uniformity, Conventicle, and Five Mile Acts of the Clarendon Code, but it did not annul either the Test Act or the Corporation Act. That is to say, Nonconformists were still excluded from military, State, and municipal offices. They were, however, now free to enjoy and develop their own religious life, and all over the country the characteristic chapels and meeting-houses of Protestant Dissenters began to make their appearance.

The bed-rock of the Revolution settlement was the Bill of Rights which, having passed both Houses of Parliament, received the royal assent on December 16, 1689. This consisted of the Declaration of Rights of February 1689—which thus received full statutory sanction—and of additional clauses excluding from the throne a papist or anyone who should marry a papist.

The Bill of Rights is justly regarded as expressing the essence of the Revolution settlement. The greatest result of the settlement proceeded from William's having no hereditary claim to the throne. His only title was his recognition by Parliament. This fact knocked away the basis of any claim to rule by Divine Right, for a sovereign by Divine Right recognized no human source of true monarchical authority. This theoretical dependence of the King upon Parliament was secured in practice, as we have seen, by such statutes as that settling the royal revenue and the Mutiny Act.

When the principles assured by the new regime were set beside the practice of the preceding Stuarts it was natural to think of them as constituting a revolution. Yet revolution is a misleading term when applied to the changes in English government in 1688–89. A revolution is a complete turning round, and this is not a true description of the results of William III's accession. Fundamentally the Bill of Rights did not introduce new principles into English government; it only reasserted and defined principles which for centuries English people had regarded as their established rights. The flagrant violation of these rights under the first four Stuarts, or under the Tudors, in no way invalidated them. Indeed, William III's supporters might well have contended that the real revolutionary had been James I, whose interpretation of Divine Right was the innovation whence the subsequent strife, both religious and political, had been derived. These views were supported by the writings of the Whig philosopher John Locke, especially his *Essay on Civil Government*.[1] Even in the matter of the succession, every effort was made in 1688 to avoid a break: on the assumption—which was then genuinely believed—that James II's infant son was a pretender, Mary was the rightful successor to her father, so that her accession, and the arrangements for the succession after her death, made the minimum of change in the normal order of hereditary succession.

One of William's problems at his accession was the choice of new Ministers. This was closely connected with the wider problem of the relationship of the political parties towards the King and their part in the country's government. Something has been said already of the formation of the Whig and Tory parties under Charles II, and of the principles for which respectively they stood. The Whigs' fortunes suffered collapse with the flight of their leader, the first Earl of Shaftesbury, in November 1682, but their principles found triumphant expression in William's accession six years later and in the consequent settlement. The corollary to these facts appeared to be that William would appoint only Whigs as his Ministers. But these were not the only relevant facts to be remembered. First, except for a few outstanding leaders on each side, the division between Whigs and Tories was much less hard-and-fast than it afterwards became, so that membership of the parties tended to be fluid. Second, before coming to England, William had

[1] See pp. 428–429.

insisted that his invitation should be signed by a number of 'representative' men. This implied a pledge of support from members of both parties, and was fulfilled in the signatories of the letter of invitation carried to William by Admiral Herbert: Herbert himself was no Whig, and of the seven names that the invitation bore, three—Danby, Lumley, and Bishop Compton—were those of Tories. Moreover, the decisive factor in William's success had been not the support of the Whigs but the defection to his cause of leading Tories—Churchill, Rochester, Clarendon, Cornbury, Charles II's son Grafton, and a host of others. It was Whig ideals which provided the Revolution with its political principles, but it was the Tories who made its achievement practicable. The third factor that William had to keep in mind in appointing Ministers was that his position as King was hereditarily anomalous and might be upset by a slight tilting of the political balance: it therefore behoved him to keep a foot in both party-camps.

For these reasons William's distribution of offices showed a nice balance between the two parties. The Tory Danby was Lord President of the Council and principal Minister; Halifax, the "Trimmer," was Lord Privy Seal; the Whig Shrewsbury and the Tory Nottingham were the two Secretaries of State; of the five members of the Treasury Board, the most notable was the Tory Godolphin; and of the six Navy Commissioners, Admiral Herbert, as the only professional sailor, was the most practically important. These appointments must not be interpreted to mean that the Tories solidly supported William. For the moment they were in a political quandary: as Anglicans they had been forced to abandon James II though he was the embodiment of their political principle of Divine Right, but they could not as yet evolve a theory adequate to their new situation. As during the preceding reigns of the first two Stuarts, so under William and Anne the primary party-divisions were religious and not political: the Tories were the party of the Established Church; the Whigs were the party of the Protestant Dissenters. The Roman Catholics were in a difficult position: since James II's flight there was no influential individual or party to champion their interests, and they would naturally lie under suspicion of Jacobitism. On the whole, they received more sympathy from the liberal-minded Whigs than from the rigid Tories.

Apart from the Whig and Tory parties, there was another political grouping which was not less important—namely, the Court and the Country parties. These were not new names but dated back to times before Tories or Whigs. The nucleus of a Court party consisted of Ministers and Court favourites; the remainder of its members were in part individuals who hoped for some sort of preferment and in part those who genuinely supported the policy of the administration. The Country party included men who from time to time were discontented with whatever administration was in office: at one time its members might be anti-Whig, and at another anti-Tory. Thus its policy was negative, but it was always a force to be reckoned with, and at moments of political crisis it was sometimes a determining element in the State. The distinction between Court and Country was more fluid even than between Tory and Whig: since neither Court nor Country had permanent leaders or organization, their respective memberships were constantly changing. Under both William III and Anne, Court and Country corresponded more nearly with reality than did Tory and Whig; for in practice it was still true that Ministers needed the King's support more than Parliament's. Ministerial change resulted not from defeats in Parliament or in a general election but from loss of the King's confidence. Even then there was no wholesale ministerial ejection such as we are familiar with in modern times: there were merely changes in certain offices at the King's discretion. It is necessary to have these political conditions in mind if events until Queen Anne's death are to be understood.

The seventeenth century was a period of expanding trade, and among trade's necessities were ready supplies of capital at a cheap rate and means for the investment of capital that was surplus to immediate needs. Hence there was a need for a more adequate banking system than then existed. In this realm the Italians and the Dutch were the pioneers. In England such banking as existed was in the hands of private individuals and firms—chiefly the goldsmiths—whose "promises to pay," based on the deposits of bullion in their strong-rooms, circulated in much the same way as modern banknotes, though of course to a much smaller extent. Schemes for a governmental bank had been mooted in England during the latter half of the seventeenth century but nothing practical had come out of them. Indeed, the Bank of England, as it came into existence in 1694, was due merely to the immediate exigencies of the Government's exchequer. William was finding difficulty in raising enough money to equip armies then fighting Louis XIV on the Continent. One source of his difficulty was that moneyed men lacked confidence in the Government's financial stability: Charles II's repudiation of his debts in 1672 was still painfully fresh in their minds.

In these circumstances Charles Montagu (afterwards Earl of Halifax), who in 1692 had been made a lord of the Treasury, put forward a scheme designed to induce such men to lend money to the Government. The scheme had been first suggested by William Paterson who was shortly to become prominent in connexion with the Scottish Darien project. The proposal was that a company should be formed to raise £1,200,000 which was to be lent to the Government at 8 per cent. The members of the company were to be incorporated into a joint-stock bank with the right to discount bills and to issue notes up to the amount of the loan, certain taxes being earmarked as security for the payment of the interest due to the company. Because lenders were assured that the profits on banking would compensate for any loss due to the government's possible defaulting in its interest-payments, the required sum was subscribed, and on July 27, 1694, "The Governor and Company of the Bank of England" was incorporated by royal charter which was to remain valid for twelve years. In 1696, in recognition of financial service rendered during the closing stages of the war against France, the Bank obtained further privileges: no new corporate bank was to be set up, and its charter was renewed until 1710 after which date twelve months' notice would be required before its dissolution.

Thus the Government achieved its purpose of securing loans to tide it over its immediate needs. But, as often both before and since in English history, far-reaching effects of the Government's action extended in directions never originally intended.

Here was, indeed, the beginning of what has come to be called the National Debt. The merchants and others who made up the company, fearful lest James II's return should mean the repudiation of loans made to William, became William's unfaltering supporters. As the merchant class was predominantly Whig, the Whigs in effect became more closely identified than ever with the Revolution settlement. Here was one of the reasons for the lack of support given to the Jacobite Rebellions of 1715 and 1745.

A further notable financial measure was the reform of the currency. Though the Stuarts were not guilty of debasing the coinage, as the Tudors had been, a large proportion of the coinage had become debased in use. Partly this was due to ordinary wear and tear; but more seriously it was due to deliberate clipping. The prevalence of poor coins meant that such coins were almost the only ones in circulation since—as Gresham's Law had long ago laid down—bad money drove good out of circulation because the good was hoarded. The result was that often traders would refuse to sell goods unless the coins tendered were weighed. This uncertainty about the value of coins seriously hindered trade both home and foreign.

How was the country to be rid of this menace to its financial stability? To call in the debased coins and to issue good ones in their place would involve a loss to the Government of the difference between the values of the old coins and of the new ones. Yet if the problem were not tackled the situation would grow worse. Already the value of taxes received was uncertain and always less than their nominal amount. So at last a re-coinage Bill was introduced and, on January 21, 1696, received the royal assent. The old coins were called in, and May 4 was fixed as the last date on which such coins would be accepted in payment of taxes. New coins were issued with milled edges so that they could not be clipped without detection. A window-tax, calculated to produce £1,200,000, was set aside to compensate the exchequer for the loss it would sustain. While the Mint, under Sir Isaac Newton, worked hard to provide the new coins in the shortest possible time, the exchequer, under Montagu, issued paper-money of various kinds to make up for the shortage of currency during the interval. Thus the country safely, even calmly, survived what might have been a dangerous financial crisis. That it did so in the midst of a war was an encouraging foretaste of the prosperity that might be expected when peace returned.

2. The Revolution in Scotland

Though William had secured the throne without civil war in England, his accession did not go unchallenged elsewhere. The challenge came from Roman Catholics who were anxious to preserve the crown for James II and his Roman Catholic heir. The resistance to William had three centres: the Scottish Highlands, Ireland, and Louis XIV of France. William had no option but to beat down this resistance by force, the resulting struggles being known collectively as the War of English Succession (1689–97).

Many Scots resented the presumption of English leaders in deciding who should be King of Scotland. The disaffected Scots still regarded James II as their rightful King. They had a redoubtable leader in Viscount Dundee, better known perhaps as John Graham of Claverhouse, who in the spring of 1690 had begun to collect supporters from the clansmen of the north. William's troops in Scotland were under the command of Major-General Hugh Mackay. On July 17 the opposing forces met near the Pass of Killiecrankie. The Highlanders, with all the advantages of position on the hillside and of familiarity with the country, swept down upon the English and drove them down the pass. Two things saved William's cause in Scotland from immediate annihilation. The first was Mackay's coolness which kept together the remaining elements of his army and so preserved a nucleus for future operations. The second was the death of Dundee in the very moment of victory: no one else possessed sufficient either of prestige or of ability to hold together the Scottish Jacobites. Dundee's death ended at one stroke the organized opposition to William's rule in Scotland.

The end of organized opposition did not mean, however, the end of disaffection; and in order to forestall further outbreaks the Government issued a proclamation that the clan-chiefs should take an oath of allegiance to the Crown not later than the last day of 1691. With surprising readiness the chieftains complied. Only one—Macdonald of Glencoe—owing to a misunderstanding, was late in presenting himself; but even he took the oath on January 7. Before news of Macdonald's belated acceptance had reached the authorities, they decided that an example must be made of the refractory clan. William's London adviser on Scottish affairs, Sir John Dalrymple, the Master of Stair, urged its extirpation, and William gave his consent. Though on January 23 it was known to Sir Thomas Livingstone, the English commander in Scotland, that Macdonald had taken the oath, a week later about one hundred and twenty soldiers were quartered in the valley of Glencoe. These soldiers were all Campbells and therefore traditionally hostile to the Macdonalds. After nearly a week's stay among the clansmen, who showed great friendliness and hospitality, the soldiers suddenly murdered in cold blood as many of their hosts as they could lay their hands on. Altogether thirty-eight were killed, including Macdonald himself. The question of the extent of William's responsibility for the massacre has never been satisfactorily answered. Whether he realized little or much of the meaning of the order before it was carried out, nothing can condone his failure to take adequate steps towards repairing the injury after it had taken place. Not until 1695 was a commission of inquiry set up, and then the only practical effect was Dalrymple's retirement from public life. Such calculated callousness was one of the few great blemishes in William's character. This example of cruelty had not even either necessity or success to justify it: two of Macdonald's sons escaped to keep alive the spirit of discontent among the clans.

3. The Revolution in Ireland

Ireland presented William with a much stiffer problem to solve than did Scotland. Whereas his Roman Catholic opponents in Scotland were a minority of the population, in Ireland they were the vast majority. Hence his enemies, both at home and abroad, regarded Ireland as the most favourable base of operations against him. The Lord Deputy, Tyrconnel, was a Roman Catholic, and refused to be won over by William's emissaries. In March 1689 James himself landed in Ireland, with French officers and supplies, and on March 24 he entered Dublin in royal state. In May he opened Parliament there. Its Members, almost exclusively Catholic, proceeded to discuss measures which would have swept away the Cromwellian plantations and have made Ireland virtually independent of England. The proposals were an embarrassment rather than a help to James: they would alienate his followers in England and would deprive him of control over Ireland when, as he hoped, he recovered the English crown. James therefore did his best to curb the Parliament's enthusiasm. For example, he insisted on the retention of Poynings' Act of 1494 whereby Acts passed by the English Parliament applied also in Ireland.

While the Dublin Parliament was thus spreading its new-found wings, the Protestants of the north had taken refuge in the strongholds of Londonderry and Enniskillen to which they brought all the cattle and stores they could gather from the surrounding countryside. Tyrconnel, lacking the siege-train necessary to reduce the towns by arms, concentrated on Londonderry which he straitly blockaded. A heavy boom was thrown across the Foyle, thus barring the city's access to the sea whence alone effective help could be brought from England. Throughout May, June, and July the siege went on until the citizens were compelled to resort to the most desperate measures to relieve their starvation. At last, after many delays, and under express orders from England, on July 28, 1689, Colonel Kirke led an attack on the boom which yielded and so allowed supplies to enter the town. On July 31, after one hundred and five days, Tyrconnel raised the siege. The joy of the besieged was further increased by the news, which reached them the following day, that the Enniskilleners had just routed a superior Roman Catholic force at Newtown Butler. This ended the first stage of the Irish resistance to William.

In August 1689 the Duke of Schomberg—formerly a Marshal of France, but the son of an English mother and now William's most trusted general—landed in Ulster with what seemed a substantial force. Owing partly to the stress of weather, partly to the ill-preparedness of the troops, and perhaps partly to Schomberg's advanced age (he was seventy-four), nothing much was achieved during the winter or even when the next spring came. In June 1690 William himself landed at Carrickfergus. The reinforcements which he brought raised the total force under his command in Ireland to nearly forty thousand. With these he marched down the coast until he reached the river Boyne. There he was faced by James' troops, Irish and French, who were drawn up on the river's southern bank near Drogheda. On July 1 William launched his attack and drove his enemies off the field. The one piece of ill-fortune that the Battle of the Boyne brought to William was Schomberg's death during the action. James, thoroughly disheartened, at once fled to France, thus ruining whatever chance of recovery his cause might have had.

Though the back of the Irish rebellion was broken, two tasks remained to be accomplished before William could feel safe. The first was to prevent the landing of further French troops and supplies. On the day before the Battle of the Boyne the Earl of Torrington (formerly Admiral Herbert), in command of a combined English and Dutch fleet, had been defeated off Beachy Head. Torrington was court-martialled for his conduct: he was acquitted but was never again employed in command. The natural inference from the action was that the French would use the resulting naval supremacy in order to invade either England or Ireland. To counter this threat, William sent back to England two regiments of foot and three of horse while he seized Waterford, which would be a vital port in the event of a French attack. Fortunately for England, Louis XIV, deciding to concentrate on his war on the Continent, recalled his fleet to Brest.

William's second task was to crush the remaining resistance in Ireland. He therefore turned west against Limerick which he tried to storm. The defence proved too strong, and on August 30, 1690, he raised the siege and then returned to England. Marlborough brought the 1690 campaign to a successful close by seizing Cork and Kinsale, thus gaining control of two more possible landing-places for troops from France.

For the 1691 campaign, William gave supreme command to

his countryman, Godert van Ginkel. During July Ginkel took first Athlone and then Galway. Then he turned against the remaining centre of Jacobite resistance, Limerick, which had successfully defied William the previous year. While Ginkel was investing the town by land, English ships were cutting off all means of relief by sea. On August 12, the first day of the siege, death robbed its defenders of their leader, Tyrconnel. Yet they held out gallantly, and not until October 3 did the town capitulate.

By the terms of the capitulation, Irish soldiers were to be allowed to cross to France in ships provided by Ginkel. More than ten thousand accepted the offer, thus entering into voluntary exile and forming the Irish Brigade in the service of Louis XIV.

The civil articles were less easily framed. As finally agreed upon, the Treaty of Limerick promised that Roman Catholics should enjoy the same religious privileges as under Charles II, that a Parliament should be summoned as soon as possible, and that the people of Limerick and other stipulated areas, as well as soldiers in the Irish Army, should have their estates restored, and should be granted a complete amnesty.

This treaty, which might have marked the beginning of a happy relationship between England and Ireland—as William intended that it should—became instead the starting-point of two centuries and more of bitter strife. Hardly was it signed when laws were passed—the first of a long, melancholy series —which contravened its terms in spirit and in letter. A declaration against Transubstantiation, in addition to an oath of supremacy, had to be taken by all Members of the Dublin Parliament and by all office-holders in Ireland. Further, the Irish Parliament of 1695 (which, in consequence of these regulations, contained Protestants only) passed penal laws to prevent Roman Catholics from becoming teachers or tutors, from sending their children overseas for education, from owning a horse worth more than £5, and from carrying firearms. Still more stringent laws were passed in 1697: Roman Catholic bishops and members of religious orders were to leave Ireland; and the marriage of Roman Catholics to Protestants was forbidden. Though the penal laws were not rigidly or uniformly enforced, while they remained on the Statute Book—which they did until the close of the eighteenth century—they fostered a bitter sense of injustice in Ireland. The injustice was the graver because it involved not the oppression of a small minority by a great majority but the oppression of a conquered majority by an alien minority. The breaches of the Treaty of Limerick were the foundation of the hostility which continued between Ireland and England throughout the eighteenth and nineteenth centuries and on into the twentieth.

4. War on the Continent

The conflict between William and the Scots and Irish had for him two aspects. First, it was the repression of rebellious subjects who were opposing his succession to the throne: it was the War of English Succession. Second, because the Scottish and Irish rebels were abetted by Louis XIV, the conflict was part of William's long struggle against France: it was part of the War of the League of Augsburg.

England's connexion with the League was the pivot of her foreign relationships throughout William's reign. Enmity between Louis XIV and William of Orange dated back to the Dutch war of 1672–78. By the Treaty of Nymwegen at the end of the war, though France made valuable gains at the expense of the Spanish Netherlands, the United Provinces had remained intact. Louis was therefore determined to seize the first opportunity to avenge himself against the Dutch who had thwarted his plans. But the Dutch were not the only people whom Louis' designs menaced. Neighbouring rulers knew that the seizure of the United Provinces would not satisfy Louis' ambition. The Provinces, once in his control, would be jumping-off grounds for further advances. This was the root reason—the more immediate reasons do not concern us here —for the formation of the League of Augsburg, in 1686. The original members were the Emperor, Spain, the United Provinces, Sweden, and Saxony. In 1687 Bavaria and Savoy joined. Though England was not directly concerned, the league had two indirect effects of the highest importance to her. First, as we have seen already, it was Louis' invasion of the Rhine

Palatinate in September 1688, as part of his operations against the league, which provided William with the opportunity to leave the United Provinces and invade England. Second, when William was installed as King of England, his great purpose was to add England to the declared enemies of Louis. Indeed, William's detractors constantly averred that this was his only real interest in England: that he had "come to England on his way to France."

Thus one of William's first aims after establishing himself in England was to gather Louis' enemies into a firm, effective alliance. In May 1689 the United Provinces and the Emperor signed a mutual treaty. Spain joined in June; and in September William was able to lead England in also. Thus was formed the Grand Alliance. Other members were Savoy and the German States Brandenburg, Saxony, Bavaria, and Hanover. The Dutch and the English, in addition to the general terms of alliance, secretly promised the Emperor that if Charles II of Spain died without an heir they would support the claims of the Imperial Habsburgs, as against the French Bourbons, to the succession to the Spanish throne. Though this scheme—of which the Spaniards were not informed—did not bear fruit for nearly ten years, its agreement in 1689 is worth careful note.

England did not intervene actively in the Continental war for two years after the formation of the alliance. This was partly because she was unprepared and partly because she was fully occupied with events in Scotland and Ireland. It was on the sea that England was first engaged. Mention has already been made of Torrington's defeat by the French off Beachy Head on June 30, 1690. Two years passed before the English were able to avenge this disgrace. The opportunity came in 1692 when a French fleet, under Count Tourville, set out to clear the Channel of English ships in preparation for an invasion of England by an army collected in the Cotentin peninsula and led by James II. The junction of the English and Dutch fleets gave them a decisive superiority in numbers over the French, and in the Battle of La Hogue, on May 19, 1692, the French lost fifteen first-rates, most of which were destroyed by fire directed by the English in the bay. This result

frustrated the projected French invasion. Even more important, it gave to the English and Dutch complete naval
supremacy which they never lost either during the remainder
of this war or during the following war of Spanish Succession.
Marlborough's ability, during the latter war, to transport his
armies unhindered between England and the Continent was
due to the supremacy established at La Hogue.

The military campaigns on the Continent were monotonous
affairs showing little genius on either side. It was mostly a war
of sieges and entrenchments. William was never a brilliant
general. Perhaps his most valuable characteristic was dauntless courage showing itself not only in personal conduct in the
field but also in his refusal to accept defeat. Though he rarely
won an action, he could never be beaten while he had an
army in being. In judging his generalship, the point should
always be borne in mind that he was continually hampered by
being at the head of forces not of one country but of a coalition
which made dilatoriness almost inevitable. Also, during the
early campaigns William's operations on the Continent were
hampered by the revolts in Scotland and Ireland.

In January 1691 William crossed to The Hague for an Allied
Conference. During its proceedings the French laid siege to
the great fortress of Mons, and though William hurried to its
relief he was unable to prevent its fall. In April he paid a brief
visit to England, but early in May he was on the Continent
once more. The campaign that year saw no further decisive
action. On balance the advantage rested with the French: they
had gained Mons and had maintained the war on their
enemies' soil.

Early in 1692 the Allies lost the services of Marlborough.
He was the centre of discontent among English officers who
were jealous of the Dutch whom William entrusted with
highest command to the exclusion, as it was believed, of the
English. Marlborough and his wife were so strongly established in the favour of the Princess Anne that action against
him was not easy to take. Indeed, they seemed to be making
Anne's household almost a rival Court to that of William and
Mary. But in January 1692 Marlborough was dismissed from
his offices and from Court. Later in the year, while William

11 + s.c.

was abroad, Mary even had Marlborough confined to the Tower, on suspicion of treason, whence, however, he was released after six weeks.

William took the field early in March. In May the English and Dutch navies won their victory at La Hogue. In June the French captured the fortress of Namur which also William had been unable to relieve. Thence the French, under the Duke of Luxembourg, advanced towards Brussels. To check this move, William launched an attack at Steenkirk but, owing partly to divided command, was compelled to retreat. His generalship saved the retreat from being a rout, and the French, in spite of their supremacy in the field, neither pursued William nor went on to Brussels.

During 1693 things were no better. Luxembourg once more took the offensive, and William, in spite of taking up a strong defensive position between Neerwinden and Landen, was driven from it in July. Even so, William's movement was orderly, and when he had gathered all his forces together he was not seriously weaker than he had been before the battle.

1694 marked the limit of French successes. For the first time since the war began, the French were outnumbered by the Allies and therefore did not attempt offensive operations. By the end of 1694 the Allies were in a stronger position than at the end of the previous campaign. If William could hold the Allies together diplomatically, and could pursue his military advantage, the next campaign might see a decisive turn in the tide of war.

But before the next campaign could open, William's position was seriously weakened by tragedy at home. His Queen was attacked by small-pox, and on December 28 she died. Mary's passing made more than a formal break in William's reign. Her popularity had done much to counteract the widespread dislike felt for William. After her death the moderate Tories, who hitherto had given general support to William, gravitated towards the opposition. The extreme Jacobites also were encouraged to take active measures against William. If they had removed William while Mary had been alive the Revolution would have remained unshaken, and might even have been strengthened, since Mary would have been left to reign alone;

and to have gone farther and used violence against Mary would have done the Jacobites' cause more harm than good because of Mary's popularity. Mary's death removed these restraints. Thus William's embarrassments increased during the remaining six-and-a-half years of his life—that is, while, in accordance with the succession clause of the Bill of Rights, he reigned alone.

For many weeks after Mary's death William was prostrate. At every turn he was made aware of the effects of his loss. For example, during his absence on each of his previous Continental campaigns the Queen had managed matters of domestic government; but from 1695 onward William had to appoint a commission of Ministers, though even so the final authority had to rest upon the King.

Thus it was May before William left for the 1695 campaign. His chief objective was to recapture Namur, which had been in French hands since 1692. The French had greatly strengthened the defences of the fortress, but in spite of its strength William laid siege to it. A French relieving army failed to move him, and in September, after a three months' siege, the town was compelled to capitulate.

Namur's surrender had immediate reactions upon William's position. It gave new heart to his troops in the field, and it gave to his war at least a momentary popularity at home. Almost at once William returned home, dissolved Parliament, and ordered the issue of writs for a new election. The election, held while William's reputation was at its height, returned a substantial majority of supporters of the war, many of them being Whigs. William opened the new Parliament, the third of the reign, on November 22. His appeal for continued support for the war resulted in a vote of £5,000,000.

There was one section of the people whom William's successes, military and political, bitterly displeased. These were the Jacobites. From the beginning of the reign there had been a series of plots for James II's restoration. They came to very little during Mary's lifetime, but they were renewed during the winter of 1695–96. On the Continent preparations were made for a French invasion of England, and during February 1696 James took up his quarters in Calais ready to join the operations. Meanwhile in England a plot was hatched to murder William in a narrow lane near Turnham Green as he returned from Richmond to Kensington after his Saturday's hunting. As usual with such plots, some of the conspirators turned informers, and the Government was able to lay its hands upon the would-be assassins.

On February 24 William personally informed Parliament of the plot. The result was a great outburst of loyalty. The Whigs, realizing how imminent had been the overthrow of the King on whom their security depended, were genuinely warm in their congratulations. The Tories were chiefly anxious to dissociate themselves from the Jacobite cause which was covering itself with infamy. Commons and Lords agreed to the suspension of the Habeas Corpus Act and to the continuance of Parliament for six months after the King's death. An association, similar to that of 1584 for Queen Elizabeth's protection, was formed whereby its members swore to take vengeance upon anyone compassing the King's death and to maintain the order of succession as laid down in the Bill of Rights. Thus the Jacobite plot, designed to overthrow William, reacted strongly in his favour.

In the war abroad 1696 was a relatively uneventful year. The only item of any consequence was that the Duke of Savoy made terms with Louis and then withdrew from the Grand Alliance. The truth was that both France and the Allies had fought until they had reached exhaustion. Moreover, Louis had particular reasons for desiring peace. The English Revolution settlement had by this time become so firmly established that there was no possibility of restoring James II by French arms: to continue to fight for that purpose was therefore futile. Also, in September 1696, Charles II of Spain became seriously ill, and his death seemed imminent. As Charles had no descendants, and the only claimants to his throne would be members of other reigning families in Europe (including the French Bourbons), his death was likely to precipitate a major political crisis. Louis XIV was anxious that, whenever this crisis should arise, he should not be embarrassed by a war and that his treasury should not be exhausted. Relative to the large possibilities of the Spanish Succession, the issues of the struggle against the Grand Alliance were of small moment. William III, anticipating the same circumstances, was similarly disposed towards peace.

Consequently, at Ryswick in September 1697, England, the United Provinces, Spain, and France agreed on terms of peace of which the chief items were that Louis renounced all his conquests except Strassburg since the Treaty of Nymwegen of 1678, that Louis should recognize William III as King of England and Anne as his successor, and that the Dutch should be allowed to garrison certain of the chief fortresses, known as Barrier Fortresses, in the Spanish Netherlands as a buffer to protect the Dutch frontier.

These terms implied that Louis restored to Spain, Luxemburg, Mons, and other fortresses in the Netherlands as well as all that he held in Catalonia including Barcelona. In part, these concessions were explained by facts that we have already considered. But there was a further highly significant factor—namely, that though Louis had not been defeated in the field, his bid to dominate Europe had been effectively checked. Louis had been the aggressor, and if his offensive was not successful he was virtually defeated. Once again his attack on the Netherlands had aroused a European coalition which had held him in check. If Louis had learned that lesson he would have been able to save not only his own country but all Europe many years of futile slaughter and exhaustion.

5. The Act of Settlement

Early in July 1698 William's third Parliament was prorogued and later was dissolved. The ensuing general election showed a strong anti-Whig reaction following the end of the Whig war. The leading individual in the new House of Commons was Robert Harley, who had been a Member since 1689. His father had been a Puritan and an officer in the Parliamentarian Army, and it was as a Whig with Nonconformist sympathies that Robert Harley had entered the Commons. It was he who had introduced the Triennial Bill of 1694. But gradually he moved to the right in both religion and politics: in the end he became a Tory, leader of the Tories, and a High Churchman. His Toryism, however, was moderate in character so that he never lost contact with the Whigs whom he had left.

The first measure of great consequence in the 1698 Parliament showed both the new temper of the country and the political change that Harley had undergone: it was a measure to reduce drastically the number of armed forces, and it was introduced by Harley. The proposal was that the Army in England should not exceed seven thousand men, and in Ireland twelve thousand, and that all these should be native-born Englishmen. This reduction in the Army could be justified theoretically as being in accordance with the Bill of Rights, which forbade the keeping of a standing army in time of peace. In practice it was an unwise move. The Treaty of Ryswick had not settled the fundamental cause of the war against France—namely, Louis' threat to dominate Europe—and a renewal of war was inevitable, none could predict when or how. This was clearly understood by William who did his utmost to dissuade Parliament from its intention. His own estimate of a safe minimum of troops was thirty thousand. But his efforts were in vain: the resolution to reduce the army to seven thousand easily passed both Houses. The stipulation that they should all be English was scarcely less of a blow to William, for it meant the ejection of his Dutch troops and the loss of the Dutch officers on whom he had largely relied.

William's first reaction to these events was that he would abandon England for ever. This determination he communicated to Heinsius (Grand Pensionary of Holland) and to Marlborough, and he even prepared a farewell address to Parliament. But calmer counsels prevailed. To separate himself from England would mean the loss of English support against France. For the sake of Holland William swallowed his disgust and retained his English throne.

In one other matter of difference between William and Parliament William played into his detractors' hands. In 1691, following the campaign in Ireland, enormous tracts of Irish land, belonging to James II and to Tyrconnel and other Jacobites, were declared forfeit. William had promised that the disposal of these lands should be left to Parliament. As time passed without Parliament's making any settlement of them,

William gave to his favourites large areas in Ireland amounting altogether to about one million acres. Chief among the recipients were his Dutch generals and friends including the Earls of Portland (Hans Willem Bentinck), of Galway (Henry de Massue de Ruvigny), of Athlone (Godard van Reede-Ginkel), and of Albemarle (Arnold Joose van Keppel), and to his mistress, Lady Orkney (Elizabeth Villars, sister of Bentinck's wife). These gifts roused antipathy on two grounds: first, they were made to foreigners; second, if they had been in the nation's control their value would have contributed substantially to defraying the cost of the war and so would have decreased taxation. In 1699, therefore, the Commons appointed seven commissioners—four Tories and three Whigs—to review the grants. In December the commission reported on the extent of the estates and on the individuals holding them. The upshot was that the Commons resolved that all grants of land since February 13, 1689 (the date of the proclamation of William and Mary as King and Queen) should be void, and that all forfeited lands in Ireland should be vested in trustees who were to sell the lands within three years. Though the Lords resisted the Bill, they had finally to give way, and William assented to it on April 11, 1700.

Another resolution of the Commons was that the King should not admit foreigners to his councils in either England or Ireland. So acutely did William feel these rebuffs that he prorogued Parliament on the same day as he assented to the resumption of the Irish lands.

During the remaining two years of William's life the greater part of his attention was occupied by problems connected with the succession to the Spanish throne. Before we turn to those problems it will be convenient to deal with one other matter of importance in domestic politics—namely, the Act of Settlement.

The primary aim of this Act was to settle the succession to the English throne by making provisions additional to those of the Bill of Rights. The latter, in arranging for the succession through William and Mary and their descendants, and through the Princess Anne and her descendants, had done all that in 1688 seemed necessary. But subsequent events had made these provisions inadequate. William and Mary had had no children; and though Anne had had numerous children, only one of them—the Duke of Gloucester—had survived infancy. Then, on July 30, 1700, the Duke of Gloucester died at the age of eleven years. Hence, though the Princess Anne remained as William's successor, if death should suddenly remove her, as it had done her sister Mary, there would be no agreed solution of the problem of succession. Should such circumstances arise, the Jacobites would seize the opportunity to try to place the Pretender upon the throne. In order to prevent strife and possible civil war, a further settlement of the succession was essential. William himself urged this in his speech from the throne to the new Parliament in February 1701.

The framers of the consequent Act of Settlement[1] took advantage of a measure defining the succession in order to include certain stipulations affecting the powers of the crown. In this respect they were following the example of the Bill of Rights. The clauses of the Act of Settlement are therefore divisible into three groups. The first, relating to the succession, stated that:

> The most excellent Princess Sophia, Electress and Duchess Dowager of Hanover . . . is hereby declared to be next in Succession . . . and the heirs of her Body being Protestants.

The second group aimed at filling up gaps in the constitutional safeguards contained in the Bill of Rights:

> That no person who has Office or Place of Profit under the King or receives a Pension from the Crown shall be capable of serving as a Member of the House of Commons.
>
> That Judges' Commissions be made *Quam diu se bene Gesserint* and their salaries ascertained and established but upon the Address of both Houses of Parliament it may be lawful to remove them.
>
> That no pardon under the Great Seal of England be pleadable to an Impeachment by the Commons in Parliament.

The purpose of the first of these latter clauses was to prevent Parliament from being overawed by the presence of Ministers

[1] Robertson, pp. 151–160.

of the crown. It would have separated sharply the executive from the legislative parts of the constitutional machinery (as later in the United States of America) and so would have introduced a practice alien to the English system of government. The clause was drastically modified in 1705. The clause making judges irremovable except by Parliament's consent was designed to prevent a recurrence of the early Stuarts' method of using the royal influence over the law-courts in order to make statutes inoperative. The invalidation of a royal pardon in case of impeachment would frustrate a Minister's attempt (such as Danby had made in 1678) to avoid responsibility for the action which had provoked the impeachment by pleading that it had been done by royal consent. The third group had no deep constitutional significance but expressed antipathy to William personally:

> That this Nation be not obliged to engage in any War for the Defence of any Dominions or Territories which do not belong to the Crown of England without the consent of Parliament.
> That no person who shall hereafter come to the possession of the Crown shall go out of the Dominion of England, Scotland and Ireland without the consent of Parliament.
> That Things . . . transacted [in the Privy Council] and all Resolutions taken thereupon shall be signed by such of the Privy Council as shall advise and consent to the same.
> That no Person born out of the Kingdom of England, Scotland or Ireland or the Dominions thereunto belonging . . . shall be capable to be of the Privy Council or a Member of either House of Parliament or to enjoy any Office or Place of Trust either Civil or Military.

The clauses of this group, being aimed at William personally, were of only temporary duration. To compel all Privy Councillors to sign all resolutions that they had supported proved unworkable, and the provision was repealed in 1705. The restriction on a sovereign's leaving Britain was repealed in the first year of George I. The clause preventing foreign-born men from being Members of Parliament or holding office was repealed early in Victoria's reign.

It was of some significance in the history of political parties that the 1701 House of Commons which passed these restric-

11*

tions on royal power had a strong Tory majority. The Act of Settlement showed unmistakably that the Tories had moved away from Divine Right and, equally, that as a party they were not Jacobites.

6. The Spanish Succession

```
                        Philip III
                         d. 1621
        ┌──────────────────┼──────────────────────────┐
Anne = Louis XIII        Philip IV           Ferdinand III = Maria
      d. 1643            d. 1665
  Louis XIV = Maria       ┌──────┴──────┐              │
   d. 1715  | Theresa  Charles II   Margaret (1) = Leopold I = (2)
           |           d. 1700       Theresa |           |
        Louis                 Elector of = Maria      Joseph      Archduke Charles
     the Dauphin              Bavaria | Antonia     Emperor    Emperor Charles V
       d. 1711                        |             1705–11       1711–40
  ┌──────┴──────┐            Joseph Ferdinand
Louis,        Philip         Electoral Prince
Duke of       Duke of          d. 1699
Burgundy      Anjou
 d. 1712      Philip V
|             of Spain
Louis XV      1700–46
1715–74
```

While the party-interchanges outlined above were taking place at home, diplomatic relationships were working to a climax abroad. These were connected with the problems of the succession to the Spanish throne, anticipation of which had been a main reason for Louis XIV's anxiety for peace in 1697. Many of the details are the concern of European, rather than of British, history. The essence of them was that Charles II of Spain was feeble in both mind and body, so that his death had long been expected, and he was childless. After him the succession in Spain would pass through one of his sisters of whom the elder, Maria Theresa, had married Louis XIV, and the younger, Margaret Theresa, had married the Emperor Leopold I. There was no certainty which of these two had the superior claim. By the Treaty of Pyrenees (1659) Maria Theresa had renounced, for herself and for her descendants, any claim to the Spanish throne; but as Spain had never paid her dowry of 500,000 crowns, which had been another provision of the same treaty, Louis held that her renunciation was invalid.

Margaret Theresa had not renounced her claim when she married Leopold; but when her daughter Maria Antonia had married the Elector of Bavaria, Leopold, who was anxious that Spain should never be added to the dominions of a fellow German ruler, forced Maria Antonia to renounce her claim. If these two renunciations held good they barred all the descendants of Philip IV.

In the previous generation Philip IV's elder sister, Anne, had married Louis XIII of France, and she too had renounced her rights on Spain; but Philip IV's younger sister, Maria, in marrying the Emperor Ferdinand III, had not renounced. Through her, Leopold I thus had a claim to Spain in his own right which he would transmit to the children of his second marriage—that is, to Joseph or to Charles. But this right existed only because Leopold had compelled his daughter to renounce her claims. That he should by this means be able to maintain his own intrinsically inferior claim, as against his daughter's superior claim, was generally felt to be unjust. On the other hand, if Maria Antonia's renunciation was to be set aside for this reason, ought not Maria Theresa's renunciation to be set aside for the more specific reason that her dowry had never been paid? In the latter case the succession would clearly fall to Louis, the Dauphin.

Even this bare outline of the situation is enough to show that none of the claimants had an indisputable right to the succession. On a strictly hereditary and theoretical basis, all that could be said was that there were three lines of claimants to the Spanish throne: the French, the Bavarian, and the Austrian. But there was a practical consideration of great weight: each of these lines was that of a ruling house so that, no matter which of them made good its claim, the effect would be to add Spain and all the Spanish dominions—in Italy, in the Netherlands, and in the New World—to the dominions of another European Power. This would upset the diplomatic balance of all Europe. Not only would the two defeated candidates be jealous of their successful rival, but every other European State would feel itself concerned, for the successful claimant would dominate Europe. Almost inevitably

Charles II's death would be the signal for a great European struggle.

Only by one method could European war be avoided: before the crisis arose, the three candidates must agree to such a division of the Spanish dominions as would satisfy not only themselves but also the other interested parties in Europe. Among these would certainly be William III as representing the security both of the United Provinces and of England. So overwhelming was the case for this solution that in 1698 William and Louis secretly signed what became known as the first Partition Treaty whereby they agreed to support a specified division of the Spanish dominions between the three lines of candidates. The particulars of this division proved in practice unimportant because one of the three beneficiaries, the Electoral Prince of Bavaria, died in February 1699 while Charles II was still alive.

Consequently in June 1699 William and Louis agreed to a second Partition Treaty whereby the Archduke Charles of Austria was to acquire Spain, the Spanish Netherlands, and the Spanish possessions beyond the sea, on condition that these dominions should never be united to the Empire: this condition was possible because the Archduke was Leopold's younger son and hence was not likely to become Emperor. The Dauphin was to acquire Naples, Sicily, and Lorraine, while the Duke of Lorraine was to be compensated by the Milanese in exchange for his own Duchy. These terms were submitted to Leopold, but he refused them because they gave the advantage to France. Hence in March 1700 William and Louis ratified the treaty without Leopold.

When the treaty-terms became known Charles and his subjects were infuriated. That foreigners should presume to decide what was to be done with his property while he was still alive was insult enough. That the decision should involve the break-up of the Spanish Empire was intolerable. To avoid this, Charles, while on his death-bed, made a will granting all the Spanish dominions to Philip of Anjou, younger son of the Dauphin, on condition that he never became King of France. Charles signed his will early in October 1700. Three weeks later, on November 1, Charles at last died. Within a week of the news of Charles' death reaching Paris, Louis announced his recognition of Charles' will and of his grandson, Philip, as King of Spain.

The reactions of the various Powers to the ensuing situation were in some respects surprising. In England there was almost universal dislike of the Partition Treaty: the Whigs, many of whom were merchants interested in Mediterranean trade, disliked it because it would strengthen France in the Mediterranean; and the Tories realized that the treaty could be made effective only by making war against both Emperor and Spain. Hence Parliament, accepting Louis' assurance that he would not use his grandson's power to increase his own, recognized Philip V of Spain, as did also the Dutch States-General.

To discuss Louis' motives in abandoning the Partition Treaty and accepting the will is aside from our present subject, though incidentally we may note that some of the details of events (such as the uncertainty of the Spanish Court as to whether he would accept the will or not) do not substantiate the suspicion that all along he was playing a double game. Doubtless the will served French interests better than the Partition Treaty would have done; but even if this had not been so it is difficult to see how Louis could have carried out the treaty no matter how much he had wished for it. To enforce the treaty would have involved using French arms to expel his grandson from Spain and to fight the Emperor, without the support of England or the United Provinces both of whom had recognized Philip.

It is necessary to have these facts in mind in order to be clear that it was not Louis' acceptance of Charles' will that caused the war. Neither the English nor the Dutch would have fought him on that account. The war was precipitated by a series of astonishingly reckless actions whereby Louis demonstrated that his virtual control of Spain would jeopardize the security of the rest of Europe. First, during the opening week of February 1701, French troops expelled the Dutch from the Barrier Forts in the Spanish Netherlands and encamped along the Dutch frontier. This was a breach of the Treaty of Ryswick and therefore was the concern of all the signatories of the treaty, including England and the United

Provinces; more than that, it indicated Louis' next move and thereby alarmed the other Powers of Europe. Scarcely less alarming was Louis' declaration, also made in February, reserving the right of his grandson, Philip of Spain, to succeed to the French throne. The weak health of the Dauphin and of Louis, Duke of Burgundy (Philip's father and elder brother) who did in fact die in 1711 and 1712 respectively—that is, before Louis XIV died—rendered Philip's succession to the French throne a real possibility. These two actions by Louis, showing that Philip's accession to Spain meant in effect the union of France and Spain, were more effective than all William's arguments in swinging over English public opinion against Louis' acceptance of Charles II's will.

No other man in England had appreciated the menace so quickly as had William, for no one else was so concerned as he for the security both of England and of Holland; and few Englishmen understood how intimately the interests of the two countries were bound together. William therefore, anticipating that the swing of English opinion would increase, began negotiations with the Emperor for a new alliance. Perhaps the supreme proof of William's statesmanship was that, in this hour of crisis, he put personal animosities behind him. Marlborough had been recalled to Court in June 1698 as Governor of the Duke of Gloucester. Now, at the end of 1701, William appointed him Commander-in-Chief of the English Army which already was being gathered in the United Provinces. A month later Marlborough was appointed as a special Ambassador to take charge of negotiations with the Emperor. At the beginning of September the Treaty of the Grand Alliance was signed between England, the United Provinces, and the Empire. Though the signatories agreed that Philip V should remain on the Spanish throne and should retain the Spanish possessions in America, the Spanish and French thrones were never to be united; and the Emperor was to receive Milan, Naples, the Spanish Netherlands, and Luxemburg. In September 1701 Sweden, under its warrior-King Charles XII, also joined the alliance.

The alliance did not make war inevitable. If Louis had taken warning from its formation peace might even at that late hour have been preserved. But ten days after the alliance had been formed James II died. Louis, not then knowing the terms of the alliance, at once proclaimed the dead King's son as James III of England. This was an insult to England, a threat to William's government, and a further breach of the Treaty of Ryswick. It was this that made war certain.

In October heavy import duties were imposed upon English goods entering France, and thus another cause of offence was given to the English mercantile class—that is, mainly to the Whigs. At the end of December a new Parliament met. It contained only a small Tory majority. The result was seen in the vote to provide for an army of forty thousand men; and during January and February 1702 preparations for war went actively forward. Then suddenly the scene was transformed by tragedy. On February 21 William was thrown from his horse while riding from Kensington to Hampton Court. He sustained a broken collar-bone which to a normally fit man would not have been unduly serious but which was too severe for William's feeble constitution. Though he rallied for some days, he suffered a relapse and, on March 8, died.

As a soldier William has had many superiors, but as a statesman he has had few. His courage, his shrewd judgement about when and how to strike in a crisis, were outstanding characteristics of this statesmanship. In foreign politics he alone had barred the way to Louis XIV's ambitions. In domestic politics his wisdom alone had tided England safely through the Revolution and laid firm foundations on which the English constitution could rise and develop.

Chapter 13

Queen Anne and Marlborough

1702–9

1. Domestic Politics

The interest of the first part of Queen Anne's reign centres chiefly around Marlborough's campaigns during the War of Spanish Succession. The issue of those campaigns depended not only upon Marlborough's military genius but also upon the ever-changing political situation at home, and not the least important of the factors shaping that situation were the characters of Anne and of Marlborough and the make-up of the rival parties.

To historians of earlier generations, Queen Anne was a lay-figure, a sort of marionette whose movements were controllable by anyone able to pull the appropriate strings, which in practice meant the Duke and Duchess of Marlborough and, later, Mrs Masham. Indeed, the phrase "as dead as Queen Anne" has come to suggest that Queen Anne was never very much alive. One of the services rendered to historical truth by the later school of historians has been the light thrown upon the character of Queen Anne and upon the part she played in shaping the events of her own day and hence in setting the course for events during the generations that followed. Dr Keith Feiling, for example, wrote that:

> In spite of ill health, vacillation, and thoroughly second-rate ability, Anne had fixed ideals on which the ablest politician ship-wrecked. She would be Queen, and in the last resort Ministers must learn to obey. . . . She never ceased to declare, directly or through her servants, that she would not be the tool of a party.[1]

[1] *History of the Tory Party, 1640–1714*, pp. 361–362.

Of Sir Winston Churchill's views on Anne's character, expressed and implied throughout his biography of Marlborough, the following may be selected as typical:

> It is astonishing that most of our native historians have depicted Queen Anne as an obstinate simpleton, a stupid, weak creature, in the hands of her bed-chamber women; and that it should have been left to foreign writers to expose her immense powers of will-power, resistance and manœuvre. On her throne she was as tough as Marlborough in the field.[1]

It is well that this more balanced view of the Queen should be fairly in our minds at the outset of our study of her reign. Its significance will become more apparent as the study proceeds.

The dominant passion of Anne's life, and the mainspring of her actions, was devotion to the Church of England. The favour that she showed to the Tories was due not to their political principles but to their being the High Church party. In addressing the Parliament that existed at her accession, she declared:

> My own principles must always keep me entirely firm to the interests and religion of the Church of England, and will incline me to countenance those who have the truest zeal to support it.

Not even her beloved Sarah, a Whig of Whigs, was able to move the Queen—or dared to try to move her—from this determination. Herein lies the key to Anne's disposition and actions.

As an individual, Anne should move us to pity. When she became Queen she was thirty-seven years of age, had buried fifteen children, and suffered from chronic gout and dropsy. To walk even a few steps was often an agony. Her husband was Prince George of Denmark whom she had married in 1683. Charles II's well-known quip about the Prince—"I have tried him drunk and I have tried him sober, but there is nothing in him"—may have been a reflection of the traits that Charles looked for in a man rather than a disgrace to the Prince. Nevertheless Anne's consort certainly lacked the

[1] *Marlborough, His Life and Times*, Vol. III, p. 219.

distinction and quality of leadership that would have been valuable as a complement to such a character as Anne's. At best he was dull and slow-witted. If we remember Anne's personal and domestic trials we need not be surprised that she welcomed the sparkling conversation of the Duchess of Marlborough.

Though earlier historians erred in reducing the Queen to be the puppet of the Marlboroughs, there can be no disputing the fact that, during the first half of the reign at least, the Marlboroughs were without rival the greatest of the Queen's servants whose influence extended to every sphere of national life. This position they owed not to the advantages of noble birth but to native genius which used to the full the opportunities that circumstances presented. John Churchill, the Duke, was the eldest surviving son (born in 1650) of Winston Churchill, a Dorsetshire squire who, during the Civil War, had been a staunch Royalist. He suffered considerable impoverishment at the hands of Parliament, but the Restoration brought a welcome turn to his fortunes. In 1661 he became a Member of Parliament, and in 1663 received knighthood; and during the following years he was employed in Government posts both in London and in Ireland. John, when about sixteen years old, became a page to the Duke of York. In 1667 he entered the Army as ensign. Thereafter he saw service in Tangier and in Flanders during the war beginning in 1672. By 1678 he had risen to the rank of colonel, in which year he married Sarah Jennings, who also was a member of the Duke of York's household. Their union proved to be indeed remarkable. Whatever truth there may have been in the allegations of treachery in Churchill's public life, his private life was one of complete loyalty. The relation of John and Sarah was that of unclouded and unspoiled affection. Sarah was the centre of John's life. Immediately after a battle, and even in the midst of battle, if a suitable courier appeared, it was to her that he wrote, and she reciprocated with equal warmth. The one sharp difference between them was in the realm of politics: John was a staunch Tory while Sarah was a vehement Whig. Even this did not divide them. Indeed, it had the practical advantage that it gave them a foot in both camps.

During Charles II's reign Churchill shared the fortunes, good and bad, of James of York, and almost immediately after James became King, in 1685, he raised his adherent to the peerage as Baron Churchill. One of his first services to the new sovereign was to help to suppress Monmouth's rebellion in his native West country. The main items of Churchill's relations with James II and William III we have already noticed. In 1689 William raised him to be Earl of Marlborough.

Marlborough's distinguishing personal characteristic was his charm of manner. Men and women of all types, ranks, and nationalities alike found him irresistible. Herein lies much of the explanation of his astounding and continuous diplomatic success. For the fact must never be forgotten that in addition to being Captain-General of the forces of the Grand Alliance he constituted himself also a sort of diplomatist-in-chief without whose exertions the alliance would have broken up in disaster many times before the common enemy was defeated. Nor did leadership of the Allied armies and management of Allied diplomacy exhaust his responsibilities and activities. He was also a party leader at home, being for several years virtually Prime Minister. This brings us back to the subject of party politics in general.

The composition of the two political parties was not directly affected by Anne's succession. The Whigs were still the party of the Revolution: they included the trading and moneyed class that was concerned to maintain the Bank of England, the various branches of Dissenters, the mass of yeoman farmers, and also a number of prominent landowning peers. Indeed, the Whigs were able to control a narrow majority in the Lords. The Tories had the support of the bulk of the landowning classes, particularly the country gentry and their dependants, and of the parish clergy of the Established Church. There was, however, one difference that Anne's succession did make to the party-situation: it tipped the balance in favour of the Tories. For this there were two reasons. First, Anne, because of her High Church convictions, was herself a strong Tory. Second, and not less important, Tory principles enabled the party to support Anne as they had not enabled it to support William; for Anne was in the line of Stuart succession, and if the Pretender was conveniently left aside—whether because his origin was doubtful or because his religion was Roman Catholic—Anne was the rightful occupant of the throne. Hence, the political ascendancy which the Tories had secured during the closing years of William became more marked during the opening years of Anne.

Almost as soon as Anne became Queen, Godolphin, who had been First Lord of the Treasury under William, received the white staff as Lord High Treasurer. Godolphin was not a strong party man. He had been in office with Whigs and with Tories. His temperament was rather that of a superior civil servant than of a party leader. But his general sympathies were with the Tories. He worked perfectly with Marlborough, and while Marlborough was campaigning abroad Godolphin represented his views and his interests at home. The two families of Godolphin and Marlborough had become united in 1698 by the marriage of Marlborough's elder daughter, Henrietta, to Godolphin's son, Francis.

The general election of July 1702 returned a substantial Tory majority in the Commons. Possibly the electorate had taken heed to Anne's hint that she would be inclined to "countenance those who have the truest zeal to support" the Church of England. Thus the Ministry which Godolphin led in 1702 was predominantly Tory, but during the period of his Treasurership (1702–10) the composition of his Ministries gradually changed from Tory to Whig. The fact was that to both Marlborough and Godolphin the one thing that mattered was to win the war against France. To this end they were willing to work with whatever political leaders could best command a majority favouring the war.

The section of the Whig party that the Queen could not countenance was the inner group of five known as the "Junto" —namely, Lord Wharton, the Whig leader in the Lords; Lord Somers, who, as Sir John Somers, had been Lord Keeper from 1693 to 1697 and then Lord Chancellor from 1697 to 1700; Charles Montagu, Earl of Halifax, the financial genius; the Earl of Oxford, who, as Edward Russell, had been the English commander at the victory of La Hogue; and Charles Spencer, who in 1701 had married Marlborough's younger daughter,

Anne, and who in September 1702 succeeded his father as Earl of Sunderland.

The measure which first provoked cleavage in the 1702–5 Ministry was the Occasional Conformity Bill which Henry St John introduced in November 1702. Its object was to prevent Dissenters from qualifying for office in either local or central government by taking the sacrament at an Anglican church though henceforward continuing to attend their usual place of worship. The Bill proposed loss of office and a heavy fine for any office-holder who attended a dissenting service. Though the Bill passed the Commons, it was wrecked by amendments in the Lords. Twelve months later it was again introduced: once more the Commons passed it, but this time the Lords rejected it outright. The repeated rejection of the Bill was a rebuff to the Tories, and some of the more extreme Tories were removed from office. Rochester, like his father, the first Earl of Clarendon, the personification of the High Church party, had been pushed into resigning his Lord-Lieutenancy of Ireland after the first rejection. In May 1704 Nottingham resigned his Secretaryship of State, and was succeeded by Harley, who was the leader of the moderate Tories: the years of his Secretaryship (1704–8) were the most prosperous period of Marlborough's and Godolphin's combined rule. In April 1704 Harley was able to introduce his friend Henry St John into the Ministry as Secretary-at-War. Though only twenty-five years of age, St John had already distinguished himself as a debater; but he was a violent Tory, and his advent to the Ministry was certain to introduce a disruptive element.

The triennial election of 1705 substantially increased the number of Whigs in the Commons. Party lines were not then hard-and-fast, and exact numbers of the respective groups are not easy to arrive at. Godolphin's estimate was 190 Tories, 160 Whigs, and 100 "Queen's Servants." Though these numbers would fluctuate from division to division, the broad result was that the Whigs plus the courtiers could comfortably outvote the Tories. Consequently there was a gradual change in the Ministry's composition involving the introducing of Whigs. The most notable newcomer was Marlborough's Whig son-in-law, Sunderland, who in 1706 was made a Secretary of State.

By this time the Ministry had become a coalition, and it soon showed a coalition's weaknesses.

There were two matters which produced increasing friction. The first was the relation between the Ministry and the Queen. Anne's Toryism, based upon her adherence to the Established Church, would mean that, as the Ministry became progressively Whig, it would tend to lose her support. The pivot of this support had been her affection for the Marlboroughs: if for any reason this affection weakened, the Ministry's security would be seriously undermined. The second matter was the war. The Whigs were the war-party because it was William's war and because one of its chief aims was to maintain the terms of the Treaty of Ryswick and the Revolution settlement. The temper of the nation was such that the Tories did not dare to oppose the war outright. Instead, they adopted the policy of urging that England should enter not as a principal but only as an auxiliary, not sending large armies to Flanders but concentrating upon naval operations against France and Spain. While the Whigs had a majority in the Commons the Tory tactics might not matter a great deal, but if the war should go badly for the Allies the Tories would be able to make capital out of the Whig failure. If this happened and if at the same time the Marlboroughs lost the Queen's favour the Whigs would be completely undone. The sequel will show that this was precisely the course that events followed.

The man who was chiefly responsible for the rift in the Ministry was Harley. Though a Tory, he was not anxious for an all-Tory Government, nor did he wish for Marlborough's fall. Harley did not wish for the complete predominance of either party. His ideal Government was a Ministry of moderates representing the balance of political views in the nation and depending upon the Queen's favour. His dislike of the 1705 Ministry was due to its strong Whiggism. He therefore aimed at himself becoming the directing influence so as to carry his ideal into effect. This would involve displacing Godolphin and hence, because Godolphin and Marlborough were inseparable, it might displace Marlborough also.

As the instrument of this policy, Harley used one of the Queen's waiting-women, Mrs Abigail Masham. Abigail, whose maiden name had been Hill, was a distant and poor relative of Sarah Churchill who in 1702 had obtained for her a minor post at Court. By 1704 Abigail had become a bedchamber-woman to the Queen. This position, though not an exalted one, gave opportunities of intimacy with her royal mistress. Though plain of feature, and without any charm of manner, Abigail knew how to make the most of other qualities that she did possess. Her quiet sympathy, in marked contrast to Sarah's haughtiness, gradually won its way into the Queen's affection. Though Abigail owed everything to the Duchess's interest and protection, she did not scruple to foster strife between the Duchess and the Queen. By 1707 Anne was leaning more upon Abigail than upon Sarah. In that year Miss Abigail Hill be-came Mrs Masham, her husband being a gentleman of Prince George's household. That the marriage took place without the Marlboroughs' knowledge was a straw which showed the direction of the wind at Court. Harley was not slow to use this back-stair means of access to the Queen. "The Church is in danger from the Whigs" was the obvious theme with which to impress the Queen. By the beginning of 1708 it was upon Harley's advice, not upon Marlborough's and Godolphin's, that the Queen was leaning.

The main attack upon the Government could not be directed by Harley since he was a Government Member. His policy was to take advantage of the Government's loss of prestige owing to attacks delivered by the opposition composed of Whigs and extreme Tories. The main attack was against the Government's war-policy of concentrating its military forces in Flanders to the neglect, so the opposition claimed, of Spain. In December 1707 a motion in the Lords proposed that twenty thousand troops should be transferred from the Netherlands to Spain. Against this motion Marlborough spoke vehemently, claiming that such a transfer would drive Holland out of the war and so play into Louis XIV's hands. Though these attacks did not defeat the Government, they made the party-divisions more definite, and convinced Marlborough and Godolphin that a coalition Ministry was not sufficiently firm-based to stand up to the wear-and-tear of government: they must ally either with Harley and the moderate Tories or with the Whig

Junto. The former alternative was impossible because the Tories disliked the war and because the Queen's confidence had already been lost. Early in February 1708 the Queen, hoping to get the best of both worlds, tried to rid herself of Godolphin while keeping Marlborough as Commander-in-Chief. But the two friends acted together and resigned. This threw the onus of government upon Harley, but he was unable to form a Ministry with a majority in the existing House of Commons. Consequently on February 11 he was compelled to resign office. With him went St John and others of his personal followers.

Marlborough and Godolphin had survived a serious crisis, but their position after it was very different from what it had been before. After February 1708 Marlborough and Godolphin were dependent upon Whig support, and, being alienated from the Queen, were therefore Whig servants.

The party-change was not given full practical support until later in the year. The general election of May produced a Whig majority in the Commons, but as the new Parliament was not to meet until November, the Queen postponed further Government changes. But as November approached, even the Queen realized that the Whig majority would be unmanageable unless its complexion was reflected in the Government. Hence, after the death of Anne's consort, Prince George, at the end of October 1708, the Whig Earl of Pembroke succeeded him as Lord High Admiral, and Lord Somers succeeded Pembroke as Lord President of the Council and was associated with Godolphin and Marlborough in directing the war.

Beyond that point we cannot further trace the course of domestic politics until we have followed the main stages of the war abroad. But before plunging into the story of the campaigns we can best at this point deal with one other subject of domestic politics within the period 1702–8—namely, the Union of England and Scotland.

2. Union of England and Scotland, 1707

The accession of the Stuarts to the English throne in 1603 meant that sooner or later the question of complete political union between the two countries over which they ruled would have to be faced. When James VI of Scotland became also James I of England his northern and southern kingdoms remained as separate as they had been before. The only difference was that henceforth one man would wear two crowns. Each country retained its own separate Parliament and law and institutions generally just as it had done previously. Such a situation was clearly absurd. It could be straightened out by one or other of two opposite courses: either the partial union must be dissolved so that each kingdom was once again separately ruled, or the partial union must become complete. James I, strongly favouring the latter course, did his utmost to bring it about, but the only result was the judgement of the English court in Calvin's case of 1608[1] relating to the *ex post nati*. The decision then was that Scots born since James' accession in England—that is, the *post nati*—should have the same rights as Englishmen. James hoped that time would accomplish what he was unable to do, and that as Scots and English grew accustomed to the idea of being subjects of the same King, they would look more favourably upon the project of union. In fact, events tended in the opposite direction. Even the Cromwellian union, being based upon conquest, ended as soon as the occupying troops marched south in 1660.

Though both countries were mainly Protestant, their respective churches, Presbyterian and Anglican, had so many points of difference that religion was no more a tie between them than if they had been Protestant and Roman Catholic. In this respect, as in others, the Civil War had left bitter memories.

There were economic difficulties also. Scotland was a poor, undeveloped country. Her population was computed to be less than 1,000,000 as compared with England's 5,000,000 and more; and Scotland's wealth was reckoned as about one-fortieth of England's. Her agricultural methods were primitive and unproductive, her manufactures feeble. Her houses were commonly hovels and, in many instances, little better than the huts of uncivilized savages. Economically, therefore, union could not be on anything like equal terms: union looked as

[1] See p. 33.

though it would really be absorption of the weaker by the stronger. English merchants were afraid that Scots would derive enormous benefits from their freedom to trade in English markets, but that English merchants would not be able to find commensurate advantages in Scottish markets. On the other hand the Scots feared that the small number of representatives to which their population would entitle them in the Union Parliament would mean that Scottish interests would be neglected or deliberately set aside. In theory, the execution of a united Parliament would bring an end to a separate Parliament for England just as it would for Scotland, but in practice, because of the predominance of English Members, the new Assembly would differ little from the previous English Parliament. Moreover, the seat of the united Parliament would inevitably be near the English capital not only for the convenience of the majority of the Members but also for the convenience of the king who normally lived in or near London. These and other similar considerations threatened to postpone the project of union indefinitely.

The Revolution of 1688, and events resulting from it, made the relations between the two countries more difficult than ever, and brought matters to a crisis. James II's flight altered the relations of Scotland and England in one fundamental respect. The Stuarts had been Scotland's royal line long before they had come to England; and though James II had ceased to be King of England, there was no constitutional reason why he should not continue to be James VII of Scotland. This fact lay at the base of much of the opposition that William met in Scotland; and though he had no serious difficulty in subduing the rebellious elements north of the Tweed, his accession inevitably widened the breach between English and Scots. Nor were William's subsequent relations with the Scots always such as to deepen the Scots' loyalty towards him. The Massacre of Glencoe in particular left a bitter taste in the mouths of Scots holding various political views.

But the events which particularly fomented Scottish antagonism towards England were those connected with the Darien Scheme. In 1695 the Scottish Parliament formed the Company of Scotland Trading to Africa and the Indies. Until that time, though many Scots were to be found in English colonies, Scotland had no colony or trading company of her own. Partly from a sense of patriotism, and partly in the hope of a large return for money invested, many Scots placed sums, large or small, in the company. A decision was made to establish a colony on the Isthmus of Darien because a colony so placed would command the trade both of the Pacific and of the Atlantic. Almost from the beginning, things went wrong. Darien had a fever-laden climate and was within the Spaniards' sphere, and the company's directors proved incapable of dealing with the difficulties of the project. Moreover, by the time that the first expedition set out for Darien in 1698, William III had brought his European war to a close, and the last thing that he wished to do was to embroil himself in a fresh quarrel, especially as the problem of the Spanish succession was already looming ahead. After vigorous protests by the Spanish Ambassador in London against the Darien Scheme, William notified the governors of all British colonies that no help was to be given to the Darien colonists. Between July 1698 and September 1699 three expeditions were sent out, and all ended in unrelieved disaster through fever, shipwreck, or Spaniards. Though the failure was due to inefficient management, the Scots vented their sense of humiliation upon William, blaming him for lack of support and even for opposition. The result was bitter Scottish resentment against England.

On the English side there was not always enough consideration of Scottish sensibilities, or even of Scottish rights. For example, when the English Parliament passed the Act of Settlement in 1701, naming the Hanoverian House as the heirs to the English throne, the Scots were not consulted or even taken into account: the Act provided for the "Succession in the Protestant Line to the Imperial Crown and Dignity to the said realms of England, France, and Ireland and of the Dominions thereunto belonging." The apparent implication was that the Scots were not important enough to be considered and that they would be content to accept as their monarch anyone whom their larger neighbour decided upon. The English Parliament was thus ignoring Scotland's complete political independence of England. Similarly, when England entered the war of Spanish Succession Scotland thereby became involved though she had not been consulted in the matter. Thus by the time that Anne succeeded to the throne the Scots were bitterly incensed against England and were seeking means of breaking from her. This would mean that Scotland must provide a line of succession to the Scottish throne different from that which the Act of Settlement provided for the English throne.

This was the position at the opening of Anne's reign, and the new Queen lost no time in tackling the problem. William III died on March 8, 1702. Three days later, when for the first time addressing her Parliament, Anne expressed her hope for a closer union between England and Scotland. On March 27 Parliament sanctioned the naming of commissioners to negotiate for a union. In June the Scottish Parliament reciprocated so far as to sanction the Queen's appointing Scottish commissioners but only on condition that the Presbyterian Church of Scotland should be safeguarded. For three months, during the turn of the years 1702–3, negotiations went on between the two sets of commissioners but without success. So suspicious were the Scots, when negotiations were indefinitely suspended, that the Scottish Parliament passed an Act of Security to provide that, on Anne's death, the successor to the Scottish throne should be a Protestant and a member of the royal line but that he should not be the same individual as the successor to the English throne unless England first gave guarantees about conditions of government and of trade. When this measure was presented the Queen's commissioner in Scotland refused his assent; but in the middle of 1704 the Act was again passed, and on August 5 Anne gave her assent. One reason for her doing so was fear of disorder in Scotland in the midst of uncertainties about the war abroad. All unknown to the Queen, three days previously Marlborough had removed these uncertainties by his victory at Blenheim. Had she known, almost certainly she would not have signed the Act.

Yet actually the Act brought union nearer than ever before; for when both countries were thereby brought face to face with the possibility of complete severance, neither liked the prospect. The Scots' economy would be ruined if their trade remained hampered by English restrictions on both sides of the Atlantic, nor could they wish to revert to the position of aliens in English territory as before James I's accession. The English, on their part, did not wish to return to the condition of providing a foothold for Jacobites or of having a permanent enemy in the northern half of the island. In order to counter the Act of Security and to force the Scots' hand, in March 1705 the English Parliament passed the Alien Act which empowered the Queen again to nominate commissioners to negotiate for union, and stipulated that, beginning on Christmas Day 1705, every Scot should be reckoned an alien in England until the Scots' Parliament should agree to recognize the successor to the English throne as the successor to the Scottish throne also. The Scots took the broad hint, and in September the Scottish Parliament resolved that the Queen should be empowered to appoint Scots' commissioners. In December, so as to encourage friendly negotiations, the English Parliament repealed the Alien Act.

Negotiations between the two sets of commissioners began in the middle of April 1706, and at the end of eight weeks they were brought to a triumphant conclusion. The chief provisions of the ensuing Act of Union were as follows:

> That the Successor to the Monarchy of the United Kingdom of Great Britain . . . be . . . the Most Excellent Princess Sophia . . . of Hanover and the heirs of Her Body being Protestants.
>
> That all parts of the United Kingdom . . . be under the same . . . Regulations of Trade and liable to the same Customs and Duties on Import and Export.
>
> That the United Kingdom of Great Britain be represented by One and the same Parliament.
>
> That . . . of the Peers of Scotland at the Time of the Union Sixteen shall be the number to sit and vote in the House of Lords and Forty-five the number of Representatives of Scotland in the House of Commons of the Parliament of Great Britain.[1]

The financial clauses of the Union Act were recognized as being especially generous to Scotland. While the taxation and customs systems were to be the same throughout Great Britain, the amount that Scotland was to raise in land-tax was to be

[1] Robertson, pp. 162–179.

only one-fortieth that to be raised by England. A further financial difficulty was the inequality of the financial debts of the two countries: England's was approaching £18,000,000 while Scotland's was only £16,000. Hence, as compensation to Scotland for the share of England's liabilities that she was to shoulder, England was to pay to Scotland what was called the "Equivalent" of £398,085 10s. 0d. This sum was to be used to repay to the shareholders of the Darien Company their losses in full, to provide Scotland with new coinage, and for certain other specified services.

The treaty-provisions received the almost unanimous consent of the sixty commissioners on July 22, 1706. Having passed first the Scottish and then the English Parliaments, on February 6, 1707, the Bill received the royal assent. The Act of Union took effect on May 1, 1707.

Both parties to the union made sacrifices. Both gave up the independence as symbolized in their respective Parliaments; for the point should not be overlooked that England no longer had a separate Parliament any more than Scotland had, and though the English Members enormously outnumbered the Scottish Members, the forty-five latter would be an important or even a decisive element when the English Whigs and Tories were nearly balanced. The English further admitted the Scots freely to the advantages of their oversea trade and possessions. But certainly both parties gained substantially. In the development of the oversea Empire, Scots have played a part greatly in excess of their relative numbers. Again, though the Jacobite Rebellions of 1715 and 1745 centred in Scotland, they failed through the lack of general Scottish support. In foreign affairs, as in economic prosperity, the United Kingdom has enjoyed a success which neither country could have achieved alone.

3. The War of Spanish Succession

By the time that the United Kingdom had come into being the War of Spanish Succession was well on its way, and Marlborough had achieved the two most notable victories of his career at Blenheim and Ramillies. Notwithstanding Marlborough's supreme genius, the limits within which he was able to work were strictly defined by the conditions prevailing in Europe. In this connexion two factors have to be considered.

First, several of the southern Powers found much to distract them. Austria in particular had the Turks on her flank. Among the smaller members of the Empire there was at first considerable hesitation as to whether they should enter the war at all and, if they did, on which side. However, during the latter part of 1701 and early 1702 most of these States joined the Allies, including Prussia under Frederick, who felt bound to uphold the dignity of the royal title which he had acquired as recently as 1700, and Hanover under its Elector George who was looking forward to succeeding in due course to the crown of England. The alliance's danger-spot was Bavaria whose Elector, Maximilian Emanuel, spent many months in negotiating with both sides, a process which enabled him to raise his price and to obtain favourable terms. In September 1702 he allied with France.

The second factor was the peculiar relationship existing between England and Holland. William III's death had severed the only personal link between the two countries and had left Holland without a ruler. The most prominent politician in Holland was Heinsius. He, however, did not succeed William as Stadtholder—a position which was left vacant— but was Pensionary—that is, he held the office formerly held by John de Witt. His authority was therefore less than William's had been, and Marlborough had to endure galling restrictions of oversight by Dutch field-deputies who, not being professional soldiers, constantly hampered his plans and robbed him of the fruits of victory. Only a man of Marlborough's superb diplomatic gifts of self-control and tact could have maintained friendly relations with such allies, and have won victories in spite of the difficulties which they imposed.

It was the middle of May before political affairs allowed Marlborough to leave England. Then occurred the first of many delays due to the English and Dutch relationship. Not until early July did the Dutch agree to allow Marlborough to command their forces as well as the English. The Dutch hesitation was not unnatural: Marlborough had yet to establish his ability to handle armies in large-scale operations; and the

Dutch had several capable generals, notably Ginkel, now Earl of Athlone. As soon as his position of command was recognized, Marlborough was anxious to expel the French from the land between the Meuse and the Rhine—that is, from the Spanish Netherlands—before they became too firmly established there. But the Dutch field-deputies raised objections to all his successive battle-plans. As a result, four years of hard fighting, culminating at Ramillies, were necessary in order to achieve what could have been achieved in 1702. In default of battles, Marlborough had to be content with siege-operations. In these he had some success, notably by seizing Venlo in mid-September and Liége a month later.

During 1702 warfare was opened in an element which was to remain a decisive one throughout the war—namely, the sea. Even before Marlborough had opened the 1702 offensive in the Netherlands the Empire had asked that an English fleet should be sent to the Mediterranean so as to induce the Italian rulers to side with the Allies. Portugal also was hesitating about which side to take, and a demonstration by a British fleet might bring her also into the Allied camp. These ideas were but a revival of a project of William III to seize either Cadiz or Gibraltar as a base for naval power in the Mediterranean. Cadiz was the place that Marlborough selected, and thither in July 1702 a combined English and Dutch fleet was sent under the command of Admiral Rooke, the English soldiers being commanded by the Duke of Ormonde. This divided command caused indecision and delays. Instead of a sudden attack before the Spaniards had time to organize defences, a landing was made in the neighbourhood and a month was spent in plundering, by the end of which time an attack was useless. In the middle of September, therefore, the fleet moved northward away from Cadiz. By a stroke of undeserved good fortune the commanders learned that a Spanish treasure-fleet was at anchor in Vigo Bay. On October 12 the English rammed the boom that had been built at the end of the bay and landing-parties at the same time rushed the land-defences. Every Spanish ship in the inner harbour was either sunk, burnt, or captured. Much of the treasure on the galleons had already been taken ashore; but a million pounds' worth was carried off by the attackers. Not less important was the destruction of fifteen first-class French men-o'-war that had convoyed the treasure across the Atlantic and were still in Vigo when Rooke sailed in. In spite of the failure at Cadiz, it was an auspicious opening to naval operations.

The Queen's appreciation of Marlborough's services to the Allied cause was shown by his being raised from an Earl to a Duke, in December 1702.

The year 1703 was more notable for changes on the diplomatic front, and hence for preparations for future campaigns, than it was for immediate warlike operations. That Marlborough accomplished very little in the Netherlands, except the capture of certain fortresses, was again due not to lack of enterprise but to Dutch obstructiveness.

The first diplomatic change was made by Victor Amadeus, Duke of Savoy. Savoy's geographical position, athwart the Alpine passes from France on the west to the Austrian possessions in Italy, had been reflected in her unstable relations with France and the Allies respectively. To all outward appearance, the interests of Victor Amadeus were firmly tied to those of France and Spain, and two of his daughters had married into the French and the Spanish royal families. During 1701, therefore, Savoy had been used as a base of French operations in Italy. But Victor was a crafty diplomatist. He had no wish to see France overwhelmingly victorious, but preferred that Austria should be strong enough to check France so that Savoy, because of her geographical importance, might be courted by both of them. In October 1703 Savoy threw in her lot with the Allies.

Even more important was the declared adherence of Portugal to the Allied cause. This was the result mainly of the efforts of John Methuen and his son, Paul, who during the reigns of William III and Anne had represented English interests at the Portuguese Court. Portugal, like Savoy, could hardly avoid being drawn into the war on one side or the other. Her accessibility from Spain seemed to suggest that her interests lay in that direction. But Portugal's main consideration was her colonies and her trade. A hostile sea-power was therefore more to be feared than even a neighbouring land-power. The Allied victory at Vigo Bay in October 1702 clinched the arguments that the Methuens had been putting forward, and finally in May 1703 Portugal joined the Allies. The Methuen Treaty arranged that English cloth should be admitted into Portugal at low rates of customs while Portuguese wines were to enter England at customs rates one-third below those levied on French wines. This is the explanation of the port-drinking—and of the gout—which soon became common in England. The treaty's immediate effect on the war was that the Allies could use Lisbon as a base of operations in the Mediterranean. But the Methuen Treaty had effects much wider than this. Portugal demanded, as a condition of her alliance, that large Allied forces should be sent to the Peninsula, that the Archduke Charles should be proclaimed Charles III of Spain, and that no peace-treaty should be signed until Charles was established on his new throne. To these terms the Allies, including the Emperor, had to agree. The whole character of the Allies' war-aims was thus changed. William's original Treaty of the Grand Alliance had promised to Austria only the Spanish Netherlands and the Spanish possessions in Italy and in the Mediterranean. This original purpose was virtually achieved by the time of the Battle of Ramillies, in 1706, and certainly by the time of Oudenarde, in 1708. The extended objective, as laid down in the Methuen Treaty, prolonged the war during several years, and even then was never achieved.

During 1703 danger to the Allies loomed up in another direction. In May the Duc de Villars had arrived on the Danube to co-operate with Maximilian Emanuel of Bavaria in attacking Vienna and so in driving the Emperor out of the war. If this could be achieved the French would be able to concentrate against the English and Dutch in the Netherlands. Villars was the most capable of all Louis XIV's generals but he lacked tact and patience. Consequently he never secured the genuine co-operation of Maximilian Emanuel, and at the end of 1703 Vienna was still in Austrian hands, and finally Villars disgustedly resigned his command. Nevertheless Vienna's danger remained acute, and in 1704 the attacks upon it would almost certainly be renewed. It was this situation which gave rise to the scheme which culminated in the Battle of Blenheim.

The scheme was that Marlborough should lead a relieving expedition on to the Danube. This attracted Marlborough all the more because of the impossibility of inducing the Dutch to engage in decisive battles near their own borders. Throughout the winter of 1703–4 the project was under discussion between him and Count Wratislaw, the Imperial Envoy in England. By the spring of 1704 Marlborough had become convinced that an expedition to the Danube was the only means of saving Austria and preserving the Grand Alliance. But to reveal this conviction even to the Allies would be to ensure its defeat. If Louis XIV learned of it a French army would invade the Netherlands as soon as Marlborough marched out; and if the Dutch suspected the project they would, for fear of a French invasion, refuse to sanction it. In March 1704, therefore, Marlborough laid before the Dutch a plan to invade France up the Rhine and the Moselle. In support of it he urged that as he moved on up the Moselle the French armies watching him would move parallel with him and away from the Netherlands. At last the Dutch gave their consent. Marlborough naturally had no objections if information of this plan leaked out to the French. The real plan was, in the first instance, known only to him and the Austrians. Not until the middle of April 1704 was it revealed even to Godolphin and Queen Anne.

The only means of transferring the bulk of the Allied Army from the Netherlands to the Rhine was on foot. Yet if the decisive blow was to be struck before the French realized Marlborough's purpose, or at least before they could adjust their strategy to meet it, the utmost possible speed was essential. Accordingly, everything was done to keep the troops fit in body and happy in mind. Depots and hospitals were established at regular intervals along the planned route, and Marlborough personally supervised every possible detail for his men's comfort.

It was just west of Cologne that in May he gathered his troops for the great march. He followed the left bank of the Rhine as far as Koblenz where he had ostentatiously collected a large store, and where he was expected to branch up the Moselle. But at Koblenz he crossed the Rhine, and then proceeded through Mainz, and thence still along the Rhine. The new theory was that he intended a campaign in Alsace. After crossing the Neckar the secret could no longer be kept. From Heidelberg on the Neckar he turned south-east across to the Danube which he struck just north of Ulm, and at Mundelsheim he met Prince Eugene for the first time.

Eugene was a prince of the House of Savoy, and had been brought up at Louis XIV's court. But, unable to tolerate Louis' domineering suppression of all who had to do with him, Eugene in 1682 fled and took service with the House of Habsburg—that is, with the Emperor, the traditional enemy of France. By sheer merit, Eugene had risen in his adopted service until he held the highest rank in the Imperial Army. He had waged a victorious war against the Turks, and now he led the Imperial Army in Marlborough's support. From the day that he and Marlborough met at Mundelsheim, the two generals formed an intimate friendship based upon mutual confidence which, in spite of varied and adverse conditions, never wavered for a moment.

Having reached the Danube, Marlborough aimed to control Donauwörth, where there was a good crossing of the river, and where he intended to establish a new depot of stores. The key to the control of Donauwörth was a great rocky hill called the Schellenberg where Marshal Marsin, the French commander, fortified himself, and so barred Marlborough's further progress. Marlborough decided that at all costs the position must be stormed, and after hours of fierce fighting the Allied troops won the height. It was a notable victory, but the real struggle was yet to come. Tallard, when he realized Marlborough's real purpose, marched rapidly eastward and joined Marsin at Augsburg whither the latter retired after his defeat at the Schellenberg. Thus Marlborough might have to face the great combined French and Bavarian armies. But the French failed to take the initiative which thus passed to Marlborough.

At dawn on August 2 Marlborough ordered battle against the French encamped at Blenheim. So precarious and feeble did the Allies' position appear that the French imagined that

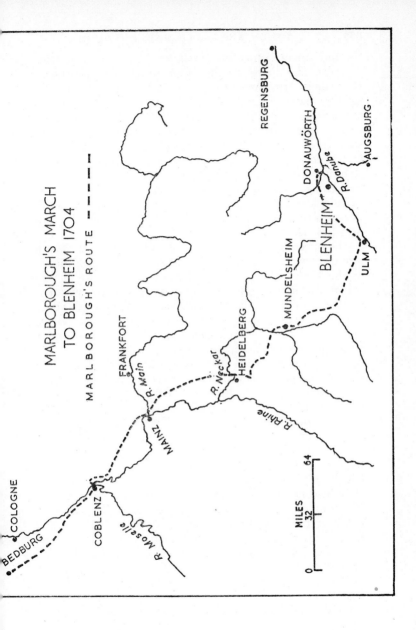

MARLBOROUGH'S MARCH
TO BLENHEIM 1704

MARLBOROUGH'S ROUTE – – – – –

REGENSBURG

DONAUWÖRTH

AUGSBURG

R. Danube

BLENHEIM

ULM

MUNDELSHEIM

FRANKFORT

R. Main

R. Neckar

HEIDELBERG

MAINZ

R. Rhine

COLOGNE

BEDBURG

COBLENZ

R. Moselle

MILES

0   32   64

the movement betokened Marlborough's retirement from the Danube, and therefore they took no counter-measures until the Allied Army was drawn up in battle-order. The consequently hasty French dispositions were unable to withstand the weight and skill of the massed Allied attack. It was past noon before Marlborough gave the order for the attack. During some three hours the battle swayed backward and forward, but in the end Marlborough's generalship and his perfect understanding with Eugene began to tell. As evening wore on, the French were driven back, and by nightfall they were scattering in hopeless rout. Tallard himself was a prisoner in Marlborough's coach; and half his army were either dead, wounded, or prisoners.

The effects of Blenheim were plain for all to see. The tradition of French invincibility was broken at a stroke; the morale of the French Army remained shattered for several years to come; Marlborough's reputation as a general was equally clearly established, and henceforward he could command where previously he had had to request; Vienna was saved, and with it the cohesion of the Grand Alliance. It was Blenheim that rescued Europe from French domination.

While the campaign was being conducted on the Danube the English fleet was winning a scarcely less significant success in the Mediterranean. One effect of Portugal's entering the war was that Lisbon became available as a base for Allied fleets. From Lisbon, therefore, early in 1704 Admiral Rooke set sail in the hope of encouraging a revolt in Catalonia against Philip V's Government. Rooke, disappointed in these hopes, turned westward to meet an English squadron under Sir Cloudesley Shovell who had been sent out to join him. The combined fleets, thus finding themselves in the neighbourhood of Gibraltar, decided to try to seize the Rock. Gibraltar was not then the great fortress that it has since become, and the Spanish garrison there was very small. After a day's bombardment, on July 21, 1704—that is, ten days before Blenheim—English marines were landed, and took the place almost without resistance. Most of the families living on the Rock took advantage of the capitulation terms and migrated to the Spanish mainland. Thus Gibraltar became almost wholly

British. The full significance of its capture, in giving to England control over the entrance to the Mediterranean, only the future could show.

But enough of its importance was realized at the time to cause the French to sail out at once to challenge Rooke and to recapture Gibraltar. The clash came off Malaga on August 13. By the end of the day both fleets were severely mauled yet neither was defeated. The English had only a small supply of ammunition left, but this the French did not know. Next day the two fleets lay and glowered at each other, and when dawn broke on the 15th the French had disappeared, having sailed back to Toulon during the night. It was the first battle that the English had to fight in defence of Gibraltar.

The French and Spaniards next decided to attack the English garrison there before the latter became too firmly established. Several thousand Spanish troops marched overland, and in September 1704 a fleet from Toulon landed a strong force of French. When Rooke had sailed home after the action at Malaga Prince George of Hesse was left in command of a mixed force of English and Dutch troops. He was a capable commander who had seen much service under William III; but not all his resourcefulness would have availed to hold Gibraltar if he had been cut off from outside help. Such help was possible because Lisbon and not some distant port was the English base of operations. Admiral Leake was in command of the English fleet at Lisbon, and three times between September 1704 and March 1705 he led relieving expeditions. At the end of that period the French and Spaniards grew tired of their repeated failures and raised the siege.

When the 1705 campaigning season opened Marlborough was confident that, if he received the genuine co-operation of his allies, he would be able to strike a decisive, and perhaps final, blow against the French. Blenheim had seen not only the military defeat of the French Army but also its demoralization. Marlborough's plan was to make a real, not a feint, invasion of France up the Moselle. This route would take him into the heart of France without having to fight his way through the fortresses of the Spanish Netherlands. But from the very outset things went wrong. The Dutch seemed unconvinced that the brilliant success of 1704 was not an accident such as might never recur, and they therefore refused to allow their troops to be taken to a distance from the Netherlands. Also the German princes failed to send their quotas to the Allied Army. Consequently Marlborough had to abandon his Moselle campaign and to revert to the operation of clearing the French from the Netherlands. His immediate objective was to force the defensive lines of Brabant which the French had built in an arc from Antwerp, in the north, to near Namur, in the south. Early in July he forced the lines, a move which so completely surprised and unbalanced the French that a resolute and concerted advance would possibly have cleared them completely from the Netherlands. But Marlborough could not sufficiently trust to Dutch co-operation in a large-scale operation, and he therefore adopted the opposite policy of deliberately remaining inactive. The result was that even the Dutch could hardly avoid a sense of shame. Though the 1705 campaign was ruined, the prospects for 1706 were somewhat brightened.

Meanwhile an attempt was being made to embarrass Philip V's Government in Spain by exploiting the permanent discontent of the subject-province of Catalonia. The Earl of Peterborough was given the command of an expedition for this purpose. It was a strange choice: Peterborough, though personally brave and fiercely energetic when once started on a course, was irresolute and changeable. In June 1705 he directed an English fleet, with a considerable body of troops aboard, into Lisbon. Thence, having picked up the Archduke Charles —"Charles III" of Spain—the fleet sailed first to Gibraltar and then to Barcelona, the capital of Catalonia. The Catalans welcomed the invaders but had nothing tangible to offer in support. Early in September Peterborough launched an attack on the citadel overlooking the town of Barcelona. After five days' struggle the action was finally decided when an English cannon-shot exploded the citadel's powder-magazine. The fall of Barcelona was followed by the surrender of other neighbouring towns, and soon Catalonia and the adjoining province of Valencia acknowledged Charles III. The future would show that the victory was a dearly bought illusion. In the eyes of the rest of Spain Catalonia was an alien province, and the

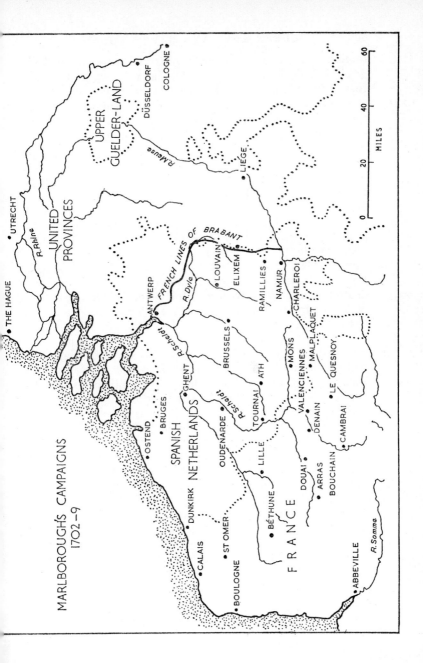

MARLBOROUGH'S CAMPAIGNS
1702-9

THE HAGUE

UTRECHT

UNITED
PROVINCES

R. Rhine

UPPER
GUELDER-LAND

DÜSSELDORF

COLOGNE

R. Meuse

LIEGE

ANTWERP

FRENCH LINES OF BRABANT

R. Dyle

LOUVAIN

ELIXEM

RAMILLIES

NAMUR

CHARLEROI

R. Scheldt

BRUSSELS

GHENT

OUDENARDE

R. Scheldt

ATH

TOURNAI

MONS

VALENCIENNES

MALPLAQUET

DENAIN

LE QUESNOY

CAMBRAI

OSTEND

BRUGES

SPANISH NETHERLANDS

LILLE

DOUAI

ARRAS

BOUCHAIN

DUNKIRK

ST OMER

BÉTHUNE

CALAIS

FRANCE

BOULOGNE

ABBEVILLE

R. Somme

0   20   40   60
MILES

foreign support upon which Charles had to rely provoked a general Spanish resentment against his rule. All that the capture of Barcelona did for the Allies was to induce them to send a stream of men and supplies into Spain in support of a cause that could not ultimately succeed. As it was for Napoleon a century later, Spain was for the Allies a running sore.

No sooner was the 1705 campaigning season over than Marlborough began to plan for the campaign to follow. The most important item of preparation was how to strengthen the Grand Alliance. With this object, Marlborough set out on a great tour of visits to the Allied princes. Starting in the middle of October 1705, he passed through Düsseldorf where he met the Elector Palatine who promised to increase the number of his troops in Allied pay from seven thousand to ten thousand. Thence Marlborough went to Vienna to visit the Emperor Joseph, who had succeeded his father, Leopold, on the latter's death the previous May. Joseph fell completely under the spell of Marlborough's charm, and hence his continued adherence to the alliance was ensured notwithstanding the mutual dislike of the Austrians and the Dutch. From Vienna Marlborough travelled to Berlin, being accompanied by Sunderland, who had previously been sent from England as a special envoy to Vienna. "Such were the pains taken to smooth and speed their journey that they covered the five hundred and thirty miles in eight days in their coaches, in spite of the bad roads and the winter weather." Finally, Marlborough "reached The Hague on December 15 after a journey by coach and barge in midwinter of nearly two thousand miles."[1] It was a stupendous feat, not less noteworthy, and not less necessary to the successful prosecution of the war, than such victories as Blenheim.

Notwithstanding Marlborough's diplomatic success, the Allies' prospects at the beginning of 1706 were not too bright. The war was entering its fourth year, and the only outstanding Allied achievement had been the Blenheim campaign. The year following Blenheim had been as barren as those that had preceded it, and the feeling was spreading that Blenheim had been a stroke of luck rather than of genius. Unless 1706 could

[1] Winston S. Churchill, *Marlborough*, Vol. III, pp. 50, 54.

show something outstanding, there was a serious danger that 'war-weariness' would creep in with fatal results. The French retained a strong hold on the Netherlands, and there was every prospect of another year of monotonous, slow siege-operations. Then suddenly the French moved. The truth seems to be that French resources were so near breaking-point that Louis resolved to make a bid for decisive victory. Early in May he ordered Marshal Villeroi to assume the offensive. Villeroi and his generals, having a splendidly equipped Army, and greatly underrating Marlborough's powers, eagerly responded. The effect on the Allied armies was no less exhilarating. Marlborough, who had never expected any such opportunity, moved at once to accept the challenge.

The clash came at Ramillies, a few miles from Namur, on May 12. The French took up a strong defensive position. Marlborough used the prominent English red-coats on his right wing to make a feint attack and so to draw the French away from the other parts of the battle where he intended to deliver his main onslaught. The first attack was opened soon after noon. Shortly after 6 P.M. the French began to break. Almost at once the retreat turned into a confused rout. Whole regiments dispersed and were never re-formed. Some of those in French pay deserted solidly to the Allies. How many men were lost to the French Army in killed, prisoners, and deserters, cannot be accurately estimated. Very possibly the losses amounted to half the French Army, and the confidence of the remaining half was so thoroughly undermined that it was useless as a fighting force during the rest of that year. Ramillies was as striking and decisive a victory in the Netherlands as Blenheim had been on the Danube.

Nor was the scattering of the French Army its only result. The remnants of the Army were given no rest but were followed westward from the battlefield without respite. During this process town after town—the siege of any one of which would normally have been spread over a whole campaign—fell into Allied hands, including Louvain, Brussels, Oudenarde, Ghent, Bruges, Antwerp, and many another. By the close of 1706 the only Netherlands fortresses remaining in French control were those on the border such as Mons, Charleroi, and Namur.

Marlborough's triumphs in the Netherlands were accompanied by a notable triumph in Italy. There the French controlled several great towns, especially Milan and Naples, and were besieging Turin, the capital of Savoy. The French hold on Italy jeopardized the Allies' control of the Mediterranean and even of the Spanish ports. If Turin was allowed to fall into their hands Savoy would be forced out of the Grand Alliance, and all Italy would soon be under French control. To relieve Turin was obviously Austria's task, but Joseph was not to be relied upon to engage in the work heartily. However, in July 1706, Prince Eugene set out with a mixed force of Austrians, Prussians, and other Germans. Marching via Lake Garda, he reached the river Po, near to Turin. There he was joined by the small army of Victor Amadeus, Duke of Savoy. Even their combined armies were smaller than that of the French. But at the end of August Eugene risked storming the besiegers' line at its weakest point. The assault succeeded: the French Marshal, Marsin, was mortally wounded, and his Army scattered across the Alps. Turin was saved, the French were expelled from the other Italian cities, and all Italy fell to the Allies.

In the third theatre of the war the Allies were less prosperous during 1706. Early in April a considerable French Army laid siege to Barcelona. The English garrison was not numerous, and but for the willing support of the Catalans, both within Barcelona and in the country around, the town could not have held out long. In the citadel the English, several hundreds strong, held out for three weeks. Though it was then overcome by superior numbers, the delay was just long enough to allow help to be brought before the town itself surrendered. On the very day that the French had planned a general attack Admiral Leake sailed into the harbour and landed five thousand soldiers. Barcelona was relieved and the besieging French driven off.

Meanwhile a combined Anglo-Portuguese force, under Galway's command, was advancing towards Madrid from the west. By mid-June it had command of the city. Philip V had fled from his capital, and if Charles III had now appeared he

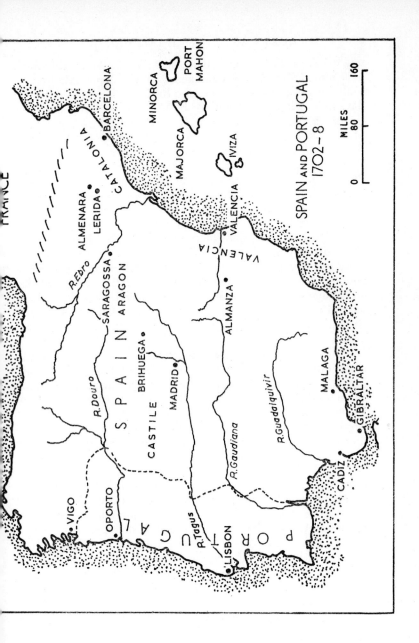

SPAIN AND PORTUGAL 1702–8

FRANCE

CATALONIA
BARCELONA
ALMENARA
LERIDA
R.Ebro
SARAGOSSA
ARAGON
BRIHUEGA
MADRID
CASTILE
SPAIN
R.Douro
VIGO
OPORTO
PORTUGAL
LISBON
R.Tagus
R.Guadiana
R.Guadalquivir
CADIZ
GIBRALTAR
MALAGA
ALMANZA
VALENCIA
VALENCIA
IVIZA
MAJORCA
MINORCA
PORT MAHON

MILES
0   80   160

might have made good his hold on it and on the crown which he claimed. But Charles remained in Catalonia. Madrid resented his continued absence, and his cause languished day by day. Before long the populace in Madrid and the peasants of the neighbourhood grew so hostile that Galway withdrew from Madrid and added his forces to those of Charles in Catalonia, thus leaving the main field clear for the French and Philip. The ground thus lost could never be recovered. The war in the Peninsula was over. The man chiefly responsible for the disastrous turn of affairs was the unstable Peterborough, who was in command in Catalonia, and by whose advice Charles had decided not to go to Madrid. No sooner was it clear that the campaign had failed than Peterborough left the Peninsula and went to Savoy for a change and rest.

In spite of these events, in 1707 plans were made for a counter-offensive. Now the Allies suffered the additional disadvantage of divided command and divided counsels. Galway wished to renew an attack on Madrid; King Charles wished to strengthen his hold upon the coastal fortresses of Catalonia. The worst possible decision was taken: they tried to do both, and the inevitable result was disaster. No sooner did Galway move out from southern Valencia in April 1707 than a combined French and Spanish Army moved towards him. The French commander was the Duke of Berwick, natural son of James II of England, and Arabella Churchill, eldest sister of Marlborough. Berwick was a worthy nephew of his distinguished uncle and, with the possible exception of Villars, the most competent of Louis XIV's marshals. Galway underestimated his opponent and, with inferior forces, brought on a battle at Almanza. In the height of the battle the Portuguese cavalry suddenly fled, thus disorganizing Galway's plan, and leaving the English forces hopelessly outnumbered. Almanza confirmed Charles' loss of Spain except Catalonia.

An attempt to seize Toulon in July 1707 was equally a disaster. It consisted of combined operations between an army led from North Italy by Eugene and Victor Amadeus and a navy sent from England under Sir Cloudesley Shovell. For once Eugene was reluctant to take the offensive, the result being that the expedition lacked the verve necessary to success. The French were able to strengthen the port's defences before the Allies arrived, and in the middle of August the siege had to be raised.

For the Allies, 1707 had been a dismal year in every sphere of the war. Even Marlborough in the Netherlands had achieved nothing valuable, and he realized that if 1708 was a mere repetition of 1707 all hope of a decisive Allied victory might be abandoned. The foundation of his plan for 1708 was that he and Eugene should again combine to bring on a pitched battle. Eugene was therefore given a command on the Moselle while Marlborough remained in the Netherlands.

The French also had a plan. The Anglo-Dutch administration of the Spanish Netherlands was provoking discontent, and the French hoped to convert this discontent into active support of their cause. In 1708 a French army was sent into the Netherlands under the Duke of Burgundy's command along with Marshal Vendôme. Their first moves promised every chance of success. While Marlborough was protecting Brussels, the French slipped northward, and as soon as they appeared Ghent and Bruges welcomed them within their gates. The disadvantage to the French was that Marlborough lay between them and France. In an attempt both to hold what they had gained and to secure their communications, the French left garrisons in Ghent and Bruges while their main Army marched towards the French frontier. Here was a situation after Marlborough's own heart. Eugene was hurried from the Moselle ahead of his men, and together the two great Allied generals prepared to force an engagement. The opportunity was provided by the French attempt to seize the fortress of Oudenarde on their way, and it was here that the Allied Army fell upon them. Without waiting to arrange an orderly field of battle, Marlborough flung regiment after regiment into action as they crossed the hastily constructed pontoon bridge over the Scheldt, close to the fort. The French fought gallantly but the memory of Blenheim and Ramillies was so powerful that, when the crisis of the battle was reached, the French broke. The result was a complete rout. The number of prisoners approached ten thousand (a sure sign of demoralization); and the killed, the wounded, and the deserters numbered nearly as many more. Even the French still at liberty were in little better plight, for their only line of retreat was away from France.

Soon after Oudenarde, Eugene's army from the Moselle arrived to join Marlborough's English and Dutch armies in the Netherlands. The Allies thus had overwhelmingly superior striking-power at the very moment when their enemy was both defeated and demoralized. This power, wisely used, might have ended the war almost at once. Marlborough was intent upon advancing against Paris without further warning. Eugene, urging the danger of leaving the Netherlands wholly unprotected, while Lille, the strongest of the French fortresses, would be in their rear, advocated the reduction of Lille before making any further advance. To besiege such a city, whose defences were believed to be impregnable, while large armies led by such commanders as Berwick and Vendôme could be sent to its relief, was an enterprise with difficulties of the first magnitude. Even if the almost impossible was achieved and Lille was captured, the season would by then be too far spent for an advance into France. However, Marlborough, with characteristic patience, yielded to Eugene's argument, and the siege began. As might have been expected, the process was long and costly. The siege operations, the repelling of attacks, the bringing up of stores, together cost the Allies fifteen thousand men, which was several times their loss at Oudenarde. But the siege was maintained, and in mid-October the French evacuated the town and concentrated upon defending the citadel. Six weeks later this also yielded. Though less dazzling as an event, the fall of Lille was more solidly notable an achievement than victory in battle: the attackers' difficulties were greater, the loss in prestige to the French was not less, and the way into France now lay wide open. In spite of the wintry season, the Allies continued operations, and before the year was out Ghent and Bruges had also capitulated. Thus all the Netherlands were at last clear of the invader. There was every prospect that the following year would see the rôles reversed, with Marlborough free to carry out his plan of attack and France being the invaded country.

Even these triumphs in battle and siege did not exhaust the Allied successes of 1708. In the Mediterranean a further advantage was gained. One of the Allies' serious drawbacks there was that their vessels had to be brought home during the winter because they had no port suitable as a winter base. So, in the middle of 1708, the English decided to land on Minorca, whose capital, Port Mahon, had a harbour splendidly suited to the purpose. Early in September Admiral Leake and General Stanhope effected a landing. Within a fortnight Port Mahon had surrendered and Minorca was in British hands, and so remained for nearly a century.

France's thorough defeat in the field and her exhaustion at home left Louis with no alternative to making overtures for peace. The exhaustion was intensified by the rigours of the 1708–9 winter which was of almost arctic intensity, and left France covered with starving peasants. On May 28 the pleni-potentiaries of Britain, Holland, and Austria signed Preliminary Articles which were handed to the Marquis de Torcy as ex-pressing the Allies' terms. They demanded that within two months of June 1, 1709, the whole of Spain and the Spanish Empire should be handed over to Charles III except that certain stipulated towns in the Spanish Netherlands should be garrisoned by the Dutch as a barrier against France. They further declared that if Philip V did not abdicate within the specified time Louis XIV was to help the Allies to expel him from Spain. It was this last article which was the rock on which negotiations split. On all other points Louis yielded; but that he should levy war on his own grandson in order to expel him from Spain and from the Spanish people who had adopted him, was more than even Louis would grant, notwithstanding his need of peace. As neither side would make any concession on the point, hostilities were inevitably renewed.

So far as Britain was concerned, there were two root reasons for the failure to make peace. First, the dominant political influence behind the negotiations was that of the Whigs who, in the previous November, had become supreme in the Govern-ment and who, being the war-party, were not likely to use their newly acquired power to make concessions for peace. Second, no party in England seems to have realized that the struggle against Louis XIV's threatened domination in Europe and the war against Philip V were two separate issues. Had the Allies been content with their complete victory in the first of the two issues, while recognizing that equally complete victory in the second would be inherently impossible, peace would have been concluded in 1708.

In refusing to make peace except on their own extreme terms the Allies were relying upon starvation to bring the French people to abject surrender. But they overlooked the moral effect that their refusal would have in France. Louis could now truthfully claim that not he but his enemies were the aggressors; and he could call for a final rally against the nation's unreasoning foes. This appeal, added to widespread hunger, drew large numbers of recruits to his armies. The Duc de Villars was entrusted with the command of these armies. He alone of the French marshals had kept the confidence of the French people undiminished.

The protracted negotiations had delayed field operations until June. Marlborough and Eugene first laid siege to Tournai, which was just on the Netherlands side of the frontier. A full two months passed before its last stronghold surrendered. This cost the Allies five thousand men killed and wounded.

Marlborough at once turned to the near-by border-fortress of Mons. While still on the way there, and before he had time to form a regular order of battle, he found himself challenged by Villars at Malplaquet, and there, on August 31, the last big battle of the war was fought. Villars took up a strong position which could be attacked only at great hazard, but the Allies had no option but to attack. At the end of a bitter struggle the French were driven from the field, thus rendering Mons a prey to the victors and leaving twelve thousand killed or wounded behind them. But the Allies, notwithstanding their victory, lost eighteen thousand killed or wounded (some estimates place the number as high at twenty-four thousand). The fall of Mons early in October was a welcome sign that the Allies still were superior, but the battle had shown also that the enemy still had fighting qualities not to be ignored. Further, the heavy price that the Allies had paid for victory would encourage the critics among their own members and would loosen the alliance.

In October 1709 Dutch and English reaffirmed their unity

in a Barrier Treaty whose terms had been under discussion for some time. In essence the treaty was a bargain whereby Britain would allow to the Dutch a number of fortresses in the southern Netherlands, and in return the Dutch undertook to support the Hanoverian succession in England. It was a one-sided agreement since, even without it, self-interest would have compelled the Dutch to support the Hanoverians as against a Jacobite Pretender: for the latter's success would have brought an Anglo-French alliance. Marlborough openly disavowed any responsibility for the terms of the treaty.

This latter fact was an indication of the course of future events. The inconclusive condition of affairs bred discontent and friction among men of all parties. Soon the members of the Government were deeply infected. Among the masses of the people the hardships due to the war were producing a revulsion against it. Rumours that Marlborough was protracting the war for the sake of his own profit became current. Though demonstrably false, such rumours, once started, were not easy to check. The Government, feeling its credit falling, tried to restore it but only with an effect the reverse of what it intended. A Government in such a condition was an easy prey to enemies both within its ranks and without. One of these enemies was the Queen. Before we can understand the negotiations which brought an end to the war we must trace the political fall of Marlborough and his friends at home, and hence the rise to power of the Government that was to conduct the negotiations.

Chapter 14

Queen Anne and the Tories

1709-14

1. Party Changes, 1709-10

At the critical stage in the Spanish Succession War when the
Allies, though supreme in the field, were uncertain how to
turn their victories into victory, English politics centred in the
strangely assorted trio of Queen Anne, Robert Harley, and
Mrs Masham. The Queen's attitude was governed by her
desire not to be dependent upon either of the political parties:
she therefore was chiefly resentful of the party that was most
strongly forcing its will in the Government—that is, the Whigs,
whose general policy also was to restrict the power of the
monarch. Harley's immediate purpose after his resignation in
February 1708 was to bring about such a Ministerial recon-
struction as would restore him to power. Because this would
involve the fall of the Whigs, the Queen and Harley for the
moment had a common political object. Mrs Masham was the
link between the two. It was she who admitted Harley to the
back stairs to see the Queen when Sarah was out of the way;
and when this was not safe it was she who conveyed to the
Queen Harley's views on current affairs. By the close of 1709
it was apparent to both Marlborough and his Duchess that
their position at Court was highly precarious. Unfortunately
for them, the Duchess in this matter was incapable of exerting
either sound judgement or self-control. Instead of responding
to the Queen's evident displeasure by keeping away from
Court except when duty demanded her presence, and so of
avoiding unnecessary occasions of increasing the Queen's
antipathy, the Duchess sought every opportunity of nagging
at the Queen, and of complaining at the injustice of the treat-

ment she was receiving. Such conduct played exactly the game that suited Harley's purposes.

Harley was too astute to make a frontal attack on the Whigs until he had weakened them by sapping their strength. This was done by detaching from the Government certain Whigs, who, though men of influence and title, either were susceptible to royal favour or had some grievance against the Whig leaders. Among these were the Duke of Somerset, who responded to the warmth of royal favour, and Earl Rivers, who as a general was jealous that Marlborough preferred the Earl of Galway to him. More notable still as a convert was the Duke of Shrewsbury. Shrewsbury had had a long career of distinguished Government service. He had been one of the most prominent leaders who brought over William III, and was William's first Secretary of State. After being suspected of complicity in the Jacobite plot of 1696, he withdrew from political responsibility and finally settled in Rome whence none of the blandishments even of Marlborough could lure him. But in 1706 he returned to his English estates. Two years later Harley opened communications with him, and during 1709 the two men formed a close political understanding. The value of Shrewsbury in Harley's scheme was that he was a nobleman who had had a long career as a Whig but had no connexions with the Junto.

These moves induced in the Whigs a state of nerves which undermined their judgement and led them to choose the wrong time and manner of making a stand against further encroachments on their power. The victim on whom they pounced was the Rev. Dr Henry Sacheverell, a Fellow of Magdalen College, Oxford. On November 5, 1709, he preached a sermon in St Paul's before the Lord Mayor on the text: "In perils from false brethren." The day was the anniversary both of Guy Fawkes' Plot and of William III's landing at Torbay, and was therefore full of significance for the Whigs. His theme was the sin of 'resistance,' coupled with the argument that the 1688 Revolution had not been 'resistance.' There was nothing new in this outburst (Sacheverell had preached almost the same sermon four years earlier without evoking comment), but this time he alluded to "false brethren"—that is, disguised enemies of the

Church—who were recognized as being Godolphin and his friends only thinly veiled. Such references at such a juncture lashed the Whigs into uncontrollable fury, and they decided to impeach the preacher. No stroke that they could have chosen would more certainly have rebounded on their own heads: an attack on a cleric would allow their enemies to raise the never-failing cry of "The Church in danger": and whatever the outcome of the trial, so portentous an action for so trivial an occasion would cover the prosecutors with ridicule. There was thus every likelihood that Sacheverell would become a popular hero and that the Whigs would be correspondingly discredited.

The impeachment-trial began towards the end of February 1710 and lasted until nearly the end of March. During that month there was a bitter and widespread pamphlet war, and the London mob expressed its sympathy with the accused by wrecking Dissenting chapels. Finally, by sixty-nine votes to fifty-two, Sacheverell was found guilty; he was then suspended from preaching for three years, and his sermon was to be burnt by the common hangman, but the motion that he was to be incapable of preferment within three years was negatived by one vote. Sacheverell's bare condemnation, followed by the infliction of only a nominal penalty, was hailed by his friends as a triumph as real as had been Hampden's conviction by a narrow majority of Charles I's judges. The Tory tide was just about to flow, and Harley would know how to advise the Queen to use it to the full.

Sacheverell's sentence was pronounced on March 23. On April 6 a piece of fortune almost too good to be true fell into the Tories' lap: on that day the Queen and the Duchess of Marlborough parted for ever. It was the Duchess herself who provoked the painful scene. She had been virtually separated from the Queen for some time, but, learning that rumours of her disparaging references to her royal mistress were being circulated at Court, she resolved to seek the Queen's presence and vindicate herself in person. After various rebuffs the Duchess at last gained her interview only to be received coldly and to be told repeatedly that she should put her complaints in writing. The result was an outburst of hysterical weeping,

which also the Queen watched coldly, and Anne and Sarah—
formerly bosom friends addressing each other as Mrs Morley
and Mrs Freeman—saw each other for the last time. As a
human episode it was a pitiful tragedy. But beyond this it had
political reactions and significance that would soon become
evident.

A week later the Queen made Shrewsbury Lord Chamberlain (without even informing Godolphin of her intention). On
June 14 Marlborough's son-in-law, the Earl of Sunderland,
was dismissed from his Secretaryship of State and was replaced
by the Tory, Lord Dartmouth. Most significant of all, on
August 7 Godolphin was ordered to break the white staff of
his office as Lord Treasurer: no Lord Treasurer was appointed
immediately but the Treasury was put into commission of
which Harley, who became Chancellor of the Exchequer, was
one of the most prominent members. The Godolphin Ministry
had passed through many vicissitudes: in 1702 it had been a
Tory Ministry; in 1705 it had been a coalition; in 1708 it had
become Whig; now in 1710 it fell altogether.

There seems no doubt that Harley, true to his political views,
intended a moderate Government, but circumstances and
prejudices were too strong for him. In September 1710 there
was a shoal of resignations: Lord Somers resigned the Lord
Presidency of the Council, Wharton resigned the Lord-
Lieutenancy of Ireland, and Oxford ceased to be Lord High
Admiral. Thus the lords of the Whig Junto were out of office.
Almost at the same time the Whig Earl Cowper resigned the
Lord Chancellorship. Harley was at the head of a Tory
administration. No surer illustration of this fact was needed
than that Somers was succeeded as Lord President by the
out-and-out Tory, the Earl of Rochester. Also, St John became
a Secretary of State.

One effect of the change of Ministry was that Marlborough's
political enemies were able to undermine his influence with
the Army and at the Courts of the Allies. A board was set up
in London, of which the president was the Duke of Ormonde,
who was Marlborough's rival for Army command, to deal with
all cases of promotion among officers. The intriguers believed
that this would cause the officers to serve the purposes of the

board rather than of the Commander-in-Chief. For example, in May 1710, by means of pressure exerted by the Queen, Mrs Masham's brother and husband, Colonels Hill and Masham, were promoted Brigadiers. If this attitude spread through the Army Marlborough's plans of campaign would be frustrated and his position in command would soon become impossible. Yet if he allowed himself to be driven from command, and if the war as a consequence ended in disaster, Marlborough would be blamed for allowing political considerations to interfere with his military duty. To goad him to resign had the further advantage over dismissing him that any disasters following his dismissal would be charged against those who dismissed him.

Of those who thus intrigued against Marlborough, the most venomous was St John. These detractors underestimated the qualities of the man they were opposing. Not only his public professions but also his private letters show that he had a genuine desire for peace with France, but peace on terms that would give to the Allies the fruits of his victories. As each campaign began, his great anxiety had been that he should be able to bring on an action so decisive as to allow him to dictate terms. For this reason, not even the gibes of St John could induce Marlborough to resign before his purpose was achieved. Moreover, events showed that the intriguers' designs against Marlborough's influence over the Army over-reached themselves: the veterans in all sections of the Allied armies resented the underhand attacks on the general and rallied to him in unprecedented loyalty.

On September 21 the Queen dissolved her third Parliament. The ensuing elections resulted in a landslide of seats for the Tories, so that when the new Parliament opened on November 25, 1710, they had a three-to-one majority. In May 1711 Harley was created Earl of Oxford and became Lord Treasurer. This did not mean that he would have everything his own way. The Tory victory had been more complete than he had either expected or desired. Harley's policy was still based on moderation, and fundamentally he had little in common with St John. This situation contained the germ of the rift that would shortly develop in the Tory ranks.

2. The War, 1710-13

Early in 1710 peace negotiations were opened at Gertruyden-berg between the French and the Dutch. The latter negotiated as representatives of the Allied Governments on the basis of the Anglo-French Barrier Treaty of October 1709—that is, they demanded "No peace without Spain", and they again insisted that if Philip V would not leave Spain voluntarily, Louis XIV must use force to expel him. Even had Louis been willing to expel his grandson, the opposition which the Spaniards would have offered would have prevented him from doing so. He had therefore no alternative to rejecting the Allies' terms. Two other factors encouraged him to do so—namely, the decline of Marlborough's authority and the new spirit of resistance displayed in the French nation after Malplaquet. So once more the hopes of the war-wearied peoples of Europe were disappointed, and the war must go on.

In the Netherlands operations were limited to a series of sieges in which the Allies were successful but only at the cost of heavy losses. The whole of May and June were needed to capture Douai; Béthune fell at the end of August, St Venant at the end of September, and Aire early in November. By this time the campaigning season was over. Its net result had been to bring Marlborough's lines nearer to the French frontier and thus afford a better base of operations for the following year.

Meanwhile the Allies were meeting with disasters in Spain. During its opening stages the 1710 campaign there had seemed hopeful. The British commander was James Stanhope, who had seen almost continuous service in the Peninsula since 1703. (He was also a staunch Whig, and had managed Sacheverell's impeachment proceedings in February and March 1710, and was later to play a leading part in bringing in the Hanoverians.) His difficulty was to persuade Charles III that the Spanish crown would never be his while he remained content merely to occupy Catalonia. At last, having re-inforcements from a British fleet, in July the Allies moved westward. At Almenara Stanhope routed Philip and the Spaniards, driving him in headlong flight westward towards Saragossa. By the end of September the Allies were in Madrid. That was the climax of the campaign: then onward the Allied cause rapidly declined.

Four facts contributed to this result. First, Louis XIV sent Marshal Vendôme to take command of Philip's army. Second, the Allies in Madrid were cut off from their base of operations, and from the possibility of reinforcements from the sea, by the increasing hostility of the Spaniards. Third, there was perpetual division of opinion among the Allied commanders. Lastly, the support which the Allies expected from Portugal failed to materialize. The Allies therefore decided to withdraw from Madrid into Aragon for the winter. Vendôme energetically took up the pursuit. He caught Stanhope's section of the Allied Army at Brihuega, and made Stanhope and a large proportion of his army prisoners. Though Starhemberg, the Austrian marshal, managed to hold his own, the defeat was irretrievable, and the remnant of the Allied Army had to be led back to Catalonia.

During 1711 the rivalry between Harley and St John became an increasingly important factor in the trend of affairs. One curious incidental result was a campaign against the French at Quebec. St John was strongly in favour of the campaign, but Harley—partly because he suspected that St John was anxious to put into his own pocket money intended for the expedition—opposed it. On March 9, 1711, while the subject was still under the Cabinet's consideration, Harley was stabbed by a French spy, whom he was examining, and was therefore temporarily unable to attend to business. During his absence St John secured the Cabinet's decision to proceed with the Canadian expedition, and General Hill, brother of Mrs Masham, was appointed to lead it. The murderous assault on Harley evoked a wave of sympathy towards him, expressing itself in a host of addresses and messages of goodwill from both Parliament and the country generally. It was at this point that the Queen, accurately sensing the feeling of the populace, conferred upon Harley the title of Earl of Oxford and made him the Lord Treasurer, thus virtually recognizing him as chief Minister of the Crown. This intensified St John's jealousy and provoked his determination to undo and outstrip his rival.

The Quebec expedition proved to be an unfortunate choice of a means to this end. It set out from England in May 1711, called at Boston, and then proceeded northward. Lack of both charts and pilots left the flotilla at the mercy of fogs at the St Lawrence mouth. Several transports got on to the rocks and hundreds of men were drowned. This so discouraged the commanders that they decided to return to England which they reached in October. The expedition did not shed lustre on either its promoters or its commanders. Harley may well have smiled at his rival's ill-fortune. The one advantage that St John gained was the friendship of Mrs Masham to whose brother he had given the command.

Another event of 1711 with far-reaching results upon the war and upon the peace to follow was the sudden death from small-pox of the Emperor Joseph in April. His successor was his brother, the Archduke Charles of Austria and Charles III of Spain. In 1700 William III and Louis XIV had agreed to the Partition Treaty which recognized Charles' claim to Spain because they had assumed that he would never succeed either to the Habsburg dominions or to the Empire. This condition was renewed by the Methuen Treaties of 1703. But now that Charles would himself become Emperor, the Allies, if they continued to support his claim to Spain, would defeat their primary object of preventing the union of Spain with one of the great Powers of Europe. As a result, to the widespread desire for peace was now added the uncertainty as to what terms of peace were desirable. Such an atmosphere was not conducive to a vigorous prosecution of the war.

The total forces under Marlborough's command in the Netherlands at the opening of the 1711 campaign consisted of British and Dutch only, Eugene having received orders to stand on the Rhine ready to take any action that the uncertainties of the Imperial election might make necessary. Marlborough's numbers were therefore inferior to those of Marshal Villars. But the latter was under orders from Louis XIV not to risk a battle if he could avoid one. Louis was convinced that political affairs in England would bring about Marlborough's fall and cause Britain to desert the Allied cause. Accordingly Villars had built enormously strong fortified lines ninety miles long from the sea west of Montreuil through Arras and Bouchain to Valenciennes. So complete was his confidence in their impregnability that he christened them the "Ne Plus Ultra Lines." Marlborough was not strong enough to force a battle, but he had no intention of allowing his movements to be restricted by Villars' Lines. He therefore made careful preparations to pierce them. These plans, until he was in the act of putting them into operation, he kept secret even from his friends. Elaborately planned feint marches and attacks, during the latter part of July, thoroughly deceived Villars. The climax of the movement was a long, forced march of fully thirty-six miles in sixteen hours. So hot was the pace that a large proportion of Marlborough's men fell out on the way, and some died of exhaustion. But those were the only men he lost in the operation, for he was able to cross the so-called Ne Plus Ultra Lines at Arleux where Villars least expected him. Thence he turned farther eastward and invested the great fortress of Bouchain. The French, though superior in numbers, were warded off while the siege proceeded. Early in September the garrison surrendered unconditionally. Of the ten consecutive campaigns that Marlborough had conducted on the Continent, this, the tenth, was militarily the most brilliant, especially when the difficulties attending him were taken into account. And it was the last of his campaigns. Before the next season began, Marlborough was no longer Commander-in-Chief of the Allied armies.

While Marlborough was investing Bouchain, secret negotiations were being carried on between Harley and Louis XIV's Minister, Torcy. These had begun as early as August 1710—that is, shortly after the failure of the Gertruydenberg conference in July 1710. The only Englishmen whom Harley took into his confidence were Shrewsbury and Jersey (through whose Roman Catholic wife a French priest was obtained to act as emissary to the French Court). In April 1711 Harley received from Torcy a statement of the terms which the French regarded as a basis for a treaty—namely, that Philip should retain Spain, that the Dutch should hold Barrier Forts, and that England should receive substantial commercial advantages. As soon as these terms were received they were laid before the full Cabinet. Only then did the Secretary of State, St John, learn of the negotiations. From that moment he became the moving and guiding spirit of the bargaining. His general policy was to hammer out with France the details of the gains that were to accrue to Britain, and then to dictate these to the full peace conference at which the Dutch and the other Allies would make what terms they could with France. St John's agent in the bargaining was Matthew Prior, an astute diplomatist with a long experience of the French Court. By the end of September 1711 detailed articles of Anglo-French agreement were signed in Britain. Britain's principal gains thereby were the monopoly of the slave-trade with Spanish America; the acquisition of Minorca, Gibraltar, Newfoundland, Acadia, and Hudson Bay; the dismantling of Dunkirk's fortifications; and the recognition of the Protestant succession in Britain as laid down in the Act of Settlement. In addition to these details affecting Britain, the articles contained more general references to matters related to Allied interests that would come under discussion at the full peace conference. The general articles—that is, omitting the secret Anglo-French details—were communicated to the Allies. At once there was an outcry that Britain had broken the undertaking given by all the Allies that there should be no separate negotiations.

Not the least important factor in the success of St John's scheme was the attitude of Marlborough. No one's opinion would carry more weight, either in Britain or on the Continent, than would his. In the middle of September 1711, Marlborough landed in England having brought his brilliant campaign of that year to a close. The opportunity to make his opinion public was soon provided. On December 7 the Queen delivered the Speech from the Throne at the opening of a new Parliament. An amendment moved in the Lords "that no peace could be safe or honourable to Great Britain, or Europe, if Spain and the West Indies were allotted to any branch of the House of Bourbon," received the support of the Whig peers and of Marlborough, and was passed by a majority of twelve. The amendment was counteracted in two ways: the large Tory majority in the Commons defeated the same amendment which Walpole had moved there; and in January 1712 twelve new Tory peers were created.

More important than either of these results was the determination of Harley and St John that Marlborough must be disgraced. While he was in command of the armies, there was always the possibility of a decisive military victory which would frustrate all their schemes and lead to their own fall. Moreover, no other event would so certainly cause dissension among the Allies and hence leave them a prey to British and French machinations. Charges were therefore laid against him of appropriating moneys which went through his hands for the conduct of the war, in particular that he had received commission on the supply of bread to his armies and had taken 2½ per cent. from the pay of Allied troops in British pay. To both charges Marlborough gave a straightforward and dignified reply: on the first he claimed that the money was a perquisite always received by the Commander-in-Chief in the Low Countries and that the bread contract had been signed not by him but by the Treasury; and on the second he was able to show that the money had been spent on the secret service, which was an arrangement made by William III shortly before his death and sanctioned by Queen Anne whose signature still stood on the relevant document. On December 31, 1711, before the charges had been examined, the Queen sent to Marlborough a letter dismissing him from all his offices. For a year after his dismissal Marlborough and his wife lived in England. As the months passed, his position, instead of becoming more secure, became more precarious. His enemies, instead of leaving him in peace now that they had obtained his fall, were preparing to impeach him. He therefore secured passports and, on December 1, 1712, crossed to the Continent where a little later he was joined by the Duchess. They finally made Frankfort their headquarters; and everywhere they went they were received with honour, both in public and in private.

Closely connected with the attack on Marlborough was a similar attack upon Walpole who had been the Whig Secretary-at-War and was the outstanding Whig in the Commons. He also was charged with peculation. Judged by modern standards, Walpole had been indiscreet, but he had done nothing that was not common among contemporary office-holders—much less, indeed, than St John—and the majorities against him in the Commons were small. He was found guilty, was expelled from the Commons, and was committed to the Tower where he remained until the following July.

Marlborough's successor in command was the Duke of Ormonde. At the moment of his appointment there seemed little likelihood that he would be called upon to conduct a campaign. In January 1712 the Peace Conference opened at Utrecht and an early settlement was anticipated. But when the French proposals were laid before the Allied representatives there was an immediate storm of protest: while British interests were conceded, those of the other Allies were flouted. Only one interpretation to these facts was possible—namely, that the British had already made their own terms with France.

While discussions were proceeding, events in France knocked away the basis of any peace settlement so far projected. In

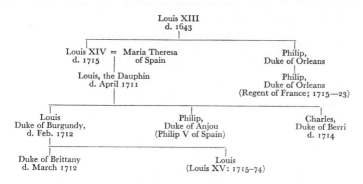

April 1711 the death had occurred of Louis XIV's elder son and heir, Louis the Dauphin. Then in February 1712 the latter's son, the new Dauphin, also named Louis and generally known as the Duke of Burgundy, died. Finally, in the following month, Burgundy's elder son died also. Thus, during the opening stages of the Utrecht Conference, two successive Dauphins died, the cause of their deaths being an epidemic of smallpox. The same complaint attacked also the last Duke's younger brother. Somehow he managed to recover, but he remained a sickly child, likely to be carried off by any passing ill. As events turned out, he survived to reign over France, as Louis XV, for nearly sixty years (1715–74). But in 1712 no one could foresee this: to the diplomats at Utrecht, the succession to the French throne hung upon the slender thread of a two-year-old child who was daily expected to follow his brother and father and grandfather to the grave. If (or, as seemed more probable, when) he should die, it was difficult to see how Philip V of Spain could be excluded from the French throne. To this, no one in Europe, other than France and Spain, would agree. But when Philip was presented with the proposition that if his claim to France materialized he should renounce the crown of Spain, he refused. He preferred to keep the throne on which he was already settled. Moreover, when the alternative proposition of renouncing the French throne was revived, the French lawyers declared that such a renunciation would not be valid. Consequently, as no solution of the root cause of the war seemed possible, the resumption of hostilities was inevitable.

Early in April Ormonde took up his command of the British and the British-paid forces of the Allies. Prince Eugene was in command of the remainder of the Allied forces, including the Dutch. It was generally expected that the Allies would follow Marlborough's plan of the previous year—namely, to push on from Bouchain to the neighbouring, though smaller, fortress of Le Quesnoy. But on May 10 St John wrote to Ormonde what became known as the Restraining Orders, which included the following instructions:

> It is the Queen's positive command to your Grace that you avoid engaging in any siege, or hazarding a battle, till you have further orders from her Majesty. I am, at the same time, directed to let your Grace know that the Queen would have you disguise the receipt of this order. . . .
> P.S. I had almost forgot to tell your Grace that communication is given of this order to the Court of France.

It is safe to say that no such dishonourable orders have ever been issued, either before or since, by a British Government to a general in the field. The peak of their shamefulness was that, while concealed from the Allies, the terms were communicated to the enemy. If Villars, being aware of the orders, had attacked Eugene, Ormonde would presumably have stood by and watched his ally being smashed. Though the primary responsibility rests upon St John, the guilt of Ormonde is only second to St John's since he acquiesced in the orders. His only protest was a series of letters to Oxford, as Lord Treasurer, asking for fresh instructions.

The new situation thus constructed could not long be disguised. No doubt could remain in Eugene's mind when he saw that, while Villars made no attempt to attack or even to take measures for his own defence, Ormonde made no attempt to seize the opportunity thus provided. Before long reports of the passive rôle being played by British forces became widely current. The subject was raised in debate in the British Parliament, where deep indignation was expressed; but the Government spokesmen, notably Lord Treasurer Oxford, either refused to commit themselves or denied the existence of the orders.

Meanwhile Eugene was pressing the siege of Le Quesnoy of which he gained possession before the end of June. Not only did the British play no part in this operation, but Ormonde informed the Allies that British and French had signed an armistice which was to last for two months, and as security the French had agreed to surrender Dunkirk to Britain. The Allies were invited to join in the armistice. When they refused, on July 5, Ormonde moved the British troops, numbering about twelve thousand, northward away from the Allies. The troops, feeling keenly the shame of their position, marched in dejected silence. In addition to Dunkirk, the British occupied also Ghent and Bruges. The Grand Alliance had ceased to exist.

Two days later St John was elevated to the peerage with the title of Viscount Bolingbroke. He had asked for an earldom, and the knowledge that the Queen had granted him the lower rank on the advice of the Lord Treasurer embittered still further the relations between Oxford and Bolingbroke. Almost at once the new Viscount was sent, with much pomp, as special Ambassador to France. The visit was a demonstration of Anglo-French relations, and it served to mollify somewhat Bolingbroke's chagrin at his Viscounty, but it achieved nothing tangible except an extension of the armistice.

13 + s.c.

Le Quesnoy was Eugene's last success. After its fall Villars took the offensive, and during the three months ending mid-October 1712 he not only defeated Eugene in the field (at Denain) but seized fortress after fortress in the Low Countries, including Le Quesnoy and Bouchain, the scene of Marlborough's last triumph. This continued defeat of the Allies, by demonstrating that they could not hold their own without Britain, compelled them to make terms with the enemy. In effect, it would compel them to accept whatever terms Britain and France would allow them.

Throughout the winter of 1712–13 bargaining went on. Finally, on March 31, 1713, peace was signed at Utrecht. The combatants were so numerous, and the issues involved so complex, that what is commonly known as the Treaty of Utrecht was really a series of treaties. Between Britain and France there was a political treaty and a commercial treaty. By the former, France recognized Queen Anne's title to the throne and the Hanoverian succession thereto as laid down in the Act of Settlement, and France further undertook to exclude the Pretender from France. Philip V's renunciation of the French throne was confirmed. Dunkirk's fortifications were to be demolished. Newfoundland, Nova Scotia, Hudson Bay, and the Island of St Kitt were to become British. By the commercial treaty, arrangements were made for a mutual lowering of customs duties on certain classes of goods. So strong was the opposition in England to the tariff clauses, especially by the Whigs who represented the interests of the commercial classes, that the British Parliament refused to confirm them.

By her treaty with Spain, Britain obtained Gibraltar and Minorca and the famous *assiento*—that is, contract—whereby she was to be allowed to export negro slaves to Spanish possessions in America. Perhaps the part of the treaty most disgraceful to Britain was her failure to stipulate for the security of the Catalans—whom she had encouraged to rise in Charles III's support—against the vengeance of Philip V's party.

The Dutch obtained the right to garrison a number of fortresses in the southern Netherlands. Though this Barrier was less formidable than the one of 1709, it was more so than that existing in 1701. Perhaps the chief security of the Dutch lay in the transfer of the southern Netherlands from Spain to Austria.

Savoy obtained Sicily. Portugal obtained security against encroachments from French Guiana on to the Amazon.

The one Power which refused to make terms at Utrecht was the Empire. The Emperor Charles VI still claimed his right to be also Charles III of Spain, and during the summer of 1713 a desultory campaign was fought in Germany. But in March 1714 the Treaty of Rastadt ended hostilities between France and the Empire: its basis was that France gave up conquests on the east of the Rhine but retained Strassburg and Landau on the west. The Empire retained Milan, Naples, and Sardinia. Bavaria had to be content with her pre-war boundaries.

Such was the treaty which brought to an end the quarter-of-a-century struggle between France on the one hand and Britain and her Allies on the other. Britain's—that is, Boling-broke's—method of making the peace can call forth nothing but condemnation: its characteristic was base and flagrant treachery to the Allied nations unequalled in British history. But the terms of the treaty, judged by the practical test of results, were at least justified by success: Britain was not involved in another major war during the quarter-century that followed. Doubtless the soundness of the treaty was not the only reason for this exceptionally long peace-period—some of the others will be reviewed in the closing paragraph of this chapter—but the other reasons would have been useless for building the peace if its foundations had been unstable.

3. The End of the Reign

The signing of the treaty removed the main subject of party-strife and left the way clear for other issues which for some time had been relegated to the background.

These issues were all concerned with the succession to the throne. The Queen's health was rapidly and seriously declin-ing, and her death could not be long delayed. This would bring into operation the succession clause of the Act of Settle-ment, and the Dowager Electress Sophia of Hanover would become Queen. The Act of Settlement, being part of the Whig Revolution, had never received Tory support; and though the Tories had latterly carried on the Queen's government, they did not look with favour upon the Hanoverian dynasty to follow. Moreover, the Hanoverian Court, being aware of the Tories' sentiments, would be likely to favour the Whigs. The Whigs strengthened their prospects by close contact with Hanover. This necessarily made them unpopular with Queen Anne; but, anticipating that the Queen's life was near its end, they judged it wise to sacrifice a brief present for the sake of a much longer future. Events were to vindicate their judgement.

The Tories, on the other hand, tried to get the best of both worlds. For the sake of the immediate present they kept on good terms with Anne; and they tried to insure themselves against the future by planning for the succession of the Stuart Pretender instead of the Hanoverians. Foremost in this scheme was Bolingbroke. Oxford, while favouring it, tried, as usual, to keep a foot in both camps: he was too anxious to secure himself against all eventualities to make a good plotter. The Tory scheme for a Stuart 'restoration' was unsound in two respects. First, the vast majority of English people would not recognize any claimant to the throne unless he was a Protestant, and the Pretender was a convinced Roman Catholic. The Tories assumed that he would regard the English throne as more valuable than his faith, but in this they misjudged him: he refused to make any concession in the matter of religion. Second, the Tories were themselves disunited. Their internal differences were typified by the relationship of Oxford and Bolingbroke, the rift between whom soon became a fissure. A party thus divided was unfit to engineer a revolution contrary to the wishes of the vast majority of the nation. Herein was the real stumbling-block to Bolingbroke's Jacobite scheme: the bulk of the nation, of whatever political views, was on the side of law and order, and amid all the fears that circumstances or policy might arouse, the dominant fear was that of a renewal of civil war. For this reason an important group of Tories consistently supported the Hanoverian Succession. These were known as the Hanoverian Tories: they were at one extreme of the party just as the members of the October Club were at the other. The latter—whose name was supposed to be derived from the strong October ale which they drank—were mainly Jacobites, and were supporters of Bolingbroke. The general election of August–September 1713 continued a Tory majority in the Commons, though its numbers were reduced, but it did nothing to heal the breach within the party.

One of the events which helped to widen and define the antagonism between Oxford and Bolingbroke occurred in April 1714 when Schütz, the Hanoverian Envoy in England, demanded that the Electoral Prince of Hanover, as Duke of Cambridge, should receive a writ to attend the House of Lords. In so doing, Schütz was acting under the instructions of Sophia, though she was acting without the knowledge of her son, the Elector. The demand caused great embarrassment to the English Court. Queen Anne had always adamantly refused to allow the presence in England of any of the line of her Hanoverian successors; and, being by this time in the last stage of bodily weakness, she wished less than ever to be reminded of her approaching demise. She was furious at the audacity of the demand, yet it was difficult to see how she could counter it. Every peer had a clear right to receive an individual summons to Parliament. Oxford, notwithstanding the anger of the Queen, advised her to issue the writ. Apart from the legality of the procedure, he doubtless realized that the opposite advice would place him in the wrong if—as seemed highly probable—the Elector ascended the throne in the near future. It was a move characteristic of Oxford's 'moderate' policy. Though the Queen saw that she had no option but to follow his advice, she could not forgive him for offering it. The writ was granted, but the Queen sent also three letters to Hanover—to Sophia, to the Elector, and to the Electoral Prince, respectively—referring in angry terms to the proposed visit of the Prince to England; and Oxford also wrote to the Elector urging its inadvisability. The Elector disavowed all knowledge of the affair. His mother, Sophia, was so shocked by the tone of the letters that, three days after their receipt, she died (May 28), being then eighty-four years of age. Thus the Elector himself became heir to the British throne.

No one would know better than Bolingbroke how to follow up his rival's incipient unpopularity with the Queen. To this end in June he promoted the Schism Bill which forbade anyone to teach, either in an institution or as a private tutor, unless he held a bishop's licence and took the Sacrament according to the rites of the Established Church. Such a measure would bring to an end the Dissenting Academies which were widespread over the country, being the Dissenters' only alternatives to the universities from which by law they were excluded. In the House of Lords Bolingbroke himself took charge of the measure. His eloquent fervour was intensified by his enjoyment of his rival's discomfiture. Oxford was genuinely opposed to the cruel extremity of the measure; nor could he rid himself of the influences of his Nonconformist upbringing. To oppose the Bill actively, in face of the Queen's strong attachment to the Church, was more than he dared risk; yet he could not bring himself to support it. He was thus reduced to silence during the debates, and to remaining neutral when the division was taken. The Bill passed both Houses and received the royal assent. It became law on August 1, 1714, and remained on the Statute Book for nearly five years though it was only laxly administered.

Oxford's neutrality could not save him from the fate which had long been threatening. On July 27, while at the Council table, the Lord Treasurer received his dismissal. Before quitting the table, in angry terms he warned the Queen against those who had schemed to remove him, and he roundly denounced the Secretary as guilty of corruption. The scene was a terrible one to take place in the presence of the Queen who, in extreme bodily weakness, sat helplessly through it. When it was over she made certain Ministerial adjustments. To appoint Bolingbroke as Lord Treasurer was impossible in view of the charges of grossly dishonest dealings in public money which Oxford had threatened to repeat in Parliament. The Treasury was therefore placed in commission. Thus, though Oxford had fallen, Bolingbroke had not yet secured his place. Events were to prove that the time available was too short to allow his plans to mature. Almost certainly the violence of the dismissal scene hastened the Queen's end.

Shortly afterwards, as though her gout had attacked her brain, she lapsed into unconsciousness. On July 30 the Council met under Shrewsbury's presidency. Shrewsbury was a moderate man, a member of what had come to be known as the Middle Party, whose views had much in common with Oxford's. On the Council the supporters of the two main parties were so evenly balanced that a resolution was passed recommending the Queen to appoint Shrewsbury as Lord Treasurer. That same afternoon he received the white staff from the Queen's hands. Whatever plans Bolingbroke may have had in mind, time defeated him. He had no opportunity to carry them out or even to secure his own position.

The Council's chief task under the new Treasurer was to arrange for the peaceful succession of the Hanoverian heir when the Queen's impending death should take place. Orders were issued for the dispositions of Army and Navy, for securing the ports, the Tower of London, and the Castle at Edinburgh. Early in the morning of August 1—the day on which the Schism Act came into operation—the Queen breathed her last, and so was released from all her troubles.

There can be little doubt that Anne died just in time to save England from civil war. For some time Bolingbroke had been in constant communication with the Pretender with a view to the latter's succeeding Anne. With the same purpose, he had been systematically 'purging' Army and Navy of Whig officers, and had secured the disbanding of certain Army units, and had united others so as to have regiments on whose loyalty to the house of Stuart he could rely. On the other hand Marlborough, soon after landing on the Continent, made contact with the Court of Hanover and, at the end of 1713, accepted from the Elector the position of Commander-in-Chief of the British forces still in the Low Countries. In this capacity he gathered leaders who had served under him—Argyle (who had been dismissed as part of Bolingbroke's 'purge'), Cadogan, Stanhope—and made preparations for armed action to secure the Hanoverian succession should there be a Jacobite move at Anne's death. In the middle of July Marlborough was at Ostend waiting for a wind to take him to England. A fortnight's delay ensued, and finally he landed at Dover on

August 2 only to be greeted with news of the Queen's death the previous day. Her sudden decease had made Marlborough's military preparations unnecessary: Bolingbroke had not had time to mature his schemes for a Jacobite succession. Whether, indeed, Bolingbroke had any clear plan of action for the accession of "James III" remains, and probably will always remain, an impenetrable mystery, and one that is all the deeper because he must have known that James' staunch adherence to Roman Catholicism made his acceptance by the nation impossible. Whatever Bolingbroke's intentions, the plain fact is that the emergency caused by the Queen's death found him unprepared: at the crucial moment he had no plan ready. Hence, without opposition the Elector of Hanover became George I of Great Britain. He landed in England on September 18, 1714, and made his way peacefully to his new capital.

Queen Anne's death marked the end of an epoch as well as of a reign. The period 1713–15 constitutes a historical boundary more clearly defined perhaps than any other in modern Europe. Each of the three years that it includes was marked by an event of outstanding importance: the Treaty of Utrecht in 1713, the death of Queen Anne in 1714, and the death of Louis XIV in 1715. The treaty brought to a close the long struggle to prevent Louis XIV's threat to dominate Europe. The deaths of the two monarchs typified the passing of the chief protagonists in that struggle (for Anne and her general, Marlborough, were the heirs of William III who had personified the challenge to Louis XIV's threat). Throughout Europe, but particularly in Britain and in France, the generation of those in whom the quarrel had originated was now dead. The succeeding generation, wearied of what in the new circumstances was a senseless struggle, was inclined to peace. In each of the two main rival nations there were also particular motives for peace. In Britain the new dynasty coincided with the beginning of a long regime of the Whigs who, representing the commercial interests, favoured peace in which alone trade could develop; and the Hanoverian monarchs were anxious lest any renewal of war between England and France should cause a French invasion of Hanover. In France, not only was

there profound exhaustion, but Orleans, the Regent for the
infant King Louis XV, desired to prevent any possibility of
the Spanish Philip V's succession to the French throne because,
if Philip was excluded, Orleans was himself the next claimant
to the throne. Orleans' policy was therefore to maintain the
Treaty of Utrecht which precluded the junction of the French
and the Spanish crowns. This policy necessarily involved the
maintenance of peace with Britain. The less powerful countries also had their reasons for avoiding further war. Holland
was exhausted by the long burden of wars far beyond her
capacity to endure; and never again did she rank as a great
Power. Spain was still torn by political and racial divisions.
The Empire was distraught by its own internal complexities.
It was these conditions in Europe generally that enabled
Britain to pass into the era of the new dynasty and, during a
quarter of century of peace, to lay the foundations for the new
economic and political society that was to characterize Hanoverian Britain.

Chapter 15

The Beginnings of Empire

The theme that has so far run through our study of the seventeenth century has been the struggle to define the relative powers of King and Parliament. The result of that struggle was to lay down the lines along which hereafter the English political constitution should develop. Less obtrusive, but scarcely less noteworthy, was the contemporary process whereby the world-wide distribution of the English-speaking people began to take shape, though the full significance of this process also could not be appreciated until enough time had elapsed to show it in its true perspective.

When James I ascended the English throne not a single English colony existed anywhere in the world. Under the Tudors there had been much maritime activity. The great seamen had opened the way for others to follow: Sir Humphrey Gilbert had taken possession of Newfoundland in the Queen's name as early as 1583, and Sir Walter Ralegh had been responsible for settlements in Roanoke Island in 1585, but neither Gilbert's nor Ralegh's experiment was permanent. Again, the East India Company had received its royal charter on December 31, 1600, and had made its first venture during the years 1601–3, but in the latter year it had no territory overseas. Yet by the end of the Stuart period there were considerable English settlements on the mainland of North America both along the eastern seaboard and around Hudson Bay, in the West Indian islands, and in India. The purpose of this chapter is to review this colonial expansion of the seventeenth century.

James I's general policy did much, though unintentionally, to produce conditions favourable to expansion overseas. The peace which James made with Spain in 1604 contained no recognition of Spanish colonies (in spite of Spanish attempts to have such a clause inserted), and thus it ended Spain's claim to a monopoly of the New World. Also, England's clear naval supremacy when the peace was signed would enable English settlers to cross the seas freely, and to establish themselves anywhere not already in Spanish hands. But Spain's decline as a world-power would not leave England free to step into her place as a colonizer unchallenged: at least two other rivals for that place arose—namely, the Dutch and the French. The result was three-cornered clashes between English, Dutch, and French in the East Indies and America. In yet another respect James I's policy, and still more Charles I's, unintentionally stimulated oversea expansion: the attempts of both kings to oppress Puritans and to restrict the powers of Parliament led increasing numbers of independent-minded Englishmen to seek religious and political freedom for themselves and their families in settlements beyond the seas.

Though Newfoundland was the first of England's oversea possessions in point of time, the colonists had to struggle hard and long against opposing elements—geographical and economic—as well as against the interest of courtiers, before they were well-established. Gilbert's expedition of 1583 had ended disastrously, Gilbert himself being drowned in a great storm off the Azores on September 9 as he was returning to England in his little ten-ton *Squirrel*. Thereafter, for a generation, the only dealings that Englishmen had with the island were those of West of England seamen who visited the Newfoundland fisheries, carrying back thence cod, mackerel, and herring. These fisherfolk used the shores of the island as a temporary base where they could repair their nets and their boats, but they built no permanent homes there. The English Government, both under Elizabeth and under James I, strongly favoured this method of temporary rather than of permanent settlement, believing that the Atlantic voyages would foster seamanship. Not until 1610 did a body of London and Bristol merchants gain incorporation to establish permanent settlements in Newfoundland. Even then the severe weather, the poor soil, and the lack of official encouragement combined to defeat the project. In spite of struggles during the century that followed, it was not until the Treaty of Utrecht of 1713, at the close of the Spanish Succession War, when the French renounced their claims to the island, that its future was assured. During the next half-century Newfoundland was of the highest strategic value as commanding the entrance to Canada.

Following hard chronologically on the heels of Newfoundland as an English colony was Virginia. Sir Walter Ralegh was Humphrey Gilbert's half-brother, and had had shares in Gilbert's joint-stock company; and Gilbert's colonizing cloak therefore fell not unnaturally upon Ralegh. In 1584 the Queen conferred upon Ralegh a patent for opening up unoccupied lands. He concentrated his efforts upon the American seaboard—which, in honour of the Virgin Queen, was named Virginia—but the two expeditions which he promoted during 1584–87 both failed, and when in 1590 a relieving expedition was sent, no trace could be found of either settlers or settlement. Some account of Ralegh's end in 1618, as the result of his ill-fated expedition to the Orinoco goldmine which he claimed to have discovered in 1595, has already been given.[1]

Not until 1605—the year after peace was signed with Spain —was the Virginia project renewed. After an exploratory expedition, in 1606 James I granted a charter for the planting of the eastern coast of North America between the thirty-fourth and the forty-fifth degree of latitude north, the whole of that long coastal strip being then included as Virginia (so that the site of Ralegh's settlement was afterwards in North Carolina). The scheme was that the part north of latitude forty should be developed by a Plymouth company, and the part south of it by a London company. During a number of years the Plymouth Company remained inactive. The London Company's first settlement in 1607 failed mainly because the wrong type of colonist was sent out. A new start, made under a new charter granted in 1609, was but little more propitious. It was the introduction of tobacco-growing in 1612 by a settler named John Rolfe which laid the foundation of the colony's prosperity. It was in 1614 that the first tobacco was shipped, and in 1690 negro slaves were introduced to work the plantations. By this latter year the colony had developed sufficiently to be granted a representative assembly on the model of the English

[1] See p. 47.

House of Commons. In 1624 James I, taking advantage of the divisions within the company's council at home and of the company's financial difficulties, confiscated its charter. Virginia was then granted a new constitution whereby she became a Crown Colony under a governor appointed by the Crown though retaining her assembly with control over internal taxation.

The settlement of the Plymouth Company's territory followed a line of its own. In 1619 the Virginia Company sanctioned a grant of land for a colony of religious refugees. The latter were English Brownists, forerunners of the Independents, who in 1608 had gone over to Amsterdam and thence to Leyden. The arrangement was that this Leyden congregation should transfer itself to North America. Thus it came about that in 1620 the 180-ton *Mayflower* carried 120 emigrants across the Atlantic. On December 21 the little company, fitly named the Pilgrim Fathers, landed at Plymouth in Cape Cod Bay. This point was actually north of Virginian territory and within the territory of the Plymouth Company. The latter, just previous to the *Mayflower's* sailing, had been reconstituted as the Council of New England, with administrative authority between the Hudson River and Nova Scotia. The infant colony passed through many vicissitudes. Not less than half the settlers died from their privations during the first winter. But the Pilgrim Fathers were men of strong character and had faced the dangers of the Atlantic inspired by a great purpose. Such men were not easily daunted. Within a few years the worst was over. Fresh colonists and fresh supplies brought encouragements both moral and material. In 1638 the colony secured representative government, every householder having the right to vote.

During the twenty years following the sailing of the Pilgrim Fathers much of the New England coastal strip was settled by various groups of colonists. Impetus was given to this process by events in England. The twenty years were those immediately preceding the outbreak of the Civil War, including those of Charles I's Eleven Years' Tyranny (1629–40) and of Laud's ecclesiastical changes. These events were an incentive to oversea colonization by English Puritans.

The first settlement thus impelled was Massachusetts. It was made by a small body of Puritans who in 1628 went out to occupy land granted by the New England Company north of Plymouth. In the next year the Massachusetts Bay Company, formed to develop this land, obtained its charter from Charles I four days before the beginning of the eleven years without a Parliament. The new colonists were able to benefit by the experience of the Pilgrim Fathers. Even more important in shaping the colony's character was the fact that its first settlers were the whole body of subscribers to the company—that is to say, its settlers were men of economic substance who had every incentive to make the venture prosper. Hence, though Massachusetts had its own early difficulties, it survived and achieved success. This in turn attracted a constant stream of immigrants so that within a dozen years of the first settlement —that is, by the time the Long Parliament met—its population numbered twenty thousand. Massachusetts thus became and remained the leading New England colony, and its capital, Boston, was the most important English town on the American mainland. In 1634 a representative assembly was set up, but the franchise was restricted to church-members: these were only a minority, probably one-fifth, of the total population so that the Government was not a democracy but a church-oligarchy.

Massachusetts' rapid growth caused a spread of colonists along the seaboard north and south of her boundaries. In 1633 settlements began to form along the banks of the Connecticut River; in 1636 a colony was formed on Rhode Island, and in 1638 New Haven was formed west of Connecticut. Many of the settlers in the new colonies were people discontented on religious grounds with the Massachusetts Government—some thought it too narrow and others too lax—while many were immigrants direct from England.

The New England colonists had to face serious dangers besides economic and geographical ones. First, the colonists lay between the French in Canada and the Dutch along the Hudson River: any movement of themselves or of their neighbours was likely to produce a clash. Also, the Indians were always a potential danger. Second, as the quarrel between

AMERICAN COLONIES 17th CENTURY

MASSACHUSETTS	1628
RHODE ISLAND	1636
CONNECTICUT	1663
DELAWARE	1664
NEW JERSEY	1664
PENNSYLVANIA	1682
VIRGINIA	1607
NORTH CAROLINA	1663
SOUTH CAROLINA	1663
GEORGIA	1732

0   240   480 MILES

Charles and his mainly Puritan Parliament grew more intense, Charles and Laud grew more and more antagonistic towards their mainly Puritan colonies. When Civil War broke out in England the news reaching the colonists of the opening campaigns suggested a rapid victory for the Royalists. For mutual defence against all these contingencies on both sides of the Atlantic, in 1643 a New England Confederation was formed, the four members being Massachusetts, Plymouth, Connecticut, and New Haven. Neither Rhode Island nor Maine was allowed to join: the former because it allowed religious toleration, and the latter because it was not exclusively Puritan. Two successes during the following years stood to the Confederation's credit: in 1652 it defeated the Dutch at New

Amsterdam, and in 1675–77 it survived a gruelling war against the Indians. One of the colonies' outstanding grievances was the restriction of trade under the Navigation Acts[1] of 1651 and 1660, the terms of which the colonists did their utmost to evade.

In 1684 Massachusetts, under a *quo warranto* writ, lost its charter. The ostensible reason was that the colony had infringed the rights of its neighbours. The real reason was that it had long been the leader of the other colonies in resisting royal interference and in evading the Navigation Acts. One effect of the forfeiture was that the New England Confederation came to an end. In 1691 Massachusetts received a new charter whereby the Massachusetts Company was dissolved, so that the colony was brought directly under the Crown which exercised its authority through its own appointed governor; there was to be an assembly, elected on a property-franchise and having rights of legislation (subject to the royal veto) and of internal taxation; finally the 1691 charter included Plymouth, Maine, and Acadia within Massachusetts.

While the New England colonies were developing to the north of the Dutch settlements round the Hudson, other colonies were developing to the south. The northern and southern colonies differed the one from the other in two main respects. First, while the New England colonies were predominantly Puritan and were founded to promote religious freedom, the southern colonies were Anglican (except Maryland) and had no religious motive for their foundation. Second, while the New England colonies were primarily coastal trading-stations (the soil inland being unfertile), the southern colonies developed in the form of large estates cultivated on a plantation-system and producing mainly tobacco. The result was that there was less friction in the south than in New England with the home Government, since both personally and religiously the southern colonies closely resembled the English gentry.

The first of the Plantation colonies was Virginia, whose early fortunes we have followed already. The next was Maryland.

[1] See pp. 215, 249.

This consisted of a strip of territory north of Virginia granted in 1632 to Lord Baltimore (formerly Sir George Calvert), who, though a Roman Catholic, was a favourite of Charles I and named his colony after the Queen, Henrietta Maria. The granting of the charter was followed almost immediately by Lord Baltimore's death so that his American estates devolved upon his brother. The first body of settlers, three hundred in number, landed at Chesapeake Bay. Notwithstanding the proprietor's Roman Catholicism, all types of settlers were allowed, and Maryland had the distinction of being the first English community in either the New World or the Old to allow complete religious toleration. One other distinction of the colony was that its administration remained in the Calvert family until the Declaration of Independence of 1776: the only dues that the proprietors owed to the English Crown were a nominal quit-rent and the tobacco duty, the payment of which ensured to the colony complete self-government.

To the south of Virginia the country remained undeveloped until the Stuart Restoration period. In 1663 Charles II granted a stretch of it to eight men (among them the Duke of Albemarle, the Earl of Clarendon, and Lord Ashley), and called it Carolina. The northern part of Carolina was the first to be populated, its settlers coming mainly from other colonies. As a large proportion of them had already been unsuccessful elsewhere, and as the soil was poor, North Carolina survived only after painful struggles. In 1670 the proprietors carried out a well-planned settlement to the south around Charleston. The effect of careful planning and choice of settlers was soon reflected in the progress of South Carolina. Though the colonists had an elected assembly of twenty members, the proprietors continued to appoint the governor and his council until in 1719 South Carolina became a Crown Colony; and ten years later North Carolina followed this example.

Georgia, the remaining Plantation colony, was not founded until 1732—that is, later than the period which at present concerns us.

The geographical link between the New England and the Plantation colonies was formed by the gradual development of a group known for convenience as the Middle colonies. The first stage in forging this link was taken when in 1664 Charles II granted to James, Duke of York, the land between the southern boundary of Connecticut and the Delaware River. As this territory included the Dutch settlements of New Netherland along the Hudson, the Duke's claim could be made good only by force of arms. Although theoretically England and the Dutch were at peace, the Duke sent out four ships in May, and on August 29 the Dutch governor of New Amsterdam was compelled to surrender, and the colony's name was forthwith changed to New York. The Treaty of Breda, at the end of the Dutch War of 1664–67, confirmed the English possession of the colony. Though the Dutch seized the territory again during the 1672–74 war, it was restored to the English by the Treaty of Westminster. The importance of the acquisition was enormous. The English colonies along the American seaboard were now in a solid geographical block. Their hold on the Hudson valley would prevent the French from descending along that valley from the river Richelieu and the Little Lakes if ever French and English were at war in America (as they would be in the Seven Years' War of 1756–63).

Another Middle colony was Pennsylvania, an inland colony west of New York and north of Maryland. It derived its name from William Penn, the Quaker leader who was a friend of Charles II and James II, whose policy of religious indulgence he supported. Penn's object was to obtain a place of refuge for the Quakers, who were subject to much persecution in England. When Penn's father, Admiral Penn, died in 1670 the Crown owed him £16,000. In 1681 King Charles and William Penn made a mutual arrangement which suited at once Charles' pocket and Penn's desire for relief for his co-religionists: the King granted to Penn forty-seven thousand square miles in North America. The next year Penn and about one hundred other Quakers set sail for the new colony of Pennsylvania whose capital was to be named Philadelphia. The regulations, religious and political, that Penn introduced were in accordance with his Quaker principles and with his ideas of freedom. All forms of Christianity were granted full toleration. With the Indians, Penn concluded a treaty of perpetual peace which was never broken on either side until

1752, by which time the Indians had become parties to the Anglo-French rivalry which culminated in the Seven Years' War. The introduction of slaves was forbidden. The Government was extremely democratic, and included a popularly elected council and assembly. The strong characters of the early Quaker settlers, and Penn's personal oversight of the colony's affairs, combined to effect its rapid development. Within twenty years of its foundation, Pennsylvania had a population of twenty thousand. Yet, unlike the typical colonial proprietor, Penn spent much more on his colony than he ever received from it in rents and dues, and it remained a constant source of worry almost to the day of his death in July 1718, in his seventy-fourth year.

The other area on the North American mainland where Englishmen were active in the seventeenth century was around Hudson Bay. This name was derived from Henry Hudson, who led a series of expeditions, beginning in 1607, with the object of discovering a northerly passage to Asia. After three failures, in 1610 he was sent out north-west by a group of English merchants. After following the Labrador coast, he pushed through what is known as Hudson Strait into the great Hudson Bay. For Hudson, the expedition ended disastrously. The ice compelled him to spend the winter of 1610–11 in the Arctic, and the next spring his crew mutinied against his intention to continue the explorations. Finally the mutineers put Hudson and some of his supporters in an open boat and turned them adrift: neither the boat nor Hudson was ever seen again. Though Hudson perished, his work had called attention to the great fur-trading possibilities of the region around the vast bay. In 1670 "the Governor and Company of Merchants' Adventurers trading into Hudson Bay" was incorporated by royal charter, its first governor being Prince Rupert. The Company's agents gradually made contacts with Indian trappers from whom furs were collected by a system of barter. Storehouses were built, but no colonizing in the ordinary sense of the term was attempted. The bay remained, however, under English influence. Clashes with the French of the St Lawrence basin were inevitable, but the Treaty of Utrecht of 1713 recognized English rights over the territory.

Though the colonies on the American mainland were to develop beyond the wildest imaginings of their pioneer settlers, the seventeenth century rated them as being much less valuable than the islands of the West Indies. The first English settlement on any of these islands was made on St Christopher (St Kitts) in January 1624, and was led by Thomas Warner who four years previously had been impressed by the island when returning from Guiana. Warner's leadership saw the colony through various vicissitudes—including Spanish attacks and wreckage by hurricane—until his death in 1649. Though other troubles continued to break over the colony, it remained English, and was so confirmed by Spain in the Treaty of Utrecht.

Quickly following on the St Kitts' experiment was the settlement on Barbados. This island was formally annexed to the English Crown in 1625 by a ship belonging to a London merchant named Sir William Courteen. In the following year Courteen sent forty settlers out to Barbados. Numerous crops suitable to the climate—including fruits, tobacco, and sugar— were soon introduced, and almost from the first the colony flourished. Within ten years of the first settlement its English population numbered six thousand; and throughout the remainder of the seventeenth century Barbados was the most important English colony in the West Indies.

The largest of the West Indian Islands to become English was Jamaica. Mention of its capture by Venables and Penn has already been made.[1] In 1658 the Spaniards tried to recapture it but were driven off, and the Treaty of Madrid of 1670 confirmed the English in their possession. The island's size and central position in the Caribbean Sea made it a favourite centre for trade, for buccaneering, and for a naval base. The result was that during the eighteenth century Jamaica surpassed Barbados as the trading-centre for the West Indies.

At a point of contact between the colonizing activities of the seventeenth century and the contemporary constitutional struggle at home, an attempt to colonize the island of Old Providence, off the Mosquito Coast, is worth mentioning.[2] The

[1] See p. 220.
[2] For a fuller account, see the author's *John Pym, 1583–1643*, pp. 114–131.

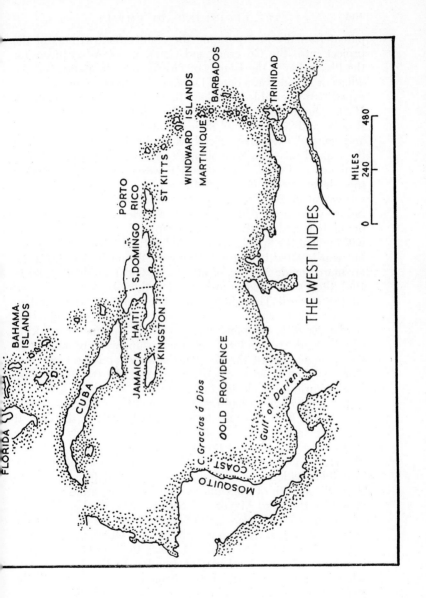

THE WEST INDIES

FLORIDA

BAHAMA.
ISLANDS

CUBA

JAMAICA
KINGSTON

HAITI
S.DOMINGO

PORTO
RICO

ST KITTS

WINDWARD ISLANDS
MARTINIQUE
BARBADOS

TRINIDAD

C. Gracias á Dios

OOLD PROVIDENCE

Gulf of Darien

MOSQUITO
COAST

MILES

0   240   480

patent formally incorporating the eighteen subscribers of the project into "the Governor and Company of Adventurers for the Plantation of the Islands of Providence, Henrietta, and the adjacent islands" was dated December 4, 1630, though the first expedition to establish a colony there had gone out in October 1629. The company included the Earl of Warwick, Lord Brooke, and Sir Nathaniel Rich; and its indefatigable Treasurer and general executive official was John Pym. In spite of all the capital raised in the colony's support, and of the ceaseless vigilance of Pym (whose attention was thus absorbed during the eleven years of non-Parliamentary rule, 1629–40), the settlement of Old Providence was never well-established. The failure was due partly to too wide a variety of elements in its population and partly to its geographical position which was within what the Spaniards regarded as their sphere of influence but was isolated from English support. From 1635 onward the Spaniards made a series of attacks on Old Providence, and in 1641 they succeeded in overrunning the island and carrying off the settlers. Though the colonizing project failed, it had one permanent effect: almost without exception the members of the English company were political opponents of King Charles and, still under Pym's leadership, were prominent in the struggle against the King in the Short and the Long Parliaments. The Providence Adventure was the training-ground for the Puritan Revolution in England.

The motive which had first sent Columbus sailing westward was that of finding a way to the Spice Islands of the east. It was this same motive which, after the Spaniards and the Portuguese had blocked the southern routes thither, led men like Hudson to try to find northern routes as an alternative. Tangible evidence of English merchants' determination to share the wealth of the Indies was afforded by a meeting convened by the Lord Mayor of London on September 22, 1599, which resolved to form a company to trade in the east. The outcome of this resolution was the charter which Queen Elizabeth I granted on December 31, 1600, to "The Governor and Company of the Merchants of London to the East Indies" whereby the members of the company were granted the monopoly of English trade between the Cape of Good Hope and Cape Horn. The monopoly was for fifteen years: nineteen years later James I made the period indefinite but subject to revocation at three years' notice. In April 1601 the company sent out four ships under James Lancaster. It is well to remember that both the company and Lancaster were thinking not of the mainland of India but of East Indian islands which were still "the Spice Islands." The first expedition reached Sumatra in June 1602, and then, having left three agents to collect goods in readiness for the next voyage, returned homeward. By the time that Lancaster brought his ships back to England, in September 1603, James I had been on the English throne six months. A second voyage began in 1604 and returned in May 1606; and several similar ones took place during following years. The chief cargoes brought home were spices like cloves and pepper.

Not unnaturally this growing English trade was resented by the Dutch who regarded the English as poachers on Dutch preserves. A Dutch association had sent out an expedition as early as 1595, since when Dutch merchants, consistently supported by their Government, had built up an East Indian trade on a large scale. In 1609 they claimed the monopoly of trade with the Moluccas, thus implying that they would use force against interlopers. A period of constant bickerings and strife inevitably followed; and when in 1618 James tried to find a basis for agreement, all that the Dutch would concede was the right to English merchants to trade but without holding any territory. This meant that the English remained only on sufferance: they could not fortify themselves or even own depots. Their utmost possibility was to maintain agents, which they did chiefly at Bantam and Amboyna. Gradually the English were elbowed out of the islands.

It was in Amboyna in 1623 that this process came to a head. Amboyna was one of the strongest of the Dutch stations. It included two hundred Dutch settlers as well as native troops under their command. The English company had only eighteen agents there, and the Dutch governor seems to have determined to oust his rivals entirely. Natives were compelled to declare that they knew of an English plot to seize the Amboyna station. That so few Englishmen could not possibly have carried out such a plot was itself enough to show the story's absurdity. Nevertheless the English were horribly tortured and then massacred. Neither James I nor Charles I could be moved to compel the Dutch Government to acknowledge the criminal nature of the act. Not until Cromwell brought the Dutch war to a victorious end in 1654 did the Dutch pay compensation to the surviving relatives of the murdered agents.

For the moment the massacre had the desired effect of bringing to an end the English trade in the East Indian islands. What the Dutch had not foreseen was that the East India Company, as an alternative, would turn its attention to the Indian mainland. Two factors especially governed its operations there. First, the whole of India was subject to the overlordship of the Great Mogul at Delhi. When the E.I.C. was incorporated in 1600, Akbar (1556–1605), the greatest of all the Great Moguls, was reigning; but by the time that the company was driven from the islands Akbar had been succeeded by his son, Jehangir, who tried to compensate for the lack of his father's greatness by avarice and terrorism. Second, just as the Dutch had forestalled the English in the islands, so the Portuguese had forestalled them on the mainland. Hence, when, as early as 1607, the E.I.C. had sent Captain William Hawkins bearing an introduction from James I, to negotiate with Jehangir for a depot at Surat, the Portuguese were able to induce the Mogul to reject his advances. The English company therefore decided upon strong measures. In 1612 two well-provided vessels were sent out, and when four Portuguese warships hove in sight the English gave fight in Swally Roads. A two-day battle saw the Portuguese completely defeated. The English then sailed into Surat where the Mogul, greatly impressed by these events, granted to the E.I.C. a site for a depot (1613).

This precedent was followed, as opportunity served, in other parts of India. In 1622 a factory (that is, a depot for the company's 'factors,' or traders) was opened at Masulipatam; and it was an agent from this latter factory who in 1639 obtained for the company the concession of a six-mile strip of coast round Madras. The first English fortifications in India were then constructed on an island off this coast and were called Fort

St George. Next year the company obtained the right to trade free from tolls on the river Hoogly, and in 1650 it built a factory at Hoogly.

Bombay, as we have seen,[1] was granted to Charles II in 1661 as part of the dowry of his Portuguese bride, Catherine of Braganza. A short time sufficed to convince Charles that to administer the place as a Crown Colony was both costly and a nuisance. In 1668, therefore, he allowed the E.I.C. to take it over in return for an annual rent of £10. The island-site made Bombay an ideal trading-centre; and after the company had improved it by drainage-works, it superseded Surat as the company's headquarters in India.

Bengal was the next area to be opened up. As a centre of operations there, in 1696 a number of villages on the Ganges were bought, and Fort William was built to protect them. One of the villages was Calcutta. Thus before the end of the Stuart era the E.I.C. already held the three pivotal points, at Madras, Bombay, Calcutta, in what was to become British India.

What was true in India was true of English settlements at large: by the time the Stuart period closed the beginnings of the first, and even of the second, British Empire had been laid. There seems ample justification for the claim that during the Stuart regime England hammered out the main lines both of her political constitution at home and of her Empire abroad. Equally clear is the fact that the Stuart kings were no more intentionally responsible for the one than for the other.

The foregoing survey has shown that during the seventeenth century the colonies were playing an increasing part in national life. Gradually the Stuarts adopted a deliberate policy which was to be known as the Old Colonial System. Its full meaning will become clearer during the next chapter in connexion with the Mercantile System and the Navigation Acts. Here we may notice briefly that in its final form that system regarded the Empire as one self-sufficing community. In this community the resources of the parts must be made available to all the members especially to the Mother-country. In practice this meant

[1] See p. 248.

that colonists existed for England's benefit. They were to provide her with cheap raw materials for her manufactures and with markets for her manufactured goods. The transport of these goods kept large numbers of English ships and sailors constantly employed at sea and so maintained a potential Navy for use in war. At the end of the seventeenth century the population of the colonies was reckoned to total about 3,000,000, the contemporary population of England being only about 4,500,000 or 5,000,000. The colonies were then sending to England goods to the value of about £870,000 a year, and were taking goods valued at £787,000 in return.

So valuable was this trade, and so considerable the possibility of its development, that Stuart Governments did their best, by a series of regulations, to secure its benefits as the monopoly of the Mother-country. The climax of these regulations, within the Stuart period, was the Navigation Acts, the details of which have been given already.[1]

The line between the Old and the New Colonial Systems is thought of as being drawn at the War of American Independence (1775–83). The fundamental cause of that war was colonial impatience with the restrictions which the Old System placed upon colonial development, especially as those restrictions were applied in the circumstances of the eighteenth century following the Seven Years' War (1756–63). The question of the rights and wrongs of the events leading to the American Declaration of Independence in 1776 is aside from our present purpose. What concerns us is that the loss of the American colonies provided England with a sharp lesson. It was at least to her credit that she learned her lesson and henceforward treated her remaining colonies with new consideration as having rights and responsibilities of their own. Gradually a new conception of Empire was evolved, its final outcome being seen in the great self-governing dominions freely associated with the framework of the Commonwealth. Thus the passing of the Old Colonial System and the loss of the First British Empire were the ashes out of which the Second Empire was to arise.

[1] See pp. 215, 249. See also pp. 419–420.

1. Classes of Society

Since the vast majority of Englishmen were still directly concerned with agriculture, we may well begin with a survey of the various classes of landowners and landworkers. The characteristic figure among seventeenth-century agriculturists was the yeoman. Properly the term referred to the middle-class freehold-farmer—that is, the man who did not rank as a gentleman and who worked his own farm. But, as commonly used, the term included also the tenant-farmer of similar class and also the copyholder and the leaseholder. Thus the yeomen can be thought of as the farmers as distinct from the gentry above them and the cottagers and labourers below. The only contemporary, systematic estimate of population that can pretend to anything like reliability was that of Gregory King whose *Natural and Political Observations and Conclusions upon the State and Condition of England* was published in 1696. King was a man of sound learning: he had been secretary to Sir William Dugdale and registrar of the College of Arms; and his statistics, based on all the information he could collate, were accepted by contemporaries as reasonable. He estimated the various categories of farmers and freeholders at thirty-one thousand, and the total numbers of their families at ninety-eight thousand. This was clearly an important element, as to both quality and number, in a total population which King estimated as high as 5,500,520. In spite of these numbers, there were widespread complaints of the decline of the yeomen. Whatever decline there was resulted probably from enclosures and larger-scale farming, the competition of which rendered unprofitable all but the largest of the yeoman-farms. Farmers of all classes continued to till their land in accordance with local customs. Over large areas of the country the customary system was the three-field rotation of crops. During the century there was a tendency to enclose land, including the common land, so as to make possible more economical cultivation. The cottager's loss of his common-land rights caused continual complaints. Moreover, because the purpose of many enclosures was to change arable land into pasture, the results were to throw large numbers of labourers out of work, and to depopulate the countryside.

Next above the yeomen in the social scale were the country gentry. These, too, were not easy to define as a class. Many of them owned estates with farms rented out to tenants. Such gentry were distinguished from the nobility only in not owning a title to the peerage. They were the magnates of their countryside and the leaders of public opinion. During the Civil War the gentry, and those whom they were able to bring from their estates, formed the bulk of the King's supporters. It was significant of the depth of conviction aroused by events leading to the war that a large proportion of the gentry's neighbours, the yeomen, supported the opposite side.

The peers, as a result of the Stuart regime, became a strangely mixed body. At Elizabeth I's death there had been only about sixty peers; yet by the time that the Civil War broke out there were nearly one hundred and forty. Of these, nearly one hundred represented new creations by James and Charles, sixty by James and forty by Charles. Two results followed this rapid expansion of the peerage. First, the peerage declined in prestige. Second, it became divided against itself: the peers of ancient lineage thought contemptuously of the upstarts in their ranks. The contempt was intensified by the knowledge that some of the new peers had obtained their titles by purchase from the King, the usual price being £10,000 which, reckoned in twentieth-century values, was a very considerable sum. On the other hand, some of the new men fully deserved their honours: Lionel Cranfield, who reorganized James I's exchequer, was not unjustly rewarded with the Earldom of Middlesex. Moreover, nobles and even members of the royal family thought it no disgrace to seek profit in mercantile enterprises such as they despised in the newly created peers: witness some of the promoters of the Hudson Bay and East India Companies.

In this connexion a general word of warning may be useful. A review of the population under classes of society is convenient as a means of clarifying ideas and marshalling certain facts about the subject, but it must not lead us into thinking that membership of the various classes was in any way fixed or permanent. Socially, in modern centuries at least, English society has always been fluid. Throughout the seventeenth century there was a good deal of movement by individuals from one class to another, up and down alike. Nevertheless social distinctions existed and had a significance which is worth noting.

2. Industries

The most important industry throughout the country was agriculture except, of course, where lack of suitable soil—owing to mountains or some other factor—rendered agriculture impracticable. The condition of seventeenth-century agriculture cannot be considered properly in isolation from other contemporary conditions—for example, the state of trade, and current tariff policies—so that to do justice to the subject would necessarily involve a detailed examination of a wide range of factors. Our immediate purpose may perhaps be better served if, in spite of the dangers of generalization, we consider a few marked tendencies only.

First, where enclosure had not taken place,[1] agricultural development was limited by the prevailing three-field system of tillage—usually wheat, barley, fallow—which meant that only two-thirds of all the arable land was under cultivation in any one year, and that, as we have seen, the cultivators were tied by the traditional custom of their locality. This generalization, like others, needs to be modified in detail. In some villages the land was divided into four fields, which would allow greater variety in the crops. Here and there were to be found patches which from time immemorial had been enclosed. Also, the process of enclosure was continually going on. Nevertheless the three-field system generally prevailed.

Second, the growth of a few of the larger towns, particularly of London, needing increasing supplies of foodstuffs, was a constant impetus to corn-growing. By about the time of the Restoration supply seems to have overtaken demand. Thenceforward there was a surplus of corn. The obvious solution of this problem was export.

[1] See pp. 15–16.

These changing conditions were reflected in the legislation of the period.[1] The first Stuart corn-law was passed in 1604. It enacted that wheat could be exported when the home-price did not exceed 26s. 8d. a quarter. The principle of this Act was not new and was continued in a series of Acts during many following years though the price-limit was raised as time went on. In Restoration-year the qualifying price was 40s. and three years later was 48s. In practice the specific limit mattered little since almost always the price exceeded the limit: in only seven years during the period 1604–63 was this condition not fulfilled. Evidence of increased corn-production is afforded by the changed policy denoted by an Act of 1670 which removed the price-limit and allowed corn to be exported whatever the home-price. This would stimulate production still further. A greater stimulus was provided by a 1673 Act granting a bounty of 5s. on every quarter of wheat exported: bounties were granted also on other corn-crops. The close connexion between bounties and exports was shown not only by export-increases after this date but also by decreases when the policy temporarily ceased in 1681 until its resumption in 1689.

Though agriculture was still the most important source of national wealth, the seventeenth century saw a significant expansion of manufacturing and trade. This was true especially of wool. As during earlier centuries, spinning by the women-folk yielded a welcome addition to farmers' incomes. What was new in the seventeenth century was the growth of large-scale operations. This took the form not of complicated machine-processes or of large factories but of operations by capitalists. These were the wealthy clothiers who gave employment to many, sometimes to hundreds of workers, in the workers' own homes. Wool was bought up over a wide area and distributed to domestic spinners, from them the yarn was collected and distributed to weavers; and so stage by stage the raw material was transformed into the finished article.

In contrast to the factory-system of the twentieth century, it was not the employers but the workers who owned the

[1] For the facts quoted in the remainder of this paragraph, the author is indebted largely to Lipson: *The Economic History of England*, ii, pp. 448–452.

various types of machines and the premises that housed them. The workers, such as the spinners and the weavers, carried through their respective manufacturing processes independently of interference, even of that of the clothier: the latter concerned himself only with the quality of the goods stage by stage. Nor were the individual workers bound to serve only one master. A weaver, for example, could contract to serve several clothiers, choosing which of them to serve at any particular time according to the state of the market and the type of weaving he preferred. The conditions of weaving varied somewhat in detail from one part of the country to another—notably between Yorkshire and the West—but those outlined above fairly describe those prevailing generally. In some instances there was greater division of control than this summary suggests. Where a clothier did not control all the processes of manufacture, middlemen of various types took advantage of the situation to make a profit by linking up the otherwise disjointed units.

Next in importance to wool in the country's industry was coal. The rapid depletion of English forests during Tudor times was causing coal to be the chief fuel not only for industry but for domestic heating. Though coal had been worked in various parts of the country for several centuries—references to coal-mining in Warwickshire, for example, occur as early as 1275—during the seventeenth century the outstandingly important source of supply was Newcastle upon Tyne and the surrounding district. Not only were many thousands of men continuously engaged in the pits there, but fleets of ships and lighters were kept busy in transporting the coal. London depended almost exclusively upon coal brought from Newcastle by sea, and hence called "sea coal." A Parliamentary Commission of 1871 estimated that by 1700 the country's total output had been no less than 2,612,000 tons and was then increasing rapidly. Not only was the industry valuable as a source of heat and power, but it was providing an increasingly valuable article of export: fleets of ships from France, the Low Countries, and the North German ports regularly carried Newcastle coal to their respective countries.

Even in Stuart times, when conditions were primitive, the

coal-trade was not without its troubles. These were connected mainly with the Hostmen, a body of men incorporated by Elizabeth to load and ship Newcastle coal. Gradually they acquired ownership of the mines and thus enjoyed a virtual monopoly of the Tyne coal-industry, from the working of the coal in the pit to its delivery at the port of sale. By mutual arrangement they used this monopoly so as to dictate, on the one hand, the wages of their workpeople and, on the other, the price of coal in London. This position already existed at the beginning of the Stuart period: and throughout that period —and long afterwards—there were struggles between what was really the Newcastle selling cartel and the London consumers.

Alongside these staple industries, a number of others, which later became more important, began to establish themselves. For example, the manufacture of cotton goods was being carried on in Lancashire; and Huguenot refugees had brought their silk industry, especially to Spitalfields. Perhaps the most important of the still minor industries was that of iron, its chief pioneer being Abraham Darby (1677–1717). He was the first of a line of Abraham Darbys who were ironmasters at Coalbrookdale, in Shropshire, where their work played a highly influential part in the industrial changes of the eighteenth century.

3. Mercantile System

The increasing industrial development of the seventeenth century led the Government to take some account of this aspect of national life, and to adopt deliberately a commercial policy which during the following century became known as the Mercantile System.

One of the signs of the Government's growing concern was its appointment of a succession of committees to deal with matters of trade policy. Perhaps the most important was that of the Commissioners for Trade and Plantations set up by William III in 1696. The members were in part officers of State and in part paid officials, and they had at their service a body of clerks. In effect, William created a Board of Trade closely resembling a present-day Government department. Its business was to keep in touch with merchants, and the effect was seen in a variety of regulations to encourage trade.

Though Mercantile System was a term not coined until the eighteenth century, it is a convenient label which has become generally applied to the principles of the system whenever they manifested themselves. Those principles had indeed been regarded as sound policy since the closing years of the fourteenth century when Richard II (1377–99) inaugurated the Policy of Power as distinct from Edward III's Policy of Plenty. The essence of the Mercantile System was so to regulate trade as to contribute towards the power of the State rather than merely towards the prosperity of individuals—'power' rather than 'plenty.' In particular, the State must encourage the production of essential goods and foodstuffs so as to be self-sufficing in time of war.

Closely connected with this idea was that of the Balance of Trade. The regulation of trade in order to maintain a favourable balance, whereby the value of exports exceeded that of imports, was regarded throughout the seventeenth century as the chief commercial function of government. This was pithily expressed in the *Discourse of the Common Weal* (first published in 1549)[1]: "We must always take heed that we buy no more from strangers than we sell them; for so we should empoverish ourselves and enrich them." The implication of this dictum was commonly accepted at the time—namely, that in every commercial transaction only one of the two parties could gain, while the other must suffer loss. One of the objects commonly adduced for maintaining a favourable trade-balance was that of keeping within the kingdom a stock of bullion. Though not all the seventeenth-century supporters of the Balance-of-Trade theory held the view, in its crudest form, that money and wealth were synonymous terms,[2] they nevertheless were anxious to prevent the draining of gold and silver from the country. In a century when a system of credit was

[1] Cunningham, *Growth of English Industry and Commerce*, i, pp. 552, 563.
[2] Lipson, *Economic History of England*, iii, pp. 62–67.

imperfectly developed, a ready supply of money was necessary for trading transactions. Similarly, ready money was necessary in the event of war.

Hence, one of the purposes of regulating trade was to maintain a store of bullion within the country. To this end, imports must be discouraged (since payment for them would take gold out of the country), and exports must be encouraged (so that they would be paid for in gold from abroad).

These ideas were the motives of various attempts to regulate trade. Some of these attempts have been mentioned already. The corn-laws, from 1604 onward, aimed at encouraging corn-production for its own sake but, in so far as they were successful, they would have the further effect of enabling England to feed herself, and of preventing the draining away of gold from the country.

The Mercantile System was also the basis of the national attitude towards colonies. These were regarded not as separate entities with rights of their own but as an integral part of the Mother-country. Their industry and trade must therefore be regulated in the interests of England, and no exports from the colonies must be allowed to compete with similar classes of goods produced in England. Thus a regulation of 1621 compelled all tobacco exports from the colonies to be sent to England before going to other countries; another of 1624 stipulated that colonial tobacco must be carried in English or colonial vessels; and yet another of 1647 extended this latter provision to all colonial exports. At the same time it must be remembered that the colonial system was not altogether one-sided. For example, after 1619 the growing of tobacco in England was forbidden, and various regulations exempted goods passing between England and her colonies from paying duties.

The outstanding examples of the Mercantile System in Stuart times were the Navigation Acts of 1651 and 1660 which we have noticed already[1] in connexion with the Dutch wars, and which also introduced further regulations affecting trade with the colonies. Their immediate purpose was to injure

[1] See pp. 215, 249, 410.

Dutch carrying-trade; but, further, they exemplified the mercantile principle that, when goods have to be imported, they must be brought in English ships. The effects of the Navigation Acts have been much in dispute. As we saw when considering the 1651 Act, there is reason to doubt whether in fact it injured Dutch trade as much as contemporaries thought it did. Certainly it was likely to hinder English trade. Dutch ships had hitherto been able to compete successfully with English ships in carrying goods to England because Dutch freights had been lower; and one effect of removing Dutch competition was that English shippers could raise their charges still higher. This could be no help to English trade. Also, English ships were unsuited to certain work, especially in the Baltic. The withdrawal of Dutch ships therefore restricted Baltic supplies for England, and so still further hampered trade. Perhaps more paradoxical of all the effect of the Navigation Acts was that the Dutch, being thereby prevented from transporting Baltic goods to England, carried them instead to Holland, where they were made into sails and ropes which, being Dutch manufactures, were then brought to England in Dutch ships, thus competing both with English shipping and with English manufactures!

4. Assessment of Wages

While Stuart Governments were trying on the one hand to control the course of trade in accordance with accepted theories, on the other hand they were trying to regulate some of the working conditions of certain staple industries. One aspect of these regulations was the assessment of wages.

The assessment of wages was no new idea. As far back at least as the fourteenth century the dislocating social and economic effects of the Black Death had led to the Statute of Labourers of 1351 which fixed maximum rates of wages. Later Acts authorized the justices to fix the wages for their respective shires. These Acts were not only important in themselves but became also precedents for the sixteenth century when the economic situation changed once again. That century was marked by what would now be called inflation—that is, by a fall in the value of money and a rise in prices. For this condition there were various contributory causes, including, for example, the debasement of the coinage by Henry VIII. The most important cause, however, was the vast influx into Europe of silver and gold from Central and South America. So steep was the general price-rise that large numbers of wage-earners, both in town and countryside, were reduced to serious poverty. This was recognized by the Elizabethan Statute of Apprentices of 1563, which once more enjoined that each year the justices should "rate and appoint" wages.

However well-intentioned this Act may have been, it was a mere palliative. During the forty years between its passing and the accession of the first Stuart in 1603 prices continued to rise and wages still lagged far behind. Hence, an Act of 1604 introduced two new principles into wage-fixing. The first was the principle of a minimum instead of a maximum wage: though justices were to continue to assess wages, any employer who paid less than the stated rate of wages was to forfeit ten shillings to his aggrieved workman. The second was that no justice who was a clothier was to take any part in wage-assessments for men engaged in the cloth industry.

We have seen ample evidence of the Stuarts' ineptitude in political matters. But in this matter of the welfare of their poor subjects there seems no reason to doubt their good intentions. Nevertheless the enforcement of such regulations was extremely difficult. The workers' poverty and ignorance, and their lack of organization and leadership, must have made them particularly dependent upon their masters. If the masters ignored the Act the workers would find great difficulty in securing redress. How common were such evasions of the law was shown by numerous workers' petitions to the Privy Council, either directly or through some powerful friend, calling attention to their grievances. The Council's general support to the workers throughout the reigns of the first two Stuarts confirms their good intentions towards the mass of their subjects in such matters.

The Commonwealth seems to have continued the Stuarts' concern. In 1649 the Commons expressly ordered justices to carry out the instructions of the 1563 and 1604 Statutes. After the Restoration also the practice of fixing wages continued to be followed.

5. Poor Law

This account of attempts to fix reasonable wage-levels has served to emphasize one cause of poverty during the seventeenth century—namely, rising prices due to increased supplies of bullion. Earlier in our study other causes also have been mentioned and need be only summarized, for the sake of convenience, at this point.

First was the growing practice of land-enclosure already mentioned, with its attendant social upheavals. Throughout the sixteenth century this practice had gone on. Even the vigour and ingenuity of the Tudors had failed to find an adequate remedy for the evil, and its effects still continued into the reigns of the Stuarts.

Second, the development of industry and trade produced what modern times would call trade-cycles of booms and slumps. Because these were then new phenomena they were neither understood nor foreseen, and the successive slumps caused periodic and widespread distress.

Third, the Civil War caused much economic dislocation. The Commonwealth Government was too preoccupied with religious and political problems to evolve a new economic policy or even to enforce the provisions already in existence on such matters as wages and apprenticeship. Nor did the restored Stuarts find it easy to re-assert the Government's powers to enforce regulations for the lives of individuals, particularly in economic affairs.

For such reasons as these, measures for the relief of poverty became urgent. The foundation for such measures had been laid in the sixteenth century, and the seventeenth-century Poor Law was little more than an application of principles already existing. A glance at earlier Poor Law is therefore useful at this point.

The first Tudor Acts dealing with poverty were passed under Henry VIII. They were concerned less with relieving poverty than with suppressing vagabonds and beggars. During Elizabeth I's long reign it became generally recognized that suppression alone was not enough because at least some people were not wilful idlers but were genuinely unable to support themselves, either because suitable work was not available, or through physical disability, or the like. Hence the Elizabethan law-makers tried to distinguish between the deserving and the undeserving poor. The relief of the deserving poor they made the responsibility of each parish.

After the various Acts passed during Elizabeth's reign the system of poor relief was summarized towards the end of her reign in the famous Act of 1601. Its main provisions were as follows:

1. In every parish "four, three, or two substantial householders shall . . . be nominated in Easter week, and that these, with the churchwardens, shall be overseers of the poor."
2. The overseers are to raise "in every parish, by taxation of every inhabitant . . . such competent sums of money as they shall think fit."
3. This money is to be used in various ways to relieve poverty, including: (a) "Setting to work all such persons . . . having no means to maintain them." (b) "For the necessary relief of the lame, impotent, old, blind, and such other among them being poor and not able to work."[1]

Thus the 1601 Act dealt with genuine poverty in that it provided for those poor people who were unable to provide for themselves—that is, the "impotent poor." The other class of poor had recently been dealt with in an Act of 1598: "An Act for the punishment of Rogues, Vagabonds, and Sturdy Beggars." By its terms, any able-bodied person found wandering or begging was to be:

> stripped naked from the middle upwards, and be openly whipped until his or her body be bloody, and shall then forthwith be sent from parish to parish . . . straight way to the parish where he was born, [or] to the parish where he or she last dwelt by the space of one year.

[1] For a fuller account of this legislation, see Sir George Nicholls, *History of English Poor Law*, Vol. I, especially pp. 103, 189–190, 211

These two Acts, passed very near the end of Elizabeth I's reign, had more than a momentary importance. Their twin principles formed the foundation of English Poor Law through all the centuries to follow—namely, a recognition of the community's duty to provide for those who cannot provide for themselves and, at the same time, to ensure that such provision shall go only to the "impotent." These were the Acts, therefore, which continued in operation under the Stuarts, though from time to time there were amendments in detail or additions to their provisions.

Thus in 1604 the 1598 Act was confirmed and strengthened with the addition that anyone convicted as a rogue under its terms should be:

> branded on the left shoulder with a hot burning iron of the breadth of a shilling, with a great Roman R, upon the flesh, that the letter R may be seen and remain for a perpetual mark upon such a rogue during his or her life.

Any branded rogue arrested for a second offence was to suffer as a felon.

As might be expected, the upheaval of the Civil War encouraged disorderliness and rendered difficult the regular and uniform enforcement of Acts depending upon voluntary local officials. Hence, after the Restoration a 1662 Act for the Better Relief of the Poor complained of the laxity in enforcing the laws relating to vagabonds and introduced fresh and more stringent provisions to remove wandering beggars to their proper parish. The effect of the Act was, in practice, to prevent poor people, unable to find work in their own parish, from travelling so as to find work elsewhere. Thus labour was made stationary, with resulting hardship to individuals and aggravation of national poverty.

The fact was that seventeenth-century England was not only still suffering from the legacy of early distresses but was also feeling the first effects of the growing industrialization of its own day. The full force of that process was not to be realized until the following century, which saw large changes in the Poor Law as a consequence.

6. Culture

A factor which affected profoundly—if less obtrusively than did industry and trade—the nature of English society was education. At the beginning of the seventeenth century education was subject to serious handicaps. The monastic schools, which had disappeared with Henry VIII's dissolution of the monasteries nearly a century earlier, had never been adequately replaced. Yet the limitations in syllabus which monastic education had implied still operated—that is, the subjects studied had had a strong religious bias. And in the Grammar Schools the main subjects of instruction were still Latin, Greek, and Hebrew grammar, these being the languages essential for study of theological treatises and of the Bible itself. That almost all these schools should have been under the control of the local Anglican clergy was almost inevitable since in most places the clergy were the only people qualified to teach, or to supervise instruction in, the required subjects.

Instruction for very poor children was provided in Charity Schools which were supported by the subscriptions of interested persons. The motives of subscribers varied much: some were anxious to remove ignorance; others were more concerned with the religious side of education. The great agency of the work at the close of the seventeenth century was the Society for Promoting Christian Knowledge, founded in 1698, under whose auspices large numbers of Charity Schools were founded throughout the country.

At the other end of the education-scale were the two universities of Oxford and Cambridge. The details of their history and customs during the seventeenth century are beyond the compass of this summary, and readers must be referred to books on the subject.[1] Here it must suffice to say that, many though the shortcomings of the universities were, judged by twentieth-century standards, Oxford and Cambridge maintained a high degree of scholarship and, what was not less important, a respect for sound learning in a not always friendly

[1] For example—Mallet, *History of the University of Oxford*, Vol. II (1924); and Mullinger, *The University of Cambridge*, Vols. II and III (1873–84).

14* +

age. Nor were the universities interested only in theology and classics and kindred subjects. It was at Oxford that the Hon. Robert Boyle (1627–91), son of the first Earl of Cork, settled in 1654 and set up his laboratory. Scarcely less important than his enunciation of Boyle's Law was the impetus that he gave to the experimental method of investigation. Boyle's younger contemporary, Isaac Newton (1642–1727), was a son of Trinity College, Cambridge, where he worked on the subject of optics and on the material published in his *Principia* in 1687, and where in 1705 Queen Anne knighted him.

Not the least noteworthy of the seventeenth-century advances in scientific knowledge were those connected with medicine. Among these the most justly famous was the discovery of blood-circulation by William Harvey (1578–1657). The foremost school of medicine in the late sixteenth century was at Padua owing to the fame of Vesalius who in 1543 had published a truly epoch-making book on the structure of the human body. To Padua, therefore, Harvey went after graduating at Cambridge. After returning to England he worked at St Bartholomew's Hospital and elsewhere. It was in a lecture in 1616 that he first made public his discovery of the systematic circulation of the blood. The discovery was the more notable because Harvey lacked apparatus that modern investigators would consider elementary and essential: even the microscope was unknown to him. Yet this was probably the most notable single discovery of physiology and was the starting-point of a vast amount of research in that branch of science which increasingly exact methods and apparatus made possible.

The universities, however, had no monopoly of learning. As the century proceeded, interest in learned subjects, especially those connected with science, grew steadily. A notable exponent of this growing interest was Sir Thomas Gresham (1519–79) who was a Lombard Street businessman and was repeatedly employed by the Crown as a business agent abroad. For the promotion of the liberal arts, he founded and endowed Gresham College and, about the time that the Civil War ended, a group of men began to meet there once a week to discuss scientific subjects. This group was the forerunner of the body of which Charles II, in 1662, became the patron, and so began the Royal Society. One of the men who helped to found the Society was Robert Boyle; and Isaac Newton, elected President in 1703, was thereafter regularly re-elected for twenty-five years.

In the realm of literature the seventeenth century was so rich that to review the whole field within this chapter would reduce the material to a catalogue of titles and authors. Most outstanding of all the books produced in the seventeenth century was the Authorized Version of the Bible prepared in accordance with James I's decision taken at the Hampton Court Conference of 1604 and published in 1611. During the greater part of the three following centuries the Authorized Version was almost the only book in a large proportion of English homes and was the staple reading of a large proportion of English people. The result was that its subject-matter became part of the literary and religious heritage of every Englishman: it helped to shape his daily language and to mould his character and that of the nation.

Among other literary works must be specially mentioned those of Francis Bacon, Lord St Albans (1561–1626), Edward Hyde, Earl of Clarendon (1609–74), Thomas Hobbes (1588–1679), John Locke (1632–1704), George Savile, Marquess of Halifax (1633–95), John Milton (1608–74), John Bunyan (1628–88), Samuel Pepys (1633–1703), and John Evelyn (1620–1706).

The scope of Bacon's genius was such that he held a pre-eminent place in at least three spheres. Of his legal career, mention has already been made in earlier chapters. In literature, his *Essays*—first published in 1598, and thereafter until 1625 several times re-issued and expanded—sufficed to place him in the highest rank. But it was as a scientist that he chiefly merited fame. The crown of his scientific writings was the *Novum Organum Scientarum* which occupied him twelve years and was first published in 1620—that is, just before his fall from the Lord Chancellorship. The book's outstanding feature was its insistence upon the discovery of causes as science's chief object, and upon the inductive method of reasoning, based upon practical experiments, as the only sure means to his end. Some of Bacon's claims were vague, and those that he put forward for the mechanical infallibility of his methods were certainly absurd. Yet this cannot alter the fact that his principle of basing conclusions upon the systematic investigation of facts was the true way to scientific knowledge, and that much of the vast scientific achievement of modern times is to be traced to the awakening that Bacon inspired.

Clarendon's *History of the Great Rebellion* is a combination of two records: the one, written during his first exile, was to be a treatise on the reasons for the overthrow of the Stuarts; the other, written during his second exile twenty years later, was to be an account of the political events in which he played a part. The history in its final form was published during the years 1702–4. As is inevitable in a book written by a partisan in the controversial events which it records, it contains serious errors of judgement and of fact; but as the reflection of the views of a prominent contemporary statesman, it remains an invaluable study of Stuart politics.

The political philosophies of Hobbes and Locke, though having much in common, were marked also by differences characteristic of their respective generations: Hobbes was born in Armada-year, and Locke not until the seventh year of Charles I. In spite of the prestige of Bacon's inductive method, Hobbes continued to use the opposite method of deducing the best governmental method from what he regarded as first principles. This was exemplified chiefly in his *Leviathan, or the Matter, Forme and Power of a Commonwealth Ecclesiastical and Civil,* published in 1651. Its main theme was that, in a state of nature, mankind had been in a constant condition of war such as could still be seen elsewhere in nature. Thence he deduced that, in order to end this warfare, men had entered into a contract to render obedience to a king who, though an absolute king, had thus owed his power not to Divine Right but to the people's Contract. Locke was closely associated with the Whigs, and after Shaftesbury's fall he had to go into exile. In 1688 he returned to England, and during the following years he wrote a number of books enunciating Whig philosophy including letters on toleration and *Essay on Civil Government.* In the latter he, like Hobbes, presupposed a contract between king and subjects but, unlike Hobbes, he deduced that if the monarch broke his contract his subjects were thereby absolved from their share in it, and were justified in rebellion against him. Of the political writings of the Earl of Halifax, enough has been said already[1] to make further details at this point unnecessary.

The diarists Pepys and Evelyn, though concerned largely with the Court and politicians, did not write to advocate particular theories. Consequently they give, if not unbiased, at least honest, reflections of such parts of contemporary life as came within their purview. Thus their books may be regarded as both historical and literary.

In the realm of pure literature the greatest seventeenth-century figure was John Milton. He was the outstanding, though by no means solitary, example of the cultured Puritan. His work was intimately connected with contemporary events in Church and State; and the changing character and content of his writings reflected the changing world in which he lived and his changing reactions to it. Even as a child he must have lived among religious questionings: his grandfather had been a staunch Roman Catholic who had disinherited his son, the poet's father, when the latter had confessed conversion to the Church of England. John's father became a man of wide culture as well as of comfortable affluence. These two circumstances enabled John to graduate at Cambridge and afterwards to spend several years in quiet study, largely of the classics, and in desultory writing. It was this early period which produced the fastidiously beautiful verse of the *Ode to the Nativity*, *L'Allegro, Il Penseroso,* and *Lycidas.* Then during 1638–39 he travelled in Italy.

This journey seems to have marked a stage in his development, for he returned to write not poetry but a stream of prose pamphlets. The twenty years 1640–60 were a well-defined, middle portion of his life during which his independent spirit moved him to assert the right of every individual to think and to speak as his conscience bade him, a right which in his view was being denied by King and bishops. Herein lay the

[1] See pp. 239, 274–275.

explanation of his Puritanism. At the same time there was growing in him a conviction that God had chosen him to play a part as a champion of the cause of freedom. Even before the Italian tour something of this note was in his work. In *Lycidas* (1638), for example, he expressed the fear that death might intervene before he could fulfil his high destiny: along with this the poem expressed his contempt for the corrupt clergy of the Anglican Church. During this middle period he was occupied in two ways. First, he wrote numerous prose pamphlets, occasioned by personal events, but all testifying to a desire to be freed from the shackles of outworn custom, bad tradition, or irksome legislation. Most noteworthy of them all was his eloquent plea for the freedom of the Press: *Areopagitica; A Speech of Mr John Milton For the Liberty of Unlicenc'd Printing. To the Parliament of England* (1644). Second, in 1649, he was appointed to be Latin Secretary to the recently formed Council of State, a position which he retained until the Restoration. It was the strain which this work entailed upon his eyesight, already weakened by intense study, that brought on blindness in 1652.

Following the Restoration, he received some ill-treatment, including imprisonment, but was soon allowed to retire to private life. Thus at last, in the third period of his career, he had leisure to compose on a grand scale. Fortunately, this opportunity came at a time when experience had matured his mind and spirit. The result was the vast epic poem *Paradise Lost*, said to have been begun as early as 1650 but not published until 1667, for which he received the sum of £10. Constructed around the story of Adam and Eve's fall, the poem represents the whole struggle between Good and Evil and the prediction of the ultimate triumph of Good in Man's redemption through the Son of God. In 1671 appeared together the epic *Paradise Regained* and the tragedy, exquisitely wrought, *Samson Agonistes*.

Though a great artist is not of an age but of all time, Milton reflected aspects of the century in which he lived. First, there is the struggle for freedom as exemplified in his own life and family, in his bitter comment, "New Presbyter is but old Priest writ large," and in the desolation of his closing years when his most cherished purposes seemed to be lost. Second, in his person was blended much that was admirable in Cavalier and in Puritan—wide culture, love of the beauty of earth, of man, and of the works of men's hands together with the austerity and sense of being "ever in his great Taskmaster's eye." Lastly, he displayed the temper of the English character—God-fearing, sober, law-abiding, yet asserting the right of the individual.

John Bunyan had this in common with Milton, that he was a Puritan propagandist. In other respects they were sharply contrasted. Whereas Milton had the best scholarly training available combined with ample means and leisure, Bunyan was the son of a tinker of Elstow, near Bedford, and grew up with only the rudiments of reading and writing. It was his marriage in 1649 to a religious woman which seems to have led to the powerful spiritual experiences that altered the whole tenor of his life. His consequent passionate Puritan preaching earned for him a term of imprisonment in Bedford gaol lasting from January 1661 until the Declaration of Indulgence of 1672. During his imprisonment he was allowed to work, to preach to his fellow-prisoners, and to write; and it was then that he began his immortal *Pilgrim's Progress* of which the first part was published in 1678 and the second part in 1684. Others of his books included *Some Gospel Truths Opened* (his first book), published in 1656, *Grace Abounding* in 1666, *Life and Death of Mr Badman* in 1680, and *The Holy War* in 1682. One result of Bunyan's lack of book-learning was that he had little contact with contemporary religious thought: the views that he held were the product of his own rugged, independent reflection on the Authorized Version of the Bible which, together with Foxe's *Book of Martyrs*, was almost his sole literary diet. Herein lay the explanation of Bunyan's unique qualities in both matter and manner. His influence upon every succeeding generation of Englishmen, as well as upon his own generation, has been incalculable. Next to the Authorized Version of the Bible, his *Pilgrim's Progress* has been the most widely read book in the English tongue.

One other feature of seventeenth-century literature needs to be mentioned—namely, the growth of journalism. The forerunners of modern newspapers were news-sheets made up by gossip-writers whose business it was to retail news-items both political and personal. Much of this news was collected in coffee-houses which grew up during the latter half of the century and were virtually clubs each with its characteristic clientèle—Whigs at the Kit-Kat, classicists at the Grecian, marine-insurers at Lloyds, and so forth. A round of such centres of social activity could not fail to yield literary articles of wide interest. The development of newspapers in the modern sense of the term was seriously hampered by the Licensing Act of 1662 whereby not only were books liable to the Archbishop's censorship, as they had long been, but the Government assumed complete control of printing: the number of master-printers was to be allowed to decline to twenty, after which printers were to be licensed either by the Archbishop of Canterbury or by the Bishop of London, and no uncensored publication was to be allowed. Originally the Act was to last two years, but before it expired it was renewed, and it continued to be renewed (with one short break) until it was allowed to lapse in 1695. The earliest daily newspaper was the *Daily Courant* which first appeared in 1702. Soon journalism widened its scope by catering for literary interest: thus in 1709 Richard Steele started the *Tatler,* and two years later Steele and Addison started the *Spectator.*

Closely related to the makers of newspapers were the pamphleteers of whom the prince was Jonathan Swift (1667–1745) whose clear, satirical prose was one of the most valuable weapons possessed by the Tory party. The great Whig protagonist was Daniel Defoe (1659?–1731). Some idea of the convincing skill of Defoe's satire can be gleaned from the fact that his *Shortest Way with the Dissenters* (1703), though in reality a skit on the Tories' intolerance, was at first treated as a serious proposition, and the Whig House of Commons ordered it to be burned—which was the highest, though unintentional, compliment that could have been paid to its satirical quality.

One other feature of seventeenth-century cultural life that calls for mention is its music. On account both of its distinguished musicians and of the large place that music occupied in the lives of ordinary people, the seventeenth has nothing to fear from comparison with any other century, either before or since.

When the century opened William Byrd (1542?–1623) was still the leading English musician. He was the link between Elizabethan and Jacobean music. He had been the pupil of the great Thomas Tallis (died 1585); had been appointed organist of the Chapel Royal as early as 1569; and had written a wide variety of music, instrumental and vocal, sacred and secular. Another musician whose career had begun under Elizabeth was Orlando Gibbons; but, unlike Byrd, he did his best work under James I. In 1604 he became organist at the Chapel Royal and was no less versatile than his older contemporary in the music that he produced. The English composer whose work in the seventeenth century was virtually unrivalled was Henry Purcell (1658–95). He was fortunate in being nurtured in a musical family: his father (also named Henry) belonged to the Chapel Royal, where the younger Henry was a chorister, and was choirmaster at Westminster Abbey. In 1680 the younger Henry was appointed organist at the Abbey, and two years later at the Chapel Royal. There was scarcely any branch of musical composition in which he did not excel: in addition to much church music, both instrumental and choral, he wrote chamber music, forty operas, and many songs. In massive choral work and in the lilt of his melodies Purcell noticeably anticipated some of the characteristics of Handel. In that sense Purcell was the link between the seventeenth and eighteenth centuries, for the works of Handel (1685–1759), whose residence in England began in 1710, were typical of eighteenth-century music.

One matter deserving attention is the position of music under the Commonwealth. The idea is still current that Puritanism was gloomily opposed to the arts as being worldly vanities, and that the Commonwealth, being fundamentally Puritan, suppressed the arts in general and music in particular. This view is a generalization based on too little, or too narrow, knowledge of the facts or is a distortion of the facts. That John Milton was a staunch Puritan should alone suffice to make us hesitate before believing that Puritanism was opposed to the arts. Moreover, throughout England there were Puritan homes where education and general culture were evident and were held in the highest esteem. Puritans varied widely one from another in their religious and ecclesiastical beliefs, but one element was common to them all: all alike believed that God must be the centre of life, both of the individual and of the community, and that every individual could have direct and personal communion with God, no intermediary of priest or ceremony being necessary to such communion. Whatever seemed to rival God as the centre of human life, and whatever seemed to hinder the intimate relationship between man and God, must be removed. It was for this reason that Puritans opposed Laud's ritual, and that, under the Commonwealth, organs were removed from churches, and that theatres were closed. But there was no opposition to the arts, including music, as such; and where the arts did not obviously conflict with what Puritans regarded as God's place in life, there was no attempt to suppress them. Typical of this fact was Cromwell's having the organ removed from Magdalen College, Oxford, to Hampton Court, where Hingston, a pupil of Orlando Gibbons, continued to play it to Cromwell instead of for services at Magdalen as he had formerly done. Similarly, though Sunday dancing was forbidden, dancing continued on other days without interference. Music was one of Cromwell's favourite recreations. During the celebrations at Whitehall following the wedding of his daughter, Frances, to Robert Rich, in 1657, there was music played by forty-eight violins, and there was mixed dancing. When peace was made between England and Holland in April 1654 the dinner to the Dutch representatives was followed by a performance of instrumental music. The encouragement, rather than the suppression, of music in the country at large is indicated by such a fact as the revival of the professorship of music at Oxford in 1656; and the evidence of diaries and other books leaves no doubt that music of all types continued during the Commonwealth to hold a large place in the life of the community. This is a fact whose significance must receive due weight in any estimate of the society and culture of seventeenth-century England.

It is remarkable that in an age when English music and

musicians reached the highest levels, English painting remained scanty and mediocre. With rare exceptions, outstanding painters in Stuart England were foreigners, and most even of their painting consisted of portraits, including miniatures. The most influential artists were the Dutchmen, Van Dyck, whom Charles I welcomed, and Peter Lely, who was knighted by Charles II. The only two Englishmen at all comparable with these in artistic ability were William Dobson, also a portrait-painter, and Samuel Cooper, a miniaturist of quite outstanding quality—indeed he is sometimes regarded as the greatest of the exponents of this type of painting.

In notable contrast to painting, seventeenth-century architecture in England was developed by Englishmen, the chief being Inigo Jones and Sir Christopher Wren. This was the period of the change from the Gothic style to the Renaissance. As in other matters, there was no sharp time-boundary between the two. The first signs of the transition were to be found not in the design of whole buildings but in the application of certain ornamental features derived from contemporary Italian style such as classical columns. Circumstances favoured architectural development. Widespread prosperity encouraged the building of large houses and especially of country mansions, and these provided designers with splendid opportunities to explore the new architectural ideas. During the Civil War and the subsequent unsettled period there naturally was little building on a big scale. But after the Restoration there was a new outburst of building to which an unintentional impetus was given by the Great London Fire of September 1666. Much of the new architecture was the result of the application in England of the Palladian style, so called because its great exponent was Andrea Palladio, an Italian architect of the latter sixteenth century, and one of those responsible for the building of St Peter's, at Rome. He aimed to recapture the fine proportions and the dignity of Roman architecture, and it was chiefly to him that Inigo Jones, Wren, and their pupils owed their success in these respects. Excellent examples of Inigo Jones' use of these ideas are the Queen's House at Greenwich and the Banqueting House at Whitehall. The best-known examples of Wren's work are in the new St

Paul's and about fifty City churches whose building was entrusted to him after the Great Fire, but many other examples of it are to be seen in houses or parts of houses scattered over the country.

It is encouraging to reflect that from a century when many features of English life were undermined and others suffered regrettable deterioration, there emerged at least one feature of permanent worth and of which Englishmen of all shades of opinion may be justly proud.

Books for Further Reading

The following is not intended as an exhaustive bibliography of books dealing with the seventeenth century. The works mentioned are those which might profitably be consulted by students for whom this volume is intended, and which should be readily available in college or school libraries or through public libraries.

BARKER, SIR ERNEST: *Oliver Cromwell and the English People.*
BRAITHWAITE, W. C.: *The Beginnings of Quakerism.*
BRETT, S. R.: *John Pym, 1583–1643.*
BRYANT, SIR ARTHUR: *Samuel Pepys: The Man in the Making.*
—*Samuel Pepys: The Years of Peril.*
—*Samuel Pepys: The Saviour of the Navy.*
—*The England of Charles II.*
—*Charles II.*
BUCHAN, J.: *Montrose.*
—*Oliver Cromwell.*
CARLYLE, T.: *Letters and Speeches of Oliver Cromwell.*
CHURCHILL, SIR WINSTON S.: *Marlborough, His Life and Times* (4 vols.).
CLAPHAM, J.: *Concise Economic History of Britain.*
CLARENDON, EARL OF: *History of the Great Rebellion.*
CLARK, G. N.: *The Later Stuarts.*
—*The Seventeenth Century.*
—*The Wealth of England.*
CUNNINGHAM, W.: *The Growth of English Industry and Commerce, Part II.*
DAVIES, G.: *The Early Stuarts.*
EVELYN, J.: *Diary.*
FEILING, K. G.: *British Foreign Policy, 1660–72.*
—*History of the Tory Party.*
—*A History of England.*
FIRTH, SIR CHARLES: *The Last Years of the Protectorate, 1656–58.*
—*Oliver Cromwell.*
—*Cromwell's Army.*
GARDINER, S. R.: *History of England, 1603–42* (10 vols.).
—*History of the Great Civil War* (4 vols.).
—*History of the Commonwealth and Protectorate* (4 vols.).

GARDINER, S. R.: *Constitutional Documents of the Puritan Revolution, 1625–60.*

—*Cromwell's Place in History.*

—(ed.) *Commons' Debates, 1625.*

GIBB, M. A.: *Buckingham, 1592–1628.*

GOOCH, G. P.: *The History of English Democratic Ideas in the Seventeenth Century.*

HEARNSHAW, F. J. C. (ed.): *Social and Political Ideas of the Sixteenth and Seventeenth Centuries.*

HOLDSWORTH, SIR WILLIAM S.: *History of English Law, Vols. IV and V.*

JONES, J. D.: *The English Revolution.*

LEADAM, I. S.: *Political History of England, Vol. IX, 1702–60.*

LIPSON, E.: *The Economic History of England, Vols. II and III.*

LODGE, R.: *Political History of England, Vol. VIII, 1660–1702.*

MACAULAY, LORD: *History of England from the Accession of James II.*

MAITLAND, F. W.: *Constitutional History of England.*

MALLET, SIR C.: *History of the University of Oxford, Vol. II.*

MONTAGUE, F. C.: *Political History of England, Vol. VII, 1603–60.*

MULLINGER, J. B.: *The University of Cambridge, Vols. II and III.*

NEWTON, A. P. (ed.): *The Great Age of Discovery.*

NICHOLLS, SIR GEORGE: *History of English Poor Law.*

NOTESTEIN, W.: *The Winning of the Initiative by the House of Commons.*

NOTESTEIN, W., AND RELF, F. H. (ed.): *Commons' Debates for 1629.*

NOTESTEIN, W., RELF, F. H., AND SIMPSON, H.: *Commons' Debates, 1621.*

NUGENT, LORD: *Memorials of John Hampden.*

OGG, D.: *England in the Reign of Charles II* (2 vols.).

PEPYS, S.: *Diary.*

PROTHERO, G. W.: *Statutes and Constitutional Documents, 1558–1625.*

RANKE, L. VON: *History of England* (6 vols.).

ROBERTSON, SIR CHARLES G.: *Select Statutes, Cases and Documents, 1660–1832.*

SAVILE, GEORGE, FIRST EARL OF HALIFAX: *The Complete Works* (ed. Raleigh).

SEELEY, SIR JOHN: *The Growth of British Policy.*

TAWNEY, R. H.: *Religion and the Rise of Capitalism.*
—*Business and Politics under James I: Lionel Cranfield as Merchant and Minister.*
TRAIL, H. D.: *Strafford.*
TREVELYAN, GEORGE M.: *England under the Stuarts.*
—*England under Queen Anne* (3 vols.).
—*English Social History.*
TREVOR-ROPER, H. R.: *Archbishop Laud, 1573–1645.*
UNWIN, G.: *Industrial Organization in the Sixteenth and Seventeenth Centuries.*
WEDGWOOD, C. V.: *Strafford.*
—*The King's Peace, 1637–41.*
—*The King's War, 1641–47.*
WILLEY, B.: *The Seventeenth Century Background.*
WILLIAMSON, J. A.: *Short History of British Expansion.*

Genealogical Tables

The Descent of Henry VII

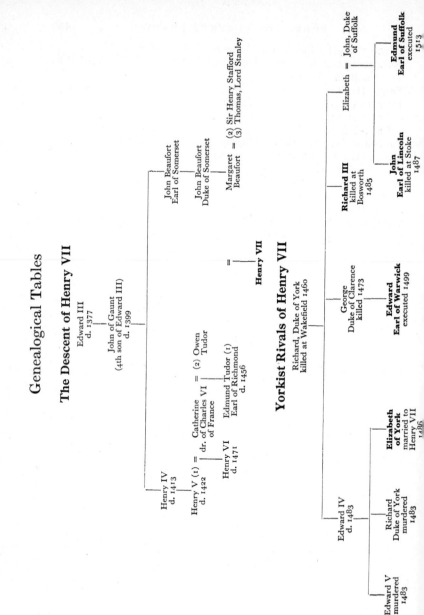

Edward III
d. 1377

John of Gaunt
(4th son of Edward III)
d. 1399

Henry IV
d. 1413

Henry V (1) = Catherine = (2) Owen Tudor
d. 1422   dr. of Charles VI
  of France

Henry VI
d. 1471

Edmund Tudor (1)
Earl of Richmond
d. 1456

John Beaufort
Earl of Somerset

John Beaufort
Duke of Somerset

Margaret = (2) Sir Henry Stafford
Beaufort = (3) Thomas, Lord Stanley

Henry VII

=

Yorkist Rivals of Henry VII

Richard, Duke of York
killed at Wakefield 1460

Edward IV
d. 1483

George
Duke of Clarence
killed 1473

Richard III
killed at
Bosworth
1485

Elizabeth = John, Duke
of Suffolk

Edward V
murdered
1483

Richard
Duke of York
murdered
1483

**Elizabeth
of York**
married to
Henry VII
1486

Edward
Earl of Warwick
executed 1499

**John
Earl of Lincoln**
killed at Stoke
1487

**Edmund
Earl of Suffolk**
executed
1513

Descendants of James I

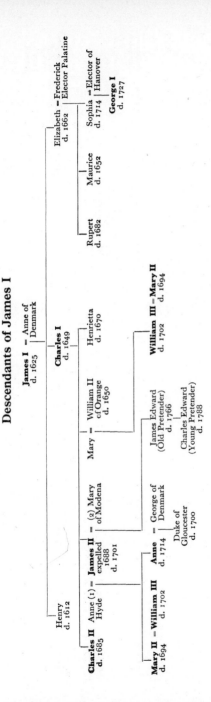

The Cromwell Family

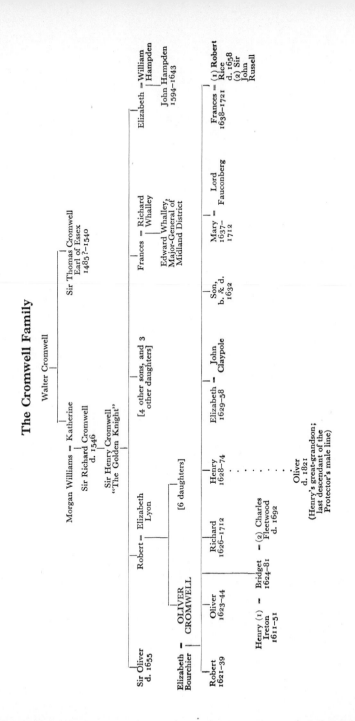

Index

Names of Battles, Statutes, and Treaties are shown under those headings respectively.